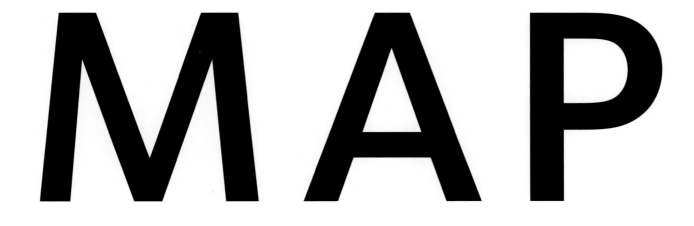

MAP

EXPLORING THE WORLD

Φ

Phaidon Press Limited
Regent's Wharf
All Saints Street
London N1 9PA

Phaidon Press Inc.
65 Bleecker Street
New York, NY 10012

www.phaidon.com

First published 2015
© 2015 Phaidon Press Limited

ISBN 978 0 7148 6944 5

A CIP catalogue record for this book
is available from the British Library.

Commissioning Editor: Victoria Clarke
Editors: Rosie Pickles and Tim Cooke
Production Controller: Adela Cory
Cover Design: Julia Hasting
Interior Design: Studio Philippe Apeloig
Layout: Studio Chehade

Printed in Hong Kong

Arrangement

The maps in this book have been arranged
in pairs to highlight interesting comparisons
and contrasts based loosely on their subject,
age, purpose, technique or appearance.
This organizational system is not definitive
and many other arrangements would have
been possible. A chronological survey of
cartography can be found in the timeline.

Editions

Many of the maps in this book exist in
multiple editions and versions. First editions
have been included where possible, and
if a later copy or edition is included this
is noted. The dates in captions refer to first
editions, except where an included copy
is substantially different.

Dimensions

Dimensions are listed by height then width.
Where differences in dimensions exist
between sources, measurements listed refer
to the illustrated version. Digital images
all have variable dimensions.

ASSEMBLING THE WORLD IN AN IMAGE

There are many different kinds of map. Part science, part artistic design, the map as a concept is complex and ever changing, encompassing a range of different forms of graphic expression and display. And even though scholars have spilled much ink trying to settle on a written definition, a map is still something that is best understood when seen as an image – whether printed on paper, chiselled on to stone, painted on an animal skin or viewed on a computer screen – rather than commented on verbally.

Undoubtedly, it is the cartographic image's intricate and abstract visual element that is the locus of its strength and lasting appeal. That is the source of its ability to assemble an interpretation of space that helps us to understand how a particular map-maker sees his or her world, or how they interpret the human activities that take place within it. Thankfully for the cartographer, all external human activities take place in some kind of geometric space: space is the container and boundary within which we live our social lives, and it provides a rich source of inspiration to map-makers. Whatever is near or far, whatever is connected or separated, whatever exists in the material or natural world, and today, increasingly, whatever is linked by the flow of bits and bytes through fibre-optic cables or crosses between mobile-phone towers at the speed of light, can be mapped.

Perhaps the best modern definition of a map is the one put forward in 1987 by the historian of cartography Brian Harley, who described maps as 'graphic representations that facilitate a spatial understanding of things, concepts, conditions, processes or events in the human world'. Yet even this broad and highly descriptive definition confines itself to the 'what' of a map rather than the 'why', 'how', 'when' or 'who'. It says nothing about the experience of viewing or using a map, about the origins of map-making in antiquity or about why these images have been so compelling throughout virtually the whole of human history.

ABOUT THIS BOOK

Applying the adage 'I know one when I see one', this book puts the emphasis back on the experience of viewing rather than of describing. Bringing together maps from many ages and many cultures on a cross-section of themes – from the first attempts at scientific cartography by the Greeks and the scroll maps of East Asia to the complex networks of today's social media, each created to assemble and symbolize the various kinds of world inhabited by humans – creates a revealing impression of how cartography has shifted, changed and developed through time.

Rather than arranging this vast array of the world's cartographic knowledge chronologically or thematically, however, contrasting or complementary images have been paired in a way that not only highlights the uniqueness of individual maps and map-makers but also reinforces some of the common structures that many maps employ. Linking the dramatic image of the many layers of historic lava flows from Mount Vesuvius (see p.168) with one showing the flooding caused by Hurricane Katrina as it came ashore in New Orleans in 2005 (see p.169), for example, leaves the viewer with the impression both of how the timelessness of human experience can be captured on a two-dimensional map, and of the vast canyon of difference in the technology needed to make these compelling and very different images of natural disasters.

It is from the cartographer's selection of graphic and artistic forms of display – from the engraving of stones in antiquity to the carving of woodblocks for the great world maps of the Renaissance and onward to the near-infinite variety of computer visualizations that map large datasets of social interaction – that map-making draws its deep creative potential and its lasting power. It is there, in the choice of form, colour and thematic emphasis, that the viewer may peer into the hidden, seldom-considered fourth dimension of cartography: the one found in the minds of the cartographers themselves. It is in this fourth dimension that the infinite potential of cartography as a means to transmit and display information surely lies.

Many of the pairings in these pages underline the myriad ways that cartographers have solved some of the little-known technical and design problems involved in making a map. Since the very beginning of cartography, one of those problems – that of the vertical or, in the language of cartographers, of 'relief representation' – has been a central frustration for map-makers trying to replicate a three-dimensional Earth on a flat plane. In the struggle to design a clear representation of mountains, cliffs and other features that extend outward from the Earth's surface, map-makers have been pushed to invent new ways of envisioning terrain.

Two classic solutions to this problem, from the many that have been tried, can be seen in a map of Switzerland by the early twentieth-century Swiss cartographer Eduard Imhof (see p.196) and in the later view of Greater Yellowstone National Park by the Austrian Heinrich C. Berann (see p.197). These two striking maps solve the problem of relief in very different ways. One abstracts from reality and attempts, through the use of colour and shading, to trick the viewer into imagining the third dimension, while the other veers towards a more realistic and mimetic rendering of the landscape by using a bird's-eye view. Seeing the Earth as if from above is one of the more popular forms of envisioning a geographic space, and during the nineteenth and twentieth centuries this approach was used in maps found everywhere from placemats in small-town diners across the American West to the illustrations of flight paths in airline magazines.

THE NATURE OF CARTOGRAPHY

Maps have been – and continue to be – used in many ways, not only as analytical tools for accurately displaying distances and boundaries and for visualizing complex and developing collections of data, but also as a form of expressive visual art that has both cultural and political purposes with deep aesthetic underpinnings. Many of the maps in this book highlight this aesthetic and design element, and the pairings may prompt new consideration of and conclusions about precisely what makes an abstract rendering into a map. Such questions have long preoccupied visual artists in general, rather than cartographers alone, and this book contains many thought-provoking responses to and developments of map-making by artists from Jasper Johns to Grayson Perry (see pp.243 and 107).

Most historians place the beginnings of modern cartography in the work of the celebrated second-century Greek-Egyptian geographer Claudius Ptolemy. It was Ptolemy, in his book *Geography*, who first seems to have codified the idea of latitude and longitude – the grid of north-south and east-west lines that is used to divide the Earth in many modern maps – and developed the idea of a projection that underpins the geometric form of maps. It is not known for certain whether Ptolemy himself produced maps, as no examples from his time have survived, but this book features the iconic world map from the 1482 edition of *Geography* (see p.139).

As early cartographers were fully aware, making an accurate map is no easy matter, since taking the three-dimensional surface of the Earth and projecting it on to a two-dimensional plane is not a simple task. In order to understand the process one might picture the Earth as an orange. Peeling back the skin of the fruit is like peeling off the features of the Earth's surface that one wants to map, but trying to lay this surface out flat makes us either distort or tear the skin of the orange: flattening the surface of the Earth, or any sphere for that matter, is otherwise an impossible task.

Ptolemy was perhaps the first cartographer to analyse this problem and propose a mathematical solution for keeping track of the inevitable inaccuracy that was introduced to a map by such flattening. Some form of his solution survives in modern maps, accounting for some of the diversity in their geometrical appearance. Many people are unwittingly familiar with the most famous of these geometric projections, which is found on the great sixteenth-century world map by the Flemish cartographer Gerard Mercator (see p.155). Mercator's map was reproduced in thousands of editions and made its way into the wall maps found in school classrooms around the world. Mercator designed his map to be useful to mariners and sailors, and to allow them to navigate the great oceans using a compass in an accurate way. To make this possible, however, he had to introduce other kinds of inaccuracy, which resulted in large distortions in the area of some of the landmasses, such as a vastly oversized Greenland. There have been many other imaginative solutions to the problem first raised by Ptolemy, including Richard Buckminster Fuller's *Dymaxion World Map* (see p.231).

The kind of mapping Ptolemy envisioned – what we might call scientific cartography – is not the only kind, and it is unhelpful to judge most map-making by Ptolemy's criteria regarding mathematical and scientific accuracy. Many maps, both in antiquity and today, encompass a wider class of visual forms and find their cultural meanings and resonance in other kinds of representation and symbology. This book contains many maps from Western, Eastern and traditional cultures that are not maps in the Ptolemaic sense at all, since they neither strive for metric accuracy nor employ any form of corrective geometric projection. Many European maps from the later Middle Ages set out to map the Christian cosmos as envisioned in the Bible, for example, even after increasing geographical discovery made such maps patently unrealistic in terms of accuracy (see p.137). Such cosmological traditions can also be seen in religions such as Hinduism (see p.43) and Jainism (see pp.146–147). A comparison of a simple road map (see p.272) with a great medieval mappamundi (see p.148) or a Marshall Islander's stick chart (see p.63) shows in an instant the large conceptual space occupied by cartography.

Many kinds of cartography – like the origin of map-making itself – still baffle scholars today. One mysterious form appeared in about 1250 and died out in the mid-sixteenth century. Modern historians know little about who originated this very pragmatic form of map-making, or where it originated. The maps take the form of medieval sailing charts, such as the great *Cantino*

Planisphere (see p.223), and were made for use on board trading vessels that sailed the Mediterranean Sea and, later, the Atlantic Ocean. These maps – known as portolans – provided mariners with the names of ports along coasts, together with compass directions and the path of the prevailing winds, but did not bother to note any inland features. Such charts generally survive as large manuscript maps on vellum or sheepskin. Because they have no ancestral forms, they appear to have sprung fully formed from the medieval mind without any models or precursors, as is shown by the earliest surviving example, the *Carte Pisane* (see p.152)

CARTOGRAPHY AND TECHNOLOGY

The history of cartography has seen many revolutions in method as technological developments have increased its range and applicability. The ancient Egyptians used cartography to plot land ownership and field boundaries after the annual flooding of the Nile; the Romans to incise on bronze tablets their newly conquered lands and to distribute tribute to their soldiers; the Greeks to plot on vellum the limits of the known world; and the dynastic leaders of East Asia to build their temples and chart their long roads for the benefit of pilgrims and tax collectors.

The largest expansion of the territory that map-makers had to encompass in their view of the world came with the great Age of Discovery (roughly from the fifteenth to the seventeenth century). The explorations of Christopher Columbus, Amerigo Vespucci and many others expanded the area of the known world that had to be mapped, and forced innovations in Ptolemy's methods of map construction. Renaissance cartographers such as Martin Waldseemüller, whose great world map is the first to show the Pacific Ocean and the New World of the Americas separated from Asia (see p.228), took full advantage of contemporary developments in mathematics, navigation and astronomy to display the world visually in innovative ways. Maps of the time developed in parallel with the scientific revolutions brought about by Nicolaus Copernicus, Galileo Galilei and Isaac Newton, and are therefore nothing short of a visual expression of the coming of our modern technological age.

For most of the history of cartography, a map was made using data from field surveys, and was then transferred to copper or steel plates or lithographic stones in order to be printed on paper. Throughout the seventeenth and eighteenth centuries and into the nineteenth this was the state of the art, as map-makers employed new technology both to measure the surface of the Earth and to print maps in innovative ways. Countless mapping expeditions, including those of Samuel de Champlain in eastern North America (see p.218) in the seventeenth century, James Cook's mid-eighteenth-century adventures in the Pacific Ocean (see p.257) and Britain's Great Trigonometrical Survey of India (see p.48), mapping its colony throughout the nineteenth century – all armed with measuring chains, surveying telescopes and notebooks – filled in the blanks on older maps.

Around the world the shifting fortunes of empire and commerce brought about new mapping centres in London, Paris and the Netherlands as cartography became intimately bound up with mercantile and colonial interests. Exploration in the cause of commerce greatly expanded the accuracy of surveying technology, and, with those developments, larger and larger portions of the globe came under the cartographer's gaze, culminating only recently with the advent of satellites, which miss few parts of the Earth's surface (see p.105).

The study and science of cartography and its related geographical disciplines underwent perhaps their most profound technological and conceptual advances in the second half of the twentieth century. These advances, brought about by technology developed in the fighting of two world wars, the advent of computers, the discovery of newer and faster mathematical and computational algorithms, the birth of satellite imagery and the widespread use of the Global Positioning System (GPS), contributed to paradigm changes that expanded the definition of a map beyond anything that could have been imagined by Ptolemy or any of the great cartographers of even the more recent past.

Today many maps seek to convey information that, while spatially displayed, is not primarily concerned with Euclidean distance. The visualization of large datasets showing information such as the number of Twitter messages (see p.17), the location of Facebook members (see p.110) or even the London Underground (see p.298) are concerned more with connectivity than with distance. What they show us is the underlying topology of a space rather than its topography, displaying the shape and form of a network of social and infrastructural interaction instead of proximity and distance.

Many cartographers and programmers now have a much wider perspective on mapping than was common even a short time ago, and are exploring new forms of data and visualization technique. Such analysis, while using many of the same underlying mathematical principles as traditional maps, is computationally and aesthetically richer, and has been applied in the intervening years to the whole range of social and natural phenomena that take place in space and time.

CHANGING DEFINITIONS

Thanks to such advances, the map-making practised today is very different from and much more varied than the traditional forms that existed for centuries. The idea that cartography is confined strictly to the mapping of the features and thematic variables associated with terrestrial and celestial objects started to unravel in the 1970s with the birth of computational geometry and spatial analysis, which led to the creation of modern computer mapping and Geographic Information Systems (GIS). The number of participants in what used to be a highly specialized discipline has also exploded: now anyone with a laptop, tablet or smartphone has access to largely free and open-source state-of-the art software, geospatial data and mapping capability through Google Earth and other providers.

Today the mapping of objects that have no material existence – such as Internet searches or social-media information flows – is commonplace. These maps (in the truest sense of the word) represent a form of cartography that deals with extremely large amounts of information and data, and are made by cartographers and GIS analysts in an attempt to understand dynamic systems that are unstable and rapidly changing. Maps like these are not static, like the paper maps of the past, and have found their place in the analysis of many important real-time events including the West African Ebola epidemic (see p.213), natural disasters and revolutions in the Middle East and Africa.

As in other periods, however, cartography is not developing in a single direction. One of the most familiar of the various parallel strands – if not the most revolutionary – is the use of web-based maps for users to generate their own driving or walking routes and follow their own process, or for runners, walkers or cyclists to chart their personal activity, together with details of speed, time, elevation and so on (see p.268). Another is the development of three-dimensional printing, which potentially allows the production of maps that replicate relief (see p.311). Yet another is the exploration of the real-world application of computer games such as Minecraft, intended as a tool for building imaginary worlds but already being used to create models of real locations – even whole countries (see p.308).

In the first decade of the twenty-first century, a mapping project began that was unlike any cartographic survey previously attempted: to chart what has been termed the human connectome (even that word did not exist a few years ago, having been coined to describe the complete set of neural connections in the human brain). The idea is simple: the human brain is a complex network just like any other, so one must understand its connections in order to get an idea of how it functions. The process is comparable to what happened with the Internet, the exact functioning of which remained something of a mystery until it was approximately mapped and its connections understood. Instead of routers and network hubs, cartographers in this survey are mapping individual neurons.

The brain's structure is still known only in its broadest form. The connectome remains a fairly theoretical construct whose topological outlines are only beginning to be mapped, using raw data from various forms of brain-imaging that can be thought of as a kind of remote sensing – the Google Earth of our inner world and consciousness (see p.111). As this technology develops and new algorithms for visualizing the data are created – brain projections, as compared to Ptolemaic map projections – more and more of the blanks on this human map will be filled in. It might be argued that this is a neurological exercise rather than a cartographic one, and yet what is its ultimate aim if not to create a graphic representation – a map – that will allow us to understand another part of our spatial world, albeit internal rather than external space? That has always been the aim of cartography, so the connectome project can justly be seen as cartography's final frontier…until the subatomic world, the outer universe, the deepest oceans or simply the intricacies of billions of daily lives present cartographers with a new challenge.

John Hessler

Specialist in Modern Cartography
and Geographic Information Science
Geography and Map Division
Library of Congress, Washington, DC

A New Yorker's Idea of the United States of America | 1939 | Daniel K. Wallingford

Printed paper. 30 × 41 cm / 12 × 16 in. Private collection

Daniel K. Wallingford first drew this pointed commentary on the geographical myopia of New Yorkers in 1936, in the midst of the Great Depression. The map was so successful that it was done in a larger and more elaborate format in 1939, perhaps to coincide with the World's Fair in New York. Wallingford did not target only New Yorkers. He also created a similar map satirizing the 'Bostonian's Idea' of the nation. All of these evoke the pictorial style of map in the mid-twentieth century, which embraced a familiar and whimsical approach. Here the style is used to comic effect, stretching the very definition of geography to capture the legendary provincialism of Americans in the urban north-east. Intentional geographical errors drive the point home: Birmingham is placed in Tennessee rather than Alabama, Lake Louise in the Great Lakes rather than the Canadian Rockies, and Yellowstone in Colorado, not Wyoming. The Texas landscape is dotted with spouting oil rigs and a cowboy, while San Francisco is granted its own state. The Wallingford map is often believed to have inspired Saul Steinberg's classic *View of the World from 9th Avenue* of 1976 (see opposite), but that credit may be due to the cartoonist John T. McCutcheon, who drew a satirical version even earlier (*Chicago Tribune*, 1922).

View of the World from 9th Avenue | 1976 | Saul Steinberg

Ink, pencil, coloured pencil and watercolour on paper. 71 × 48 cm / 28 × 19 in. Private collection

Saul Steinberg's map of 1976 is one of the most familiar and widely imitated of all maps and an unquestioned modern classic. This most famous *New Yorker* cover by Steinberg – a self-confessed 'writer who draws' – highlights the way in which many of those living in great cities imagine that their concerns are all that matters, and have a correspondingly narrow perspective on the world. It has a precursor in the work of Daniel K.

Wallingford in the 1920s and 1930s (see opposite). In common with Wallingford and cartographers such as James Francis Horrabin (see p.277), Steinberg employs an amusing image as social comment. But Steinberg's drawing also raises the question of how our mental maps affect the way we relate to the world. Steinberg wants viewers to imagine viewing the world from their own street. What is valued looms large; what interests us is

close by and easy to get to. Places that mean little to us are small, peripheral and empty. As Steinberg points out, we always place ourselves at the centre and focus of our own maps (as of our worlds). Perhaps the hardest question he raises concerns what is omitted from any personal map – from a slum just around the corner or a major problem we cannot face. Maps can often reveal as much by what they leave out as by what they include.

Silos Apocalypse | 1109 | Beatus of Liébana

Ink on parchment. 32 × 43 cm / 12½ × 17 in. British Library, London

Early European cartographers were guided as much by theology as by geography, and this map and others that accompany the biblical commentaries of the eighth-century Spanish monk Beatus of Liébana are some of the earliest pictures of the Christian world. The map-maker orientated his world with east at the top and featured in India an illustration of Adam and Eve ashamed of their nakedness in the Garden of Eden. The world is divided into four: Asia, Europe and Africa, each of which the Bible relates to one of the three sons of Noah, and, to the right, *deserta terra,* an uninhabitable continent populated by monsters or Antipodeans. A blue line in the centre represents the Mediterranean Sea, with the River Nile bending off it to the right, and a red line indicates the Red Sea. The text indicates important biblical places, including Babylon and Sodom, as well as major European cities, such as Constantinople, Rome, Tarragona and Alexandria. The most important city, Jerusalem, is indicated by a temple with an Islamic-era horseshoe-shaped doorway that reminds the reader that both Spain and Jerusalem had been conquered by Muslims, exposing the Spanish artist to Islamic influences. Encircling the known world is the vast ocean that was considered the limit of the habitable Earth.

Hereford Mappa Mundi | c.1300 | Richard of Haldingham

Ink, gilt and pigments on vellum. 163 × 132 cm / 64 × 52 in. Hereford Cathedral, Herefordshire

This renowned mappa mundi uses the basic device – familiar from many modern maps – of looking down on a particular point on the globe from a great distance. At the exact centre of this map is Jerusalem – described in the Bible as being placed by God 'in the centre of the nations, with countries all around her' – with the crucifixion shown above it. Around the city lie the three inhabited continents, orientated with east at the top, with grotesque animals and monstrous peoples filling the margins. With illustrations of scenes from ancient and classical history and retellings of Bible stories, the map sets out to provide a visual encyclopedia of the world, details of peoples (known and unknown), animals (real and imaginary) and wonders (natural and artificial). The cartographer presents a unified vision of the world as viewed by medieval Christians in which everything has its proper place and all is within the domain of Providence. But the map's unity is illusory. It reflects Europeans' confidence in their knowledge rather than communicating information, reminding us that this is, primarily, a map of a world view, rather than of the world, that leads the reader to a spiritual destination – the Christian heaven – rather than an earthly one.

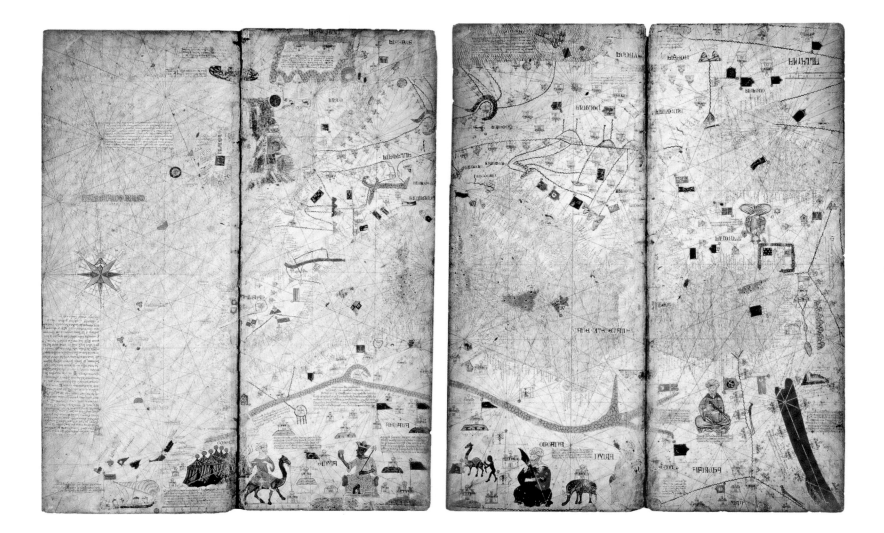

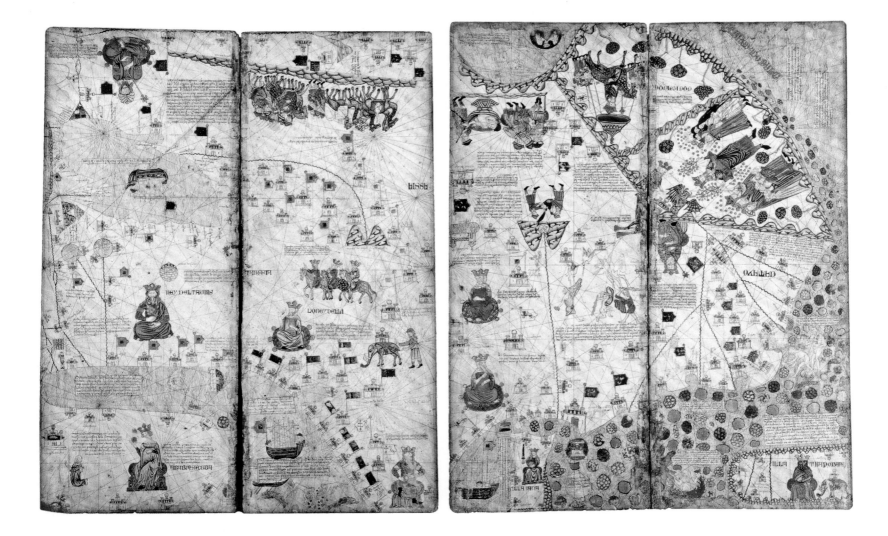

Catalan Atlas | c.1375 | Cresques Abraham

Manuscript in ink and pigments with gold highlights on parchment mounted on 12 boards. 65 × 300 cm / 25½ × 118 in. Bibliothèque nationale de France, Paris

The king seated in West Africa in the second panel of this part of the Catalan Atlas is Mansa Musa, who ruled Mali from about 1312 to 1337. Stories of the wealth this Islamic ruler spent on a pilgrimage to Mecca so impressed Europeans that he was often depicted on portolan charts seated upon a throne with an orb and sceptre. The magnificent atlas was probably presented as a gift by Pedro IV of Aragon to Charles VI of France.

It is believed to have been made by the Jewish cartographer Cresques Abraham – also known as Abraham Cresques – of the Majorcan school of cartography. It is one of the earliest examples of the incorporation of a portolan chart into a circular medieval mappa mundi. Four of its panels – not shown – contain cosmographical and astronomical illustrations and texts in the Catalan language of south-east Spain. The four central panels

(above, left) are a standard portolan chart of the Atlantic, Mediterranean, Black Sea, Europe and North Africa. The last four panels, depicting Asia, are based on medieval mappa mundi with additional information from *The Travels of Marco Polo*, written in the 1290s (Polo and his father and uncle appear in the sixth panel above). The first compass rose ever depicted on a map is shown here in the Atlantic Ocean.

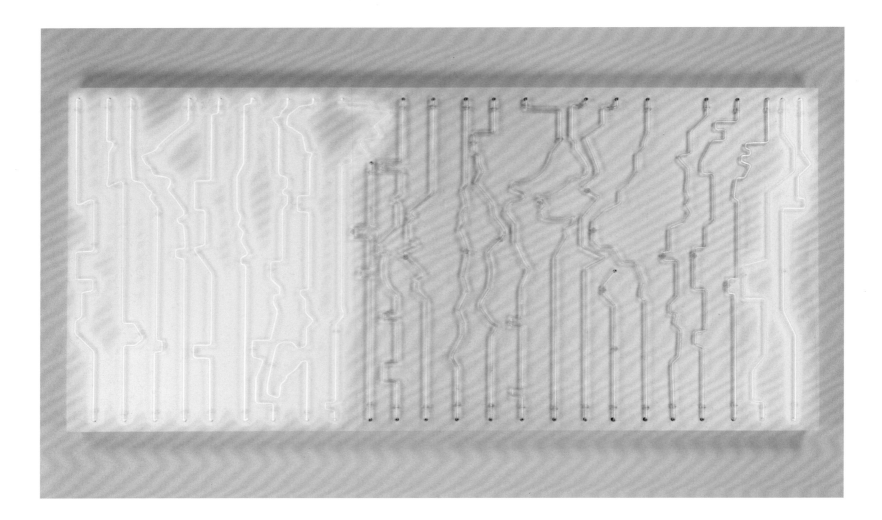

Daylight Map | 2005 | Olafur Eliasson

Neon, sintra box, transformers, controllers, sequencer, timers. 122 × 254 × 15.2 cm / 48 × 100 × 6 in. Private collection

Taking as its starting point the Mercator projection world map (see p.155), which is centred on the zero hour of Coordinated Universal Time (UTC), Eliasson's map uses twenty-four neon tubes for the evenly spaced vertical lines that divide international time zones. Presented without the context of the familiar shapes of countries, it is striking that the lines are not uniformly parallel but, rather, remarkably crooked. This reminds the viewer that while the organization of world time is notionally based on a natural phenomenon – the Earth's complete rotation on its axis divided into twenty-four hours – in practice, artificial national boundaries demonstrate political factors at play, which complicate the structure. At any one time, about half of the neon tubes are illuminated, indicating places in the world that are experiencing daylight. Indeed, the map functions in real time, so that as the sun sets on a region and one neon tube switches off, another automatically comes on where the sun is rising. Seen in the context of the Danish-Icelandic artist's wider art practice, which is concerned with the environment and ecology, this map also highlights the fact that at any one time, somewhere on the globe, electric lights are always on.

Tweetping | 2013 | Franck Ernewein

Digital. Dimensions variable

Since the early 2000s, the mapping of Internet activity, tweets and other information flows that have no material reality in space has become important in the study of everything from natural disasters and epidemics to political revolutions. This map, which comes from the Tweetping website, developed by Franck Ernewein, displays tweets from around the world. Ernewein's map is dynamic, with tweets firing across the screen as they occur in real time. As the tweets are recorded, the map builds and grows in luminescence until it resembles the more familiar 'Earth at night' maps that were popular at the beginning of the satellite remote-sensing revolution. Even though the map fills quickly, it does not even attempt to map the entire Twitter feed from around the world – clearly an impossible task. It includes only public tweets, which account for perhaps no more than 1 or 2 per cent of the total Twitter traffic. Maps such as this have been useful, when limited to particular hashtags, in keeping track of messages associated with important events happening around the world, and have also been used by journalists and crisis cartographers interested in knowing where messages originate and their quantities.

The Whole World in a Cloverleaf | 1581 | Heinrich Bünting

Coloured woodcut. 27 × 37 cm / 10⅝ × 14½ in. Norman B. Leventhal Map Center, Boston Public Library

Heinrich Bünting drew this map during the long struggle between Catholicism and the new Protestant theology in the sixteenth century. Bünting studied theology, philosophy and mathematics before becoming a Lutheran minister. He conceived of a volume about the Holy Land written for the Protestant reader. Although there is no evidence that Bünting went to Palestine himself, from its first edition in 1581 his *Itinerarium Sacrae Scripturae*

(Travel through Holy Scripture) was something of a bestseller. The book, complete with descriptions of topography and the wanderings of the Patriarchs and Apostles, was printed in many languages for more than six decades. Most editions contain several curious maps. One shows Asia as Pegasus, the winged horse; another is Europe in female form. This one depicts the world as a cloverleaf, an emblem of Bünting's home town, Hanover.

The three leaves echo the Trinity, as well as medieval maps, but not all the world fits: England and Scandinavia lie outside, while America can be seen in the lower left. If Europe, Asia and Africa – in the Bible, the domains of Noah's three sons – constitute the leaves, Jerusalem may be the flower. The map shows Hanover and the world with a theological core: Jerusalem, representing the holy city of God, is the centre of the world.

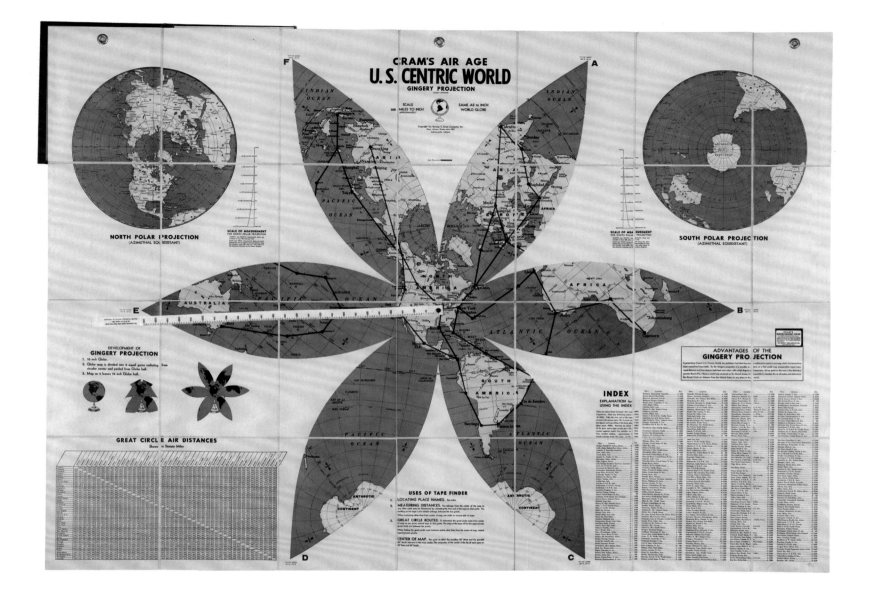

Cram's Air Age U.S. Centric World Gingery Projection | 1943 | George F. Cram Company

Printed paper mounted on linen with measuring tape. 122 × 172 cm / 48 × 67¾ in. Private collection

In the 1940s, Indiana high-school principal Walter Gingery confidently believed he had cracked a problem that had obsessed cartographers since the beginning of mapmaking: how to convert geographic information accurately from a round globe to a flat map. All previous projections had involved compromise but Gingery's attractive, flower-shaped projection, as his publishers boasted on the map itself, 'achieved a result ... which has heretofore been considered impossible'. The map was released just as passenger air travel was becoming practical for greater numbers of people, and Gingery provided tools directly on the map to assist users planning journeys: a measuring tape (connected to Chicago), written directions to calculate air routes and miles, a distance table and special pencils with which users were encouraged to write on the washable surface. The map could be either hung on the wall from its three sturdy grommets or folded along its fabric grid. Although Gingery patented his projection, however, it turned out to be neither very useful nor repeatable. While the map may be technically flat, it is as difficult to read as any other peeled globe gores that are disconnected from their usual spherical shape.

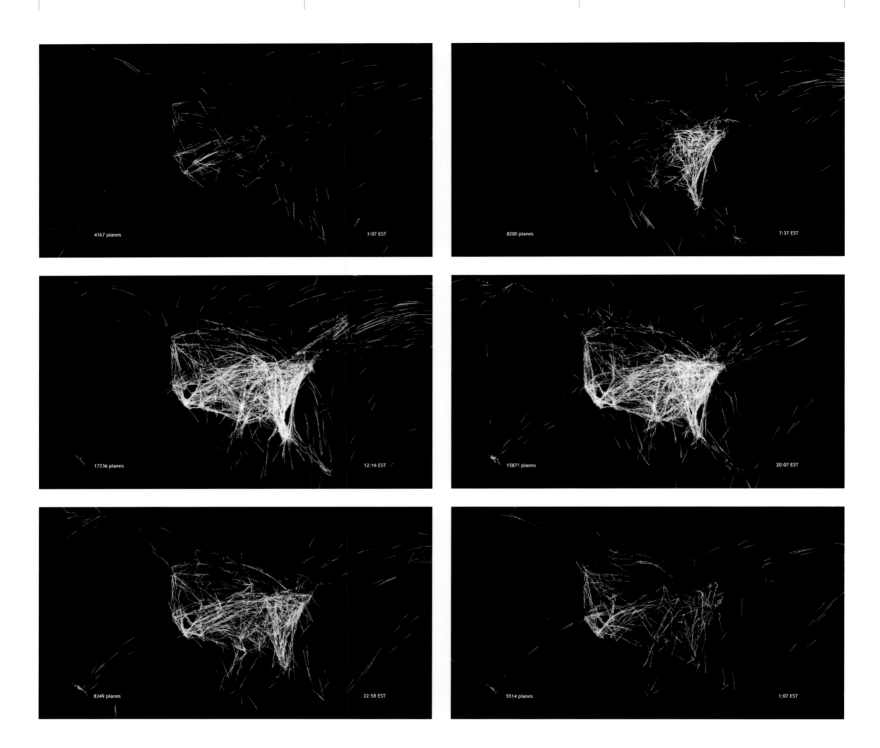

Flight Patterns | 2005 | Aaron Koblin

Digital. Dimensions variable

These maps are some of the most beautiful examples of a recent trend in cartography that uses massive amounts of data to produce network patterns and large graphs that show the connections between human-generated technology and the space people occupy. Created by Aaron Koblin, a US artist and designer specializing in the visualization of large digital datasets, the project *Celestial Mechanics* from which these maps come shows

the paths of nearly 20,000 aircraft in flight in US airspace in an array of colours keyed to the type of aircraft. To create the map – this version is actually a snapshot of a dynamic flow map that shows the flight paths in motion in real time – Koblin plotted data from the United States Federal Aviation Administration using the Processing programming environment. This specialized software allows designers and visual artists to explore the aes-

thetic possibilities encapsulated in large datasets. Maps like Koblin's can be considered part of a trend that has injected large amounts of cross-disciplinary interaction into the field of cartography, and that use real-world and community-generated data to display graphically the changing relationship between humans and the technological systems they create.

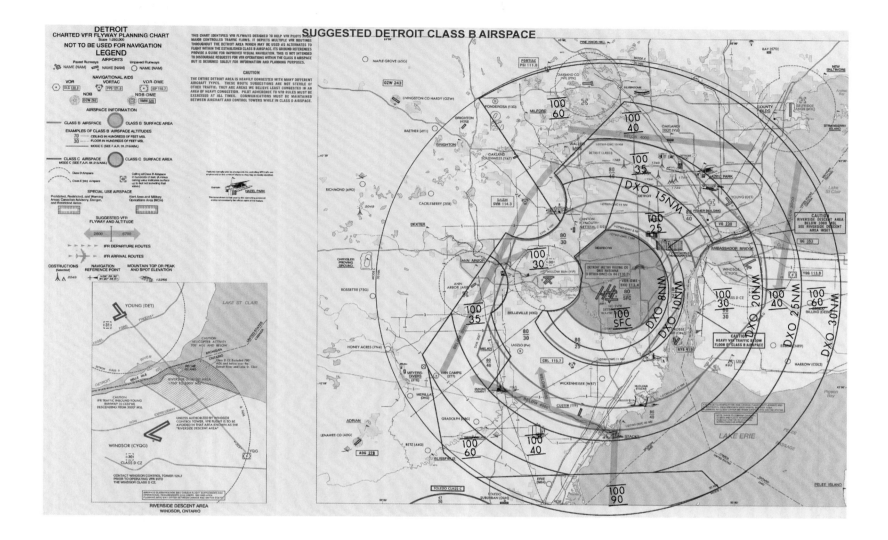

Detroit Charted VFR Flyway Planning Chart | 2010 | United States Federal Aviation Administration

Printed paper. Dimensions variable

In theory, this map allows an experienced pilot to plot his or her way safely around Detroit without any instruments – in fact, by doing little more than looking out of the cockpit window (although not all airspace allows total freedom). America's Federal Aviation Administration (FAA) produces Visual Flight Rules (VFR) Flyway Planning Charts to assist pilots in planning routes around key urban areas, with recommended flight paths and altitudes that allow them to bypass busy routes and steer towards regions that are less likely to be clogged up with air traffic. The charts, which are designed at a scale of 1:250,000 and are updated every six months, feature notable local landmarks – skyscrapers, bridges, race tracks, anything that can easily be picked out from the air and their scale may be increased to aid visual orientation. The FAA adds a crucial caveat: 'Flyways are not devoid of Instrument Flight Rules [IFR] or military traffic. They represent flight paths that are believed to have the least IFR or military activity.' In many ways this is a modern, urban map of the sky.

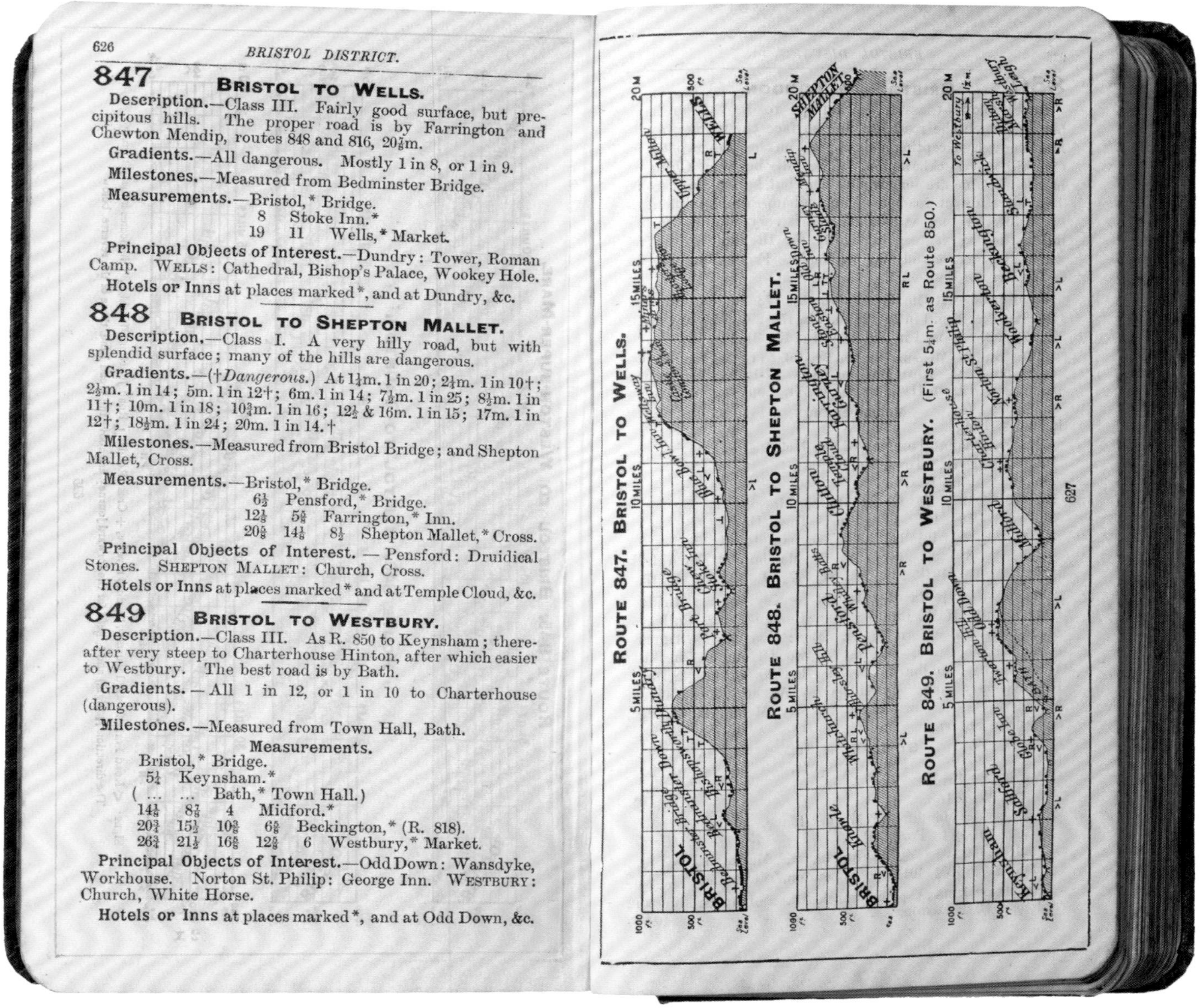

626 BRISTOL DISTRICT.

847 Bristol to Wells.

Description.—Class III. Fairly good surface, but precipitous hills. The proper road is by Farrington and Chewton Mendip, routes 848 and 816, 20¾m.

Gradients.—All dangerous. Mostly 1 in 8, or 1 in 9.

Milestones.—Measured from Bedminster Bridge.

Measurements.—Bristol,* Bridge.
8 Stoke Inn.*
19 11 Wells,* Market.

Principal Objects of Interest.—Dundry: Tower, Roman Camp. Wells: Cathedral, Bishop's Palace, Wookey Hole.

Hotels or Inns at places marked*, and at Dundry, &c.

848 Bristol to Shepton Mallet.

Description.—Class I. A very hilly road, but with splendid surface; many of the hills are dangerous.

Gradients.—(†*Dangerous.*) At 1¼m. 1 in 20; 2¼m. 1 in 10†; 2⅝m. 1 in 14; 5m. 1 in 12†; 6m. 1 in 14; 7½m. 1 in 25; 8¼m. 1 in 11†; 10m. 1 in 18; 10¾m. 1 in 16; 12½ & 16m. 1 in 15; 17m. 1 in 12†; 18¾m. 1 in 24; 20m. 1 in 14.†

Milestones.—Measured from Bristol Bridge; and Shepton Mallet, Cross.

Measurements.—Bristol,* Bridge.
6½ Pensford,* Bridge.
12⅛ 5⅝ Farrington,* Inn.
20⅝ 14⅛ 8½ Shepton Mallet,* Cross.

Principal Objects of Interest. — Pensford: Druidical Stones. Shepton Mallet: Church, Cross.

Hotels or Inns at places marked* and at Temple Cloud, &c.

849 Bristol to Westbury.

Description.—Class III. As R. 850 to Keynsham; thereafter very steep to Charterhouse Hinton, after which easier to Westbury. The best road is by Bath.

Gradients. — All 1 in 12, or 1 in 10 to Charterhouse (dangerous).

Milestones.—Measured from Town Hall, Bath.

Measurements.
Bristol,* Bridge.
5¼ Keynsham.*
(... ... Bath,* Town Hall.)
14⅛ 8⅞ 4 Midford.*
20¾ 15½ 10⅝ 6⅝ Beckington,* (R. 818).
26¾ 21½ 16⅝ 12⅝ 6 Westbury,* Market.

Principal Objects of Interest.—Odd Down: Wansdyke, Workhouse. Norton St. Philip: George Inn. Westbury: Church, White Horse.

Hotels or Inns at places marked*, and at Odd Down, &c.

Bristol District, Routes 847, 848, 849 | 1896 | Harry R. G. Inglis

Printed in *The Contour Road Book of England* (1906 edition). 15.5 × 9.5 cm / 6 × 3¾ in. Private collection

The 'lines' of these gradient cycle maps resemble music rather than traditional road maps based on a view from above. In what was still a relatively early age of cycling, they told cyclists about the hills they would face, information that was irrelevant to motorists. The rest of the book included more conventional strip maps, showing places of interest immediately on the routes, together with brief information about gradients and distances, and details of hotels and inns. The main selling point of Harry Inglis's pocket books for cyclists, prominently advertised on their waterproof covers, was that they never had to be unfolded. The large-scale maps – up to a total length of 4.8 metres (16 feet) long across numerous pages – came in a compact book that could slip into a pocket. It allowed cyclists to see quickly where they had just been and what lay immediately ahead. The strip maps are not orientated to a particular direction. All the information relates to a single message: follow the line to reach the destination. The maps can be seen as a modern equivalent of the strip maps developed for highway travel by John Ogilby in the United Kingdom in 1675 (see p.60), which set the standard for nearly two centuries, and were the precursor to the American Automobile Association's TripTik Travel Planner.

The 22 Stages of the 44th Tour de France | 1957 | Miroir-Sprint

Printed paper. 61.5 × 49.5 cm / 24¼ × 19½ in. Private collection

This souvenir map of the 44th Tour de France, held in 1957, was published in the French sports magazine *Miroir-Sprint* so that enthusiasts could chart the progress of the race for themselves. The magazine reported the cyclists' progress every other day during the race at a time when few stages of the race were broadcast – and few households had televisions, although the central advertisement for a TV set was a telling sign of the future. The Tour de France began in 1903, following stages around France – and from 1954 into neighbouring countries – on a course that varied every year, although the gruelling test of endurance did not. Readers used this outline map to update the results of each stage as it happened, thereby creating a living record of the race from 27 June to 20 July of that year. Dynamic, participatory cartography first became popular in the nineteenth century during times of conflict. Maps were circulated with coloured pencils so that readers could mark progress as reports of battles, victories and defeats reached them from the front. Today we take it for granted that maps depicting current events are updated in real time, but for the fans of the Frenchman Jacques Anquetil, who won the 44th Tour, following his progress was an exciting act of recording history in the making.

Peutinger Table | C.AD 300–350 | Unknown

Ink on parchment. 30 × 675 cm / 1 ft × 22 ft 1¾ in. Österreichische Nationalbibliothek, Vienna

This unique map of roads in the Roman Empire is named after Konrad Peutinger, who owned it in the early sixteenth century. It takes the form of a long scroll that shows the world from the Atlantic to India and the connections and distances between various places. It distorts distances – compressing those from north to south but stretching those from east to west – to highlight those links. It was compiled from itineraries showing, in effect, the roads that led to the central cities of the empire and, above all, to Rome. The roads between the 4,000 named places are annotated with distances in red Roman numerals. This version is an incomplete thirteenth-century copy of an original that may have dated from the time following Diocletian's reforms of 293 AD, so there is some question about when various elements first appeared. It is unclear why a map would be created that is too large – and too expensive – to use in actual wayfinding. The original was probably produced as a celebration of the restoration of order and peace within the empire as a consequence of Diocletian's administrative changes. As such, the map is a political statement that all is well with the world. It was later updated and used simply as a distance chart, its original purpose forgotten.

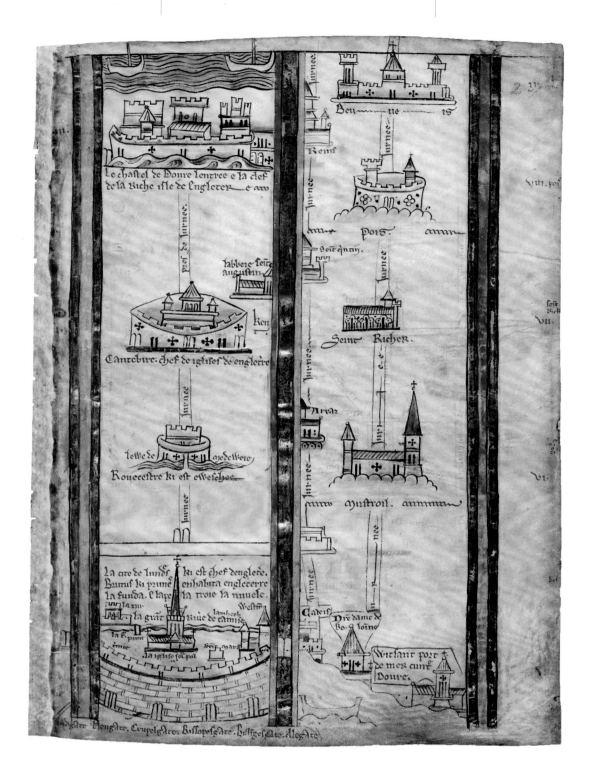

Itinerary from London to Beauvais | 1250–9 | Matthew Paris

Ink on parchment from *Chronica majora*. 36 × 24.5 cm / 14¼ × 9⅔ in. British Library, London

The thirteenth-century historian and Benedictine monk Matthew Paris drew this graphic itinery map of the pilgrimage route from London to Jerusalem around 1250. It is uncertain where he acquired this detailed, although sometimes confused, information since he is not known to have been to Italy or the Holy Land himself. Few medieval Europeans could afford to make the journey, and monks rarely travelled far from their cloisters, even

if their orders allowed them to do so. Paris arranged the journey to the Heavenly City as a straight line over six pages, each divided into two columns designed to be read from bottom to top, and left to right. In this, he pioneered an approach not seen again for more than 400 years, when John Ogilby published his strip maps of the roads of England and Wales in 1675 (see p.60). The illustrations depict the major cities and towns of Europe

as well as other locations with religious significance to form a pictorial evocation of the route. The landscape is not represented at all, however, in part because Paris's map was not intended for practical use. Instead, it was a guide to an interior journey with a spiritual goal: the viewers who used it to stimulate their imaginations believed that Jerusalem itself was only an image of the actual Heavenly City.

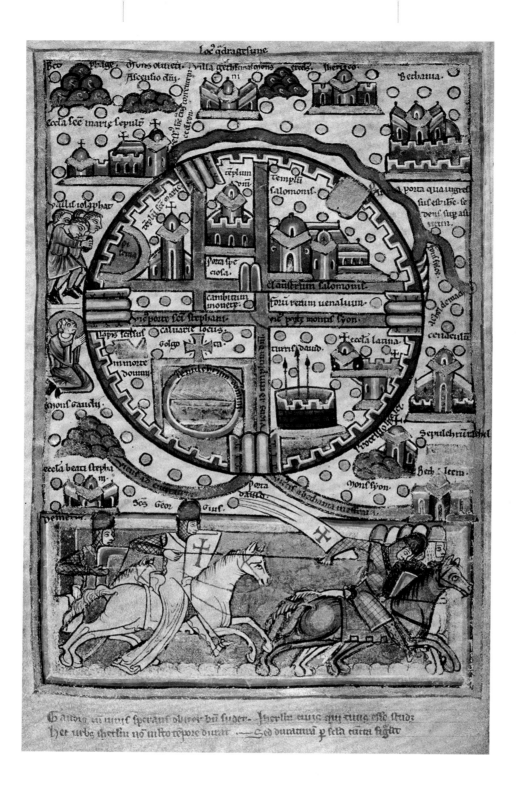

Map of Jerusalem as the Centre of the World | c.1200 | Unknown

Ink on vellum. 21 × 30 cm / 8¼ × 11¾ in. Koninklijke Bibliotheek, The Hague

Jerusalem was often placed at the heart of medieval maps, reflecting its spiritual centrality to Christians, but this early, stylized plan of the city and its region underlines its disputed status. Both Christians and Muslims claim the city as a spiritual centre. The city had been captured by Europeans from Muslims during the First Crusade (1096–9), but before the map was drawn a century later the city was recaptured by Saladin in

1187. This beautifully illuminated Crusader map simplifies Jerusalem's fortified walls into a circle, orientated with east at the top and surrounded by nearby towns such as Bethlehem. The simplified streets forming a cross within the circle, and the blue of the city walls, echo the medieval T-O style of world maps, making Jerusalem a microcosm of the world. The map labels important biblical locations, including the Holy Sepulchre, the

Tower of David, the Latin Church and the *calvarie locus* ('place of crucifixion') at Golgotha, marked with a gold cross. The artist has carefully removed or renamed Muslim places, such as the al-Aqsa mosque, which is replaced by 'Solomon's Temple'. In the war scene set outside the sanctuary of Jerusalem's city walls, two Crusaders on horseback chase Saracens along the bottom of the page.

Jerusalem | 1733 | Juan Bautista Villalpando

Copperplate engraving. 34.5 × 42.3 cm / 13½ × 16⅝ in. National Library of Jerusalem, Israel

Juan Bautista Villalpando's beautiful map of Jerusalem was widely copied and translated, and used for over a century – yet it bears no relation to any real city. Villalpando was a man of many parts: a Jesuit priest in Rome, he was an expert on geometry, an architectural theorist, a biblical exegete, a cartographer and a dreamer. Little wonder, then, that he found the subject of the Holy City irresistible. Jerusalem is a physical city that can be visited and surveyed; it is a key location in the history and sacred writings of Jews and Christians that can be studied as literature; and it is a sacred image in itself, as in the dreamlike, mystical account of its Temple (with complex dimensions) given in the biblical book of Ezekiel. Villalpando attempted to combine all facets of the city by using all the available information to draw his map. He believed he was demonstrating the divine origins of classical architectural proportion and geometry – exemplified for him in the writings of the first-century author Vitruvius – as well as discovering the Bible's deeper meaning. In reality, he jumbled empirical topography with geometrical idealism, and confused mystical imagery with historical contingencies. The result is a cartographic curiosity that, notwithstanding its aesthetic appeal, answers no one's questions.

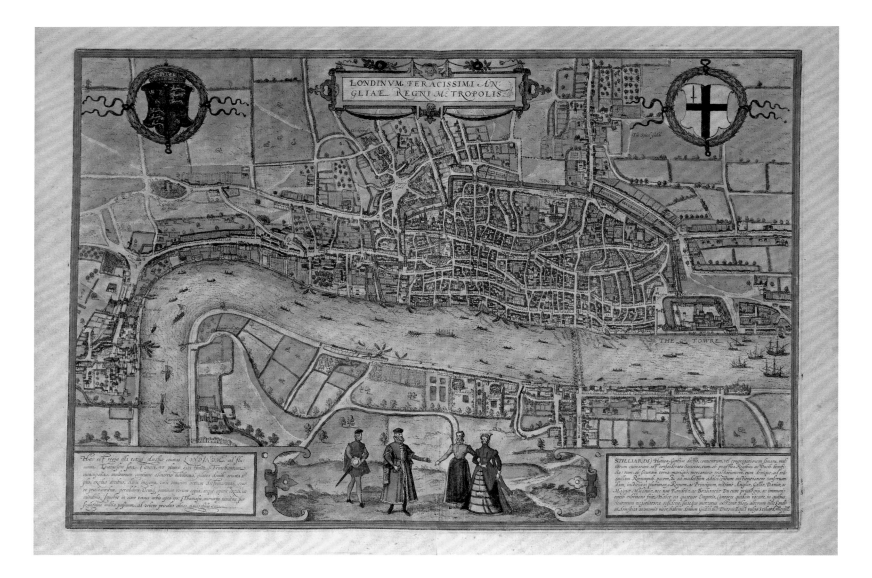

Illustrated Map of London | 1575 | Georg Braun & Frans Hogenberg

Hand-coloured engraving. 42 × 54 cm / 16½ × 21¼ in. Museo Navale di Pegli, Genoa

The royal barge of Mary Tudor sails along the Thames in the middle of this bird's-eye view of London from the south. The earliest existing plan of the city, the map was included in the first systematic town atlas, *Civitates Orbis Terrarum*, published in 1572. The German team behind the atlas – the clergyman Georg Braun and artist Frans Hogenberg – seized on the new fashion for books of maps started two years earlier by Abraham Ortelius

(see pp.134 and 229). Given the map's German origins, it is not surprising that prominence is given to the Stilliard, the London trading hall of the German-based Hanseatic League of merchants. The map's Latin title is flanked by the royal arms and those of the City of London. In the foreground are four figures in Tudor dress, together with two cartouches containing text praising both London and the League. On the south bank of the river is the

new district of Southwark, with its theatres and bull- and bear-baiting pits. To the left is Westminster, with Westminster Abbey clearly visible. The plan is based on out-of-date information (St Paul's is shown with its spire, which was destroyed in 1561; the cross shown in St Botolph's Churchyard was destroyed in 1559), but that did not affect the popularity of Braun and Hogenberg: their atlas eventually expanded to fill six volumes.

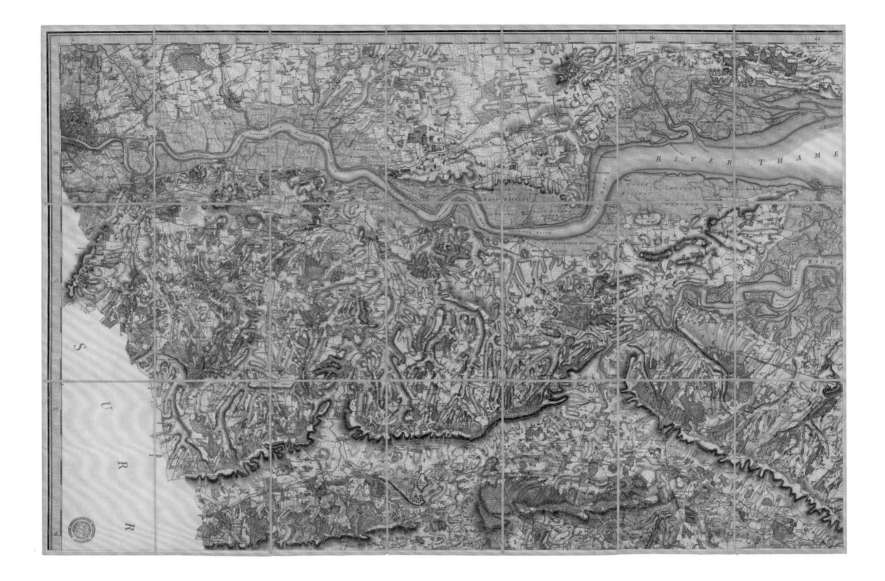

An Entirely New and Accurate Survey of the County of Kent | 1801 | William Mudge for Ordnance Survey

Copperplate engraving. 117 × 173 cm / 46 × 68 in (whole map). Royal Geographical Society, London

The publication of Captain William Mudge's 1-inch map of Kent by the Ordnance Survey was a landmark in the history of British mapping. Before the French Revolution of 1789, the British government had consistently refused to fund a national survey of Britain and Ireland, but the fear of a French invasion led to the decision by the Board of Ordnance to establish the Trigonometrical Survey in 1791. As the likely target of any French invasion, Kent was the first county to be surveyed at 2 inches to the mile (and incorporating earlier, larger-scale surveys). The map of the country was initially published in four large sheets, one of which is shown here. The various drawings were reduced to a common scale of 1 inch to the mile and engraved on copper by William Faden, a commercial map publisher who, for reasons of security, did the work inside the Tower of London. This sheet shows the area of the Isle of Dogs with the West India Docks, still under construction when the map was published, and also includes the earlier Brunswick Dock, which was later incorporated into the East India Docks. The construction of the docks encouraged rapid development of the area – leading to the necessity for a new edition of the map in 1820.

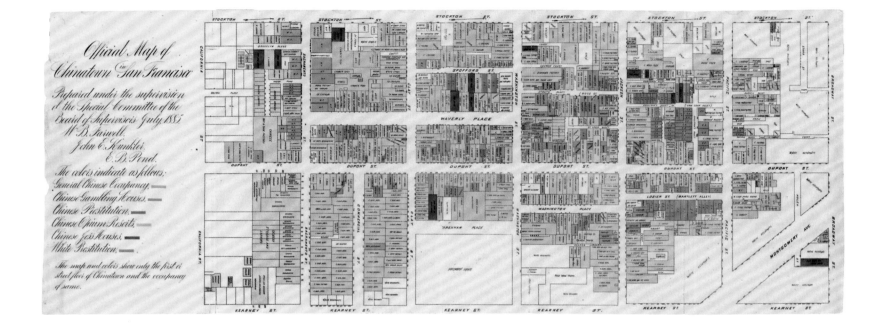

Official Map of Chinatown in San Francisco | 1885 | Willard B. Farwell

Printed in *The Chinese at Home and Abroad* by Willard B. Farwell (1885). 22 × 54 cm / 8¾ × 21¼ in. Private collection

The elaborate title of this elegant map belies its rather dark purpose, which was to detail the vice allegedly introduced to San Francisco by the Chinese in the decades after the American Civil War (1861–65). The map resembles the Sanborn Fire Insurance maps common at the time (see p.190), but rather than identifying building materials and dimensions, it identifies each property by its trade, including prostitution houses, opium dens, joss houses (places of worship) and gambling premises. The map – perhaps the earliest attempt to chart the distribution of vice – accompanied an investigation of the sanitary conditions of Chinatown that was full of salacious detail purporting to reveal the complex geography of the district. The colour-coding identified various types of vice: gambling houses in pink, Chinese prostitution in green, white prostitution in blue. More than anything, the map captures the height of anti-Chinese feeling in California in the 1880s. A few years earlier, the construction of the transcontinental railway had produced a huge demand for labour in the American West, which Chinese workers filled. During the recession that followed, the Chinese were accused of displacing white labour in California, making them an easy scapegoat for the economic crisis.

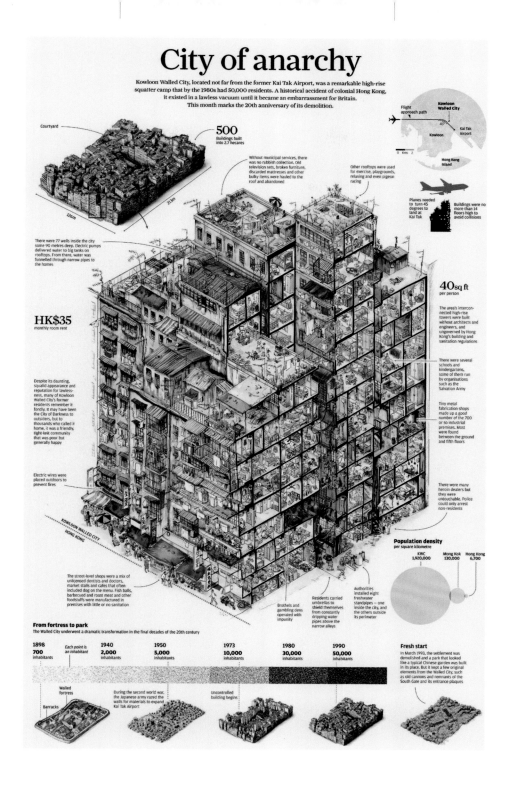

City of anarchy

Kowloon Walled City, located not far from the former Kai Tak Airport, was a remarkable high-rise squatter camp that by the 1980s had 50,000 residents. A historical accident of colonial Hong Kong, it existed in a lawless vacuum until it became an embarrassment for Britain. This month marks the 20th anniversary of its demolition.

Courtyard

500
Buildings built into 2.7 hecares

Without municipal services, there was no rubbish collection. Old television sets, broken furniture, discarded mattresses and other bulky items were hauled to the roof and abandoned

Other rooftops were used for exercise, playgrounds, relaxing and even pigeon racing

Flight approach path

Kowloon Walled City

Kai Tak Airport

Kowloon

Hong Kong Island

Planes needed to turn 45 degrees to land at Kai Tak

Buildings were no more than 14 floors high to avoid collisions

There were 77 wells inside the city some 90 metres deep. Electric pumps delivered water to big tanks on rooftops. From there, water was funnelled through narrow pipes to the homes

40 sq ft
per person

The area's interconnected high-rise towers were built without architects and engineers, and ungoverned by Hong Kong's building and sanitation regulations

HK$35
monthly room rent

There were several schools and kindergartens, some of them run by organisations such as the Salvation Army

Tiny metal fabrication shops made up a good number of the 700 or so industrial premises. Most were found between the ground and fifth floors

Despite its daunting, squalid appearance and reputation for lawlessness, many of Kowloon Walled City's former residents remember it fondly. It may have been the City of Darkness to outsiders, but to thousands who called it home, it was a friendly, tight-knit community that was poor but generally happy

There were many heroin dealers but they were untouchable. Police could only arrest non-residents

Electric wires were placed outdoors to prevent fires

KOWLOON WALLED CITY
HONG KONG

Population density
per square kilometre

KWC 1,920,000 — Mong Kok 130,000 — Hong Kong 6,700

The street-level shops were a mix of unlicensed dentists and doctors, market stalls and cafes that often included dog on the menu. Fish balls, barbecued and roast meat and other foodstuffs were manufactured in premises with little or no sanitation

Brothels and gambling dens operated with impunity

Residents carried umbrellas to shield themselves from constantly dripping water pipes above the narrow alleys

Authorities installed eight freshwater standpipes – one inside the city, and the others outside its perimeter

From fortress to park
The Walled City underwent a dramatic transformation in the final decades of the 20th century

1898 700 inhabitants	1940 2,000 inhabitants	1950 5,000 inhabitants	1973 10,000 inhabitants	1980 30,000 inhabitants	1990 50,000 inhabitants	Fresh start

Each point is an inhabitant

Fresh start
In March 1993, the settlement was demolished and a park that looked like a typical Chinese garden was built in its place. But it kept a few original elements from the Walled City, such as old cannons and remnants of the South Gate and its entrance plaques

Walled fortress

Barracks

During the second world war, the Japanese army razed the walls for materials to expand Kai Tak Airport

Uncontrolled building begins

City of Anarchy | 2013 | Adolfo Arranz

First printed in the *South China Morning Post* (2013). Dimensions variable.

This unconventional yet beautiful map brings back to life the now demolished Kowloon Walled City in Hong Kong, a dystopian place that harboured extreme poverty and unsanitary conditions. Urban landscapes and the rich stories of inhabited places are often not effectively captured by standard mapping techniques. Large-scale planimetric maps of the order of 1:2000 and above nearly always reduce a place to a clinical, surveyed chart. Such an approach would never be able to capture the detail or provide a sense of this walled city next to the old Kai Tak airport. Kowloon measured only 213 × 126 metres (700 × 413 feet), but its densely packed high-rise buildings suited an isometric cutaway diagram (a three-dimensional map). The vertical is more important than the horizontal here (planes used to take a 45-degree turn to avoid Kowloon on their landing approach). The city had more than 500 buildings and some 50,000 residents by the 1980s, with a population density some 280 times greater than that of Hong Kong itself. The layout of the page is well crafted, with small maps, complete isometric maps and detailed annotations surrounding the remarkable main illustration. The maxim of adding detail to improve clarity is well evidenced in this map's sense of what the place would have been like to live in.

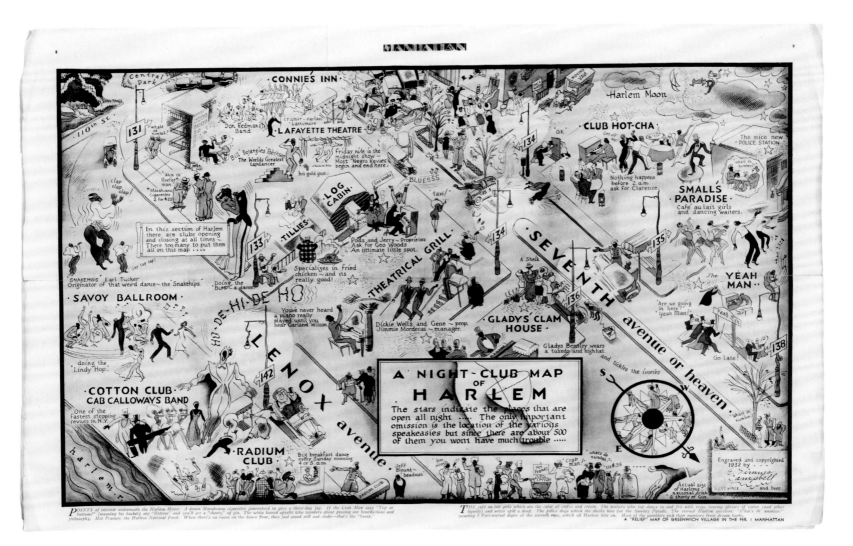

A Night-Club Map of Harlem | 1932 | E. Simms Campbell

Printed in *Manhattan: A Weekly for Wakeful New Yorkers*, 18 January, 1933 . 40.6 × 61 cm / 16 × 24 in. Private collection

Even those who have never picked up a copy of *Playboy* magazine are likely to recognize the stylish women drawn by African-American cartoonist E. Simms Campbell. But before he became a regular contributor to *Playboy*, *Esquire* and *The New Yorker*, Campbell created this map of Harlem in the midst of a cultural explosion for the first and only issue of *Manhattan: A Weekly for Wakeful New Yorkers*. During the late 1920s the 'Harlem Renaissance'

had seen a flowering of African-American literature, art and theatre, and jazz music and dance had crossed the racial line to become popular with urban white Americans. This map of the hot spots around Lenox and Seventh Avenue – including the famous Cotton Club – captures the excitement and energy of night scenes centred on characters such as dancer and actor Bill 'Bojangles' Robinson, bandleader Cab Calloway and blues singer

Gladys Bentley. The map celebrates the clandestine side of Harlem – drinking, marijuana smoking and gambling, in which even the police officers are complicit. Campbell's personal tips for readers going out on the town, such as 'ask for Clarence' or 'Specializes in fried chicken – and it's really good!' convey a sense of intimate knowledge of a cultural scene to which the artist had close ties.

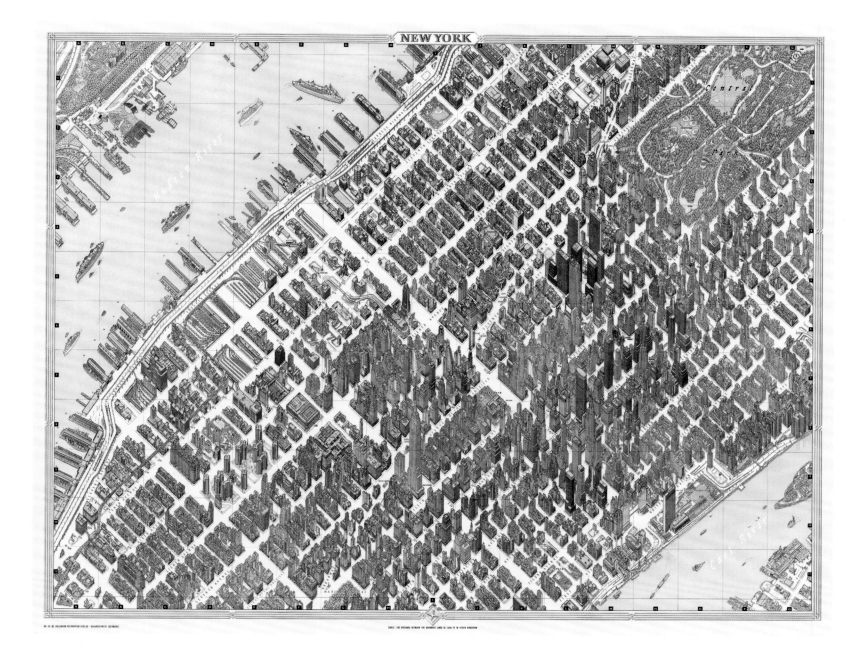

New York | 1963 | Hermann Bollmann

Printed paper. 107 × 85 cm / 42 × 33½ in. Private collection

This map by Hermann Bollmann uses an axonometric projection, a technique developed in the fifteenth century for showing three-dimensional detail while preserving scale across the image. It differs from single-point perspective, in which the foreground is shown larger than the background. Bollmann wanted to create a map that showed all streets and buildings equally. A graphic artist by training and a woodcutter, he drew this spectacularly detailed map by hand from 50,000 ground and 17,000 aerial photographs. The map exaggerates the widths of streets to create a perfect amount of white space in which buildings sit, both representing the dense fabric of the city and giving clarity to individual buildings. Vertical exaggeration also gives a sense of the skyscrapers soaring. The street numbering is consistently placed and beautifully letter-spaced. The detail invites inspection and the colouring, predominantly in pastel shades that identify building function with grey rooftops, mimics the grey skyline of Manhattan. Small features such as windows, architectural detail and trees are included, proving that omission is not the only tenet of cartographic design. Here, Bollmann proves that detail can also give clarity and a keen sense of place in map form.

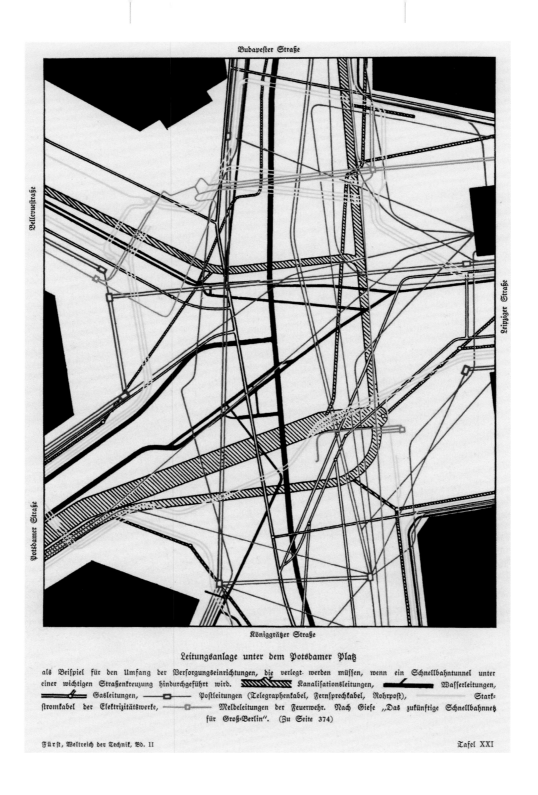

Budapefter Straße

Belleuestraße

Leipziger Straße

Potsdamer Straße

Königgräßer Straße

Leitungsanlage unter dem Potsdamer Platz

als Beispiel für den Umfang der Versorgungseinrichtungen, die verlegt werden müssen, wenn ein Schnellbahntunnel unter einer wichtigen Straßenkreuzung hindurchgeführt wird. Kanalisationsleitungen, Wasserleitungen, Gasleitungen, Postleitungen (Telegraphenkabel, Fernsprechkabel, Rohrpost), Starkstromkabel der Elektrizitätswerke, Meldeleitungen der Feuerwehr. Nach Giese „Das zukünftige Schnellbahnnetz für Groß-Berlin". (Zu Seite 374)

Fürst, Weltreich der Technik, Bd. II   Tafel XXI

Supply Lines Under Potsdamer Platz | 1924 | Artur Fürst

Printed paper. 31.7 × 23 cm / 12½ × 9 in. Private collection

The German-Jewish writer Artur Fürst's representation of the underground infrastructure found beneath Potsdamer Platz in the centre of Berlin in 1924 was not only ahead of its time in its overall design – in many ways it echoes abstract art – but also one of the first maps to treat a city's technical infrastructure as a system of networks. Fürst was fascinated by technology and wrote a series of books on the scientific and technical innovations taking place in the early twentieth century, culminating in the four-volume *The Empire of Technology* (1924). This map, taken from the second volume, uses striking symbology – rendered without labels that might clutter the map – to indicate the various networks that underlie the operations of modern urban Berlin: sewers (shaded black), water mains (solid black), gas mains (unshaded black), telegraph and telephone cables (red), high-voltage electric cables (yellow) and fire-alarm cables (green). Fürst's image is a remarkable illustration of the complexity of the technological web of life that sustains a city. In this sense the map transcends its time. It ignores the problems facing Germany after World War I (1914–8) – a time of political and economic chaos – to depict Berlin as a set of clean, ordered networks that shape the city's urban form and life.

Industrial Map of Portland, Oregon | 1945 | Portland City Planning Commission

Printed paper. 47 × 123.2 cm / 18½ × 45½ in. City of Portland Archives, Oregon

This colour-coded map of the waterfront along the Willamette and Columbia rivers in Portland, Oregon, was created in 1945 after the city's population had risen dramatically as workers were drawn to war industries during World War II (1939–45). The city's local timber resources and its strategic location on a major water route to the Pacific made it ideal for shipbuilding, and as part of the war effort the federal government took over the docks to build more than 1,000 ocean-going vessels. The vast areas in black on this map reveal the industrial areas recently vacated by the government; the pink stripes show areas under temporary use. Red marks, functioning industry, and the map also shows railoads (red), arterial routes (yellow) and tramlines (green). Prepared by the City Planning Commission, the map served as a starting point for the next phase of city planning, to ensure that the industrial areas were carefully repurposed and incorporated into growth projections. The scheme was at least partly successful. Today Portland is widely hailed as the most environmentally conscious city in the United States, owing in part to its robust history of tightly controlled urban planning.

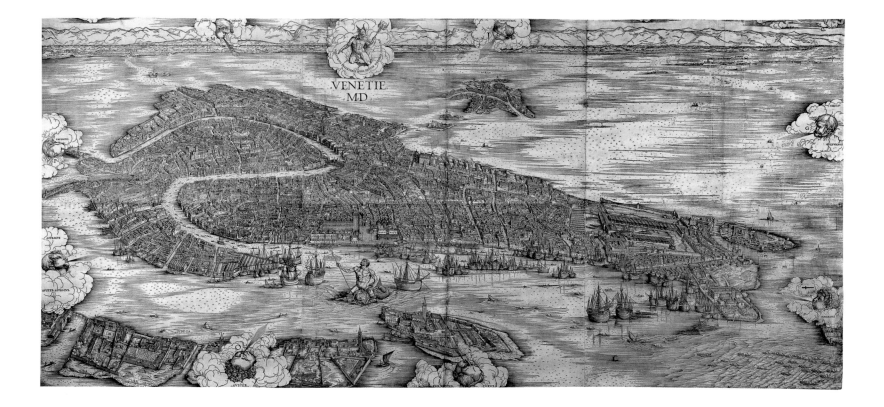

Map of Venice | 1500 | Jacopo de' Barbari

Woodcut. 134 × 281 cm / 4 ft 4¾ in × 9 ft 2½ in. Museo Correr, Venice

Imagined from a vantage point above the island of San Giorgio, Jacopo de' Barbari's bird's-eye view of Venice is both a masterpiece of Renaissance art and a celebration of what was at the time one of the most powerful states on Earth. Venice's commercial and maritime prowess is symbolized by the presence of the messenger god Mercury, who looks down from a cloud at the top of the map towards Neptune, god of the seas, trident in hand

and astride a sea monster in the mouth of the Grand Canal. De' Barbari's vast map shows Venice on the day of the regatta and illustrates scores of boats, including the Doge's *Bucintoro*, built in 1449. Close inspection of the ramshackle buildings lining the canals reveals a population involved in all the activities associated with shipbuilding, navigation, fishing and rowing. The only exception is the gruesome image of the former Senate

Secretary Antonio Landi, who hangs by his neck in Canal de San Secondo as a warning to anyone else who might be considering revealing state secrets. The map shows the temporary flat roof built for the great bell tower in St Mark's Square after a fire in 1489. When the original was restored in 1511–13, de' Barbari altered the woodblocks for his map accordingly.

Venezia, Venezia | 2013 | Alfredo Jaar

Metal pool, resin model and hydraulic system. 100 × 500 × 500 cm / 3 ft 3¼ in × 16 ft 4¾ in × 16 ft 4¾ in. Site-specific installation, Chilean Pavilion, 55th Venice Biennale

The miniature buildings and trees of this accurate 1:60 scale model of the Giardini Park, the main site of the Venice Biennale, permanently glisten with wetness. The Chilean artist Alfredo Jaar created a replica of the whole park – its twenty-eight pavilions instantly recognizable by their varied architectural styles and set in authentic, watery surroundings – which slowly sinks beneath the murky green water, then rises again. On one level, the work highlights Venice's well-publicized ongoing battle against the forces of nature that seek to reclaim land to the lagoon. Yet on another level, it is Jaar's response to the politics of the international art world. Venice has hosted a biennial international art exhibition since 1895 and over the first half of the twentieth century, twenty-eight countries – dictated by political and diplomatic arrangements of the time – built permanent pavilions in the park. By 2013, however, more than seventy countries staged national presentations at the Biennale, and the majority had to find spaces outside the Giardini. Jaar's work, created for his 'off-site' exhibition – Chile has only participated since 2009, so is excluded from the 'main' Biennale site – is a humorous response to the inherited inequality, suggesting a rather drastic solution to the outdated hierarchy of world powers.

The Course of the River Nile | 9th century | Muhammad Ibn Musa Al-Khwarizmi

Ink on vellum. 33.5 × 41 cm / 13⅛ × 16⅛ in. Bibliothèque Nationale et Universitaire, Strasbourg

This is the oldest surviving map that can be positively identified as belonging to the Islamic tradition. Drawn by the eighth-century mathematician, astronomer and geographer al-Khwarizmi, the map provides a realistic view of the course of the Nile from its two sources in the legendary Mountains of the Moon (right) to its delta on the Mediterranean Sea. Al-Khwarizmi based his map on the accounts of the second-century Egyptian–Greek geographer Ptolemy, but mainly labelled features with their contemporary Arabic names (the exceptions are the Mountains of the Moon and Alexandria, Ptolemy's birthplace, near the river's mouth). The vertical lines on the map mark different climate zones, starting with the equator on the right. Although the text reads horizontally, the map would be turned in order to be read, with south at the top. Al-Khwarizmi served as head of the celebrated House of Wisdom in Baghdad, which brought together outstanding scholars from throughout the Islamic world. He led a team that measured one degree of latitude with remarkable accuracy and reported his findings in a revised and updated version of Ptolemy's *Geography* named *Book on the Appearance of Earth*, from which this map comes.

The Dagua River Region, Colombia | 1764 | Unknown

Ink and watercolour on paper. 60 × 86 cm / 23¾ × 34 in. Library of Congress, Washington, DC

The striking colours of this manuscript map, which shows the lower reaches of the Dagua River and the town of Sombrerillo on the Pacific coast of what was then the Spanish Viceroyalty of New Grenada, give the immediate impression of a lush river valley and watershed – but the Spaniards were not purely interested in its natural beauty. The map (orientated with south at the top) was signed as being authentic by three vice-regal officials in December 1764, a period of intensive mining and farming in the region, and might have been part of a larger survey and cartographic series showing houses, settlements and waterways. Its extensive legend describes the vast mineral resources of the region and the settlement of miners. In the centre of the map stands Sombrerillo, a small settlement that emerged in the eighteenth century. Sombrerillo's roughly 200 residents were former slaves who had escaped from the lowland mines and farms and now lived by transporting goods from the Pacific coast to the town of Cali using pole-driven canoes and overland transport. Their efforts were successful enough that Sombrerillo came to be recognized as a refuge for escaped slaves, especially those coming from the farms to the north.

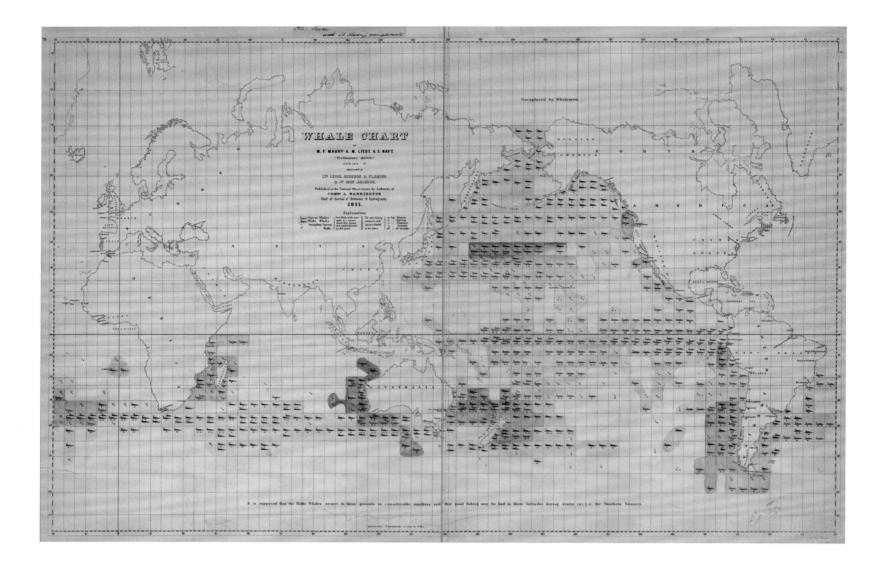

Whale Chart | 1851 | Matthew Fontaine Maury

Hand-coloured lithograph. 60 × 91 cm / 23 ⅜ × 36 in. Library of Congress, Washington, DC

In the early nineteenth century whaling was an important industry – many lamps used oil from sperm whales, which burned more brightly than most other lamp oils – and it took American ships farther out to sea than any other enterprise. The US Navy cartographer Matthew Fontaine Maury (see also p.163) noticed in his study of ships' logs that patterns of whale activity appeared to correspond with currents and temperatures in particular locations,

and he charted the information because of its obvious economic value. Maury marked the frequency of whale encounters with codes and illustrations, and the types of whale with different colours. The work quickly became widely known: this copy is inscribed to the then Secretary of State Edward Everett, and Maury's whale-charting project was mentioned in Herman Melville's classic novel *Moby-Dick*, published the same year as the map.

Yet while this chart enabled greater profit for whalers, it may also have hastened the decline of whale populations, already under way by 1851. Ultimately, the field of oceanography, which Maury's various charts and studies played an important part in developing, would take this work in a new direction in the twentieth and twenty-first centuries, informing efforts to protect and conserve whales and other ocean life.

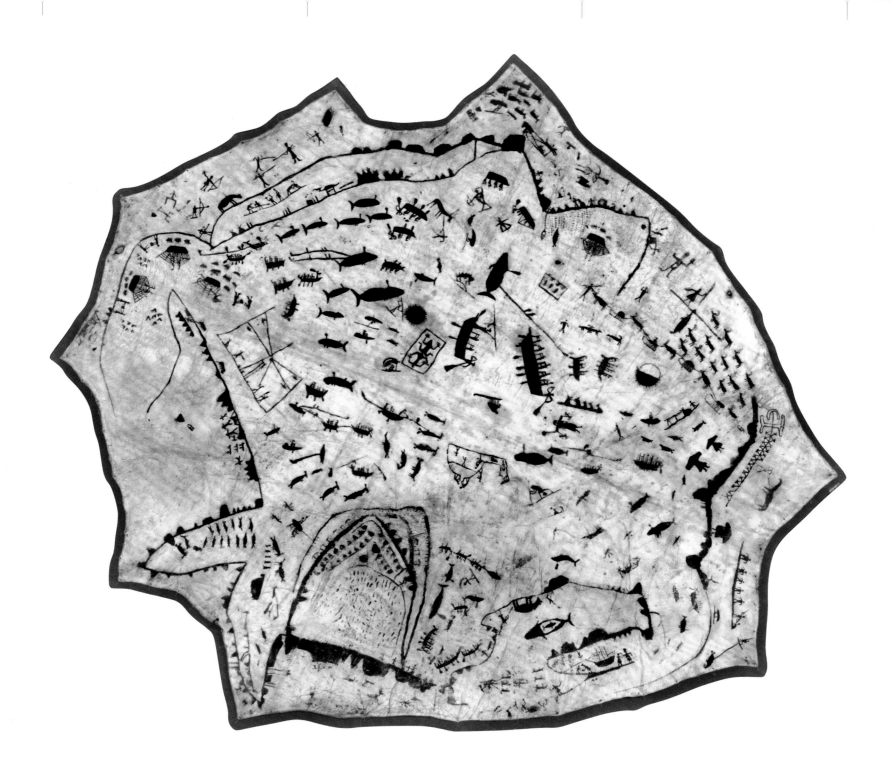

Chukchi Sealskin Map | c.1870 | Unknown

Manuscript on sealskin. 114 × 119 cm / 45 × 47 in. Pitt Rivers Museum, University of Oxford

The peoples of Arctic Eurasia and North America have a long tradition of making pictographs and maps, and the Chukchi sealskin map was obtained from the people of the Chukchi Peninsula by the crew of an American whaling ship in about 1870. The Chukchi Peninsula is the most north-easterly point of Asia, separated from Alaska by the Bering Strait. Some geographic locations along the coast of the peninsula have been identified on the map,

including St Lawrence Bay, Cape Chaplino, Michigme Bay and Providence Bay. The many scenes on the map may show the everyday life of the Chukchi people or they may represent a calendar of events of one year. There are many scenes of the hunting of whale, walrus, bear and seal. The artist depicts herds of reindeer, along with many people – including possibly Russians, Europeans and Americans – scenes of daily life, villages, dwellings,

shamans, fighting scenes, whaling schooners, umiaks (open canoes) and kayaks. Because of the unusually large number of pictures and the large size of the map, this example may have been made specifically as a trade good to sell to European traders or American whalers. It was made either by the Chukchi people or by the Sireniki Eskimos of Siberia.

The Herdsman | 1250–75 | ʿAbd al-Rahman ibn ʿUmar al-Sufi

Ink on parchment. 33.3 × 23.4 cm / 13 × 9¼ in. Bibliothèque nationale de France, Paris

This map of the constellation known as the Herdsman, the Plowman or Boötes is a copy from c.1250 of the tenth-century original drawn by the Persian scholar al-Sufi, a follower of the mystical branch of Islam known as Sufism. Working at the court of ʿAdud al-Dawla in Isfahan, al-Sufi drew on both Islamic and classical sources to compile his *Book of the Constellations of the Fixed Stars*, one of the most influential star catalogues

of the late Middle Ages. A talented astronomer, al-Sufi measured the brightness of each star in the forty-eight major constellations in the northern sky and accompanied each of his drawings with a carefully constructed list of the stars composing the individual constellation in order of brightness. Al-Sufi's Arabic text was translated into Hebrew, Latin and Persian, while his distinctly Arabic figures were copied by Christians and Jews throughout

Europe, North Africa and the Middle East (this copy, the closest to the original, may have been made in Bologna, Italy). Al-Sufi's identification of the constellations was based on an Arabic translation of the *Almagest* by the second-century Greek-Egyptian writer Claudius Ptolemy (see p.138). Al-Sufi's version of Ptolemy's star catalogue was introduced to the West by translation by Gerard of Cremona and Alfonso X of Castile.

Table of Asterisms | 19th century | Unknown

Watercolour and ink on paper. 61 × 57 cm / 24 × 22½ in. Private collection

This nineteenth-century Hindu astrological chart – with its striking bright colours and the meditative expression on the figure's face – is a table of asterisms: recognized patterns of stars within a larger constellation. An example from Western astronomy would be Orion's Belt, but other cultures traditionally connect the stars in their own ways – and therefore recognize different constellations and asterisms in the same sky.

Regardless of historical approach, almost every culture has used the sky to determine time, seasons and tides, and some have also used it for more ritualistic or mystical purposes. Hindu charts of this kind depict the stars that define the twenty-eight lunar mansions, or moon cycles, that comprise the months of the lunar zodiac. They are important in lunar astrology, which is invoked, for example, to choose a propitious name for a child.

At the top of the figure's chest is a star cluster called Krittika which in the West is part of the constellation Taurus. The map can be looked at from any direction, as the writing is anchored to the image rather than to the viewer's position.

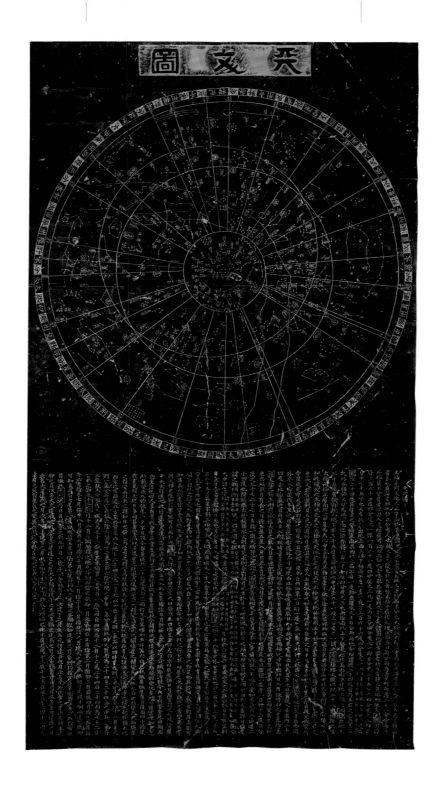

A Map of the Stars | 1247 | Wang Zhiyuan

Ink rubbing. 183 × 100 cm / 72 × 39¼ in. Collection Daniel Crouch Rare Books, London

This unusual map from an inscribed stele at the Confucian Temple in Suzhou in Jiangsu province represents nearly all the stars visible from China in a series of concentric rings. It was originally carved during the Song dynasty by engraver Wang Zhiyuan to help instruct a future emperor in astronomy and shows a total of 1,436 stars, with intersecting circles representing the celestial eqator and the ecliptic and an irregular band across its centre that represents the Milky Way. For the Chinese, the names and locations of the stars mirrored the political hierarchies on Earth, so the emperor was at the the centre of the heavens as he was at the center of the kingdom. The inner circle contains the queen, four advisors and the king's chariot, with decreasingly important government functionaries to the outer edges of the circle and the lower orders of society. At the same time the circle is divided vertically into twenty-eight pie-shaped sections called the 'houses' or 'mansions', the boundary of each was fixed by a single star. The Chinese achieved great accuracy in measuring the location of stars by fixing their distance from the Pole Star and the western boundary of their mansion. This ink rubbing was made from the original, probably during the nineteenth century.

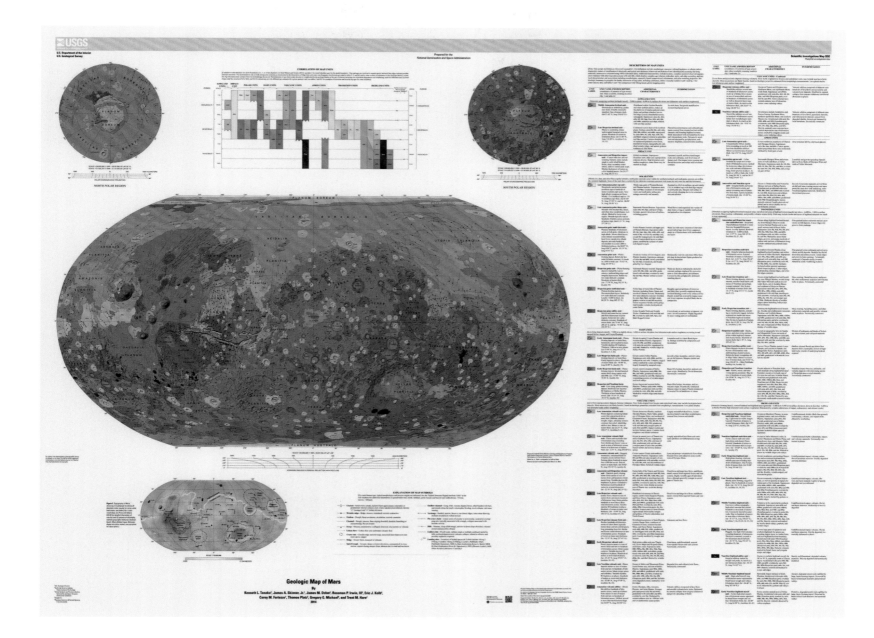

Geologic Map of Mars | 2014 | Kenneth Tanaka, US Geological Survey

Digital. Dimensions variable

Humans have been fascinated by the 'Red Planet' for over 400 years, partly because its orbit is within a range of the Sun that would make it potentially inhabitable. But the Red Planet is anything but in this colour-coded geological map of Mars, the result of seven years' work by Kenneth Tanaka and a team at the US Geological Survey. Collating information about materials and terrain gathered by orbiting sensors onboard three NASA spacecraft and one from the European Space Agency, Tanaka put together the most detailed map yet of the Martian surface (previous maps were produced in 1978 and 1986). The 1:20,000,000 map divides the surface into forty-four 'units': greens represent lowland and basin units, reds and purples are volcanic, brown tones are transition and highland units and yellow denotes impact basins. Blues indicate the polar regions. The impact basins comprise relatively young material, but overall the map revealed the surface to be older than previously thought: the dominant browns show that nearly half was formed over 3.7 billion years ago. The map also shows that Mars was geologically active until recently and that there was once liquid water on the surface – a tantalizing hint of the planet's future potential for astrobiology.

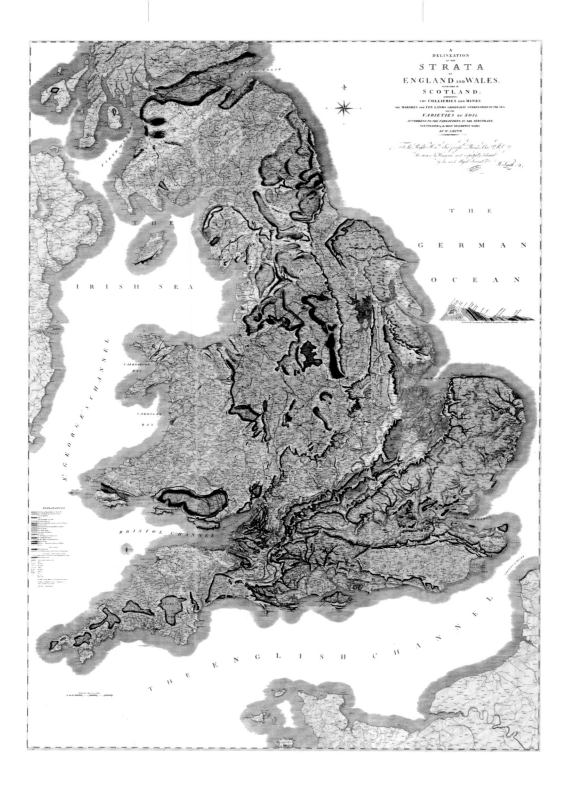

A Delineation of the Strata of England and Wales, with Part of Scotland | 1815 | William Smith

Hand-coloured engraving. 259 × 176 cm / 5 ft 10 in × 8 ft 2½ in. The Geological Society, London

This startlingly beautiful map of something previously unseen – the geological make-up of England, Wales and Scotland – had its origins in the boom in canal construction in the late eighteenth century. The surveyor and geologist William Smith began to take an interest in the different layers of rock he uncovered while digging canals in Somerset. Unconvinced by theological explanations of the rock 'strata' and the fossils within them, Smith began to theorize about the process of their formation and came to understand the distribution, consolidation, deposition and dissolution of minerals as a dynamic process that would allow him to classify the rocks. Different strata had been formed at different times, and Smith believed that understanding the processes involved in their formation should make it possible to establish some idea of when they were formed. The map Smith created after decades of excavation all over Britain represented different rock strata with twenty hand-painted tints, using darker and lighter tones to indicate older and younger rocks within the strata. Smith's landmark map – widely acknowledged as the first geological map of a country ever produced – laid the foundation for future geological research.

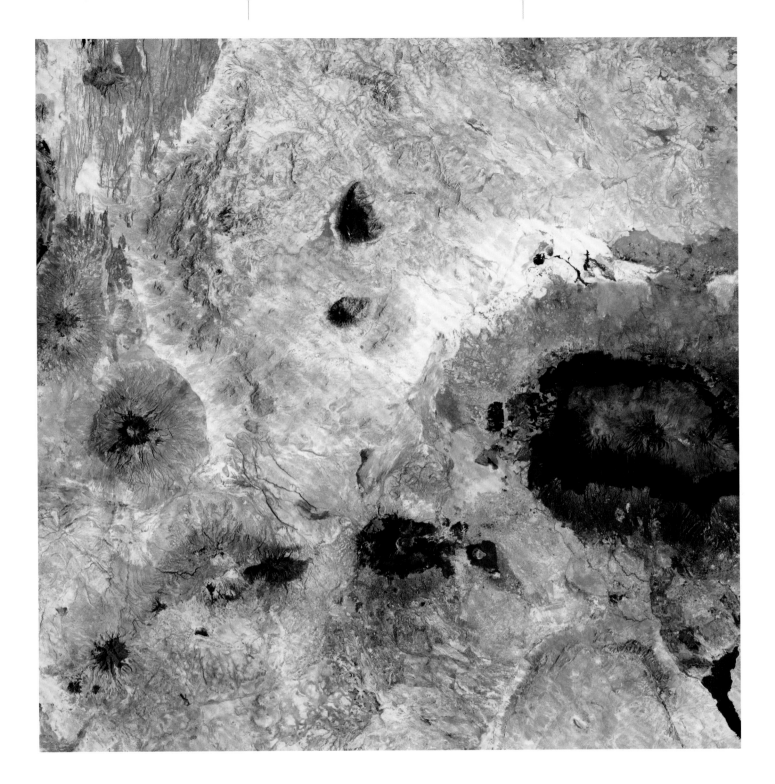

Mount Kilimanjaro, Tanzania | 2000 | United States Geological Survey

False-colour satellite image. Dimensions variable.

It might be argued that this image created by Landsat 7 is not a map – yet it closely echoes relief maps by cartographers such as Eduard Imhof (see p.196). Certainly, it is no mere photograph, as this view is not what would be seen from space. The image was created by using visible and invisible wavelengths to bring out differences between the light green grasslands of the Amboseli and Arusha national parks, the dark green forested slopes of Kilimanjaro and the bare rock and snow of the upper parts of the volcano. Early images of Earth taken by astronauts created great excitement as they revealed features that were too large to be observed even by aerial photography. In 1972 the United States launched Landsat 1, the first satellite designed for studying the Earth. Landsat used scanners operating at different wavelengths of the visible and near infrared parts of the spectrum, recording each band as a separate image. The individual bands can be combined to create different colour images. First-generation satellite images were suitable for mapping large-scale phenomena, such as vegetation patterns, but lacked the detail for mapping urban areas. By Landsat 7, satellites carried much higher-resolution scanners, with more bands operating over a wider part of the electromagnetic spectrum.

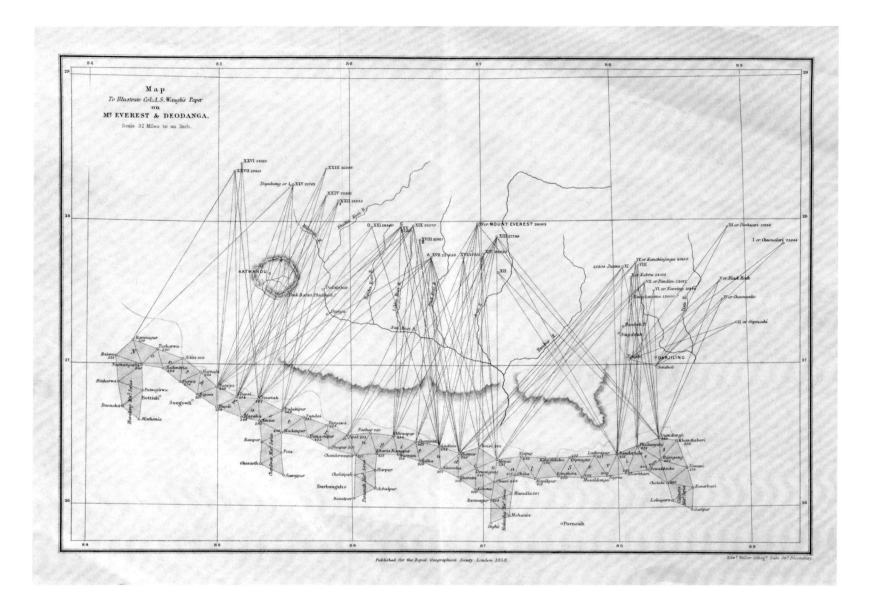

Map to Illustrate Colonel A.S. Waugh's Paper on Mount Everest and Deodanga | 1858 | Andrew Scott Waugh

Lithograph on paper. 30 × 42 cm / 11 ¾ × 16 ½ in. Royal Geographical Society, London

In 1847 British surveyors working in the foothills of the Himalaya to fix the heights of the main peaks first observed what they labelled Peak B. Five years later the Indian mathematician and surveyor Radhanath Sikdar used their calculations to determine that this was the tallest mountain in the world. It was named by the Surveyor General, Andrew Scott Waugh, after his predecessor, Sir George Everest. Although Everest himself objected that

the mountain already had local names, 'Everest' soon became a kind of shorthand for the greatest challenge to human endeavour. This map – drawn to accompany Waugh's talk about the discovery to the Royal Geographical Society – shows a series of triangulations to establish the heights of various peaks. It represents part of the Great Trigonometrical Survey of India, first proposed by the British soldier and surveyor William Lambton in 1799.

Lambton proposed to survey along a meridian from Cape Comorin (Kanyakumari) in the south to the foothills of the Himalaya in the north, with a series of latitudinal surveys across India. By the time of Lambton's death in 1823, the scheme had been elaborated to include more meridian arcs, and it was under his successor, Everest, that the meridian arc finally reached the Himalaya.

Water Line and Blue Lake Pass | 2006 | Maya Lin

Aluminium tubing and paint (*Water Line*), Duraflake particleboard (*Blue Lake Pass*). Dimensions variable. Installation view, PaceWildenstein, New York

For these two installations – displayed as part of *Three Ways of Looking at the Earth* in 2009 – the American artist Maya Lin used models, grids and topographic drawings as well as more advanced technology (sonar and radar mapping, satellite photographs) to study parts of the world that are inaccessible or impossible to observe in their entirety. *Water Line* is a scale map of the ocean floor along the Mid-Atlantic Ridge as it ascends to Bouvet Island, one of the world's remotest places, located roughly 1,600 kilometres (1,000 miles) north of Antarctica. Lin transforms data gathered by scientific expeditions into a three-dimensional, suspended-wire line-drawing, enabling viewers to pass beneath the undulating terrain. *Blue Lake Pass* refers to a specific area of south-western Colorado familiar to the artist from family vacations. Lin imposed a 91 cm × 91 cm (3 ft × 3ft) grid on a section of terrain from the Rocky Mountains, which was then scaled down and sectioned into twenty individual units arranged in a grid with narrow passageways between. The uneven, rugged peaks contrast with the uniform grid, reminding viewers of the contrast between the disorder of the natural world and human attempts to systematize and order it through mapping.

Geography of Plants in Tropical Countries: A Study of the Andes | 1807 | Alexander von Humboldt

Colour lithograph. 53.5 × 83 cm / 21 × 32⅝ in. Humboldt-Universität zu Berlin

The early nineteenth century was the age of the plant-hunter. Inspired by the eighteenth-century Swede Carl Linnaeus, who began classifying plants and animals into families, genera and species, scientists and adventurers set out to explore the implied mechanism by which plants were related. Linnaeus's *System of Nature* was on the minds of the German geologist Alexander von Humboldt and the French botanist Aimé Bonpland as

they travelled through South America between 1799 and 1804. The pair would cover thousands of kilometres, accumulate thousands of specimens and record vast amounts of astronomical, geological, meteorological, botanical and oceanographic data. This cross-section of Mt. Chimborazo in Ecuador – then thought to be the world's highest mountain – was drawn to accompany their *Essay on the Geography of Plants* of 1807. It

illustrates differences in vegetation that seem to correspond to elevation and differences in conditions, such as air temperature, humidity and intensity of sunlight, as explained in side panels. The names of species appear in the mountain cutaway, corresponding to the elevations at which they live. It was this correlation of distribution and conditions that, according to Humboldt and Bonpland, constituted the 'geographical' study of plants.

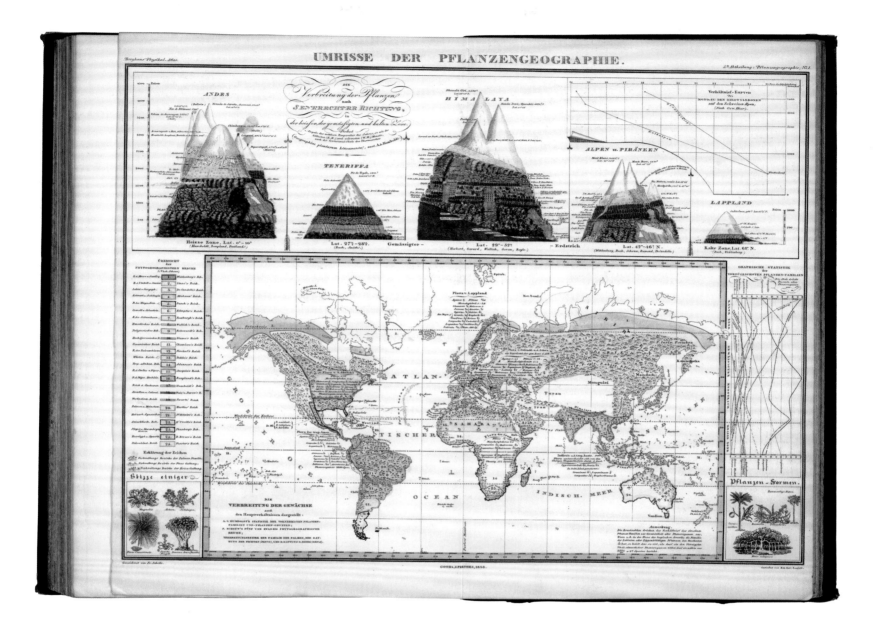

Outline of Plant Geography | 1852 | Heinrich Berghaus

Coloured engraving. 34 × 44 cm / 13⅓ × 17⅓ in. Private collection

The *Physical Atlas* of 1845 by the German cartographer Heinrich Berghaus (second edition shown) was the first comprehensive physical atlas of the world and the first systematic compilation of how plant types correspond to both the isothermal (temperature) bands circling the Earth and to degrees of elevation above its surface – a correspondence suggested by his compatriot Alexander von Humboldt. The *Physical Atlas*, intended to accompany

Humboldt's multi-volume *Cosmos* (1845–62), contained maps devoted to all manner of Earth's surface conditions, including plant geography. Like William Woodbridge's map of 1923 (see p.167), Berghaus's map divided the world into climatic regions in which plant families were drawn or labelled, identified by the colour key at lower left. A graph on the right corresponded with the map, showing the dominance of particular plant families at

various latitudes. The cross-section illustrations of some of the world's highest mountain ranges carried on the theme of Humboldt's study of Mt. Chimborazo in 1807 (see opposite) by showing the correspondence of plant types to various elevations, which also vary according to the latitude of the ranges. The curve at upper right charts the correlation between flowering plants and conditions at particular elevations in the Swiss Alps.

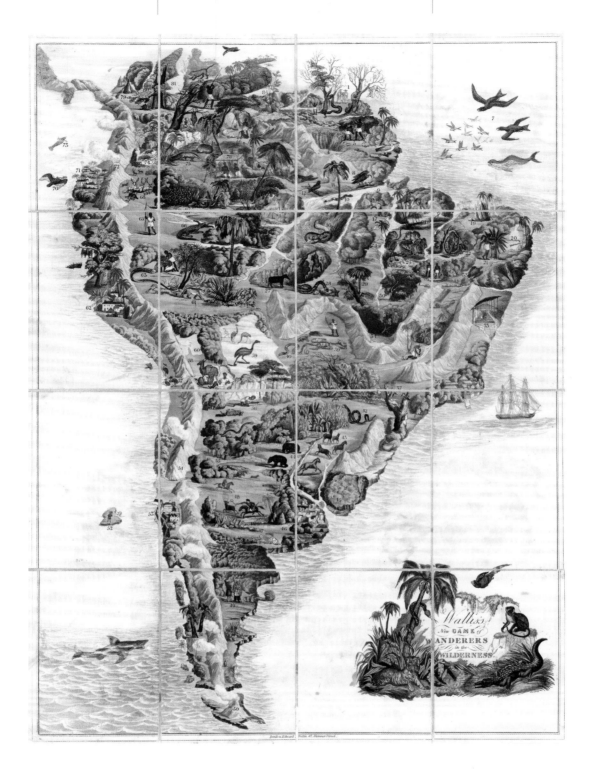

Wallis's New Game of Wanderers in the Wilderness | c.1844 | Edward Wallis

Hand-coloured engraving on paper, mounted on linen. 68 × 50 cm / 26¾ × 19¾ in. Collection Daniel Crouch Rare Books, London

The whole of South America is characterized as 'wilderness' in this British children's board game that took the form of a race, with rules similar to those of such games as Snakes and Ladders. The board's hand-coloured etching is assembled from sixteen sections to create a board with eighty-four numbered places. Following a circular route, beginning and ending on the north coast, players make an intrepid tour across high mountains and immense rivers, encountering exotic animals and 'primitive' peoples. In the lower right corner, the lavishly ornamented cartouche is surrounded by birds, palm trees, monkeys, jaguars, an alligator and a bucolic landscape. The game was one of a series dedicated to the different continents that was intended to teach children about unknown lands overseas. To some extent, such adventure-travel games are highly stereotyped, only loosely sketching physical features and tending to ignore urban centres or human impact on the landscape. On the other, their simple rules made them popular, and players presumably acquired a not-entirely-misleading idea of the world's varying landscape and wildlife. The series was a financial success, in any case, and the London firm of Edward Wallis produced several editions of 'Wanderers in the Wilderness' between 1818 and 1847.

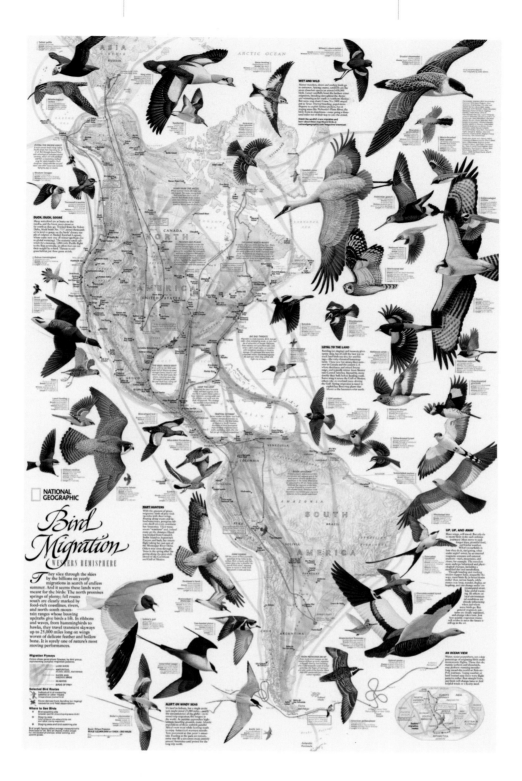

Bird Migration in the Americas | 1979 | National Geographic

Printed paper. 91.4 × 58.4 cm / 36 × 23 in. Private collection

This complex thematic map of the paths of bird migration, brimming with bird images and information, at once calls to mind *National Geographic* magazine, which pioneered such richly detailed fold-out supplements. The magazine published *Bird Migration in the America*s in August 1979 to accompany an article entitled 'Mysteries of Bird Migration'. The map highlights the migratory routes of sixty-seven species, ranging from large raptors to tiny hummingbirds, and includes paintings created by the renowned US wildlife artist Arthur Singer. The map uses four colours to represent the migratory routes for four groups of birds: Seabirds, Gulls and Terns (light blue); Shore and Wading Birds (dark green); Waterfowl (brown); and Land Birds and Birds of Prey (light tan). The migration routes connect nesting grounds and wintering areas, and each route is labelled with the name of the bird. One example is the Blackpoll Warbler, which flies south over the Atlantic Ocean from eastern Canada to South America – travelling some 4,000 kilometres (2,485 miles) at an altitude of up to 6,400 metres (21,000 feet). The map's innovation and popularity launched a whole range of *National Geographic* bird-related products, including migration posters, field guides and picture books.

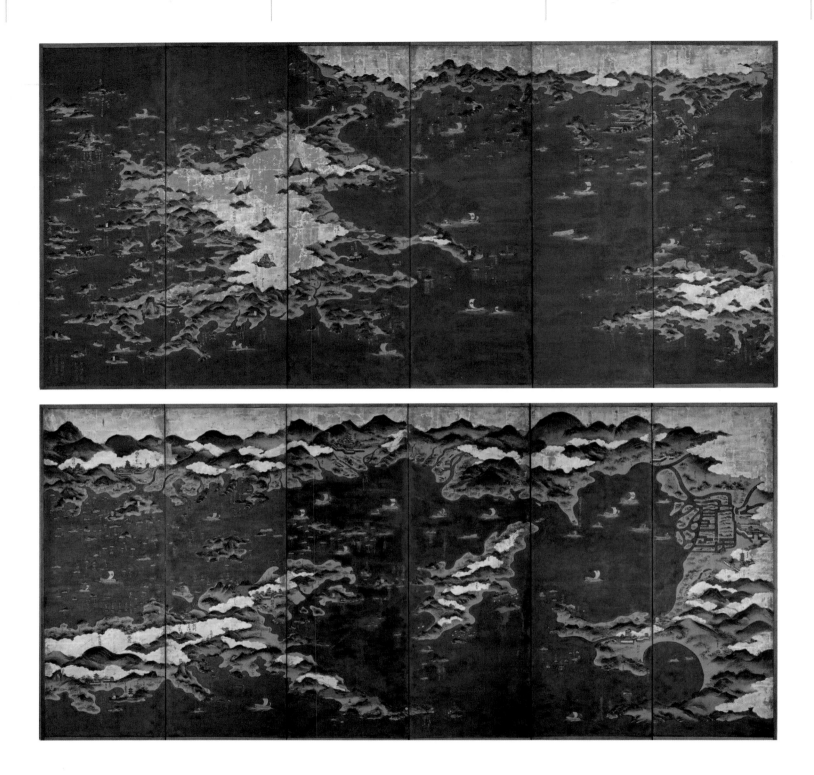

Osaka to Nagasaki Sea Route | Late 17th century | Unknown

Colour and gold on paper. 137 × 282 cm / 4ft 6 in × 9 ft 3 in. Art Gallery of South Australia, Adelaide

This beautiful six-panel screen – one of a pair – depicts the sailing route from Osaka to Nagasaki through the Japanese Seto Inland Sea, which is bordered by three of Japan's four main islands: Honshu, Shikoku and Kyushu. The Inland Sea connects the Pacific Ocean to the Sea of Japan, providing a maritime transport link to commercial centres in the Kansai region with its almost 3,000 islands. It was also part of the official Chosendentsushi route, which Korean emissaries used to travel to the headquarters of the shogunate. Similar screen maps enjoyed a vogue in Japan in the decades either side of 1800. Although they were based largely on European examples, they were painted in the established Japanese style known as *Kimpeki*, which used brilliant colours on a gold background. In style, they tended to follow that of Japanese Gyogi-type maps rather than of European-style maps, reflecting greater local knowledge. The hills and forests near the shore are painted in a highly stylized way, and the islands in the water are shown partly in planimetric fashion and partly in an oblique three-dimensional bird's-eye view, adding an impression of depth to the scene.

Map of Shiogama and Matsushima in Oshu | 1840 | Katsushika Hokusai

Woodcut. 41 × 55 cm / 16 × 21¾ in. Private collection

For much of the nineteenth century, Japanese citizens were banned from travelling abroad. Partly for that reason, domestic tourism flourished in renowned beauty spots such as the settlement of Shiogama and the Matsushima islands in the adjoining bay on the eastern coast of Honshu. The seventeenth-century poet Matsuo Basho is commonly credited with a haiku celebrating the beauty of the latter: 'Matsushima ah!/ A-ah, Matsushima, ah!/

Matsushima, ah!' The renowned *ukiyo-e* woodblock artist Katsushika Hokusai was somewhat more expressive when he captured the region in this panoramic map. Hokusai created this work about a decade before he produced his most famous print, *The Great Wave* (*c.*1830–2), and the map demonstrates the artist's capacity for depicting landscape. Some years earlier Hokusai had produced a similar view of the Tokaido Road, which ran between

Kyoto and Edo (present-day Tokyo); a few years later, he created a panorama of mainland China, despite never having visited the country. Like those maps, this is not intended as a practical work of cartography but instead as a souvenir, to be bought by Japan's growing urban classes, for whom travel and mass-produced pictorial art went together as new leisure pursuits.

Von der alten Heimat zu der neuen Heimat!

From the Old Homeland to the New Homeland! | 1938 | Federico Freudenheim

Coloured pen and pencil on paper. 21 × 27.5 cm / 8¼ × 11 in. Private collection

This child's map in a school exercise book shows one family's odyssey from Europe to South America in the late 1930s, but could represent the journey of all those refugees – the Freudenheims were German Jews fleeing the Holocaust – who must embark on their journey without knowing their destination. Federico (then Fritz) was still in Germany when he drew the first stages of the journey, in which they travelled from the family

home in Mulhouse to Berlin, probably to obtain the correct papers to allow them to leave the country. From Hamburg they took a ship down the Atlantic coast of Europe to Morocco, then across the Atlantic to Brazil and ultimately Uruguay. Freudenheim's childish map disguises the horror that presumably motivated his parents' decision to emigrate, although in hindsight the carefully drawn trains are chilling reminders of those that carried

other German Jews to the death camps. The map is also striking testimony to children's early absorption of the conventions of cartography. From the strip map across the top of the page, Freudenheim works out how to fit in Belgium, France and Spain in the usual orientation, with north at the top, even at the cost of accurate scale. The bright colours in which he depicts South America seem to echo the schoolboy's optimism about the future.

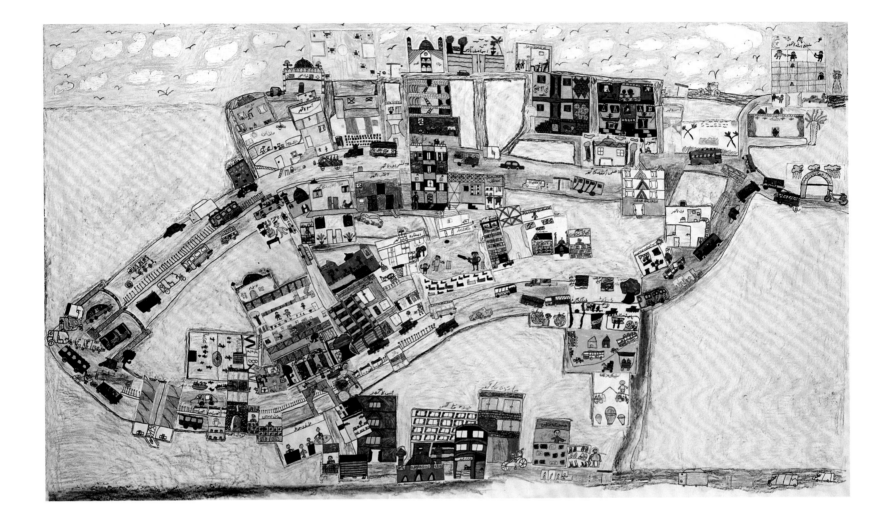

Lyari, Karachi | 2014 | Madiha Sikander & Pupils of B.F. Cabral Government Boys' Primary School, Karachi

Mixed media on paper. 107 × 198 cm / 42 × 78 in. Private collection

Even the most playful maps can have a serious purpose. In Karachi – Pakistan's largest city and one of the fastest-growing cities in the world – neighbourhoods such as Lyari have developed so quickly that they have lost most of their public places. However, children continue to claim ownership of the streets, transforming ordinary places into dynamic public spaces for play and recreation. For them, the city holds endless possibilities for play, adventure and discovery. This children's map charts those hidden places, using bright colours to highlight the playgrounds – real and improvised – where their adventures take place. Bachon se Tabdili ('Change Through Children') is a group of artists who use maps to help children visualize the city, in the belief that this will help adults become more aware of Karachi's current needs and of the potential of its young people. For this map, the artist Madiha Sikander collaborated with fifth-grade pupils from a local primary school. The children's exuberant map shows their perception of the places and people around them and embodies a pragmatic approach to the present as well as hope for the future.

Beijing-Shanghai High-Speed Railway | 2012 | Dong Zheng

Pencil and paint on paper. 95.3 cm × 19 cm / 37½ × 7½ in. Private collection

Dong Zheng's hand-painted map, created to promote the high-speed rail line running between Shanghai and Beijing, is a beautiful application of an historical Chinese style – a strip map with a painted, three-dimensional landscape – to the modern urban world. Inspired in particular by an early eighteenth-century map of the Yellow River, Dong does more than simply chart the various stops along the railway. He illustrates the landscape through which the train passes, combining detailed depiction of the line and the features it passes – including old pagodas and bridges and modern stations and high-rise blocks – with blurring fog and clouds in a background that echoes traditional Chinese styles. Dong Zheng's varied distortion of objects serves to compress the actual distances along the line while emphasizing how close to it the points of interest are. Transit maps are frequently sterile; they present an abstract network of connections that might be in any country or on any planet (see p.299). This map, however, is about the journey as much as it is the destination. It is designed not only to tell a traveller how to get around, but also to make a viewer want to undertake the journey, staring out of the window the whole time, watching the landscape and history of the country unfold.

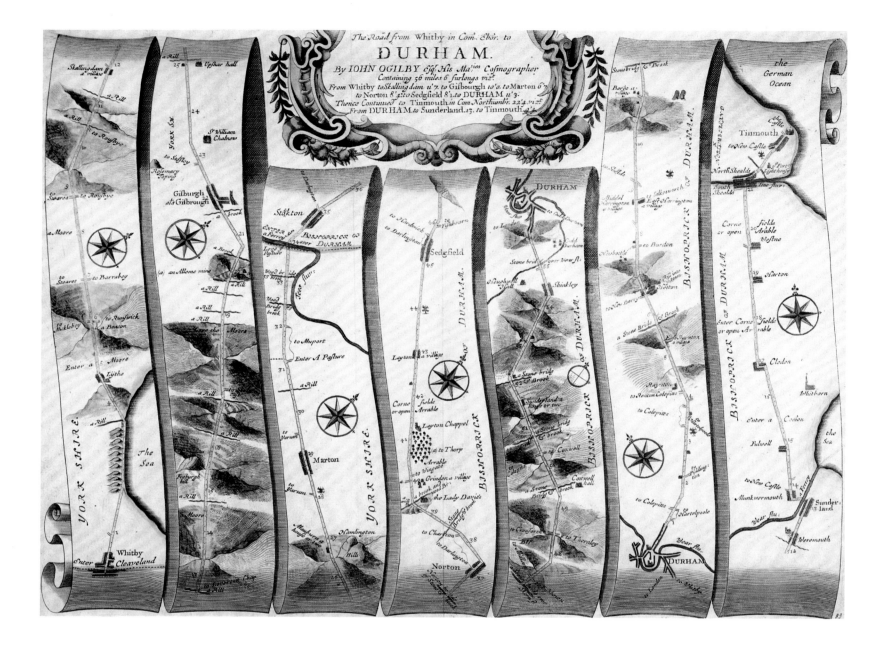

The Road from Whitby to Durham | 1675 | John Ogilby

Engraving on paper, from *Britannia* by John Ogilby (1675). 31.6 × 24.6 cm / 12½ × 9¾ in. Private collection

Road travellers need to know only the towns, distances, place names and topography immediately along their route. That was the insight of John Ogilby, the English publisher who in 1674 was appointed His Majesty's cosmographer and geographic printer. Ogilby's 300-page atlas *Britannia* – one of the first European national road atlases – contained more than 100 folio-size strip maps of Britain's roads at a scale of 1 inch to 1 mile (1.6 kilometre),

accompanied by text, and set the standard for many years to come. Strip maps were not new (see pp.24–25), but the innovative scale was later adopted by Ordnance Survey for its map series (see p.29). Ogilby's maps are linear cartograms, and travellers orientate themselves in the direction of travel regardless of the true direction (north varies between the strips). Lines have been straightened to fit into the strip, but the essential

details are maintained, although any extraneous detail is omitted. Hills – orientated according to the direction of travel to depict whether one would be ascending or descending – are included. Ogilby's ingenious style is still used today to show the linearity of route networks. The use of straightened lines has become a common cartographic approach to showing transport networks (see pp.298–299).

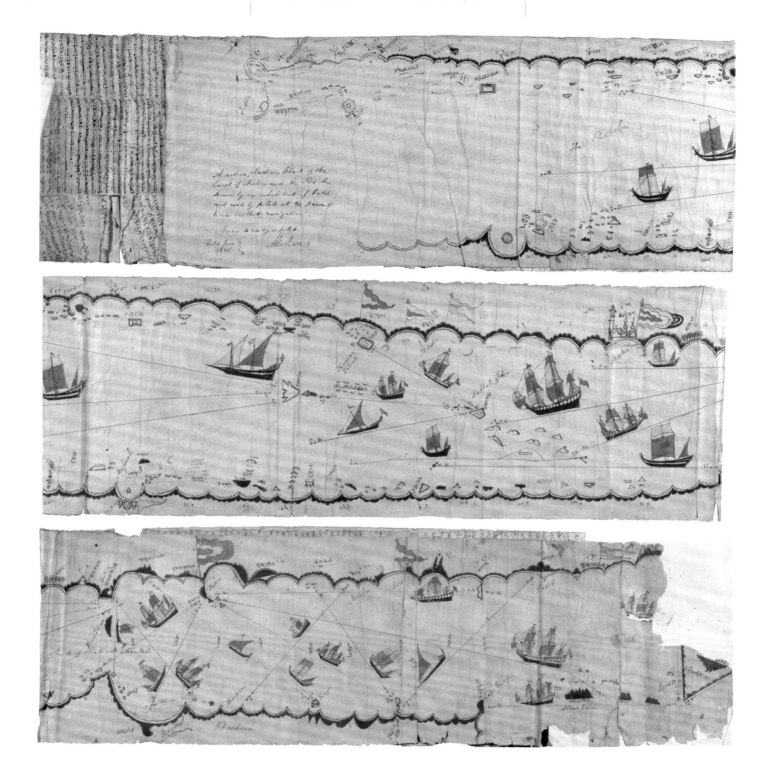

Nautical Chart of the Red Sea and Gulf of Aden | *c.*1790 | Unknown

Coloured ink on paper. 24 × 195.5 cm / 9.5 × 77 in. Royal Geographical Society, London

Although it might appear strange to Western eyes, this Gujarati chart would have been an effective means of navigation for Asian pilots along the notoriously difficult coast of the Red Sea and the Gulf of Aden as they carried pilgrims to Jedda (far left, middle strip), the port for Mecca, for the religious Hajj pilgrimage (see p.207). Believed to date from the 1790s, the chart has a stylistic similarity to Indian charts at least 100 years

older, and its schematic style may go back much further. Clues to its age lie in the stellar rhumb lines, which have constellation symbols at each end to indicate sailing directions, and the altitude of the Pole Star regularly placed along the African coast and elsewhere. Drawn with coloured ink on paper, the chart has been torn from a manuscript text. No great importance was attached to the apparent direction and length of the rhumb lines, as

their compass direction was indicated by symbols and their distances in *zam* (roughly three hours) of sailing time. The characteristic right-angle bend in the Red Sea coast at the straits of Bab-el-Mandeb does not appear, but that poses no problem to the Gujarati pilot. The chart stresses sea features such as islands, shoals, reefs and shallows, but also shows important mosques and the flags of local rulers, annotated in Gujarati and Hindi.

The Molucca Islands | 1594 | Petrus Plancius

Copperplate engraving. 36.7 × 53 cm / 14½ × 21 in. Mitchell Library, Sydney

This map by Petrus Plancius (Pieter Platevoet) of the Molucca Islands of Indonesia – the famed Spice Islands of the European Age of Exploration – was one of the earliest maps to use the new projection developed by Gerard Mercator (see p.155). The development of the Mercator projection was of huge significance for navigators: for the first time they could plot the bearing between two points on the map as a straight line,

making it much easier to steer a course between them. Plancius's map was also a small part of an international power struggle. He had been able to acquire a map of the Moluccas from the Portuguese, who had a virtual monopoly over the trade in spices from the islands. The Dutch were eager to obtain a share of the trade, and eight years after this map was published the Dutch East India Company was established to develop trade in the

region, which subsequently became a Dutch colony. Plancius's chart is both practical – rhumb lines are plotted on it to aid navigators – and highly decorative, with an ornately bordered cartouche and illustrations of the spices that were in such high demand in Europe. The Mercator projection has been much criticized for being Eurocentric, but Plancius's chart is a reminder of its original usefulness, which survives to the present day.

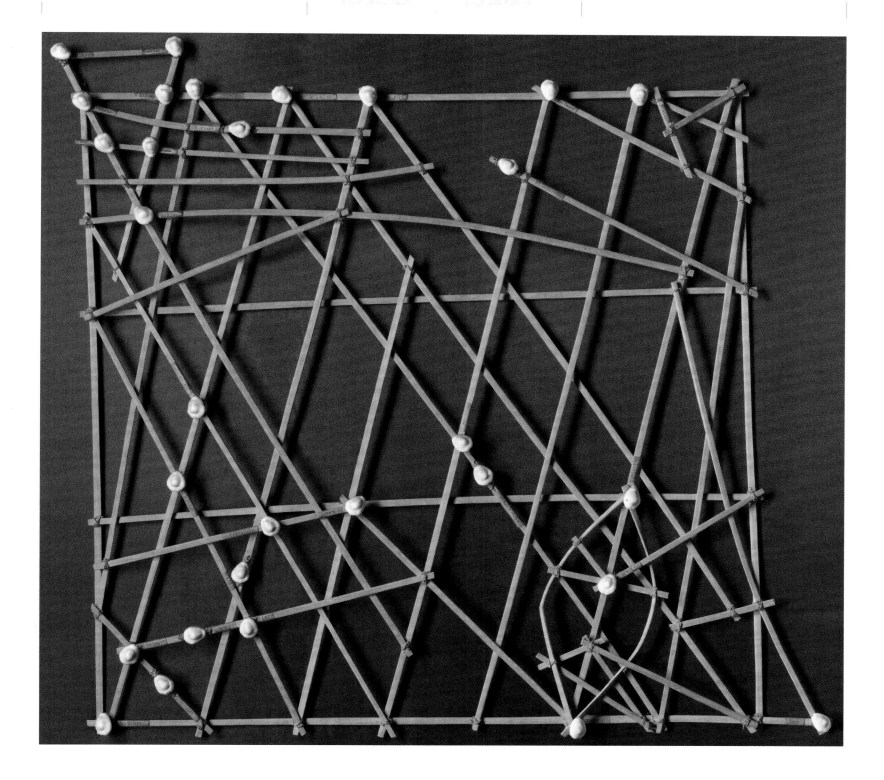

Stick Chart of the Marshall Islands | 1974 | Unknown

Sticks and shells, tied with palm fibre. 55 × 56 cm / 21¾ × 22 in. National Library of Australia, Parkes

Stick charts like this were used by navigators of the pre-literate society of the Marshall Islands of the South Pacific until about the time of World War II (1939–45). Shells and pieces of coral recorded the positions of islands, while the palm ribs show the locations and directions of ocean swell patterns. Such charts were probably used in conjunction with celestial observations to sail outrigger canoes between the hundreds of islands and atolls in the group. These distinctive maps were first reported by missionaries in 1862, when the islands were still a Spanish colony; after Spain sold the islands to the German Empire in 1884, the charts were comprehensively described by a Captain Winkler of the German Navy in 1898. Winkler identified three types: *mattang* charts were for the instruction of future navigators and did not necessarily correspond to real geography; *meddo* charts were actual maps, locating islands, currents and swells; *rebbelith* charts resembled *meddo* charts, but had greater detail. The charts were created by individual navigators and were specific to their maker, varying in shape, size and scale. Although no longer in use, stick charts are such an important part of the iconography of the Marshall Islands, which achieved independence in 1986, that they are featured on the national seal.

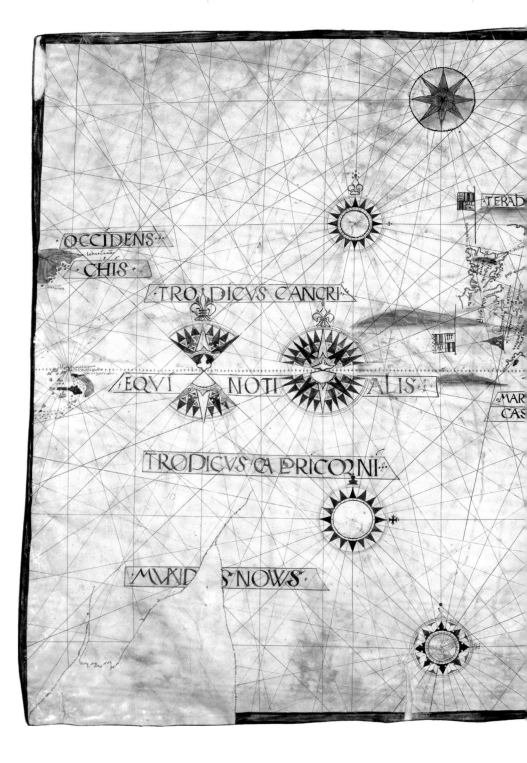

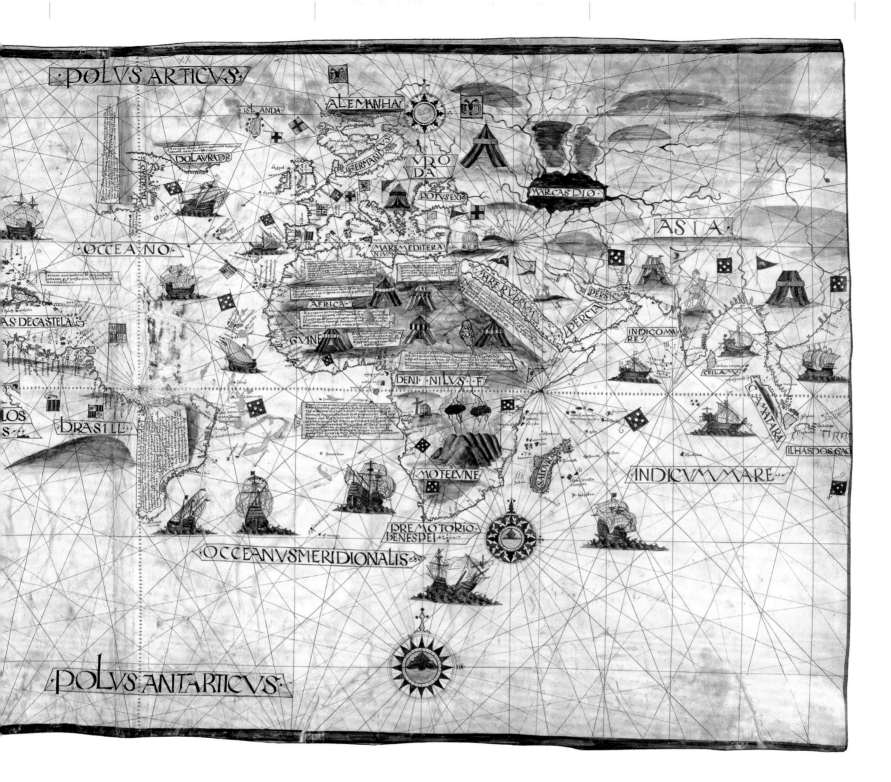

World Map | 1519 | Jorge Reinel

Illuminated manuscript on vellum. 65 × 124 cm / 25 ½ × 49 in. Bibliothèque nationale de France, Paris

This portolan represents both an attempt to solve a vital commercial problem and a remarkable story of preservation. When it was drawn in the sixteenth century, one of the most pressing geographical questions was the longitude of the Moluccas Islands, also known as the Spice Islands, the source of such valuable spices as nutmeg and cloves. The Portuguese had developed a virtual monopoly over the spice trade via their sea routes around southern Africa to the Indian Ocean. In 1513, however, the sighting of the Pacific Ocean by Vasco Núñez de Balboa offered the possibility of a new route to the Spice Islands that would avoid the Portuguese – as long as the islands could be shown to lie outside the Portuguese sphere of influence as defined by the Treaty of Tordesillas in 1494. In 1517 the Portuguese navigator Ferdinand Magellan proposed to King Charles I of Spain that he would sail west to find a passage through the Americas and across the Pacific to prove that the Spice Islands lay on the eastern, or Spanish, side of the longitude dividing the two spheres. This chart by Jorge Reinel, places the islands safely – but erroneously – within the Spanish sphere. The original chart was kept in Munich, but was lost in 1945. This exact copy was made in 1843 by Otto Progel.

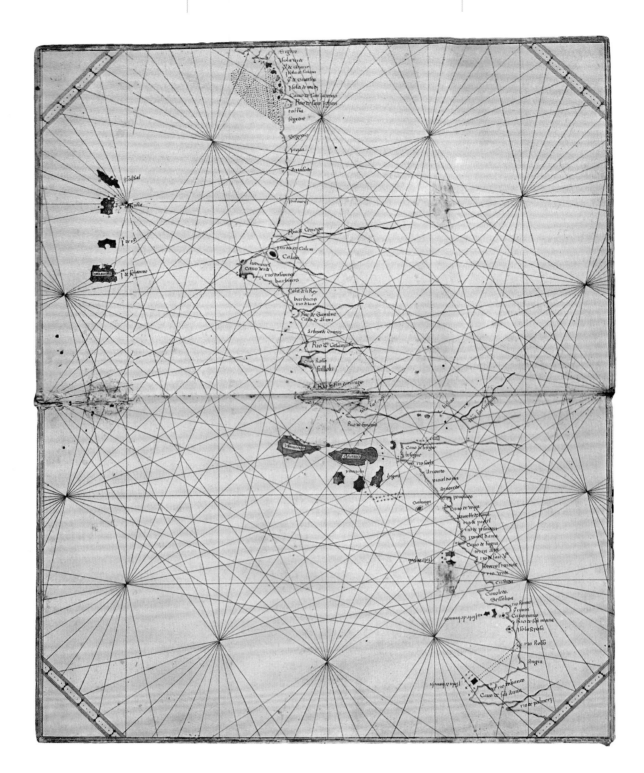

Chart of the Coast of West Africa | 1471 | Grazioso Benincasa

Ink on vellum. 34.6 × 44.2 cm / 13¾ × 17⅓ in. Biblioteca Apostolica Vaticana, Vatican City

By the middle of the fifteenth century, Portuguese ships – some under the command of Venetian or Genoese captains – were making their way along the Atlantic coast of Africa in a drive to discover the unknown southern extent of the continent and the route to India and the East. The surviving cartographic record of this odyssey is limited owing to the official Portuguese Policy of Secrecy, but thanks in part to the Italian captains,

some details leaked out. The leading chart-maker of this coast was Grazioso Benincasa of Ancona, a sea captain-turned-cartographer working mostly in Venice. Between 1463 and 1480 he produced seventeen atlases, many depicting Portuguese exploration. One of the most visible features of the chart is Cabo Verde, the westernmost point of Africa, and the islands off the Cape. Although latitude measurements are sometimes

ambiguous and place names still varied, this chart reaches from about 19°N to about 7°N, even though Portuguese voyagers had already reached the equator by this time. Benincasa's sources of information are not known with certainty, but one Italian captain in the employ of the Portuguese was Alvise Cadamosto – discoverer of the Cabo Verde islands – who had returned to Venice in 1463 after his service in the Atlantic.

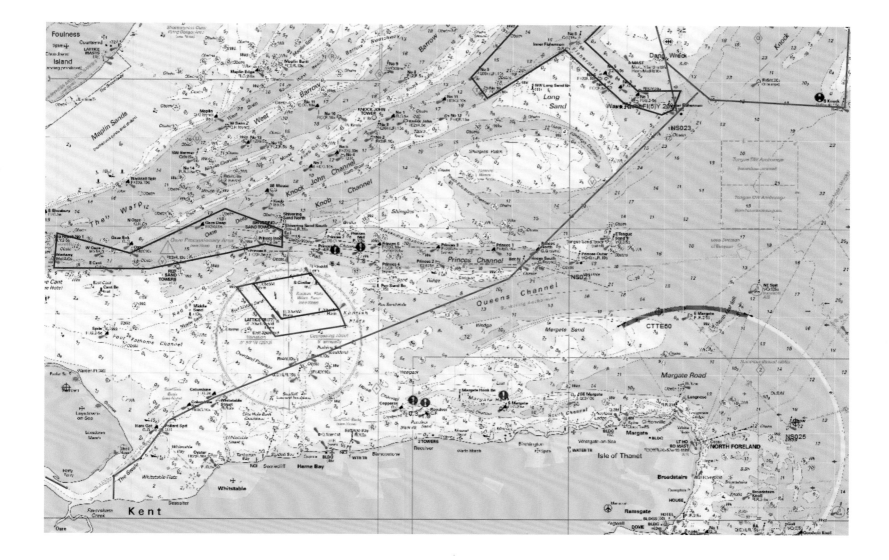

Crossing the Thames Estuary | 2012 | Roger Gaspar

Digital and printed paper. 21 × 29.7 cm / 8¼ × 11¾ in. Private collection

This map of the Thames Estuary in south-east England – specifically to illustrate a notice to mariners to show the routes of power cables (in orange) for the London Array Wind Farm, which opened in 2013 – is based upon a chart for leisure craft produced by Imray Laurie & Wilson Ltd derived from an updated version of Admiralty Chart 1183, published in 1983. Admiralty charts contain up-to-date information for both commercial and recreational vessels about water depths, navigable channels and obstacles. While digital charts are gradually replacing paper versions, the Hydrographic Office continues to produce printed versions for the few ships that do not yet use digital devices. Printed nautical charts are at a clear disadvantage over digital versions, however, because of the delay in receiving updated warnings of new or shifting hazards. The conventions for both printed and digital charts are identical. This chart shows the many shoals and sandbanks – outlined with dots – with the safest routes labelled as 'channels'. Magenta shapes indicate areas to proceed with caution. The numbers printed all over the chart tell the depth of the estuary at each particular point.

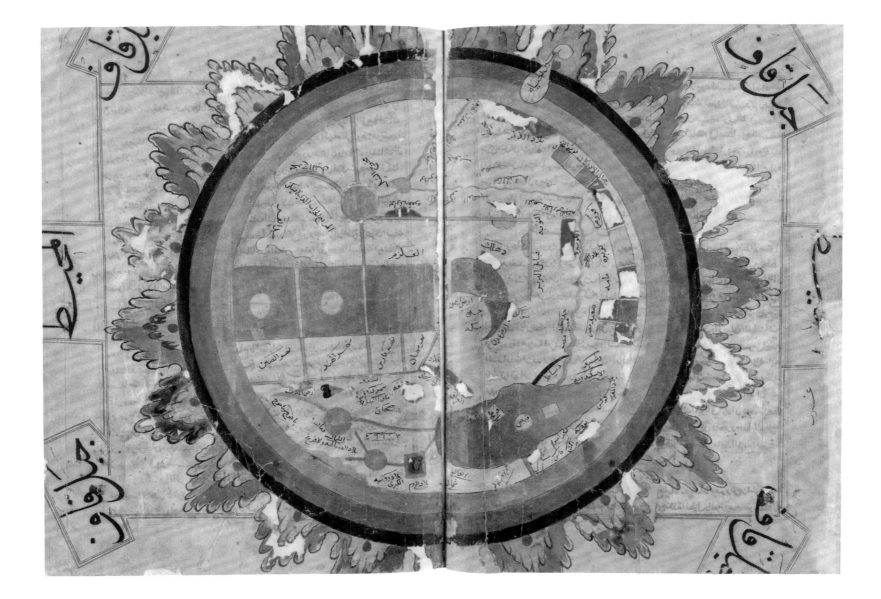

Islamic World Map | c.1280 | Zakariya Ibn Muhammad al-Qazwini

Ink and pigments on paper. 22.9 × 35.6 cm / 9 × 14 in. Forschungsbibliothek, University of Erfurt, Gotha

This seventeenth-century map is based on a thirteenth-century original by Zakariya Ibn Muhammad al-Qazwini, an Arab or Persian physician, astronomer and geographer, and the greatest medieval Muslim cosmographer. Taken from *The Wonders of Creation*, a treatise on cosmography, the circular map is a schematic representation rather than an attempt at an accurate depiction of the world. It is orientated with south at the top, and Africa dominates the upper half. The River Nile runs from its source in the legendary Mountains of the Moon to the Mediterranean Sea, the smaller body of water at the bottom. The Indian Ocean, the larger body of water in the centre, is open to the world-encircling ocean. This is an advance on the ideas of Claudius Ptolemy, the influential second-century Greek-Egyptian geographer, who believed that Africa and Asia were joined and that the Indian Ocean was therefore a landlocked sea (see p.138). Al-Qazwini drew on more than a hundred literary works, histories, legends, geographies and travel accounts from ancient Hebrew, Greek and Roman, and medieval Islamic, Arab and Persian sources. Many copies of this book were made over the centuries with different versions of the world map based closely on al-Qazwini's geographical and cosmographical ideas.

Indian World Map | c.1759–1800 | Unknown

Tempera and ink on cloth. 260 × 261 cm / 8 ft 6 in ×8 ft 6¼ in. Museum für Islamische Kunst, Staatliche Museen zu Berlin

This large Indian map is a unique and important piece of cartography that documents the spread of Islam into Asia and preserves information from a long-lost commentary. Based on the *Secrets of the Ocean*, a geography of the world by the fifteenth-century Arab sailor Ibn Majid, the map also draws on a variety of cartographic traditions, including the work of the second-century Greek-Egyptian geographer Ptolemy (see

p.138) and medieval mappa mundi, whose circular form it resembles. The map is orientated with south at the top and the geographic outlines are painted in a style that was common in western India – then ruled by the Islamic Mughals – in the eighteenth century. Filled with mythological characters and depictions of important Islamic centres such as Mecca, the map also highlights large cities important to world history. The main narrative

is the life of Alexander the Great, known in the Islamic tradition as 'Iskandar', the Macedonian ruler who in 329 BC reached the Oxus River on the borders of India. The map includes three languages. The descriptive insets are written in Arabic, while the names of countries and towns are in Persian. Within India, the place-names are in both Arabic and the Hindu Devanagari script, making the map a truly multicultural object.

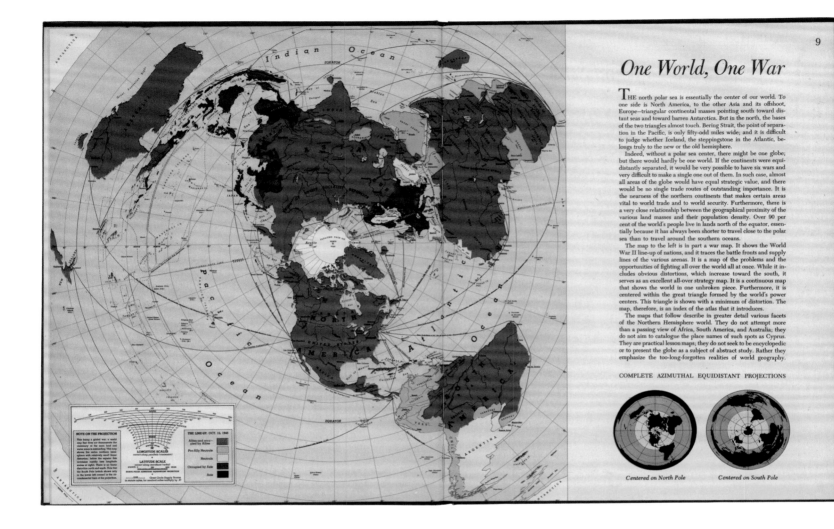

One World, One War

THE north polar sea is essentially the center of our world. To one side is North America, to the other Asia and its offshoot, Europe—triangular continental masses pointing south toward distant seas and toward barren Antarctica. But in the north, the bases of the two triangles almost touch. Bering Strait, the point of separation in the Pacific, is only fifty-odd miles wide; and it is difficult to judge whether Iceland, the steppingstone in the Atlantic, belongs truly to the new or the old hemisphere.

Indeed, without a polar sea center, there might be one globe; but there would hardly be one world. If the continents were equidistantly separated, it would be very possible to have six wars and very difficult to make a single one out of them. In such case, almost all areas of the globe would have equal strategic value, and there would be no single trade routes of outstanding importance. It is the nearness of the northern continents that makes certain areas vital to world trade and to world security. Furthermore, there is a very close relationship between the geographical proximity of the various land masses and their population density. Over 90 per cent of the world's people live in lands north of the equator, essentially because it has always been shorter to travel close to the polar sea than to travel around the southern oceans.

The map to the left is in part a war map. It shows the World War II line-up of nations, and it traces the battle fronts and supply lines of the various arenas. It is a map of the problems and the opportunities of fighting all over the world all at once. While it includes obvious distortions, which increase toward the south, it serves as an excellent all-over strategy map. It is a continuous map that shows the world in one unbroken piece. Furthermore, it is centered within the great triangle formed by the world's power centers. This triangle is shown with a minimum of distortion. The map, therefore, is an index of the atlas that it introduces.

The maps that follow describe in greater detail various facets of the Northern Hemisphere world. They do not attempt more than a passing view of Africa, South America, and Australia; they do not aim to catalogue the place names of such spots as Cyprus. They are practical lesson maps; they do not seek to be encyclopedic or to present the globe as a subject of abstract study. Rather they emphasize the too-long-forgotten realities of world geography.

COMPLETE AZIMUTHAL EQUIDISTANT PROJECTIONS

Centered on North Pole   Centered on South Pole

One World, One War | 1944 | Richard Edes Harrison

Printed in *Look at the World: The Fortune Atlas for World Strategy*. 36 × 58 cm / 14 × 23 in. Private collection

On 1 September 1939 the Germans invaded Poland, and by the end of the day a map of Europe could not be bought anywhere in the United States. War has perennially driven interest in geography, but the truly global dimensions of World War II (1939–45) fundamentally changed the look and shape of the world on a map. Much of this was driven by Richard Edes Harrison, an artist who stumbled into mapmaking when a friend at

Time magazine asked him to fill in for an absent cartographer in 1935. Harrison subsequently drew dozens of eye-catching maps for *Fortune* magazine, combining an aerial perspective with an artistic style in order to convey the way that aviation and war had transformed geographical relationships. In 1944 the editors of *Fortune* capitalized on Harrison's immense popularity by commissioning a world war atlas of sixty-six maps.

These richly executed images brought home new geographical truths. Here Harrison disrupts conventional views of the world by centering the map on the North Pole, thereby demonstrating the proximity of Europe to North America. Harrison adopted this particular view to demonstrate the continuity of land and water in the northern hemisphere, where most of the war took place. World geography would never look the same again.

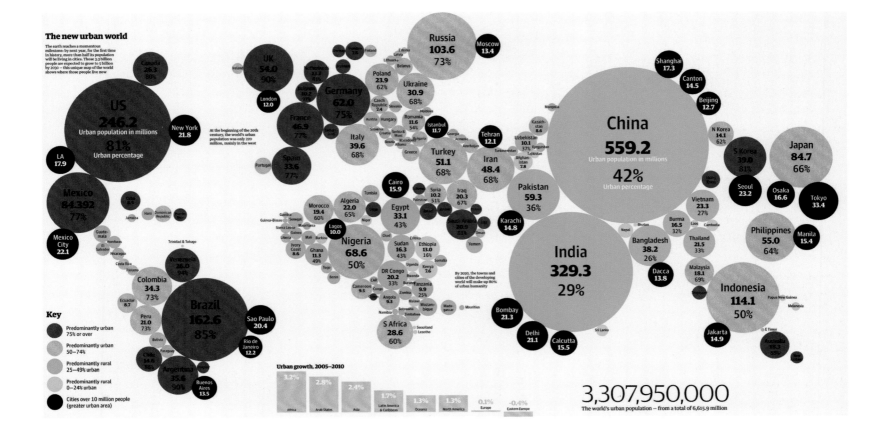

The new urban world

The earth reaches a momentous milestone: by next year, for the first time in history, more than half its population will be living in cities. Those 3.3 billion people are expected to grow to 5 billion by 2030 – this unique map of the world shows where those people live now

Key

- Predominantly urban 75% or over
- Predominantly urban 50–74%
- Predominantly rural 25–49% urban
- Predominantly rural 0–24% urban
- Cities over 10 million people (greater urban area)

Urban growth, 2005–2010

3.2% Africa · 2.8% Arab States · 2.4% Asia · 1.7% Latin America & Caribbean · 1.3% Oceania · 1.3% North America · 0.1% Europe · -0.4% Eastern Europe

3,307,950,000
The world's urban population – from a total of 6,615.9 million

The New Urban World | 2010 | Paul Scruton

Digital map. Dimensions variable

The megacity has arrived. By the end of the twenty-first century the vast majority of the world's population will live in a city environment – and in most of Europe and the Americas they already do. Paul Scruton, a graphic artist for the British newspaper *The Guardian*, made this map in order not only to show the trend towards city living but also to help readers examine how that trend is distributed around the globe. Countries are arranged broadly geographically as simple circles, sized proportionally depending on their urban population. Colour-coding indicates the percentage of the population living in cities, from the highest (red) to the lowest (bright green). The black circles indicate the world's twenty-five cities – in 2010 – with a population of over 10 million people. Scruton's map was influenced by some of the great French statistical atlases of the nineteenth century, which use circles and bars of varying sizes scaled to display demographic information on trade, population and disease. According to Scruton's map, more than half the world currently lives in a city, and the rate of urbanization is increasing. Countries such as China and India, however – although nearly half their people live in cities, including some of the largest cities in the world – still have larger rural populations than the rest of the globe.

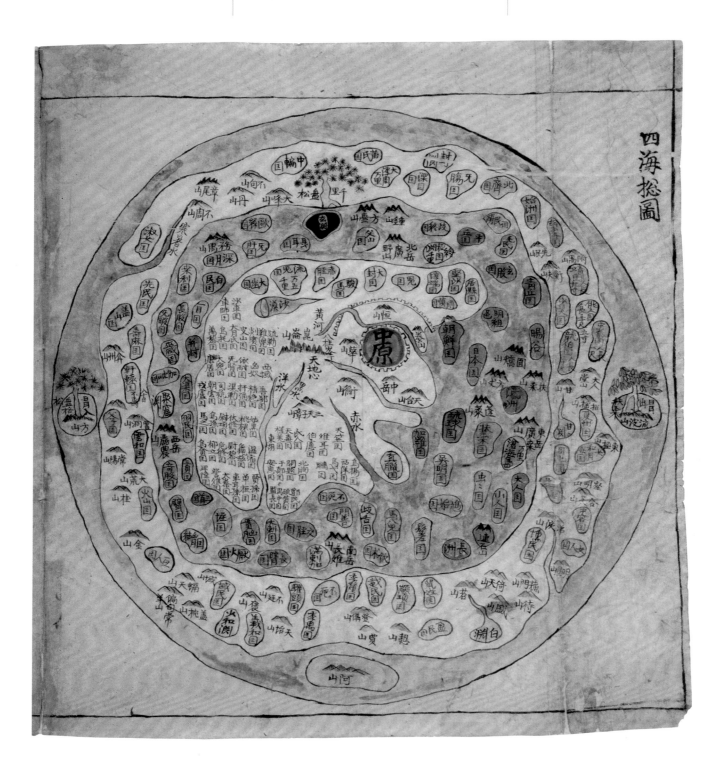

四海總圖

Map of All Under Heaven | c.1800 | Unknown

Ink on paper. 45 × 45 cm / 17¾ × 17¾ in. British Museum, London

Circular Ch'onhado ('All Under Heaven') world maps are unique to Korea, where they were produced from the early sixteenth to the nineteenth centuries. Rather than merely geographical maps, they are true cosmographies depicting both the known Earth and the imagined Heavens. The maps originated as a reaction to the introduction of Western geographical knowledge. Korean map-makers turned to older East Asian works that described more outlying areas for their new maps, which then took the form of an internal continent with China at its centre, surrounded by an internal sea, in turn ringed by an outer continent and finally enclosed by an external sea. This scheme was based on the idea that Heaven is round and the Earth is square. Although they themselves were primarily Confucianists, the map-makers incorporated place names from the older Taoist texts about an imaginary land where immortals live, along with actual place names. Sacred mountains and trees mark the centre of the Earth, the four cardinal points, the poles and the locations of the rising and setting of the sun and moon. The portrayal of the three powers – Heaven, Earth and humans – symbolizes the unity of the three before the complementary opposites of yin and yang were divided in the mythical past.

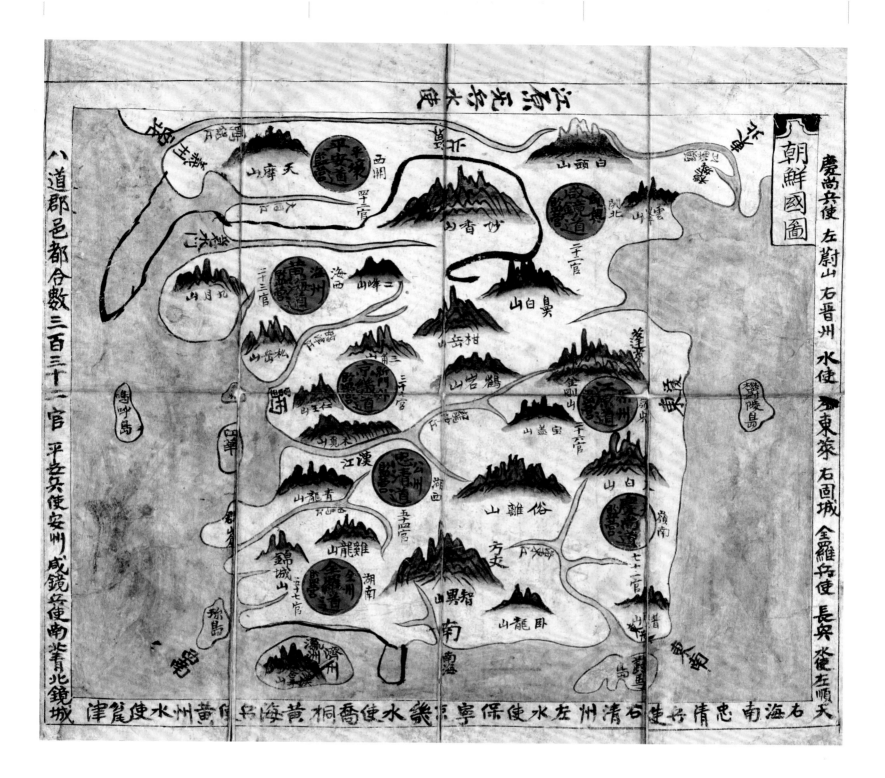

The Administrative and Political Divisions of Korea | 19th century | Unknown

Ink and watercolour on rice paper. 30 × 33 cm / 11¾ × 13 in. Library of Congress, Washington, DC

This nineteenth-century map of the administrative and political divisions of Korea during the late Choson dynasty (1392–1910) is also a demonstration of status and exclusivity. It is written in *hanja* – the technique of using Chinese characters to write down the Korean language – and must therefore have been intended for an elite readership. Four centuries earlier, in the 1440s, King Sejong had created a phonetic Korean alphabet known as *hangul*, which – being far easier to write – increased literacy in Korea dramatically and led to the creation of a popular literature. Even 400 years later, however, elite aristocrats, such as the probable maker of this map, continued to use the more difficult *hanja* for no other reason than to display their status and education. The first in a series of thirteen maps that illustrated the peninsula in ever greater detail, this map provided an overview of Korea's major divisions: the eight provinces. Each is identified by a uniform red circle typical of Korean cartography. On the left-hand side of each circle is a stamp and in the middle is the name of the province; the final column in each circle contains the name of the province's capital.

Babylonian World Map | *c.*700–500 BC | Unknown

Clay. 12.2 × 8.2 cm / 4¾ × 3¼ in. British Museum, London

This clay tablet is small – it fits into the palm of the hand – but it is one of the earliest world maps whose content we can read. It was probably made in Babylon, the city at its centre. This version was made some time between 700 and 500 BC, but the cuneiform text states that it is a copy of an older tablet. With north at the top, the Babylonians' lands are imagined as surrounded by a great 'Bitter River' (the ocean) with distant regions beyond, shown as radiating triangles. In the middle area two parallel lines running north to south represent the Euphrates, the river that gave Babylon life, and at the approximate centre is a rectangle representing the city itself, around which the whole Babylonian world – indeed the whole cosmos – revolved. Around Babylon, small circles indicate eight other cities of the Mesopotamian empire. The tablet suggests the Babylonians had a sophisticated understanding of how maps work and had evolved a set of cartographic conventions. Strikingly, it also betrays the tendency – famously parodied by Saul Steinberg's twentieth-century map of the United States as perceived by New Yorkers (see p.11) – of those dwelling at the heart of empires to imagine that everything revolves around their concerns and location.

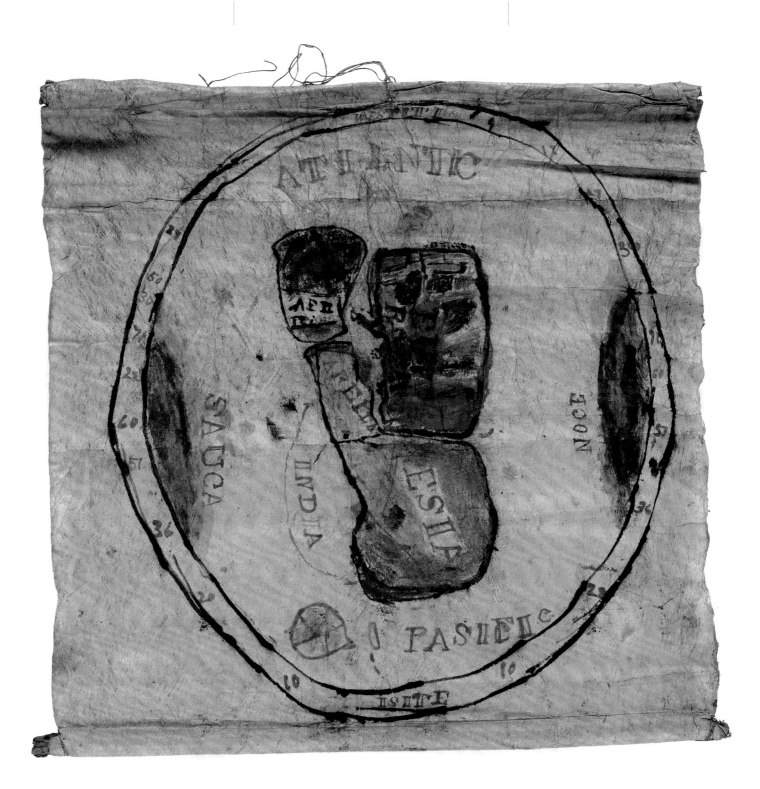

Fijian World Map | c.1896 | Unknown

Paint on white tapa fitted with wooden rollers tied on with fibre string. 56 × 54 cm / 22 × 21¼ in. British Museum, London

This world map drawn by schoolchildren from the Fijian archipelago in the South Pacific is an unwitting echo of maps from the medieval period or even earlier (see opposite). Even by comparison with contemporary Fijian works, it is notable for its poor spelling, crude design and lack of abstract symbolism. The map is oriented with east at the top, and its scale is confused. The large rectangle on the top right is Europe, while Africa

appears split in two, with the mainland forming the top rectangle and Eritrea on its own beneath it. Asia occupies the bottom half of the map, with a faint red semicircle below labelled as India. To the right appears to be Moce, an important island in the Southern Lau group of Fiji. The map was drawn on tapa, a type of cloth made from small strips of bark from the paper mulberry tree which are soaked in water to soften. The softened bark

is the beaten with hardwood clubs until it forms long textured strips, which are overlapped and beaten again to make the fibres fuse into larger sheets. Tapa comes with its own conventional symbolism, the absence of which suggests that no professional tapa designers were involved in the making of this map beyond the preparation of the cloth itself.

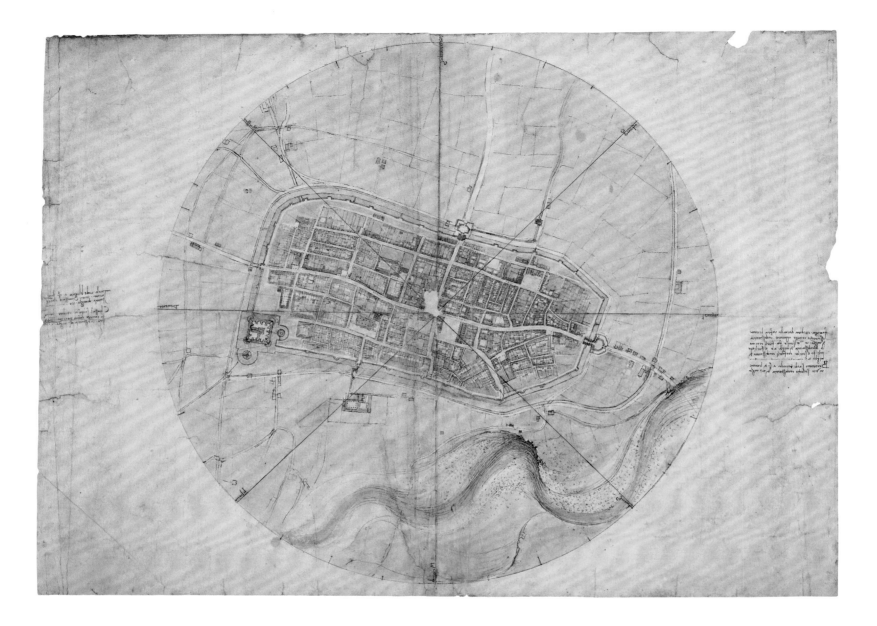

Plan of Imola | 1502 | Leonardo da Vinci

Pen and ink, pencil, chalk and coloured washes on paper. 44 × 62 cm / 17½ × 24½ in. Royal Collection, Windsor

Leonardo da Vinci is renowned as an artist, engineer and general Renaissance man, but this plan of the city of Imola – made while he was employed as an architect by Cesare Borgia, whose siege had badly damaged the fortress at Imola three years earlier – shows him to be also an innovative cartographer. Rather than following the oblique persepective common at the time and showing buildings in elevation, Leonardo's plan looks directly down on the town (an approach known as ichonographic). The plan is enclosed by a circle with crossing lines that form the eight points of the compass with the names of the winds. The plan's circumference is further subdivided into the thirty-two compass points. The technical aspect of the drawing is augmented by the artistic rendering of the surrounding fields in pale green, the delicate blue of the Santerno River and the pink houses and green gardens within the city. The artist shows every street, plot of land, church, colonnade, gate and square, the whole encompassed by the moat. Comparisons with actual details of the city suggest that Leonardo may occasionally have sacrificed accuracy for artistic simplicity, but the increased accuracy of his plan allowed for improved military planning to defend the town from further attack.

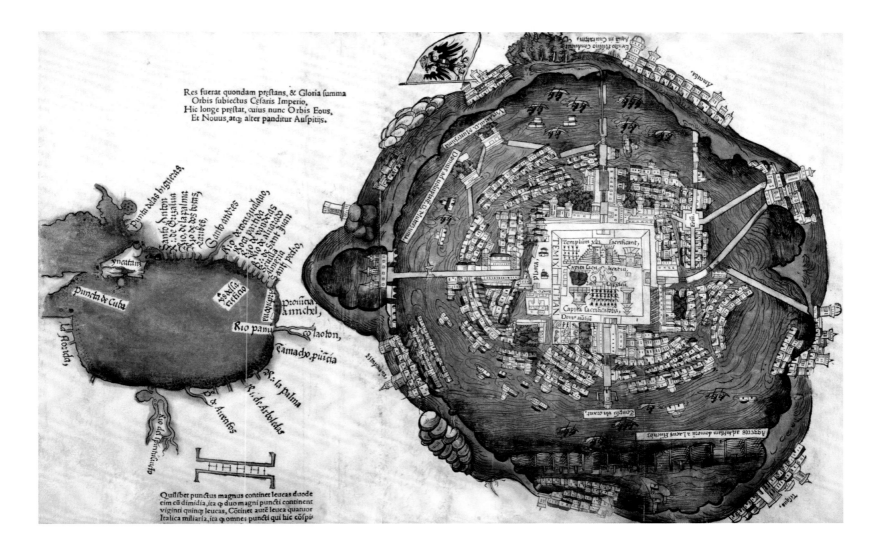

Res fuerat quondam prestans, & Gloria summa
Orbis subiectus Cesaris Imperio,
Hic longe prestat, cuius nunc Orbis Eous,
Et Nouus, ateq alter panditur Auspitijs.

Quilibet punctus magnus continet leucas duode
cim cū dimidía,ita cp duo magni puncti continent
viginti quincp leucas, Cōtinet autē leuca quatuor
Italica miliaría,ita cp omnes puncti qui hic cōſpi

Map of Tenochtitlán and the Gulf Coast | 1524 | Hernán Cortés

Hand-coloured woodcut. 31 × 46.5 cm / 12¼ × 18⅓ in. Newberry Library, Chicago

This woodcut map was the first indication most Europeans had of the greatness of the Aztec capital, Tenochtitlán (Mexico City). It accompanied a letter written by Hernán Cortés, who conquered the city in 1521, to the king of Spain. A city built in a lake, Tenochtitlán was compared by the Spanish newcomers to Venice, while European illustrators struggled to represent the foreignness of Aztec urban development, electing instead to show European-style houses and towers. The city, which was connected to the shore by a series of causeways, featured a zoo, a number of temples and the palace of the emperor Moctezuma. The Spaniards were intrigued by Aztec rituals – not least human sacrifice – so the illustrator dedicates considerable space to the main temple, where the rituals took place. A small cross to the left of the pyramid (under the word *ubi*) represents the new religious norms post-conquest. On the left is a regional map depicting the Gulf of Mexico from Florida and Cuba to the Yucatán peninsula, and the coastal features and settlements in between. One of these, the Rio del Espíritu Santo, would become the Mississippi River. This may be one of the first indications that Europeans were aware of the entrance of a large river into the Gulf in the sixteenth century.

BIRDSEYE VIEW OF THE NATIONAL CAPITAL
INCLUDING THE SITE OF THE PROPOSED
WORLD'S EXPOSITION OF 1892 AND PERMANENT EXPOSITION OF THE THREE AMERICAS.

Birdseye View of the National Capital | 1888 | E. Kurtz Johnson

Coloured lithograph. 60 × 90 cm / 23⅜ × 35⅜ in. Library of Congress, Washington, DC

This lithograph showcases the monumental landscape of Washington, DC, and expresses plans for further development. Panoramic maps had become highly popular in the United States by the late nineteenth century and were particularly associated with the 'boosters' whose task it was to attract settlers to the growing towns of the Midwest and West; even the most modest townships had their panoramic map. Johnson used the format to promote the capital's bid for the World Exposition of 1892 and Permanent Exposition of the Three Americas. Planners intended the proposed fair to celebrate the centennial of the United States Constitution, the 400th anniversary of Christopher Columbus's discovery of America and the theme of Pan-Americanism, with exhibits from the 'Three Americas': North, Central and South. The map's fairgrounds include red building outlines near the Washington Monument (the world's tallest building when it was completed in 1884) and a star-shaped location for a future monument to Columbus. Johnson, treasurer of the Board of Promotions for the exposition, included a row of three proposed cruciform buildings of massive size to house exhibits. Despite his visionary map, however, in 1890 the US House of Representatives awarded the exposition to Chicago.

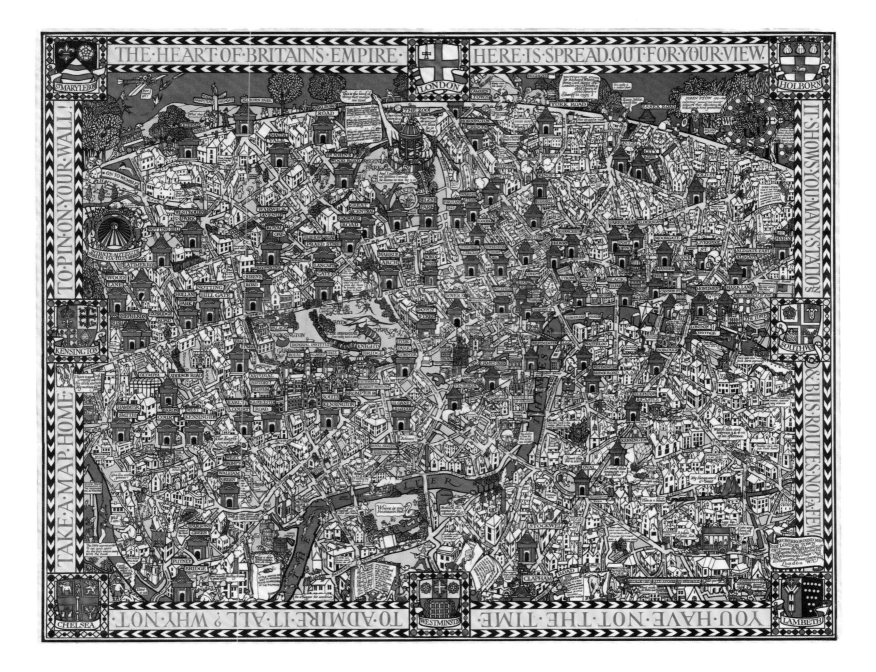

The Heart of Britain's Empire here is spread out for your view. To pin on your wall! It shows you many a station & bus routes not a few. You have not the time to admire it all? Why not take a map home. London. St. Marylebone. Holborn. Kensington. Southwark. Chelsea. Westminster. Lambeth.

The Wonderground Map of London Town | 1914 | MacDonald Gill

Chromolithograph. 75 × 94 cm / 29½ × 37 in. Collection Daniel Crouch Rare Books, London

Before the mapping of London's Underground network was changed forever by Harry Beck's schematic map of 1933 (see p.298), various approaches had been used to explore the city's transport network. Rather than the routes, the stations play a central role in this detailed and humorous map from 1914. Drawn by MacDonald Gill, the map was designed not for any functional use but to present a range of incidental details of London's attractions.

The Underground Electric Railways Company Ltd. commissioned the map as part of an attempt to overcome a perception of the Underground as overcrowded, dirty and inefficient. The company was losing money because the trains were empty at weekends, and the map presented a romantic vision of travel by Underground in an attempt to lure passengers to use the service. The poster, which was displayed at every station, became extremely

popular for its mixture of topographical inaccuracy and cartoon style. It became the first poster to be sold to the public (the Tube still retains a strong connection to public art). Gill himself went on to design official Underground maps between 1920 and 1924. *The Wonderground Map* invites the viewer to engage with the landscape, proving that detail is often key to making a good map.

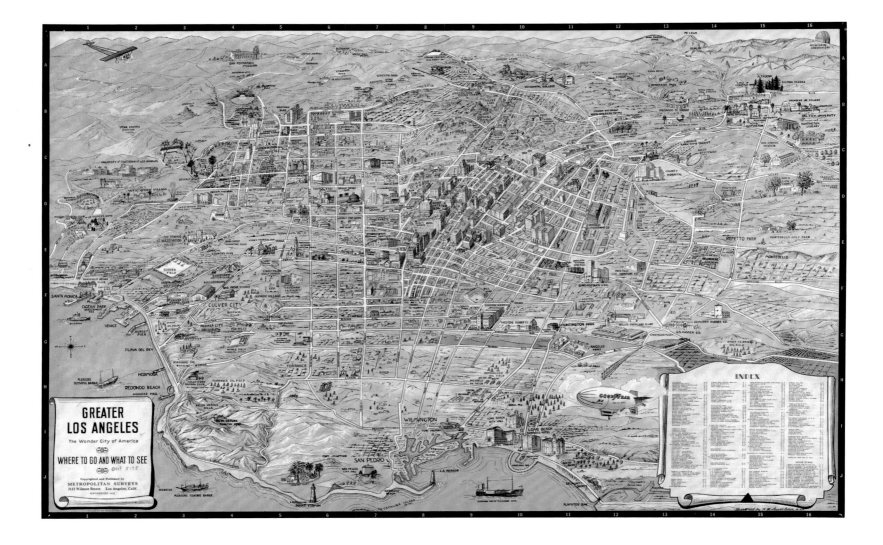

Greater Los Angeles: The Wonder City of America | 1932 | Karl M. Leuschner

Lithograph. 54 × 84 cm / 21¼ × 33 in. Library of Congress, Washington, DC

This map celebrates Los Angeles as 'The Wonder City of America', and was designed when the city was at the height of its interwar glamour. It was published in 1932, the year of the Los Angeles Olympics, and includes Olympic locations – the Olympic Auditorium and the Stadium – as well as the homes of seventeen film stars and miniature illustrations of local attractions, from Santa Monica Pier and the Hollywood Bowl to the Fox Studios, all of which are listed in an extensive index. Although illustrated city views and maps have been made for centuries, from the 1920s to the 1950s highly decorative, often whimsical, almost cartoonlike pictorial maps – sometimes called illustrated maps, panoramic maps or bird's-eye views – enjoyed an unparalleled vogue with the public and with advertisers. The artist Karl M. Leuschner, a German immigrant to the United States, earned his doctorate in art from the University of California. Leuschner's design reflects the Art Deco style of the period. Off the coast near Long Beach is the *Johanna Smith*, the most notorious floating casino of the time, which burned and sank later in the same year the map was made. Peppered across the southern parts of the city, oil wells pump the 'black gold' that played such an important part in the city's history and economy.

Silicon Valley 1991 | 1990 | Silicon Valley Map

Printed paper. 99 × 68 cm / 39 × 26¾ in (whole sheet including calendar; detail shown). Private collection

California's Silicon Valley – widely seen as the heartland of the digital revolution – might seem an unlikely location for a throwback to the seventeenth and eighteenth centuries, when publishers raised money to create maps by selling subscriptions, in return for which purchasers were included on the map. In 1989 Jill Amen – then working for semiconductor manufacturer Micro Linear – tried to find a promotional map of Silicon Valley to give to customers. Frustrated, she created the first in a series of calendar maps, bringing together a colourful, busy view of the valley full of tiny vignettes with the locations of new technology companies. Amen had so much success that she launched Silicon Valley Map in a move suitably in keeping with the area's entrepreneurial spirit. Every year, local businesses buy the right to have their logos displayed on the map, and so the chronological editions of the calendar – all by different artists and thus in different styles – have become a cartographic record of the changing fashions and staying power of companies in the unstable world of new technology. Some companies featured on this early map – such as Apple, IBM and Intel – are still world leaders while others flourished only briefly, such as the computer manufacturer Everex, which went bankrupt in 1993.

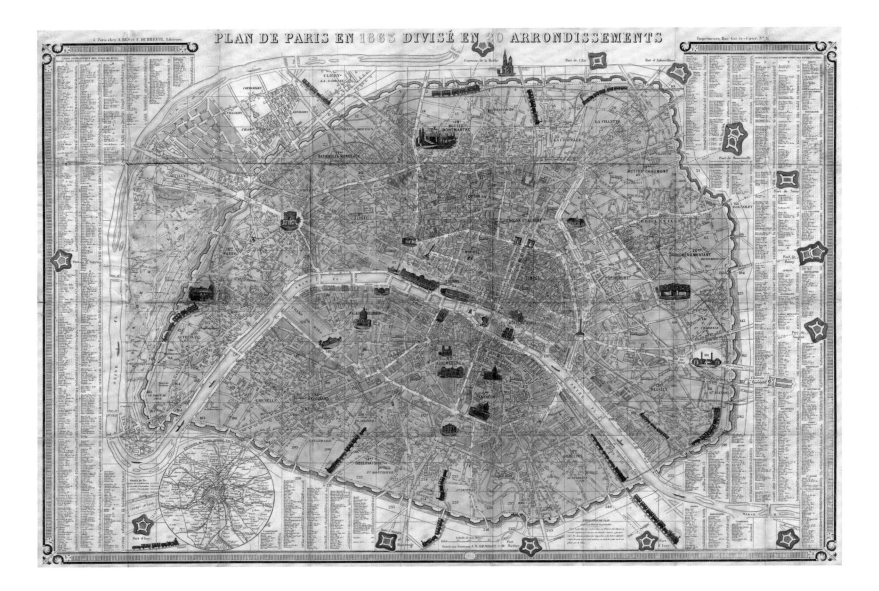

Map of Paris in 1863 Divided into Twenty Arrondissements | 1863 | J. N. Henriot

Engraving with colour on paper. 86.3 × 59.6 cm / 34 × 23½ in. Private collection

French engraver and printer J. N. Henriot drew this map of Paris three years after Emperor Napoleon III ordered the expansion of the French capital to include its former suburbs. The city's neighbourhoods ('*arrondissements*') rose from twelve to twenty – shaded in four pastel tones – arranged in a new spiral design that became known as the snail. By then, Napoleon and his prefect of the Seine, Baron Georges-Eugène Haussman, were midway through their project to convert Paris from a medieval town to an international city by creating boulevards, parks and squares (the boulevards were said to be wide so that potential revolutionaries would not be able to block them with barricades, and militaristic concerns are also reflected in the fourteen forts encircling the city). Henriot's pocket map lists all of the city's streets, while an inset circular map also shows its environs. The map extends an enthusiastic invitation to visitors by illustrating important buildings in profile and showing passenger trains – then still relatively novel – heading into the city. Such easy-to-read maps were intended to make cities more approachable at a time when they seemed to contemporaries to be changing at bewildering speed.

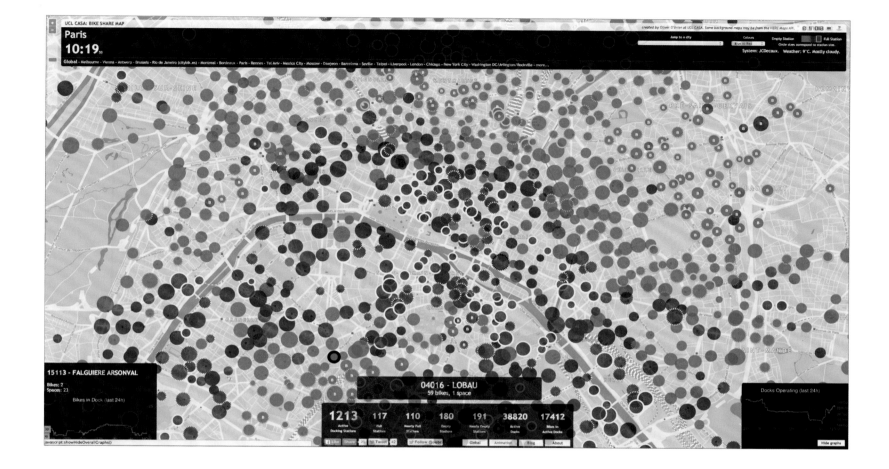

Vélib Docking Stations Map | 2015 | Oliver O'Brien

Digital. Dimensions variable

Traditionally, maps show situations that are relatively fixed. The British researcher Oliver O'Brien's web map of the bike-share scheme in Paris, however, is never out of date as its data is renewed every two minutes. Developed from a map of 2010 showing London's bike-share scheme, O'Brien's live map provides links to around 100 similar schemes across the globe. Technically, the map shows the potential of tapping into real-time data feeds that make it not only interesting but also useful. A key aspect of web mapping is the ability for a map to update when data changes. O'Brien demonstrates how to harness that and create an informative product that captures change approximately every 120 seconds. The map uses proportional symbols to indicate the size of the bike station, and colour – which can be modified to the user's liking – to show whether a station is relatively full or empty. The addition of statistics on each bike station (revealed by a mouse rollover), the overall statistics for a city, usage graphs and animations that show the ebb and flow of daily use patterns add to the utility of the map. Detail is key, and the map gives the user a number of ways to consume the changing patterns of bike use, as well as allowing them to modify the viewing experience to their own taste.

LCC Bomb Damage Map | 1945 | London County Council Architect's Department

Printed paper with hand-colouring. 60 × 100 cm / 23¾ × 39½ in. Metropolitan Archives, City of London

The unintended beauty of this map of bomb damage in the London neighbourhoods of Holborn, Farringdon and St Paul's both masks untold human suffering and celebrates hope for the future. Even while World War II (1939–45) continued to rage in Europe, local authorities in Britain planned the country's post-war reconstruction. Before rebuilding could begin, it was necessary to know the extent of the damage. The London County Council

Architect's Department recorded bomb damage in hand-coloured maps based on the 1:2,500-scale Ordnance Survey maps from 1916. The standardized colours indicated the degree of damage: black meant that a building had been destroyed totally; purple, that it was damaged beyond repair; dark red, that it was doubtful if repairable; light red, repairable at cost; orange, general, minor blast damage; yellow, minor blast damage; light green,

a clearance area. Circles were added where appropriate to differentiate the sites of V1 and V2 explosions. This map shows the extent of damage around St Paul's Cathedral, with most of the buildings damaged beyond repair and some damage to the cathedral itself. However, it also shows that a large part of the City of London had escaped relatively unscathed.

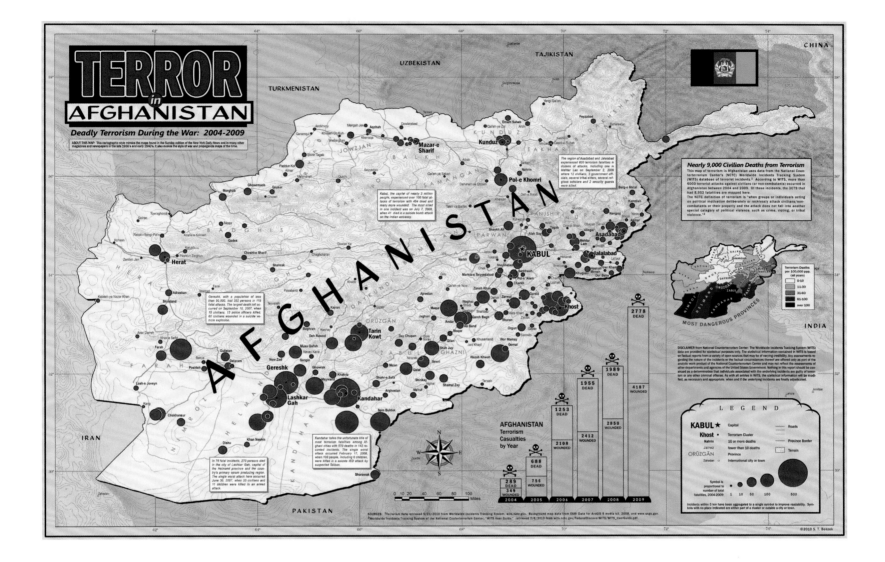

Terror in Afghanistan | 2010 | Stephen Benzek

Giclée print. 50.8 × 76.2 cm / 20 × 30 in. Private collection

This map of terror attacks in Afghanistan is unusual because it uses modern computer-mapping methods, including data analysis from the United States National Counterterrorism Center, to create a retro-style map of Afghanistan that appears to be hand-drawn. The cartographer Stephen Benzek wanted to evoke an emotional response by mimicking a style reminiscent of war maps in newspapers of the 1930s and early 1940s. *Terror in Afghanistan* uses

typography and symbols from World War II-era maps to illustrate civilian deaths (red circles) from terrorist attacks between 2004 and 2009. Taliban and al-Qaeda insurgents have killed thousands of Afghan civilians since US-led forces deposed the Taliban government following the 11 September 2001 terrorist attacks. The map reveals the spatial extent of nearly 9,000 fatalities from some 6,000 attacks, highlighting the loss of life in the capital, Kabul, and

areas south. A graph, complete with skulls and crossbones, records the grim civilian toll, which reached 2,778 dead and 4,187 wounded in 2009. Next to the graph, a small map uses dark tints to depict the most dangerous provinces, all of which are in southern Afghanistan. Map notes, outlined in red, provide details about attacks, such as one in Kandahar that killed 100 people in 2008.

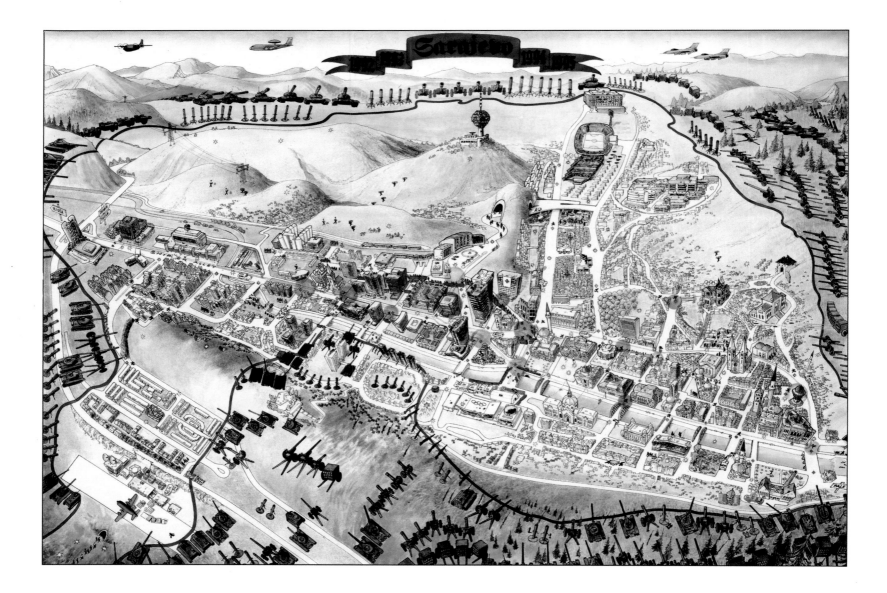

Survival Map 1992–1996 (The Siege of Sarajevo) | 1996 | Suda Kapic and Ozren Pavlovic

Pencil, ink and watercolour on paper. 70 × 100 cm / 27½ × 39⅜ in. Private collection

How could a city go from hosting the Olympics to being under deadly siege in less than ten years? This map of the Bosnian capital, Sarajevo, illustrates the city during the Bosnian War (1992–5), when it was held under siege by Serbian forces. While its initial purpose was to document the ongoing event, it also became a guide to surviving siege conditions, a memorial – almost a souvenir for those who lived through the longest siege in modern

history – and a warning. Between snipers and starvation, the people of Sarajevo struggled to survive for almost four years. The bird's-eye-view rendering almost makes the map resemble a board game, but the tanks and artillery surrounding the city behind the thick blood-red line were quite real, as was the secret 'tunnel of hope' through which food was brought into the city and early versions of this map, drawn under siege, smuggled out

to be printed in Croatia. The map depicts strategically important elements, such as water sources, a functioning bakery, food gardens and sniper zones. The Bosnian artists went on to found a media company called FAMA, which became a collection of information open to anyone researching the former Yugoslavia. Suda Kapic and Ozren Pavlovic have since compiled their projects and archives and made them available online.

Iraq War Rug | 2003 | Unknown

Wool. 246 × 162 cm / 8 ft 1 in × 5 ft 4 in. Private collection

This outline of Iraq – filled with aircraft, tanks and rockets painted for desert camouflage – was woven into a rug proclaiming support for the arrival of United Nations troops in the country in 2003. The weavers have labelled Iraq's major regions and cities and its neighbours, but have not attempted to show any geographical information beyond the country's shape. Far more attention has gone into the representation of military hardware, including black Apache attack helicopters and a detailed Humvee (bottom left). The military imagery echoes that of earlier rugs woven in another war zone – Afghanistan – where this rug was produced by weavers of the Turkic Uzbek minority. For centuries, Uzbeks have woven rugs with traditional patterns and motifs. For women living in seclusion – the Islamic tradition of *purdah* – weaving was one of the few available means to communicate their lives and thoughts to the outside world. After the Soviet invasion of Afghanistan in 1979, weavers began to feature aircraft and other images of conflict, and went on to depict the 9/11 attacks on the World Trade Center (the images were based on propaganda leaflets dropped by Coalition aircraft). The popularity of the rugs with Western collectors led to a rapid growth in rugs being woven specifically for export, like this one.

Waterloo Map | 1814–5 | Colonel Sir John Carmichael-Smyth and Major John Sperling RE

Pencil and ink on paper. 135 × 99 cm / 53 × 39 in. Royal Engineers Museum, Chatham, Kent

The map the Duke of Wellington is said to have used to plan his victory over Napoleon Bonaparte in June 1815 had a dramatic history. Knowing of Napoleon's advance into Belgium from the south, Wellington called on the Royal Engineers for a map of a broad area (Waterloo itself is to the right of the map). With the final map still unfinished, Wellington requested the four preparatory sketches be stitched together. The officer bringing the map from Brussels was unhorsed in a skirmish with French cavalry, but managed to get the map to Wellington, who pencilled on it his troop dispositions. He passed it on to his chief of staff, from whose body it was recovered after he was fatally wounded by a cannonball (his bloodstains are still on the map). Wellington was adopting the tactics of the enemy: Napoleon was so reliant on maps that he had a special cart made to carry them on campaign, and he studied them each evening, often spreading the maps out on the floor. Since the sixteenth century, military officers had been trained to sketch the main features of a battlefield. Later, the task passed to more specialized engineers who reconnoitred and recorded terrain.

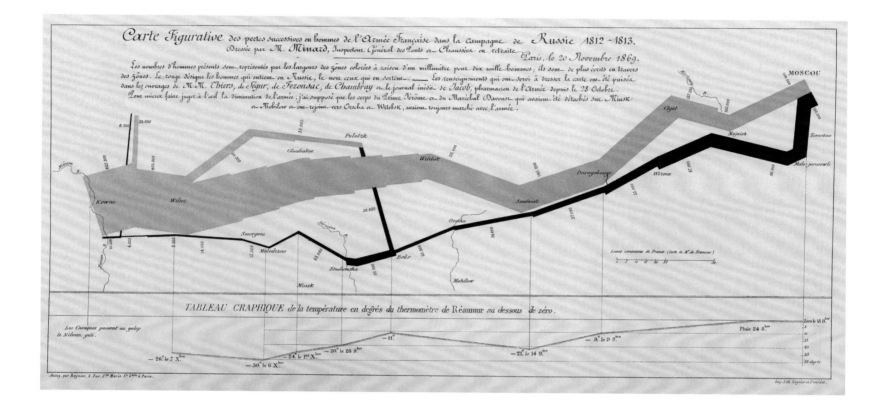

Figurative Map of Losses of the French Army in the Russian Campaign, 1812–3 | 1861 | Charles Joseph Minard

Copperplate engraving on paper. 21 × 24 cm / 8¼ × 9½ in. École nationale des points et chaussés, Champs-sur-Marne

This classic infographic depicting Napoleon's ill-fated invasion of Russia in 1812–3 has been acclaimed as possibly the best statistical graphic ever drawn. Originally produced in 1861 by the French civil engineer Charles Joseph Minard, it is a thematic data map that shows the geography and timing of the overwhelming defeat of the French Grand Armée by a combination of the Russian military and popular resistance in a cruel winter campaign.

The upper, beige shape charts Napoleon crossing the Neman River from Poland into Russia in late June 1812 with 422,000 men and reaching Moscow with a dwindling force of 100,000; the lower black line follows the retreat back to Poland in late December with approximately 10,000 men remaining. The failed invasion helped to bring Napoleon's dominance over Europe to a swift end. Minard skilfully represents six variables graphically.

In addition to time and space – indicated by the names of cities and rivers and a scale – the diminishing size of the expedition is shown by numbers and the shrinking width of the lines. At the foot of the map the retreat is coordinated with the progress of the Russian winter. Minard's pioneering infographic proves that a picture can indeed paint a thousand – or several thousand – words.

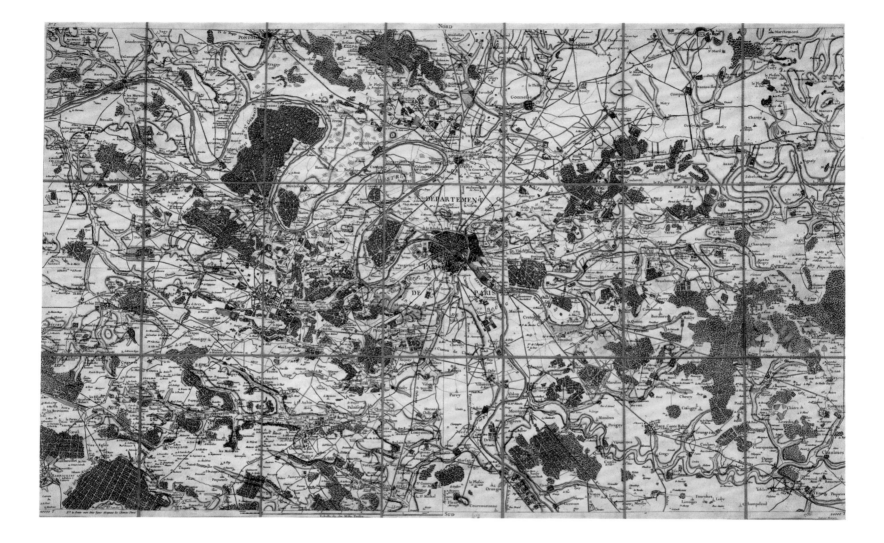

General Map of France: No 1, Paris | 1756 | César-François Cassini de Thury

Hand-coloured engraving. 60 × 95 cm / 23½ × 37½ in. Bibliothèque nationale de France, Paris

In 1744 César-François Cassini de Thury prepared the first systematic, nationwide survey of a nation-state, France. Three years later Louis XV commissioned him to produce a more detailed map of the nation (the king later dropped out, leaving Cassini to raise funds for the venture). Ultimately consisting of 180 separate sheets, the feat was the culmination of a century's work by three generations of the Cassini family, and achieved a level of detail that far outshone other European cartographic dynasties. Cassini's monumental series was based on the triangulation of France begun in 1669 by his forebears and laid out in his map of 1744. The more detailed new topographic map series, *Carte de France Levée par Ordre du Roy* ('Map of France Produced at the Request of the King', of which this map is part), was begun in 1748 and was intended to last eighteen years. In the event, the first two maps took eight years to complete, but were the first scientifically surveyed, planimetrically accurate maps of any country. Colours highlight different land use, while shadows emphasize and raise elements. Topography is shown with shading and fine hachure, and shadows add depth to rivers. The typography is beautifully applied, and pictorial symbols show the positions of churches and other landmarks.

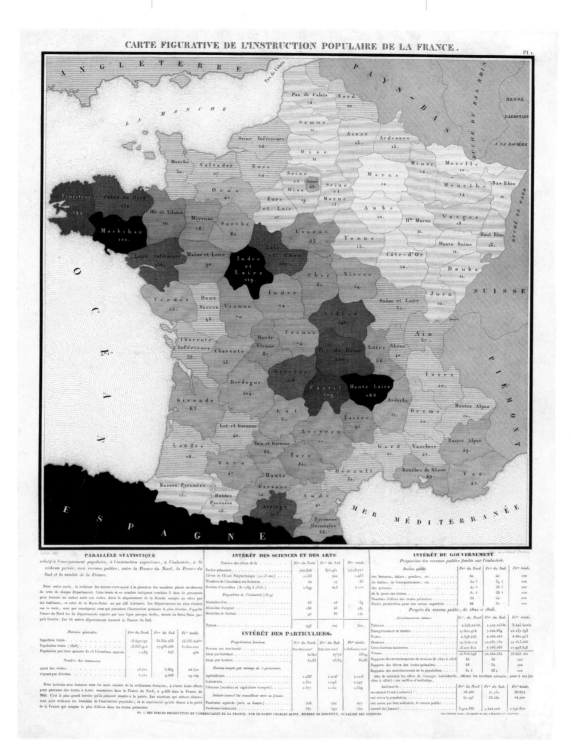

Figurative Map of Public Education in France | 1826 | Baron Charles Dupin

Lithograph. 51 × 53 cm / 20 × 20⅞ in. Bibliothèque nationale de France, Paris

Nineteenth-century social reformers energetically tackled the ills of industrial society, and Charles Dupin's innovative map was an outgrowth of that movement. His map of the rate of school enrolment across France broke new ground in terms of cartographic form and content. It initiated 'choropleth mapping,' in which a variable is averaged in a given geographic area: here Dupin used shading to represent the proportion of male children enrolled in the public schools across each *department*. His goal was to investigate the relationship between literacy and prosperity, and his map is credited with increasing the number of schools in France. Subsequently, Andre-Michel Guerry used newly gathered statistics to explore and map the relationship between crime and education; the results suggested that crime was not in fact concentrated in areas with lower levels of education. Guerry's and Dupin's experiments with mapping data sparked great enthusiasm for statistics across Europe, and later in the United States. Many reformers hoped that such data – properly visualized – might reveal social trends and patterns that would lead to reform and improved governance.

DESCRIPTIVE MAP OF LONDON POVERTY 1889.

Descriptive Map of London Poverty | 1889 | Charles Booth

Coloured engraving. 160 × 223 cm / 5 ft 3 in × 7 ft 3¼ in. British Library, London

This map graphically depicts the haves and have-nots of London at the end of the nineteenth century. The largest industrial city in the world – its population grew from almost a million in 1801 to nearly 4,700,000 by 1901 – London suffered extreme inequality in wealth, with many inhabitants in abject poverty. Their neighbourhoods and lifestyles remained hidden from most Londoners until 1885, when Charles Booth, a wealthy philanthropist, hired a team of investigators to collect data on the condition of the city's poor. The investigators walked the streets of inner London taking notes, which were published in a series of volumes entitled *Life and Labour of the People in London* (1889–91), accompanied by maps showing the distribution of different socio-economic classes. This map shows the city's distinctive patchwork of housing with Booth's descriptive key, which shows how closely the 'Upper-middle and Upper classes. Wealthy' live close to the 'Lowest class. Vicious. Semi-criminal'. Much of north London – then still a relatively new part of the city – is shown as being occupied by people who were 'fairly comfortable', 'Middle class' or 'Well-to-do'. Booth's work played an important role in future campaigns for social reform.

Human Poverty | 2006 | SASI Group and Mark Newman

Digital. Dimensions variable

The dramatic distortion in this map shows graphically, in a way that numerical values alone could not, the striking differences in worldwide poverty: the larger a country, the more poor people it has. Such maps are a form of cartographic visualization known as cartograms, introduced to the world of analytic geography in the late 1960s by the cartographer Waldo Tobler, who took advantage of the statistical and computational capabilities of early computers. The principle underlying cartograms is that the area contained within particular landmasses, or country boundaries, can be weighted and distorted according to any thematic or statistical variable for which a numeric value is available, such as poverty, food production or population. The Social and Spatial Inequalities Group (SASI) at the University of Sheffield produced this cartogram using specially developed WorldMapper software, based on an updated version of Tobler's cartogram algorithms and employing a model akin to physical diffusion processes to produce these striking images. SASI has produced many such maps and conducts interdisciplinary quantitative research to help in the development of policy directly aimed at reducing social inequality and poverty around the world.

The Great Tartary: Drawing of the Lands of Siberia | 1701 | Semyon Ulianovich Remezov

Hand-coloured pen and ink on paper. 57 × 76 cm / 22½ × 30 in. Russian State Library, Moscow

The first map of Siberia drawn by a Russian native is fully titled 'Drawing of the Lands of Siberia, the Town of Tobolsk and All Various Towns and Settlement, and the Steppe'. It was created at the start of the eighteenth century, shortly after the completion of Russia's conquest of 'The Great Tartary', the common medieval name for this huge area of northern and central Asia. The orientation of the map resembles Arab maps, with south towards the top. At the bottom of the map, black areas represent the Arctic Ocean, which is bordered by areas identified as being inhabited by Samoyeds, a term for a group of related indigenous peoples, including the Nenets, Enets, Nganasans and Selkups. The main part of the map focuses on three major river systems: the Lena (far left), Yenisei (centre) and Ob (far right). These key highways for Russian settlers are outlined in thick black, flowing from the bottom towards the top. The eastern Kamchatka peninsula appears on the far left, with 'Korea' in mustard colour at the very top. The red shape just to the right of Korea is labelled as China, with two groups of Mongols below. On the right-hand edge of the map a red semicircle is labelled as 'The Great Land of Muscovy' – the power that was by then firmly in charge of the whole of Siberia.

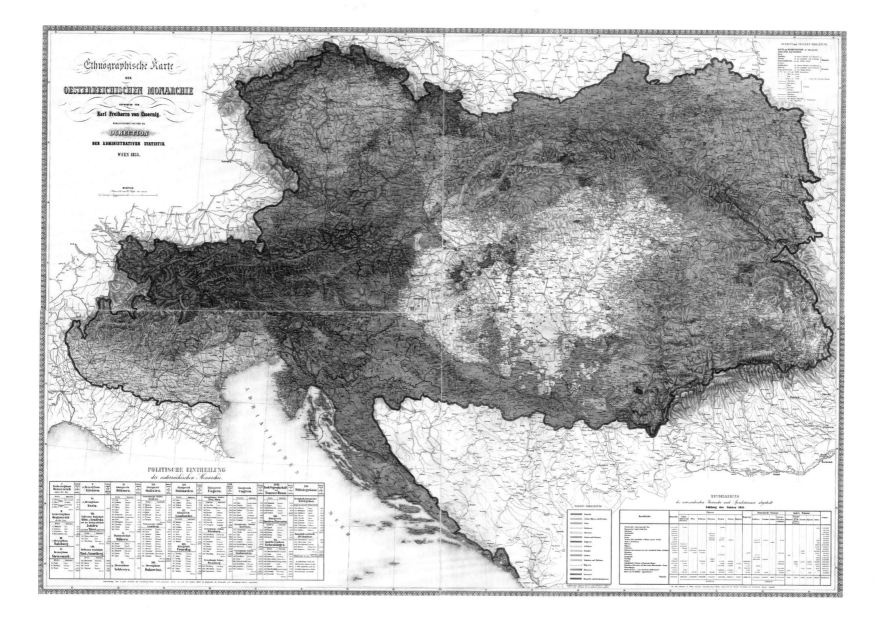

Ethnographic Map of the Austrian Monarchy | 1855 | Karl von Czoernig

Lithograph. 102 × 144 cm / 40⅛ × 56⅝ in. Museum of Military History, Budapest

Although speculating about differences among 'peoples' is an age-old practice, the systematic attempt to map such perceived differences is a more recent phenomenon. The Austrian imperial official Karl von Czoernig's ethnographic map of lands and peoples controlled by the Habsburg Empire was among the earliest of such attempts, but set the tone for those that would follow. The romantic idea that certain territories were 'natural'

homes for particular 'peoples' had become popular during the nationalist revivals of the mid-nineteenth century, and presented a challenge for imperial rulers who governed peoples from different ethnic and language groups. Czoernig began his map in the service of the Austrian imperial chancellor Klemens von Metternich, who adopted a policy of 'divide and rule' in the face of gowing nationlism. Czoernig territorialized linguistic

differences, representing in colour areas where German, Czech, Hungarian and other languages were most prominent. In the fashion of the time, he argued that these differences were not just linguistic but 'ethnographic'. His map ushered in an era of ethno-linguistic cartography that would culminate in the influence of such maps in the redrawing of European boundaries after the collapse of the empire after World War I (1914–8).

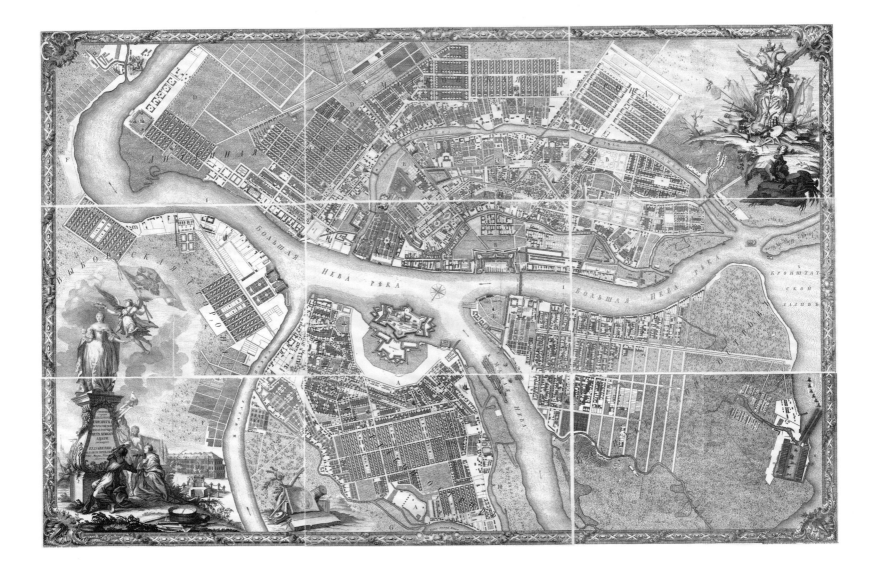

Plan of the Capital City of St Petersburg | 1753 | Mikhail Makhaev

Engraving. 141 × 206.5 cm / 55½ × 81½ in. Collection Daniel Crouch Rare Books, London

It is a measure of the rapid growth of St Petersburg that the city founded by Czar Peter the Great in 1703 filled nine sheets of this map published in limited numbers to mark its first jubilee in 1753 and dedicated 'to the glory and honour of the Russian Empire'. Mikhail Makhaev's map was commissioned to commemorate the city's first fifty years – and to anticipate its future. Produced on a scale of 1:3,350, the map gives an accurate view of the

city's existing streets, palaces and public buildings, as well as prospective building projects. The decoration includes the arms of the city and attributes of the sciences, arts, commerce and the art of war at top right. Most of the design was by Makhaev, and so his name is usually attached, correctly, to the whole work. However, numerous artists contributed to the views and panoramas, and the map itself was prepared at the Geographic

Department of the Russian Academy of Sciences, where it was supervised by the junior scientific assistant Ivan Truskott under the guidance of Ivan Sokolov, who also engraved the figure of the Empress Elisabeth Petrovna after a portrait by the French artist Louis Caravaque. Only 100 prints were taken; they were distributed among major library and palace collections throughout Europe.

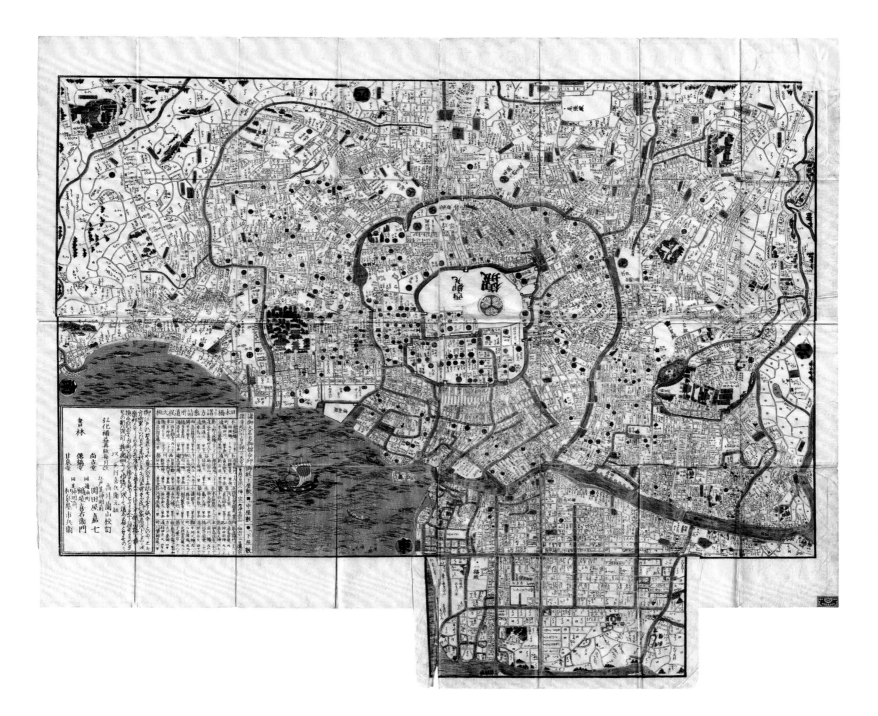

Map of Edo, Japan | *c.*1844−8 | Unknown

Woodblock on rice paper. 99 × 71 cm / 39 × 28 in. Perry-Castañeda Library Map Collection, University of Texas at Austin, Texas

This illustrated map from Japan's Koka Period (1844−8) celebrates the beauty of Edo (modern-day Tokyo). The map celebrates the city and its attractions for visitors by combining surveying techniques based on Dutch cartography with the vibrant colours and characteristic style of traditional Japanese woodblock prints (*ukiyo-e*). The chart in the lower lefthand corner lists city events and distances to points of interest from Nihonbashi Bridge,

the endpoint of two roads that ran between Edo and Kyoto. At the same time as it provides practical information for visitors the map also reinforces feudal authority at a time of increasing tension in Japanese society. Edo had been the center of power for the ruling Tokugawa shogunate for two centuries, and the family's clan symbol (*mon*) lies at the very heart of the map. Alongside are two Japanese ideograms (*kanji*) representing Edo

Castle and the living quarters of the family and ministry officials. Outside the central circle of the city, in areas not directly referring to religious or public spaces, more *mon* and *kanji* refer to close hereditary vassals. For most Japanese citizens, the map graphically reinforced traditional feudal authority just before the Meiji Period began in 1868 with the introduction of a western-style constitutional monarchy.

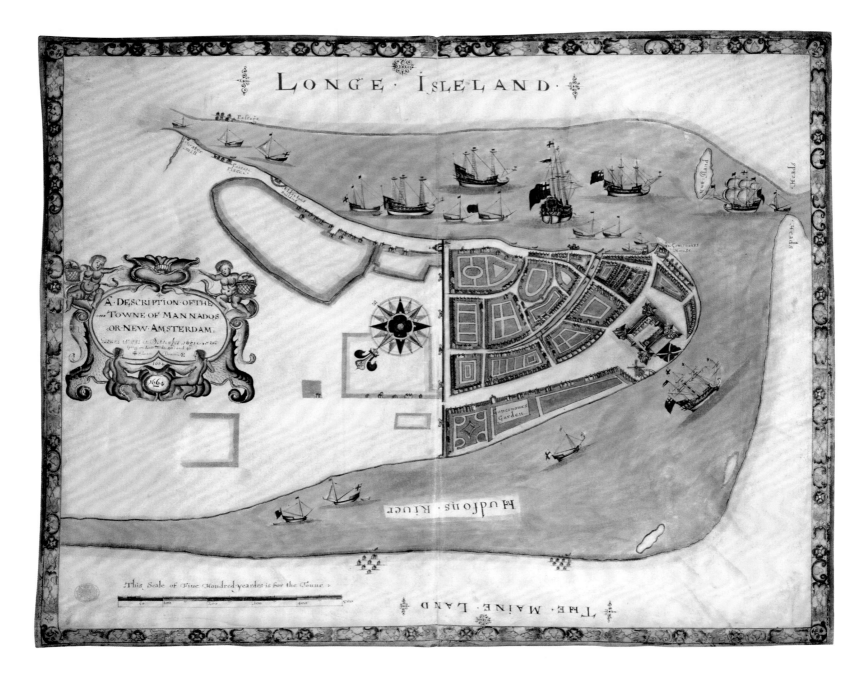

The Duke's Plan | 1664 | Unknown

Ink and watercolour on parchment with gold highlights. 69 × 55 cm / 27 ¼ × 21 ¾ in. British Library, London

The draughtsman who drew this early view of Manhattan is unlikely ever to have seen the settlement. The cartouche indicates that he was a member of the Thames School of chart-makers and draughtsmen working in the docklands east of the Tower of London. 'A Description of the Towne of Mannados or New-Amsterdam, as it was in September, 1661' was created as part of a request by the town for the patronage of James, Duke of York

(later King James II), in 1664. Earlier that year four English warships had sailed into the harbour of the Dutch colony and demanded its surrender, and the city was renamed New York after its new royal patron. This map is based on a survey by Jacques Cortelyou, the Dutch colonial surveyor-general, with English place names replacing the Dutch and the North River renamed 'Hudsons River'. Fort Amsterdam – now Battery Park – is prominent,

reflecting the harbour's military importance. Stretching north (to the left) is the Native American trail widened by the Dutch into a roadway, now the renowned Broadway. Wall Street is named after the wall marking the northern edge of the settlement. Broad Canal, the curved inlet piercing the island, was filled in to create what is now Broad Street. The English flags on the ships in the harbour underscore the country's victory over the Dutch.

Plan of the City of New York in North America | *c.*1770 | Lt Bernard Ratzer

Hand-coloured engraving. 122 × 91 cm / 48 × 36 in. Brooklyn Historical Society, New York

Drawn by a military surveyor working as an officer in the British Army, this delicate map of Manhattan surrounded by the countryside of New Jersey and Long Island recorded a world that was about to vanish. New York had prospered as a port for supplies during the Seven Years' War (1754–63) with the French in Canada, and Ratzer labels the wharfs of the waterfront, while his detailed panorama of the city from Governor's Island shows the harbour busy with British ships. The legend lists a range of places of worship, plus places of military interest such as barracks and arms stores. But Britain's attempt to impose new taxes on its American colonies to pay for the war led to protests and a series of punitive British measures to limit American shipping and commerce. Within five years Americans had taken up arms against their ruler; in 1776 they declared independence. A copy of Ratzer's map was given by the publisher to King George III, the monarch who was widely blamed for losing the American colonies. When Ratzer surveyed the city in 1766 and 1767, New York still occupied only the southern tip of Manhattan, Greenwich was a separate village and Brooklyn – 'Brookland' on the map – was a small town surrounded by farms that provided food to support the growth of the city.

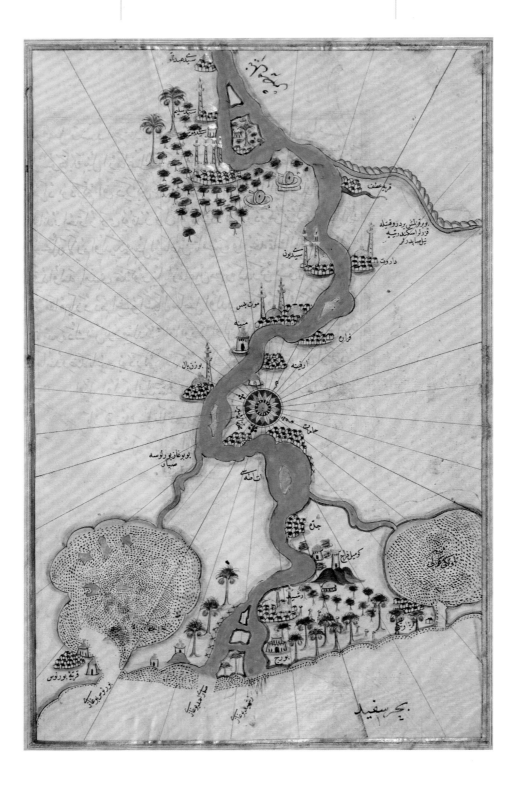

Map of the River Nile from its Estuary South to Cairo | 1525 | Piri Reis

Ink and pigments on paper. 34 × 24 cm / 13⅜ × 9⅜ in. Walters Art Museum, Baltimore

This seventeenth-century copy of an exquisite map of the Nile, orientated with south at the top and the Mediterranean at the bottom, is so highly stylized that it might seem to tend towards iconography rather than cartography. There are numerous inaccuracies. Most of the outlets of the Nile are missing. The abstract images of the two brackish lakes of Burullus and Manzala – denoted by stippling either side of the delta – are unrealistic. The

width of the river is greatly exaggerated along its entire course. Single buildings represent entire cities, including Rosetta, Cairo and Port Said. This map comes from a later copy of the *Book of Navigation*, an Ottoman atlas and sailing manual for the Mediterranean Sea created by the early sixteenth-century admiral Piri Reis. For more than a century, such luxurious manuscript copies were produced as opulent Renaissance coffee-table books.

Piri Reis is famous for his two world maps and charts of the Mediterranean. In 1517 he sailed up the Nile to Cairo to present his first world map of 1513 to Sultan Selim I (see p.154). Many years later, when he was almost ninety years old, Piri fell victim to the court intrigues of the Sublime Porte – the Ottoman bureaucracy – and was brought to Cairo for the last time to be beheaded.

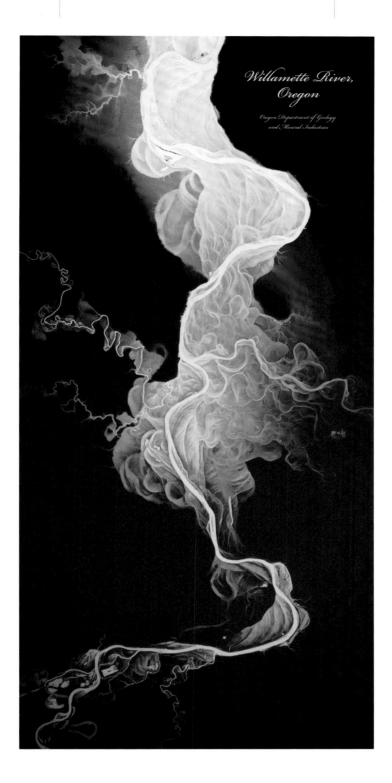

Willamette River, Oregon | 2013 | Daniel Coe

Printed on paper. 43 x 96.5 cm / 17 x 38 in. Private collection

Geologists and physical geographers are fully aware that the history of the landscape is often etched into its present form, but this electric image by Daniel Coe underlines the point. His map reveals the historical channels of the Willamette River in Oregon, and is all the more remarkable for the fact that it is, in truth, nothing more than a map of elevations: higher elevations appear in darker shades of blue. This simple symbology reveals the river's past clearly. As the Willamette has shifted, its historical channels have left behind eroded valleys, which light up on Coe's map as areas of lower elevation. This fingerprint of the past was made possible by the increasing availability of Lidar (a remote sensing technology) data. By bouncing lasers off the land, lidar can measure elevations at much finer detail than ever before. These better data not only allow Coe to reveal the past of the Willamette River but also allow other map-makers to reveal the planet's landforms at a scale never seen before. An elevation dataset may seem unremarkable at first glance, but a good cartographer knows how to sort, sift and style it to reveal the information it contains – and how to present that information in the most beautiful way.

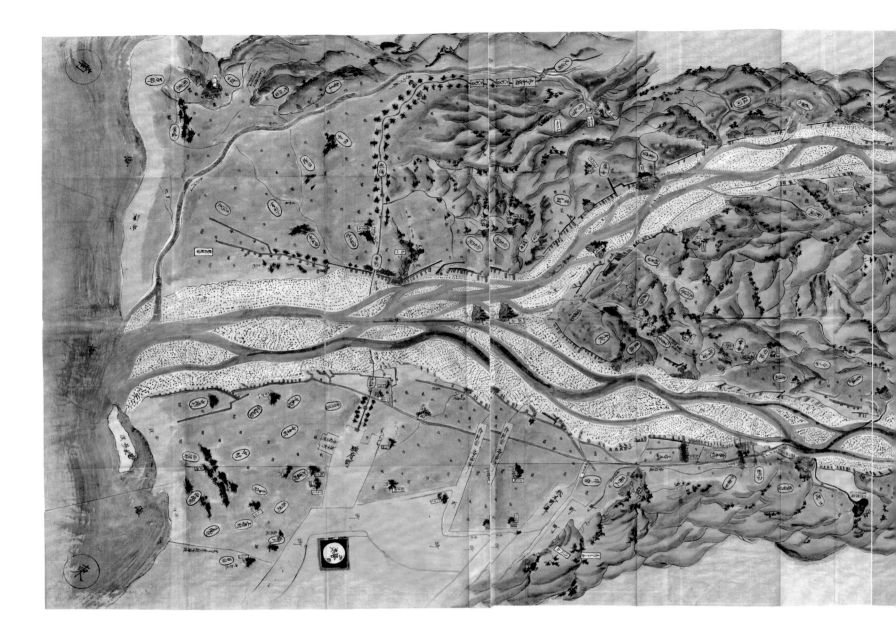

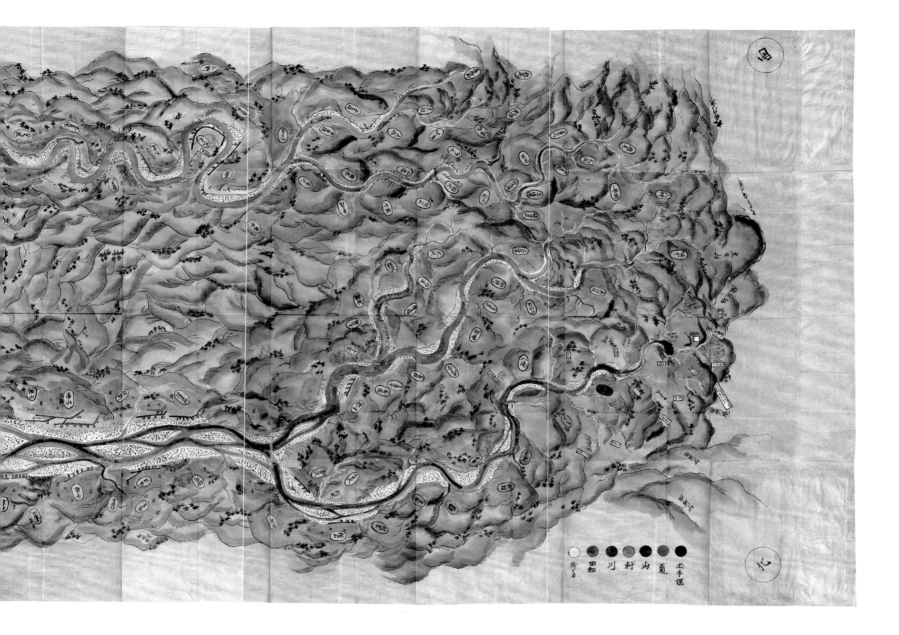

Abe River Region | 1862 | Ichiryutei Shoraku Dojin

Watercolour and ink on paper. 106 × 304 cm / 41¾ × 119⅝ in. Library of Congress, Washington, DC

The Abe River itself defines the shape and scope of this mid-nineteenth-century map of Shizuoka Prefecture, Japan. The river's course from north-west to south-east is depicted from right to left across the map, its path straightened where necessary (north is in the lower right rather than directly at the top). The highly illustrative pictorial map is generally planimetric, with relief drawn in aspect – a fairly typical approach for

Japanese cartography of the period. The mountains are not drawn uniformly with their bases towards the bottom and peaks towards the top. On the right-hand side, they are rotated right by 90 degrees to mark the source of the river and to ensure that its course makes more sense visually. There is very little text on the map itself, although the reverse gives notes on the geography of the region. Villages are marked with

yellow labels, and fields – key for taxation purposes for the ruling Tokugawa shogunate – are brown. The braided river stands out among the rich colours of the surrounding mountains as it flows through alluvial deposits and floodplains, with flood walls depicted along its course. The map has no frame as such, so the river simply washes out into the sea to the right.

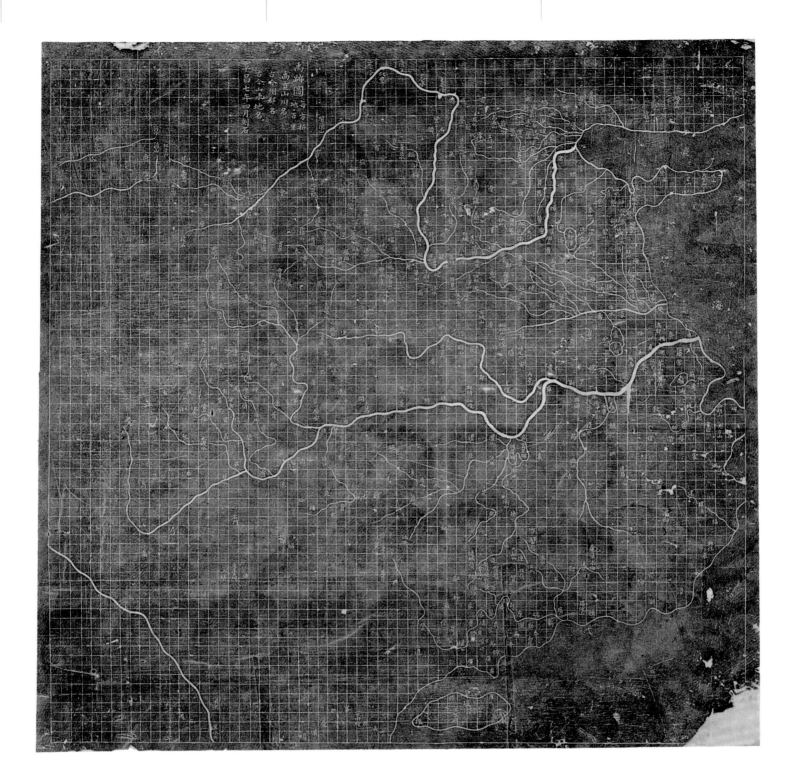

Map of the Tracks of Yu | *c.*1137 | Unknown

Carved stele. 84 × 82 cm / 33 × 32¼ in. Beilin Bowuguan, Shaanxi

The *Map of the Tracks of Yu*, a map of China's river net- work produced during the Jin or Jurchen dynasty (1115– 1234), is remarkable for a number of reasons, not least for being the oldest surviving Chinese map. The map was carved on to a 1-metre-square (3-foot-square) *stele*, or stone pillar, so that visitors could make copies by taking rubbings. It was the first map to use a grid, with lines 1 li (approximately 50 kilometres/31 miles) apart, and has

an approximate scale of 1:4,500,000. Its accuracy varies considerably. The Yellow (Huang He) and Yangtze (Chang Jiang) rivers are shown far more accurately than similar features were being mapped at that time in Europe, but the Heishui River in the west is not. Despite its apparent geographical fidelity and indication of Jin cities, the map was not intended to show contemporary China. Its title relates to a classical Chinese text, the *Yugong*, which

describes the efforts of the legendary King Yu in taming a flood by clearing river channels in about 2000 BC. The text was believed to have been edited by Confucius himself, so the map should therefore be thought of as referring to a golden age when China was a unified state, rather than the China of the twelfth century, which was divided between the Southern Song and the northern Jin dynasties.

The Great Wall of China | 1994 | NASA, Jet Propulsion Laboratory

Digital image. Dimensions variable

A familiar urban myth has long claimed that the Great Wall of China is the only built structure visible from space. The claim is erroneous – other structures can also be seen – but this image taken in May 1994 during the voyage of the space shuttle *Endeavour* confirms that the wall is indeed visible, forming a notably straight orange line across the hilly landscape. As part of NASA's Mission to Planet Earth, *Endeavour* carried a brand new radar instrument, the Spaceborne Imaging Radar-C/X-Synthetic Aperture Radar (SIR-C/X-SAR), to measure levels of carbon dioxide in the lower atmosphere. Orbiting about 350 kilometres (220 miles) above the Earth, the instrument collected data about an area equivalent to about 20 per cent of the planet's surface. Scientists at the Jet Propulsion Laboratory in Pasadena, California, used the data to create images of more than 400 sites, including this very small portion – less than 5 per cent – of the Great Wall of China. This section of the wall some 700 kilometres (435 miles) west of Beijing was built during the Ming Dynasty in the fifteenth century and today stands between 5 and 8 metres high (16 to 26 feet). The areas near the centre of the image are dry lake beds used for salt extraction. The geometrically organized patterns in the upper right are wheat fields.

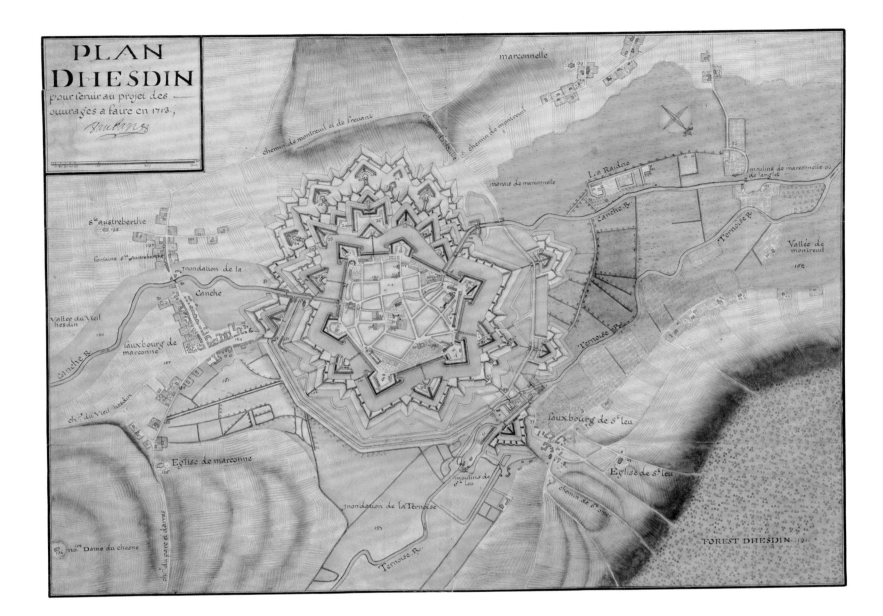

Plan of Hesdin | 1713 | Sébastien Le Prestre de Vauban

Ink and watercolour on paper. 64 × 47 cm / 25 × 18½. Bibliothèque nationale de France, Paris

The fractal-like defences at the heart of this manuscript plan for the rebuilding of the fortifications of Hesdin, near Calais in northern France, were drawn up by one of the leading military engineers of European history, Sébastien Le Prestre, Seigneur de Vauban. The system of concentric angled walls, ditches and redoubts – strongpoints – was designed to give the defenders clear lines of fire on any besiegers. Hesdin had been absorbed into the French dominions from Habsburg Burgundy only in 1639, and it was one of a group of towns that Vauban set out to re-fortify in the early 1690s, using his defensive theories and the latest technology to protect France's northern borders. In all he would upgrade the fortifications of around 300 towns, cities, ports and canals, and build more than thirty new fortresses for King Louis XIV between 1667 and 1707. Vauban was as adept at overcoming defences as he was at building them, and as a soldier directed about fifty successful sieges of enemy cities and castles in the wars of the late seventeenth century. Born into a minor noble family, he was later apprenticed to the foremost engineer of the age, the Chevalier de Clerville, before being commissioned as an Ingénieur du Roi (King's Engineer). Vauban was made the Marquis de Vauban and a *maréchal* of France in 1693.

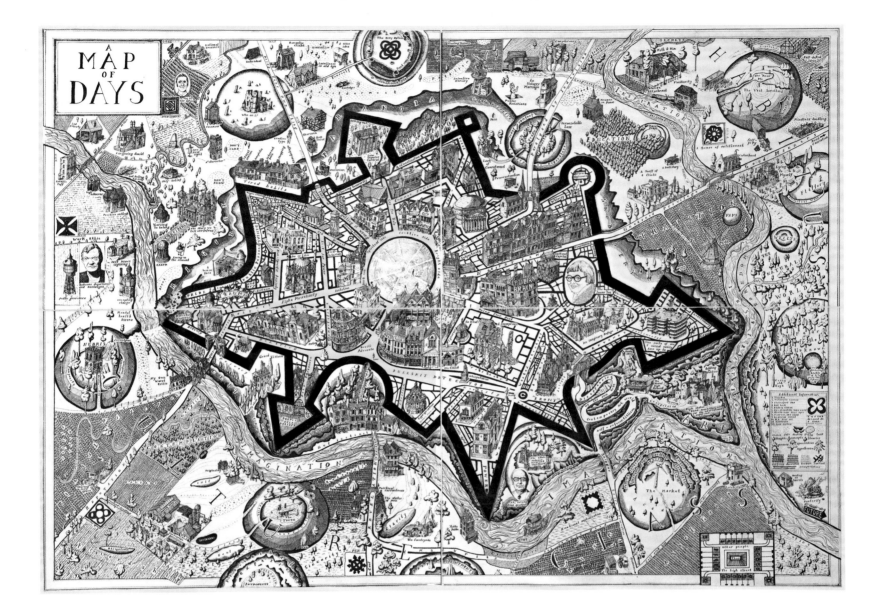

A Map of Days | 2013 | Grayson Perry

Etching from four plates. 111.5 × 151.5 cm / 43⅞ × 59⅝ in. Victoria Art Gallery, Bath

Inspired by a map from an eighteenth-century edition of *The Pilgrim's Progress*, which charted the imaginary places in John Bunyan's allegorical journey from the City of Destruction to the Celestial City, Grayson Perry's *A Map of Days* is a self-portrait depicting the artist as a walled city using the iconography of early-modern fortification diagrams (see opposite). It paints a self-critical, tongue-in-cheek picture of how Perry sees himself:

the settlement is located at a fork where the rivers Imagination and Inspiration meet. The surrounding countryside comprises aspects of the outer self – Charisma, Education, Good Manners, Pomposity and Work Ethic – and miniature portraits of inspirational figures, from the cyclist Bradley Wiggins to the poet Philip Larkin. The city within the walls represents the inner self, with streets and buildings labelled Self-Esteem, Churning Insecurity,

Fury and Denial. The streets converge at a central piazza, empty except for a tiny figure kicking a drinks can along, labelled 'A Sense of Self'. Perry suggests that an individual's identity has no fundamental core but, rather, has a relationship with everything around it. Despite first appearances, the boundary is not impenetrable – many roads lead in and out through the walls, so that inner self and outer world are connected.

SCENTS OF GLASGOW 2012

Perfume
Fast food outlets
Wet moss
Building dust
Diesel fumes
Carbolic soap
Lorne (square) sausage
Hot bovril at the footy
River Clyde at low tide
Subway

Glasgow's scents reflect the pride of the people of the city and their ability to renew, regenerate and reinvent themselves and their buildings. The large dots represent the source of the smell as the smaller dots show its range and intensity. Glasgow's prevailing south-westerly wind causes the scents to drift away to the north-east.

Scents of Glasgow | 2012 | Kate McLean

Digital print on tracing paper. 119 × 84 cm / 47 × 33 in. Private collection

Ephemeral cartography – the mapping of an elusive, non-physical world in a visible way, often from an artistic perspective – is a relatively new field. Its subjects may include memories, stories, topics or concepts. The artist and designer Kate McLean links aromas to places with her urban scent maps. As in all maps, what she leaves out is just as important as what she portrays; there are no boundaries, streets, landmarks, topographic or geographic features or even words to identify precise locations. Large dots indicate the source of each aroma, while smaller ones show where the wind carries the smell and how it dissipates. Local sausage, the climate (wet moss) and even the subway have their own breeze-carried routes presented as elegant rings. When McLean's aroma maps are exhibited, they are backlit and accompanied by bottles of scent that re-create those on the maps. There is an action component to the mapping, too: McLean leads 'smell walks' along routes in different cities. Her smellscapes show how aromas move and mingle, while also evoking memories, events and people. Ephemeral maps push the viewer to consider the world in a new, yet familiar way that often incorporates a level of aesthetic design rarely found in traditional location-driven maps.

Mapping Manhattan | 2013 | Becky Cooper

Mixed media, from *Mapping Manhattan: A Love and Sometimes Hate Story in 75 Maps* (2013). Each: 8.8 cm × 24.4 cm / 3½ × 10 in. Private collection

One could argue that every map is subjective to some degree: all are products of individuals' experiences and approaches to map-making. At one end of the spectrum are maps made as, say, part of a national mapping series, which contain less of the individual; at the other are maps that are purely subjective. These maps exist in our minds and are only rarely committed to paper. Becky Cooper's work is designed to capture the emotion of Manhattan as

seen through a variety of lenses by bringing to life some of those maps that exist in individuals' minds. She sets out to capture subjective portraits, each of which tells a part of the bigger story. To create *Mapping Manhattan*, her collaborative portrait of the city, Cooper handed out printed outlines of Manhattan and asked people to make a map and send it to her. The result is a fascinating, colourful and hugely varied collection of beautiful maps.

Some contributors approached the task topographically and some thematically, while some used it as a canvas to note memories and personal experiences. Cooper published seventy-five of the maps in a book (published in 2013) that offers a revealing insight into the personal world of its contributors – and that also includes a blank map at the back, inviting readers to add their own personalized cartography.

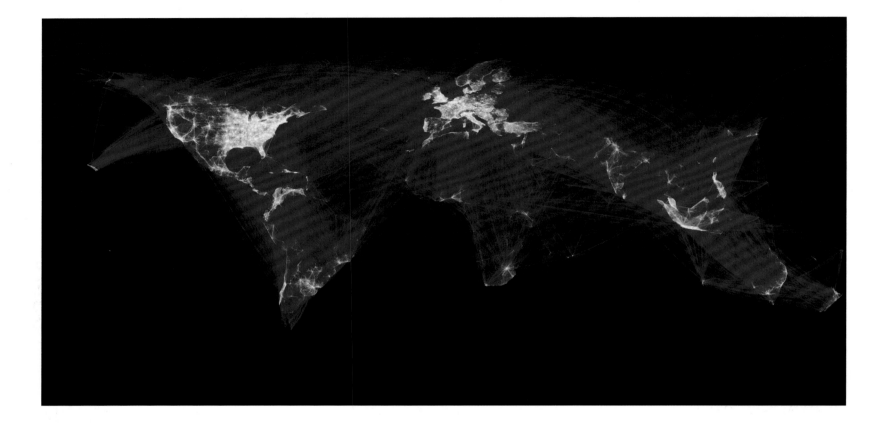

Visualizing Facebook Friends | 2010 | Paul Butler and Facebook

Digital. Dimensions variable

In the past, maps tended to be all about distance and material objects: not so any more. Paul Butler, an engineering intern at Facebook, used the data concerning how the social networking site's 500 million users at the time were connected to produce this map, which displays worldwide social connectivity but neither land-masses nor oceans. Even without a terrestrial base map to guide the viewer, Butler's map shows very clearly the outline of most of the recognizable continents and gives some indication of how entrenched social media are in the lives of most of the world. There are, however, large gaps in this connectivity, as shown by regions in China and Russia, the outlines of which are scarcely recognizable. To create the map, Butler sampled information from about 10 million pairs of friends around the world and then weighted the data based on the distance between the cities in which they lived and the number of friends to which they were connected. This statistical exercise produced this surprisingly accurate-looking map of virtual, rather than material, human social interaction.

Mapping the Brain | 2014 | Human Connectome Project

Digital. Dimensions variable

The striking beauty of this map is a by-product of one of the most ambitious cartographic projects ever undertaken: mapping the complexity of the human brain – and thus of what makes us human. This image shows the architecture of the brain using a technique called diffusion spectrum imaging. This type of magnetic resonance imaging uses the diffusion of water molecules to represent the main neural pathways that link the brain's 500 or so major regions, illuminating the connection between brain structure and function. The fibres are colour coded to show the direction of flow. The connectome – the word was only coined in 2005 – describes the complete set of neural connections in the human brain. As with other complex networks, it is necessary to understand these connections in order to get an idea of how the network functions (in the same way that the exact functioning of the Internet remained somewhat of a mystery until it was approximately mapped and its connections understood). This survey maps individual neurons (the nerve centres of the brain) in a network that is currently known only in its broadest form, which is just starting to be mapped with raw data from various forms of brain imaging, the Landsat of our inner world and of our consciousness.

Cuauhtinchan Map 2 | c.1540 | Unknown

Polychrome paint on bark paper. 109 × 204 cm / 43 × 80⅜ in. Museo Amparo, Puebla

This map prepared by an indigenous artist features, on the left, the origin myth in which the ancestors of the Aztec and their people followed the goddess Itzpapalotl to Cholula in the twelfth century and (on the right) the town they founded, Cuauhtinchan, and its environs. The map represents the people's complex history as much as the place they had inhabited until the fifteenth century, before the arrival of Spaniards in Mexico in 1519. The map itself may have been intended to demarcate native territory for Spanish authorities, although it was uniquely targeted at a native audience. Rather than European iconographic practices for the architectural representation of places, the artist employs pre-Hispanic practices involving rectilinear edifices featuring columns and square entrances, as well as pyramid-shaped temples. The towns are connected by a series of roads that contain footprints, revealing the route taken by the migrants as well as the means of transportation from place to place. Several battles – and some sacrifices – are depicted among the more than 700 glyphs in both sections of the map. The map, which is also known as the *Mapa de Cuauhtinchan 2* (MC2), was rediscovered in Cuauhtinchan in the late nineteenth century.

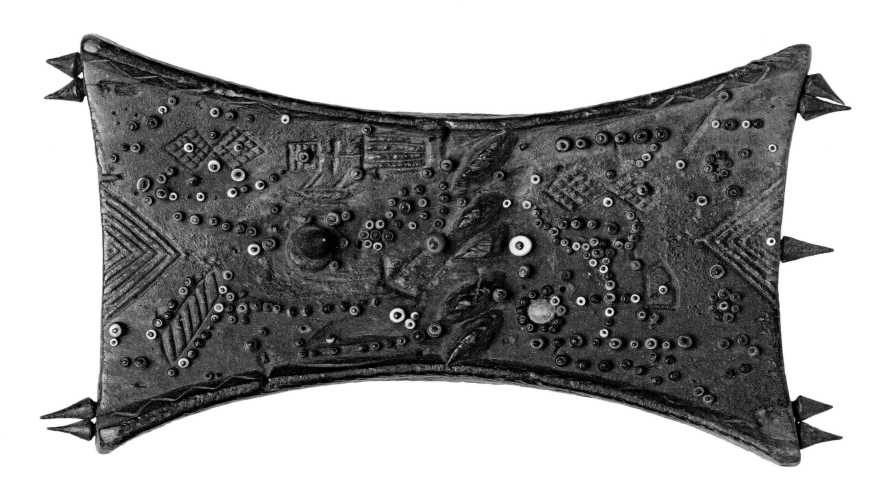

Lukasa Memory Board | c.1880–1920 | Luba Culture

Wood, beads, shells and metal. 25.4 × 14.6 × 4.4 cm / 10 × 5¾ × 1¾ in. Brooklyn Museum, New York

The *lukasa* produced by the Luba people of what is now the Democratic Republic of Congo are sculptural maps and unusually they map not geography but concept. The *lukasa* map is an open secret, and their telling is a performance. 'Reading' a *lukasa* involves holding the board with the left hand and touching it with the right. The task of interpreting the maps' telling of the Luba kingdom's hidden history, political organization, key events and migrations fell to a special Mbudye society, men and women who spent their lives learning the maps' mysteries. The carvings, beads and other features serve to stimulate and connect the Luba's collective memory of events, people and time. When the Mbudye disbanded at the end of World War II (1939–45), the former members became more open with researchers about their history. They revealed that one of the main principles of Luba political organization was a balance between the elder leader (the most senior Mbudye) and the chief (or popular leader). There were three types of *lukasa*, each containing a different kind of knowledge. One held information about early rulers and heroes, a second described how society was organized and a third recorded divine secrets.

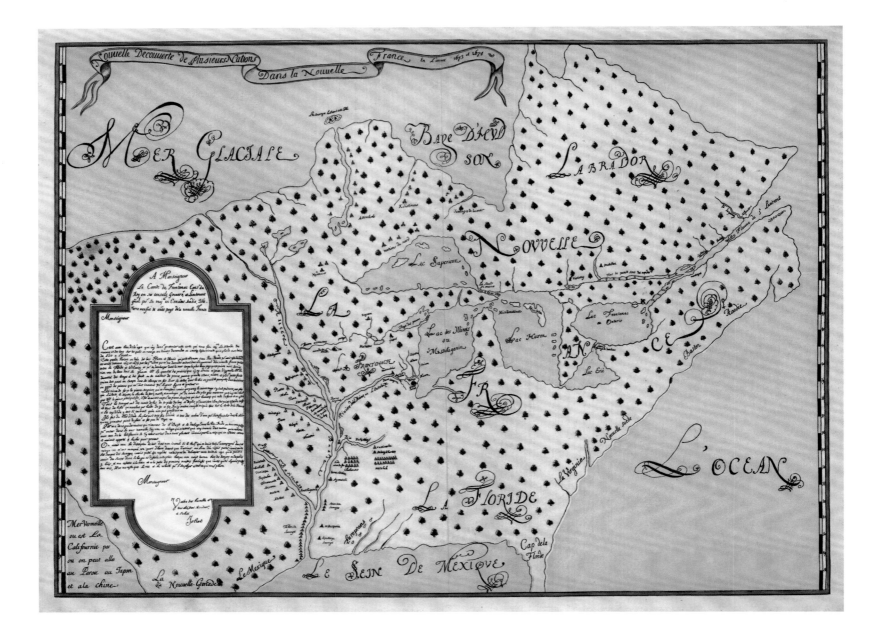

New France | c.1674 | Louis Jolliet

Ink on paper. 88.5 × 67 cm / 34⅞ × 26⅜ in. Library of Congress, Washington, DC

This French map – the first to show the course of the 'Buade', now known as the Mississippi River – may resemble a child's drawing in its style, but, given its story, the information it reveals is remarkable. It was drawn by the fur trader Louis Jolliet, who in 1673 set out to explore the Mississippi in the hope of finding a water route west to China. Born in Quebec, Jolliet probably knew several native languages, which helped him to receive friendly welcomes from native peoples and even the company of a chief's son to guide his small group along the river. After discovering vast expanses of valuable arable land, noting the location of native settlements and recording the shapes of the Great Lakes and the course of the Mississippi south to present-day Arkansas (where he turned back in fear of Spaniards), Jolliet set out to return to Montreal. Near the end of the journey, the canoes capsized in the Lachine Rapids. All was lost, including maps, notes – and the chief's son. Jolliet drew this map from memory, with an explanation of his adventures on the left addressed to the Comte de Frontenac. Knowledge of the course of the Mississippi and the location of native peoples was vital to traders and missionaries, and Jolliet's information tightened the French grip on Canada and the Mississippi valley for many more years.

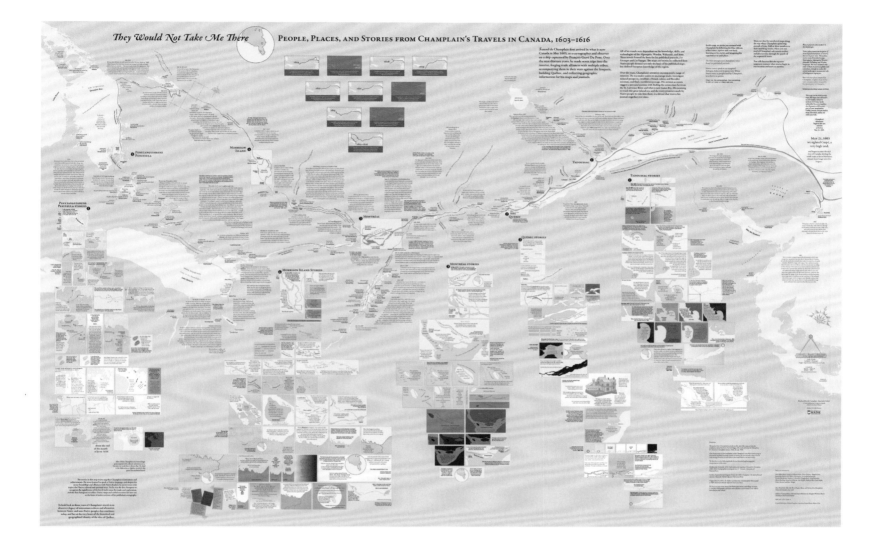

They Would Not Take Me There | 2008 | Michael James Hermann and Margaret Wickens Pearce

Printed paper. 99 x 150 cm / 39 x 59 in. Canadian-American Center, University of Maine, Orono

The title of this map – subtitled *People, Places and Stories from Champlain's Travels in Canada, 1603–1616* – refers to a complaint by the French explorer Samuel de Champlain, who over thirteen years made seven journeys into the interior of New France – now eastern Canada – as far as the Great Lakes. Champlain believed that the native peoples he met were obstructing his discovery of the Northwest Passage, the fabled water route to Asia. Meanwhile, he drew numerous maps and wrote reports describing many Indian cultures in great and often erroneous detail (he never learned any Indian languages). Four centuries later, the Canadian-American Center of the University of Maine commissioned Michael James Hermann and Margaret Wickens Pearce to create a map of Champlain's travels. They made a hydrological base map and drove across Canada using the journals to follow his routes and map key stories from the journals at the places where they happened, using not just Champlain's words but also the missing native counter-narratives. The map reveals that the indigenous people were in fact taking Champlain everywhere, if only he had recognized it. As a Canadian-Canadien endeavour, the map and its blocks of text are printed in English on one side and French on the other.

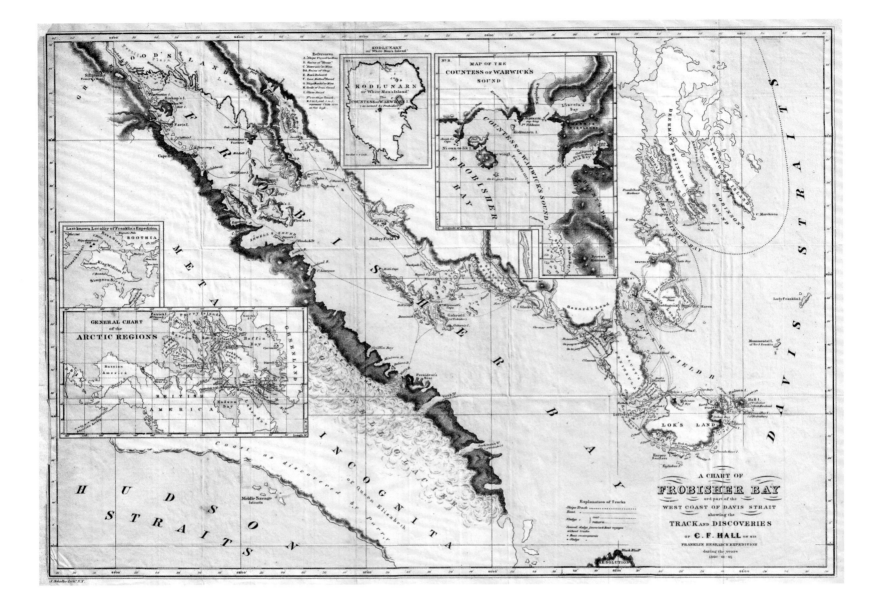

A Chart of Frobisher Bay | 1864 | Charles Francis Hall

Printed paper, from *Arctic Researches and Life Among the Esquimaux* by Charles Francis Hall (1865). 41.9 × 57.2 cm / 16 ½ × 22 ½ in. Private collection

The disappearance of the British naval explorer Sir John Franklin in 1845, while trying to find the North-West Passage from the Atlantic to the Pacific through the Arctic, gripped the world. Over the next decades dozens of expeditions set out to look for him, leading to a boom in the charting of the Arctic. The American Charles Francis Hall – a former blacksmith and newspaper reporter – was so intrigued by Franklin's fate that

in 1859 he raised funds for his own Arctic expedition. North of Hudson Bay he became icebound and lived with the Inuit for two years, finding relics of the Elizabethan explorer Sir Martin Frobisher's expedition of 1576. Hall's map of his findings in 1860–2, published in 1865, is one of the first accurately to show Frobisher Bay, which Hall identified as a bay rather than a strait, as previously thought, and part of the Davis Strait, near Baffin Island.

It also includes the tracks of the ship and of sledge and boat expeditions. Hall spent another five years with the Inuit from 1864 to 1869, and in 1871 attained the then highest latitude of 82 degrees 11 minutes north. He died later that year in Greenland after drinking a cup of coffee. He was known to have rowed bitterly with the scientists on the expedition – and an autopsy in 1968 showed that he had died of arsenic poisoning.

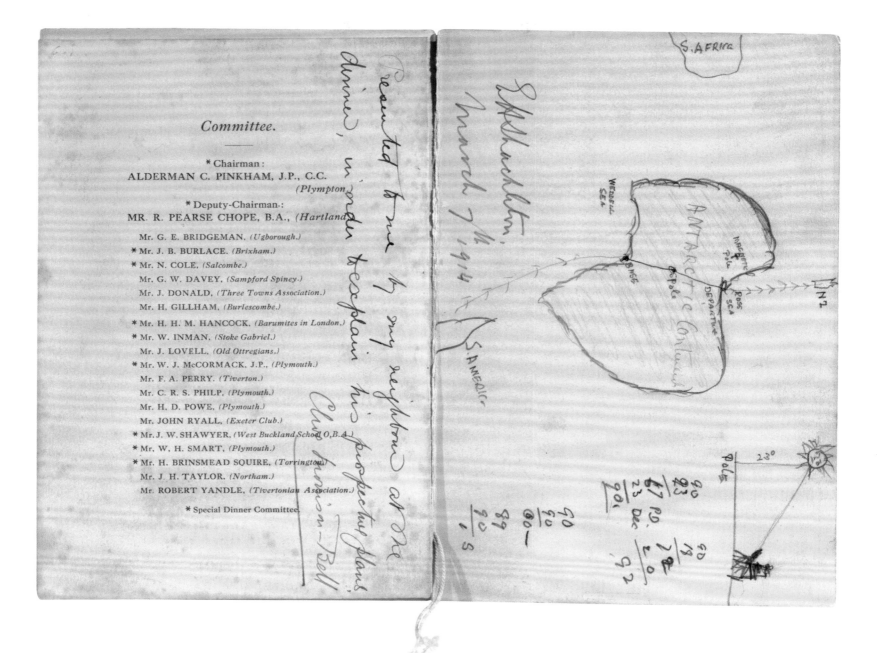

Shackleton's Imperial Trans-Antarctic Expedition Route | 1914 | Ernest Shackleton

Pencil on menu card. 18 × 24 cm / 7 × 9½ in. Royal Geographical Society, London

At the London Devonian Association's annual dinner on 17 March 1914, Sir Ernest Shackleton was seated next to an MP, Sir Clive Morrison-Bell. Shackleton wanted the MP to contribute funds for his Imperial Trans-Antarctic Expedition, so, on the back of a programme with the menu and order of ceremonies, he sketched out his plan. He would land his team on the nearest coast to South America at the edge of the Weddell Sea, cross via the South Pole to the pre-established base in the Ross Sea, then sail to New Zealand. Shackleton added a small diagram showing how to determine the location of the South Pole. In fact, things turned out differently. Shackleton's ship, *Endurance*, was trapped in the pack ice and crushed. After a month-long walk and sail across the frozen Weddell Sea to Elephant Island, Shackleton, Frank Worsley (the navigator) and four of the crew made a remarkable 1,500-kilometre (930-mile) voyage in a small boat to a whaling station on South Georgia. They reached Chile and returned to Elephant Island to rescue the remainder of the crew. Shackleton's was to be the last of the nationalistic expeditions to the Antarctic of the Edwardian era and in his failure Shackleton perhaps displayed even greater courage than Robert Falcon Scott and Roald Amundsen.

Map of a Journey Across the Coast Mountains and Yukon Plateau | 1869 | Kohklux

Pencil and ink on paper. 109 x 67 cm / 43 x 26½ in. Bancroft Library, University of California, Berkeley

This nineteenth-century Tlingit map of the Coast Mountains and Yukon River and plateau in north-western Canada is a masterpiece of indigenous cartography. It was drawn by a chief named Kohklux or Shotridge and his two wives as a record of a journey he had made nearly two decades earlier, and was given to the US surveyor George Davidson. The two men had first met two years earlier, when Davidson had journeyed to Russian

America to evaluate its proposed sale to the United States and travelled to the Chilkat River, the stronghold of Kohklux's Tlingit band. Davidson returned in 1869 to witness a total eclipse of the sun, by which time Russian America was part of the United States. After the eclipse, Davidson painted the event, while Kohklux and his two wives drew this large map of the complex geography of about 800 kilometres (500 miles) of terrain from

the coast over the mountains and down the tributaries of the Yukon to Fort Selkirk. Kohklux travelled there in about 1852 in a war party sent to burn down a Hudson's Bay Company store. Davidson and Kohklux exchanged the map and painting; the painting later went missing, but the map of the route into the Yukon interior, with more than 100 important place names and Davidson's annotations in ink, survives.

Crown Prince Islands, Disko Bay, Greenland | 1925 | Silas Sandgreen

Painted driftwood on sealskin. 89 × 61 × 4 cm / 31⅞ × 24 × 1⅝ in. Library of Congress, Washington, DC

This three-dimensional map of the Crown Prince Islands – a small group of rocky outcroppings in Greenland's Disko Bay, itself an inlet of Baffin Bay – was created by an Inuit fisherman named Silas Sandgreen. Sandgreen fashioned pieces of driftwood to represent the shape and size of the individual islands, then painted them to show the colour they appeared from a kayak at sea. He affixed the wood onto a piece of sealskin and nailed it to a piece of wood. Although Sandgreen created this particular map specifically for a US visitor – it is too large for practical navigation, and was donated to the Library of Congress in Washington, DC – it reflects the indigenous mapping traditions of the Greenland Inuit, many of whom earned their living by fishing and had to know how to navigate along the rocky shores of often fog-bound seas, avoiding the many hazards. Inuit sailors also carved profiles of the coast into the edges of pieces of driftwood to help them identify landmarks from the sea. Some of these coastal maps were small enough to be carried inside a mitten, and were tactile, so they could be 'read' with the fingertips, even in the dark.

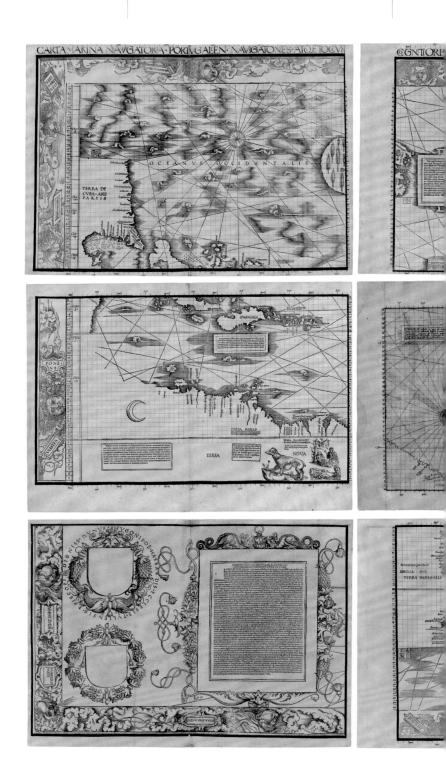

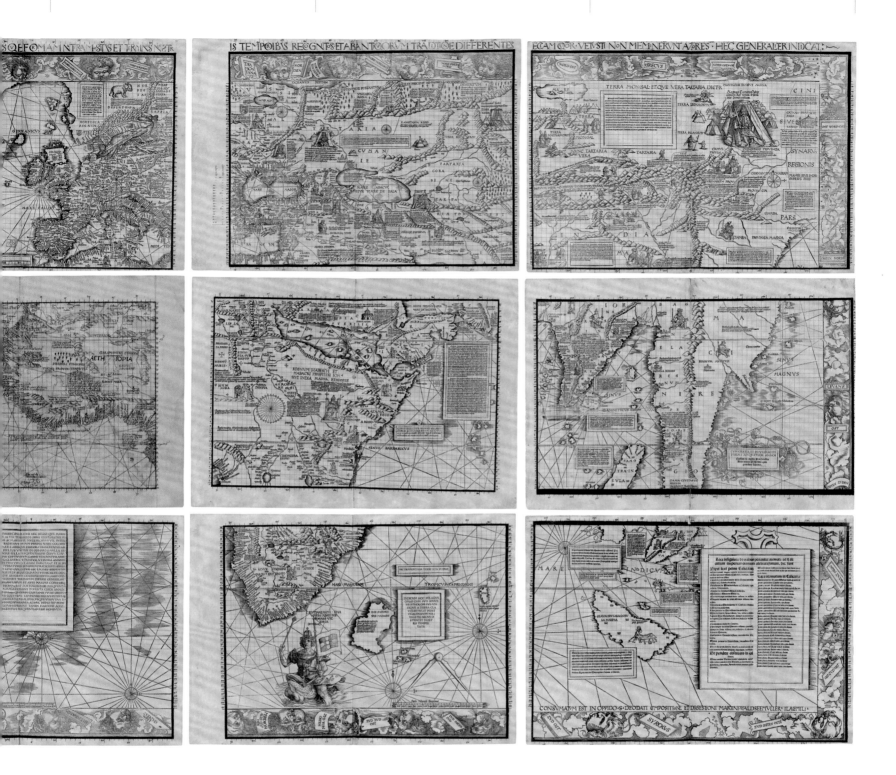

Carta Marina | 1516 | Martin Waldseemüller

Woodcut on 12 sheets of paper. 133.5 × 248 cm / 52½ × 97½ in (combined). Library of Congress, Washington, DC

Nine years after the German Martin Waldseemüller published his first world map in 1507 (see p.229), he created this even more innovative map. Instead of relying on the ancient text of Claudius Ptolemy, he based his new work on the *Caverio Planisphere* of 1505, an Italian copy of a Portuguese world map drawn as a nautical chart. Waldseemüller strictly shows only what is known; unknown and hypothetical lands are omitted. To this up-to-date

geography he added an impressive amount of notes, illustrations and ornamentation teeming with encyclopaedic details, many of which come from recently printed books and narratives describing the exotic new lands and peoples of Africa, Asia and America: the Great Khan in China, a rhinoceros, the earliest image of an opossum, *sati* – the Hindu practice of a widow casting herself upon the funeral pyre of her husband – and so on. On his

earlier map, Waldseemüller had named the new continent 'America' after Amerigo Vespucci, whom he supposed to have discovered it. In this map, Waldseemüller renames South America 'Terra Nova' – 'New Land' – and North America is named Cuba and shown to be part of Asia, which was the mistaken belief of Christopher Columbus, who discovered the 'New World'. As with the earlier map, only one copy of this work has survived.

Mappa | 1972–3 | Alighiero Boetti

Hand embroidery on linen. 163 × 217 cm / 64¼ × 85½ in. Museo Nazionale delle Arti del XXI Secolo, Rome

Flags fill in countries in this embroidery by the Italian artist Alighiero Boetti (1940–94), one of a series created between 1971 and 1994 that reveals a changing geopolitical world. The series – Mappa – emerged from previous projects in which Boetti used newspaper maps of war zones and occupied territories as a starting point for artworks. The first 'Mappa' was conceived during a trip to Afghanistan, where Boetti commissioned local craftswomen to embroider a world map in which nations were filled in with the relevant flag. Over the next two decades, until his death, he directed the creation of more than 150 maps – each taking up to two years to make – forming a record of passing time and shifting world politics. During that time, production was disrupted, moved and sometimes halted owing to events such as the Russian invasion of Afghanistan. In 1979 the embroiderers, who were unfamiliar with map conventions, used the thread colour they had the most of for the oceans: pink. Boetti was delighted with this chance subversion and, from then on, left it to the makers to choose the colour for the seas. In the 1980s Boetti switched from the Mercator to the Robinson projection – itself a reflection of changing political attitudes (see p.155) – to represent more accurately the relative sizes of landforms.

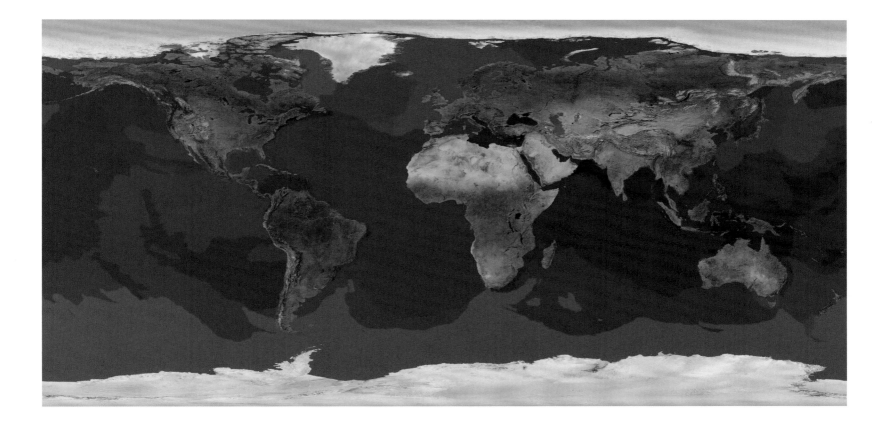

Satellite Map of Earth | 1990 | Tom Van Sant

Digital. Dimensions variable

It is hard to imagine that such a familiar view of the world is only a few decades old and was the creation of an artist, Tom Van Sant. It occurs everywhere, from flight-path displays and bedroom posters to weather reports: almost anywhere an overview of the world is needed that uses geophysical information rather than political borders (although those and other information can be added to it). To create the map for the National Geographic *Atlas of*

the World (1990), Van Sant – with collaborators at NASA and specially developed software – trawled through four years worth of infrared satellite data, digitally stitching together a view of the Earth's surface minus its cloud cover. Van Sant believes the second, higher-resolution version, completed in 1997, to be the bestselling image in the world. The digital composite can be adapted to a variety of map projections and uses, even if it is most often

seen in conventional formats such as this one. For all its apparent objectivity, however, this map remains, like any other, a cultural artefact. It is not as artless as it may appear. It shows the planet with maximum vegetation – it is summer everywhere, at the same time. More than a quarter of a century later, we must wonder whether the world would look the same if the image were remade.

Map of Brazil Divided into Captaincies | 1574 | Luís Teixeira

Coloured manuscript on paper. 35.5 × 50.5 cm / 14 × 20 in. Biblioteca Nacional da Ajuda, Lisbon

This map of the administrative divisions, or captaincies, of the early Portuguese colony in Brazil was produced by Luís Teixeira, a member of an illustrious family of Portuguese mapmakers. After seafarers sighted the coast of Brazil in 1500, Portugal's rulers claimed the territory under the 1494 Treaty of Tordesillas, which divided newly discovered lands between Spain and Portugal. The thin vertical line in the middle of the map marks the Tordesillas boundary: Portuguese territory is to the west. Almost from the outset, French traders continually launched illegal incursions into the Portuguese territory to bring back the valuable red dyewood (brazilwood) that would eventually give the land its name (Brazil). When the cost of military expeditions to root out out the French exceeded the region's revenue, King John III put prominent Portuguese figures in charge of defending the area from the French, making each of them responsible for an area known as a captaincy. The nine captaincies shown on this map are divided by latitudes. Most of the nine had successfully defeated French incursions by the 1560s.

Manuscript Map of North, Central and South America | 1596 | Evert Gijsbertsz

Ink on vellum. 87 × 112 cm / 34¼ × 44 in. Koninklijke Bibliotheek, The Hague

When the Dutch *caertschrijver* (map-writer) Evert Gijsbertsz created his map of the Americas from New France to Antarctica, he drew on a wide range of maps and written accounts to sum up the state of European knowledge. Characteristic of the North Holland school of cartographers, Gijsbertsz relied heavily on Iberian sources, but also he provides many place names in both Spanish and Dutch, and some of the miniatures – including the Patagonian giants near the Strait of Magellan and the giant sloth above them – were copied from Dutch sources. The two inset maps depict the Spanish vice-royal cities of Cuzco (centre) and Mexico (top left); the former is based on a drawing by the Italian geographer Giovanni Battista Ramusio and the latter on the map prepared by Hernán Cortés and published in 1524 (see p.77). Both those original city maps had been printed by the German firm operated by Braun and Hogenberg in 1572; their version of Mexico City placed Islamic crescent moons on top of Aztec temples to denote non-Christian places of worship, a feature Gijsbertsz retains. More than anything else, his map demonstrates how maps became encyclopaedic digests of multiple sources of information – texts as well as maps and drawings.

Map of Hispaniola | *c.*1492 | Christopher Columbus

Ink on paper. 35 × 70 cm / 14 × 27½ in. Fundación Casa de Alba, Palacio de Liria, Madrid

This map may be tantalizing evidence of one of the most significant events in world history – the first European encounter with the 'New World' since the age of the Vikings – by the man whose remarkable skill as a mariner made the achievement possible. This anonymous, hand-drawn sketch-map of the north coast of Hispaniola (la española) was supposedly made by Christopher Columbus during his first voyage to the New World, just before his return to Europe in January 1493. The map shows the first Spanish settlement of Natividad (Navidad) on the north coast while, slightly inland, Civao marks the location where Columbus's men found gold. It is curious, however, that the map includes the coastline of the Gulf of Gonave at the western end of the island, because Columbus did not sail into the gulf on his first voyage. It has been suggested that the chart is a modern forgery created on an old parchment to take advantage of the Columbian quadricentennial in 1892, the year the map was acquired by the Duke of Alba, a descendant of Columbus. The question of authenticity remains open until future non-destructive tests can be devised and carried out. If authentic, however, this would be the only extant map from the hand of Columbus and the earliest surviving map depicting a part of the 'New World'.

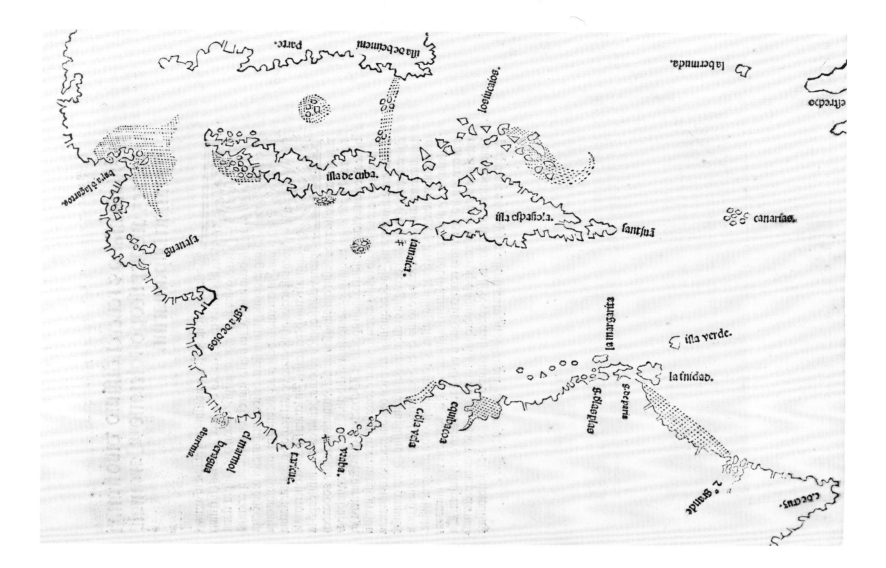

Map of the West Indies and Caribbean Sea | 1511 | Peter Martyr of Anghiera

Woodcut. 19.5 × 27.8 / 7½ × 11 in. British Library, London

'To the north there have been discovered marvellous countries and marvellous lands.' The inscription on the back of this map published in Peter Martyr's book *On the New World* hints at possible Spanish explorations of Florida before its official 'discovery' in 1513 by Juan Ponce de Léon. Martyr was an Italian-born official in the Spanish court, where he tutored the royal children and became the first chronicler of Spanish discoveries in the

'New World'. This map of the Caribbean was probably drawn by the leading Spanish cartographer Andrés de Morales. It was an insert in one of Martyr's several books chronicling the voyages to the New World. The map shows an area from Belize in Central America to the Amazon and the elbow of Brazil, as known from the explorations of Columbus, La Cosa, Vespucci and others. Martyr knew many of the explorers, and based his work

both on their accounts and on records in the official archives (he never visited the Americas, but was later a member of the Council of the Indies). This map was the first to show Bermuda, discovered by Juan de Bermúdez in 1505. Biminy – 'Isla de beimeni parte' – was a name the Spanish learned from the Taínó of the Bahamas and may have referred to Florida. It was specified as Ponce de Léon's goal in the royal patent authorizing his voyage.

The Valley of Mexico | c.1542 | Unknown

Polychrome painting on bark paper. 42 × 48 cm / 16½ × 19 in. Bibliothèque nationale de France, Paris

The settlement of the Chichimec in the Valley of Mexico under their leader, Xolotl, is one of the founding narratives of Mexico and later gave rise to the great city of Texcoco in 1224. This map forms the backdrop for the historical narrative that unfolds upon it, which is communicated pictographically and via abstract shapes, while also showing topographic and hydrographic features – the lakes of the valley appear in the lower half of the map – as well as hieroglyphic place names. The Aztec artist clearly identifies the lakes of the valley with blue near the bottom of the map, while the thick, wavy range of volcanic mountains near the top represents the valley's eastern extreme (in common with many medieval European maps, native Mexican maps were normally east-orientated). The map uses a pictographic form of expression that visualized words in Nahuatl and other local languages and dialects. The Chichimec entrance to the valley at the bottom left is represented by an illustration identifying Xolotl with an animal head, dressed in skins and carrying a bow and arrow. The series of footprints that circumnavigate the map reveal his exploration of the area as he sought a suitable settlement for his people. Other illustrations show the different peoples inhabiting the valley.

Pictorial Map of the City of Mexico and Surroundings Yesterday and Today | 1932 | Emily Edwards

Lithograph. 29 × 26 cm / 11⅜ × 10¼ in. Private collection

This bright map combines early and twentieth-century cartographic styles to depict the oldest capital city in the Americas, making its technique a nod to both history and design. Modern-day Mexico City sits atop the centre of ancient Aztec civilization – the old city of Tenochtitlán (see p.71) – which continues to be explored and excavated. The map was published by the Mexican Light & Power Company and the Mexican Tramways Company, suggesting that it was intended to help promote the modernization of the city. Artist Emily Edwards, originally from San Antonio, Texas, studied art in Mexico with the celebrated mural painter Diego Rivera. Edwards represented the city as a warrior eagle – one of the major Aztec warrior clans – and used Aztec glyphs around the map's perimeter and in the background of the modern city. The combination of ancient emblems and insignia with images of industrialization, particularly Mexico's new railways, captures the rising tensions between the modern city and its historic foundations. Pictorial maps convey information with illustrations, and are meant for popular consumption. The use of images enables such maps to reach a wider and often marginalized audience across lines of language, age, and literacy, allowing for a broader reach and understanding of the content.

Plan of Nippur | c.1500 BC | Unknown

Engraved clay tablet. 18 × 21 cm / 7 × 8¼ in. Friedrich-Schiller-Universitat, Jena

The Mesopotamians created the earliest surviving maps. They used sharpened reeds to inscribe clay tablets with world maps, property surveys and plans of land, houses and temples, labelled in the first type of writing, cuneiform ('wedge-shaped'). This plan of the fortified town of Nippur – the first town plan drawn to scale – was found in 1899 during excavations at the site by the University of Pennsylvania. The map dates from the Kassite period (14th–13th century BC), when Nippur was revitalized after being abandoned for several centuries as the most important religious centre of the Sumerians in Babylonia, for whom it was the earthly residence of the god Enlil. The tablet shows Nippur's principal temple to Enlil (the E-kur), with storehouses, a park and another enclosure. The Euphrates lies on the left-hand side of the map, while an irrigation canal runs above the city and another through its centre. The walls that protected the city had seven gates, each labelled with its name (including the Ur-facing gate and the Uruk, Gula and Nergal gates). Many features are given measurements in standard Sumerian rods or nindans (a rod measured about 6 metres / 19 feet 7 inches). Aerial photography of the modern site and modern reconstruction of the site plan both confirm that the plan was drawn to scale.

Map of Maine | 1837 | Samuel P. Ruggles and Samuel Gridley Howe

Embossed paper printed in *Atlas of the United States Printed for the Use of the Blind* (1837). 27 × 44 cm / 10⅝ × 8⅝ in (page). Private collection

This map recalls a brief period before Braille came to dominate publishing for the blind. The New England Institute for the Education of the Blind (later the Perkins School for the Blind) acquired its own printing press in 1835 and introduced an innovative technique of publishing materials with embossed letters. One of its first publications was this atlas, in which this was the first map. The designer, Samuel P. Ruggles, intended the atlas to be used without the help of a sighted person, including pages of narrative description opposite the maps to help students orientate their fingers. Lines show the main path of rivers, dotted lines indicate the borders with Canada and New Hampshire and numbers and letters indicate topographical and other geographical features. The stylized letters are clear and direct, and creative use of embossing indicates mountain regions.

The New England school's first director, Samuel Gridley Howe – husband of the noted anti-slavery activist Julia Ward Howe and colleague of the educational pioneer Horace Mann – believed Ruggles's technique would allow the blind to learn geography. Braille – invented in 1824 – soon displaced these embossed maps, but this atlas stands as an elegant example of visual knowledge, without the use of ink.

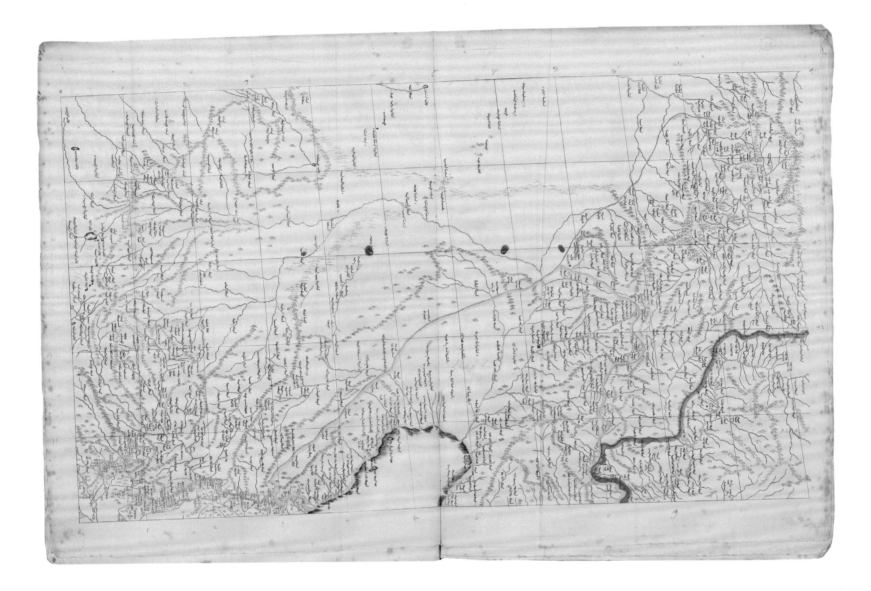

Overview Maps of Imperial Territories | 1717–9 | Unknown

Engraving on silk paper. 48 × 70 cm / 18¾ × 27½ in. Royal Library of Belgium, Brussels

When China's imperial workshops created the 'Overview Maps of Imperial Territories', or *Huangyu quanlan tu*, early in the eighteenth century, the atlas of East Asia constituted the largest mapping project based on scientific field practice the world had ever seen. The result of nearly a decade of collaborative surveying between officials of the Qing and European missionaries, the atlas greatly impacted contemporary cartography in both

Asia and Europe, revealing continental East Asia to the rest of the world. This sheet of the atlas – there were forty-one in all – shows a small part of the Great Wall north-east of Beijing and the region to its north, broadly coinciding with what are now China's Liaoning province and north-western parts of Korea. Place names south of the Great Wall are recorded in Chinese, but those to the north are in Manchu, the other official language of the

Qing empire. Although several editions of the atlas were printed, the full version was reserved for imperial use. In the 1720s, the atlas reached Paris, where the cartographer Jean-Baptiste Bourguignon d'Anville published a version adapted for the European public in 1735. In later decades, both the Qing and the European editions were improved upon, ensuring that the atlas remained the standard map of continental East Asia until the mid-nineteenth century.

Map of China | 2006 | Ai Weiwei

Iron wood (Tieli wood) from dismantled temples of the Qing Dynasty. 200 × 200 × 50 cm / 78⅔ × 78⅔ × 19¾ in. Private collection

One of the world's best-known living artists, Ai Weiwei frequently uses the recognizable outlines of countries and maps in his work to make social or political critiques of contemporary Chinese life – often angering the ruling authorities, who have found ways to limit his personal freedom if not his artistic output. This large and heavy-looking sculpture was created from beams of iron wood (tieli wood) salvaged from Qing Dynasty (1644–1911) temples that were dismantled to make way for modern construction. Using traditional joinery techniques, the perfectly smooth surface reveals supreme craftsmanship and celebrates the beauty of a natural material once ubiquitous in public architecture, but now most often replaced by concrete, steel and glass. The work can be read as a comment on the way in which the cultural legacy of China's last imperial dynasty was demolished by later authorities who, in contrast to the heritage-conserving governments of the West, have prioritized forward-looking industrial progress over the preservation of old customs and habits. Yet the map can also be considered as a positive reflection on the People's Republic of China, its solid, fused form symbolizing political unity in a vast nation built from many different cultural and historical elements.

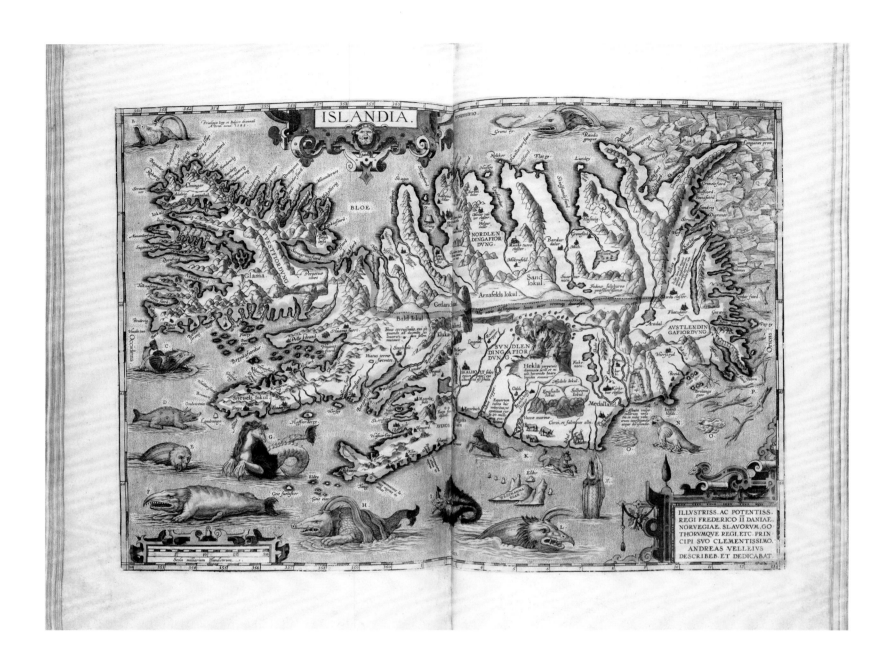

Islandia | c.1590 | Abraham Ortelius

Hand-coloured engraving. 49 × 34 cm / 19¼ × 13¼ in. British Library, London

This highly decorative map was also the first relatively accurate map of Iceland available outside the island. It was published by Abraham Ortelius in various editions of his masterful *Theatrum Orbis Terrarum* (see also p. 229). The map first appeared in the 1587 edition of the *Theatrum*, but later versions were refined, particularly in relation to the hand-colouring. The content suggests that Ortelius used many sources to compile his version of Iceland, and most likely based his map on one drawn by the Icelander Gudbrandur Thorláksson. The mountains, fjords and glaciers are depicted in remarkable detail – Mount Hekla is shown erupting – and the map contains a wealth of detail about settlements and other points of interest to reveal not only the landscape but also the way in which it is populated. In that sense this is an accurate, albeit stylized, topographic reference map. Perhaps its most interesting aspect, however, is its depiction of a fantastic array of legendary and mythical sea monsters from the fifteenth and sixteenth centuries. There are early depictions of sea horses and manta rays, walruses and even polar bears atop icebergs. Some fanciful creatures also appear; each is lettered, and has a short piece of associated descriptive text on the reverse of the map.

Iceland Illustrated | 2012 | Borgarmynd

Digital. Dimensions variable

This map by the Icelandic design studio Borgarmynd might seem little more than a tourist product, but it is also a highly successful marriage of old and new. Combining the artistry of a hand-drawn map with modern digital publishing might seem paradoxical, yet there is no rule that states that a hand-drawn map must be on paper or that a digital map must consist of nodes and vertices. Some of the most interesting modern cartography comes from combining techniques that might not appear well suited to one another. This three-dimensional, beautifully rendered terrain map originated as a printed map but has been repurposed as the backdrop to an online map that uses clickable modern pictograms to show the location of geotagged photographs of Iceland's spectacular scenery or of restaurants, shops or hotels. Borgarmynd's map is highly detailed, showing rock drawing, colour and features where comparable digital maps leave empty space. The studio took the same approach for its map of Reykjavík, the capital city, again using pictograms to mark the locations of photographs and other points of interest. While the country map is planimetric, however – with some oblique rendering of mountains – the city map is an isometric drawing in greater detail.

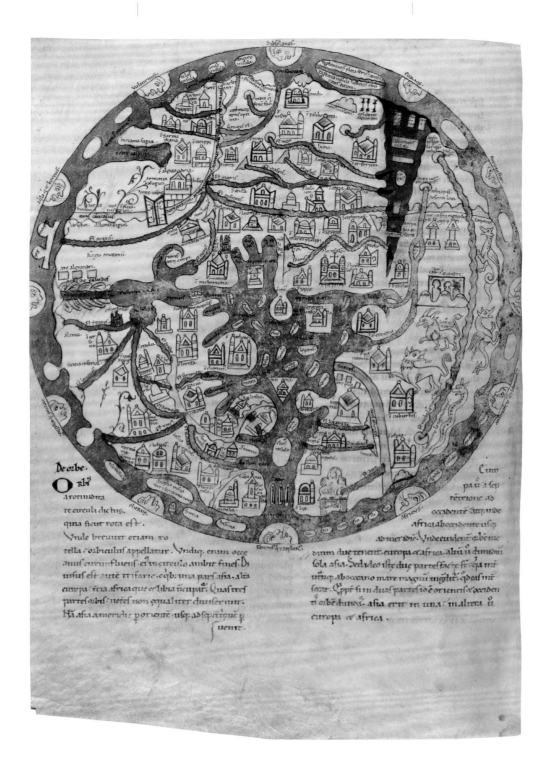

Mappa Mundi | *c.*1130 | Isidore of Seville

Ink on parchment. 29 × 42 cm / 11 ⅜ × 16 ½ in. Bayerische Staatsbibliothek, Munich

This twelfth-century map was based on an original that had already been popular for some 500 years. *Etymologies*, by the historian Isidore of Seville, circulated throughout Europe in various manuscript forms for centuries. This world map portrays Isidore's description of an Earth with three continents, making it representative of the medieval T-O style of map in which the world is represented as a circle (*orbis*) containing the letter T, which cleaves apart the three continents (*terrarum*). The map summarizes the world's history from a Christian perspective, but also includes important geographical features, such as the Mediterranean Sea, the Nile and the Red Sea, the last of which was boldly coloured in red. The artist includes the classical Pillars of Hercules separating Europe from Africa in the Strait of Gibraltar, and fantastic beasts in southern Africa. These illustrations, along with biblical references to Gog and Magog and to Noah's Ark in Armenia, reveal the medieval tendency to populate the extremes of the Earth with the monstrous and marvellous. Typically orientated with the east at the top, this map exceptionally omits the Garden of Eden, and Jerusalem is not at its centre, reflecting the advance of knowledge about the world five centuries after Isidore first prepared his description.

The Division of the Earth Between Noah's Sons | c.1459–63 | Simon Marmion (attrib.)

Illuminated manuscript on vellum. 30 × 22 cm / 11¾ × 8⅝ in. Bibliothèque royale de Belgique, Brussels

This map illustrated *La Fleur des Histoires*, an account written by the fifteenth-century chronicler Jean Mansel for the dukes of Burgundy that recounted history from the Creation to the 1420s, combining secular events with a drama of salvation in which the world's 'Second Age' began after Noah's Flood. The map – attributed to the painter Simon Marmion of Valenciennes – reflects the biblical story that the nations were descended from Noah's three sons: the nations of Asia from Shem (upper half of map); Africans from Ham (lower right); and Europeans from Japheth (lower left). This map shows the three patriarchs just after they leave the ark, which rests on 'the Mountains of Armenia' or 'Ararat'. The belief that Earth was made up of three continents shaped the unrealistic but highly symbolic medieval T-O map (see opposite page). Marmion's 'O' is formed by the ocean and the 'T' by the Mediterranean Sea and part of the Nile. The sense that this is a factual map is enhanced by Marmion's addition of the labels for the cardinal directions (east is at the top). Only a few decades after this map was drawn, new discoveries would challenge not only this map but also the whole basis of classical geography and the Bible-based history it represented.

World Map | c.540 AD | Cosmas Indicopleustes

Manuscript on vellum in a 10th-century copy of *Christian Topography*. 25.5 × 19 cm / 10 × 7½ in. Biblioteca Medicea Laurenziana, Florence

All medieval geographers faced the conundrum of producing a cosmology that was compatible with both religious authority and natural philosophy: the world described in the Bible and the world as they observed it. A much-travelled Alexandrian merchant-turned-monk, Cosmas Indicopleustes (meaning 'the sailor to India'), came up with one of the stranger solutions. Convinced that the classical spherical cosmos – with the Earth as the central sphere amid the

rotating heavens – was incompatible with Christianity, Cosmas published his polemic, *Christian Topography*. A mixture of Hellenistic and biblical materials, with several maps, the work adopted biblical ideas without any attempt to harmonize them with ordinary learning. Cosmas imagined a chest-shaped universe and the Earth as a flat layer within it. On the right-hand (east) side of the map, a strip of land beyond the ocean cordons off Paradise. The inhabited lands

lie in the indented central area surrounded by a rectangular ocean with the 'Roman Gulf', or Mediterranean, entering from the west. The other indents represent the Caspian and Red seas and the Persian Gulf. Cosmas's idiosyncratic approach did not catch on – his world view survives in only three manuscripts.

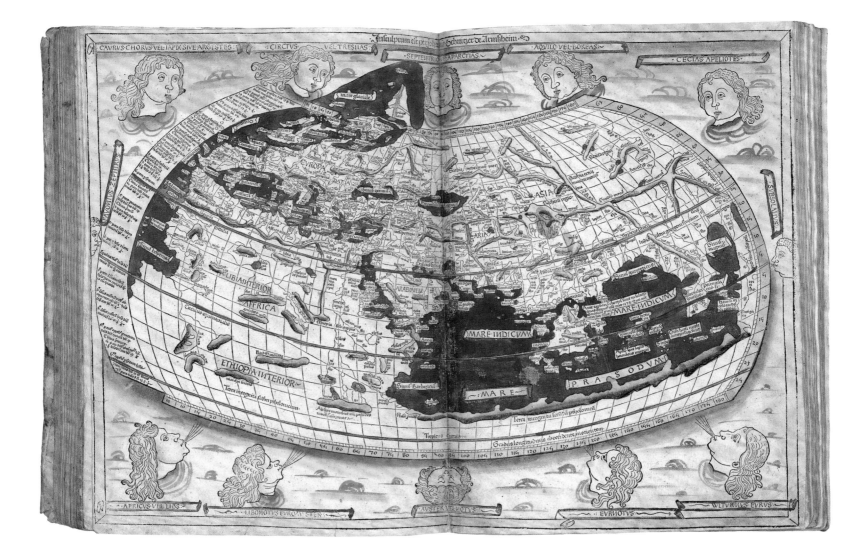

World Map | 1482 | Claudius Ptolemy

Hand-coloured woodcut by Johannes Schnitzer in a 1482 edition of *Geography*. 41.4 × 60 cm / 16⅓ × 23¾ in. Collection Daniel Crouch Rare Books, London

This late fifteenth-century world map is based on a projection suggested by coordinates detailed some 1,300 years earlier by one of the most influential names in the history of cartography: the Egyptian-Greek Claudius Ptolemy. Ptolemy's second-century work *Geography* – a guide to mapmaking with coordinates for 8,000 places – described three possible ways to project Earth's inhabited lands on to a flat map using mathematical principles. Only the text

of *Geography* survived; soon after it was rediscovered around 1400, the German Benedictine monk Donnus Nicolaus Germanus extended Ptolemy's conical projection to show the first printed cartographical representations of Greenland, Iceland and the North Atlantic. The world is shown with the Indian Ocean bound on four sides by land, and with brown mountains rising in chains across the three known continents. The tropics and equator are coloured

red, and the sea a rich blue. Ten wind heads surround the Earth, set against a light blue background. Germanus's map, which reflects Ptolemy's importance in the Renaissance, came from the first atlas to include woodcut maps. The artist identifies himself at the top as Johannes Schnitzer ('wood-cutter') of Arnsheim, thereby making it also the earliest datable printed map to bear a signature.

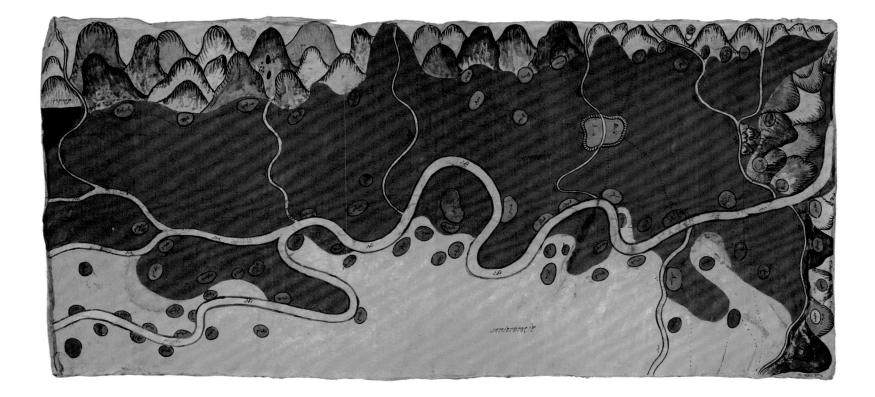

Shan Map Showing Border Dispute Between Burma and China | 1889 | Unknown

Tempera on paper. 152 × 76 cm / 60 × 30 in. Cambridge University Library

By modern standards, there is considerable cartographic license in terms of the precision of the topographic record in this map by an anonymous artist of the Shan people of Myanmar (Burma). In design terms, however, the map is a work of art – and one that also fulfils its purpose, to resolve a border dispute between Burma and China. The map covers an area of 122 square kilometres (47 square miles) along the Nam Mao (Shweli) River and

shows about eighty villages and hamlets in green. The map text is in Chinese Shan, with red areas representing the British Shan state of Möng Mao and yellow showing Chinese territory. The vibrant colours leave the reader in no doubt as to land ownership. Most of the map is plani-metric, but the upper and right-hand borders show the bounding mountain ranges in aspect, again with rich col-our. By the late nineteenth century the Burmese already

had a good appreciation for topographic mapping and cartography in general. They used maps for taxation and land use and also as a way of plotting military campaigns. Many of these maps, together with those by the indig-enous Shan and T'ai peoples, were collected by British diplomats and colonial officials.

| Palestine prior to partition | 1947 UN partition plan | 1949 Rhodes armistice line | 1967-2008 Israeli incursions |

Maps of Palestine | 2011 | Richard Hamilton

EFI VUTEK inkjet solvent print on canvas. 220 × 345 cm / 86⅝ × 135¾ in. Private collection

Flat primary colours and precise borders chart one of the most protracted geographical and political stories of the second half of the twentieth century: the growth of Israel at the expense of Palestinian territory. The British Pop artist Richard Hamilton (1922–2011) selected four moments to represent the process: Palestine before the foundation of Israel; the lines of the UN Partition plan of 1947; the Rhodes armistice line of 1949, drawn after the

Arab–Israeli War of 1948; and the Israel incursions into Palestinian territory between 1967 and 2008. Hamilton's original work involved only two images – from 1947 and 2010 – but this expanded version increases its stop-motion, snapshot quality. The artist was struck by both the importance of the Israel-Palestine conflict and the fact that all the events that shaped Israel had taken place within his own lifetime. Hamilton, who died shortly after

he completed this work, began his career as an engineering draughtsman, and his technical background is evident in the precision and apparent neutrality of what is in fact an intentionally inflammatory, politically inspired image. He made his first maps of Palestine in 2010 at the invitation of London's Serpentine Gallery, which was hosting a maps event.

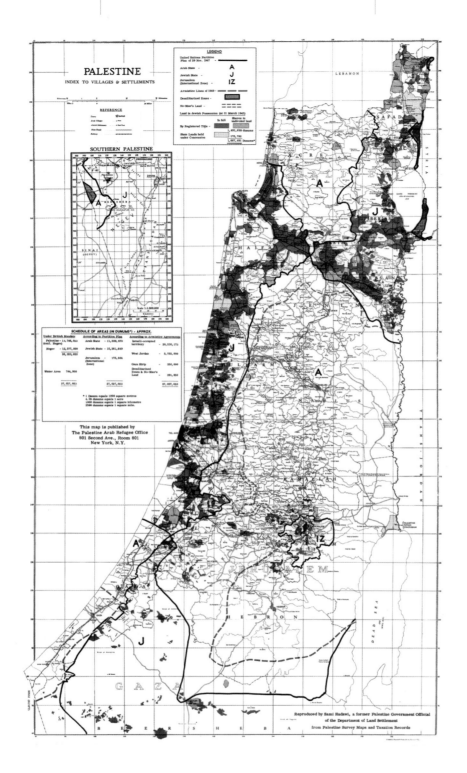

Palestine Index to Villages and Settlements, Showing Jewish-Owned Land | 1945 | Sami Hadawi

Lithograph. 40 × 69 cm / 15¾ × 27⅛. Library of Congress, Washington, DC

This map, reprinted by the Palestine Arab Refugee Office in 1956, contains the seeds of more than sixty years of dispute and conflict. Its red blooms mark what have become known in the parlance of the modern Arab-Israeli dispute as 'facts on the ground', in this case the increasing area owned either wholly or in part by Jewish settlers: a total of some 6 per cent of British Palestine, particularly along the coast and towards the Sea of Galilee. Less prominent on the map are the letters 'J' and 'A' – Jewish and Arab – marking the United Nations' proposed partition of the territory in acknowledgement of the Jewish claim to a homeland in their ancestral lands, particularly in the aftermath of the world's failure to prevent the Holocaust in Europe. (Jerusalem, deep inside proposed Arab territory, is marked IZ, or International Zone). The UN adopted the plan on 29 November 1947 – and civil war between Jews and Arabs broke out in Palestine the next day. On 14 May 1948, with the struggle ongoing, Israel declared its independence, sparking a war against Egyptian, Syrian and Jordanian forces. Ten months of fighting followed that left Israel in control not only of the land proposed by the UN but also of 60 per cent of the proposed Arab land, leaving 700,000 Palestinians to become refugees.

Present Tense | 1996 | Mona Hatoum

Soap and glass beads. 4.5 × 241 × 299 cm / 1¾ × 94⅞ × 117¾ in. Tate, London

Across a grid of 2,400 square blocks of soap, wavering lines of tiny red glass beads embedded into the surface trace out an unfamiliar map. It depicts the disconnected territories agreed to be returned to Palestinian control in the Oslo Accords of 1993. The maker, Mona Hatoum, is a Palestinian artist who has lived her whole life in exile. She was born and raised in Lebanon after her parents fled Haifa and since 1975, when civil war broke out while she was in the United Kingdom, has been based in London. Geography, nationality and dislocation are central to her varied artistic practice, through which she invites viewers to consider their place in the modern world and their relationship to its conflicts. Her unorthodox material for the map – olive-oil soap from Nablus in the West Bank, north of Jerusalem (where she was undertaking a residency at the time she made it) – is a poignant choice. Hatoum called it 'a particular symbol of resistance', soap being a traditional Palestinian product that has been made for centuries and yet also a substance prone to dissolve, echoing the potentially impermanent nature of borders and agreements. The title reiterates the temporary here and now, and also references the everyday tension in this long-disputed region of the Middle East.

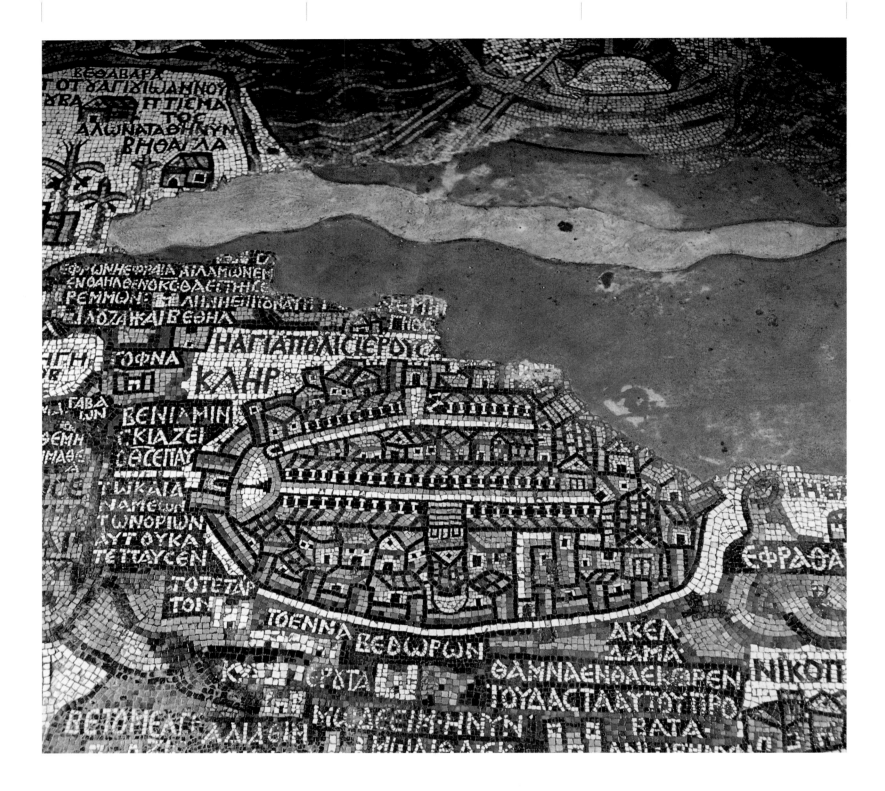

Madaba Mosaic Map | c.560 | Unknown

Mosaic tiles. 5 × 10.5 m / 16 ft 5 in × 34 ft 6 in. St George's Church, Madaba

This mosaic floor from a church in Madaba in Jordan depicts the lands of the Bible story, as remembered by Christians, reaching from lower Egypt to Damascus. It uses a variety of scales, but the largest is reserved for Jerusalem, which is pictured in such detail that twenty sites can be identified, most famously the Holy Sepulchre (drawn upside down in the middle of the colonnade). More than 150 other places are named in Greek, and there are scenes of fishing boats, animals and episodes from the Bible. The map draws on early geographical writings – itineraries – combined with later Christian authors, but its purpose is more complex. It had an educational value for worshippers, but it is also a statement that their liturgy takes place both in Madaba and in other spaces and times: their ritual brings them to the very places and events they are celebrating. On the upper right, at the end of the central colonnade, stands a structure shaped like a classical temple: this is the Nea Church, dedicated in 542, so the mosaic was made after that date. Other clues suggest it was created before the death of the Byzantine emperor Justinian I in 565. Discovered in 1884 in a badly damaged state, the mosaic was originally much larger, but it remains the best surviving example of classical mosaic mapmaking.

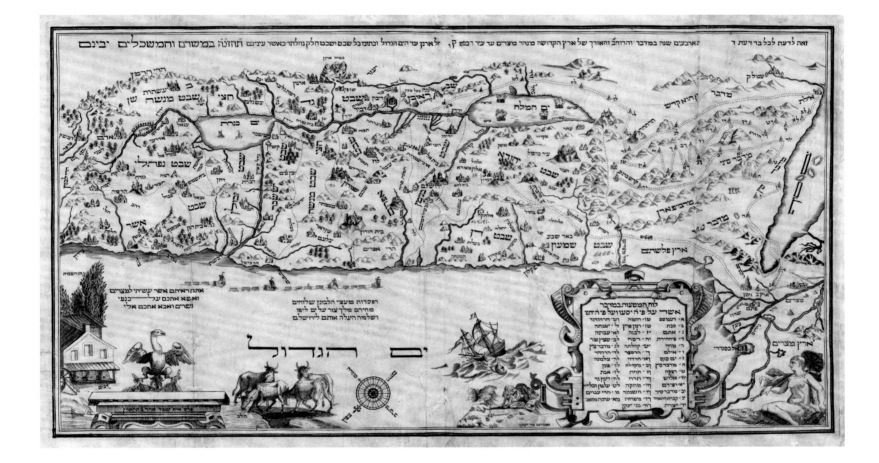

Map of the Holy Land with the Route of Exodus | 1695 | Avraham bar Ya'akov

Woodcut. 48.3 × 26.7 cm / 19 × 10½ in. Private collection

Avraham bar Ya'akov was a convert to Judaism, and his map of 1695 was, until recently, often cited as the first printed map in Hebrew. Its geographical shape is taken from a Latin map produced in about 1590 and often copied in seventeenth-century Amsterdam, but its details are based on the verbal map found in the biblical book of Numbers 33:1–49 (known as 'The Wilderness Itinerary'), which lists the Israelites' camps on their forty-year journey ('the

exodus') from Egypt, as also listed in Ya'akov's legend. The map also depicts Canaan, the 'land of milk and honey' – as referred to by the vignettes of a herd of cows and a beehive – which was divided between the twelve tribes as recounted in the book of Joshua. But this fold-out map is not simply a visual presentation of two biblical texts. It appeared in a service-book for celebrating the Passover each year. As such it is both a celebration of the festival's

origins in the Israelites' escape from Egypt and of God's promise of a time of rejoicing in the promised land, and a potent reminder of the future orientation of all such remembering. Here is what God has done, it suggests – the route out of Egypt – and what his promises still hold for his faithful. A confession and celebration of religious identity, the map proclaims: 'Next year in Jerusalem.'

Manusyaloka | c.1850 | Unknown Jain artist

Gouache on cotton, on modern cloth backing. 91 × 95 cm / 35⅞ × 37⅜ in. Library of Congress, Washington, DC

At the heart of this Jain map of Manusyaloka – the human world – lies the sacred Mount Meru, the cosmological and physical centre of the Jain cosmos, as painted on cloth by an unknown artist in Rajasthan, probably in the nineteenth century. Mount Meru was said to be the location of the anointing of Mahavira, the holy man who created the present form of Jainism in sixth-century BC India. In the central part of the map, Mount Meru is shown as being flanked by symmetrical series of other mountains – denoted by the sixteen upright rectangles forming a band across the middle of the map – beyond which are two concentric circular oceans (blue) and two circular continents (white), surrounded by a red ocean that encloses the entire middle world of humans and animals. In Jain theology, there are actually eight circles of ocean and land, but only two are conventionally portrayed on maps. The map does not portray the other parts of the five-part Jain universe, which include the heavenly abode of celestial beings above the middle world and the seven levels of hell beneath it, which are home to demons and lower forms of life.

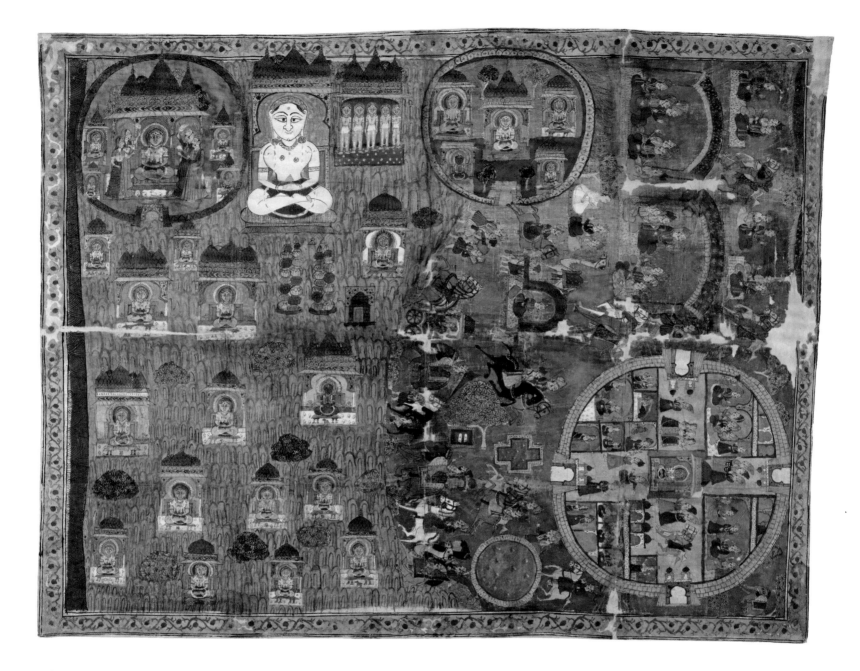

Jain Pilgrimage | c.1750 | Unknown

Watercolour on cotton. 87.9 × 108.3 cm / 34½ × 42⅔ in. Brooklyn Museum, New York

This wall-hanging was created to guide Jain pilgrims through an earthly landscape to a spiritual destination: the temple at Mount Shatrunjaya, on the left. The two parts of the map are shown from different viewpoints. The temple is seen from above, although the different figures – including the large white figure of Adinatha, whom Jains believe was the first man to be liberated from the cycle of life and death – are seen from the front. To his right stand five brothers from Indian mythology, the Pandavas. Beyond the temple's carved marble sanctuaries and shrines flows a river (left). For the viewer to see the pilgrimage part of the map properly, the image must be rotated to place the horse riders and land-marks at the top. There are hundreds of carved Jain temples around India, each one important and worthy of pilgrimage for a range of reasons having to do with attaining spiritual liberation. Also shown on this map is a circular diagram in the lower right, a representation of a village laid out in the shape of a samavasarana, or Jain preaching hall. As is clear from the workmanship, this map was not meant for practical navigation. Like medieval Christian itineraries in Europe (see p.25), it would have guided Jains on a mental rather than physical pilgrimage.

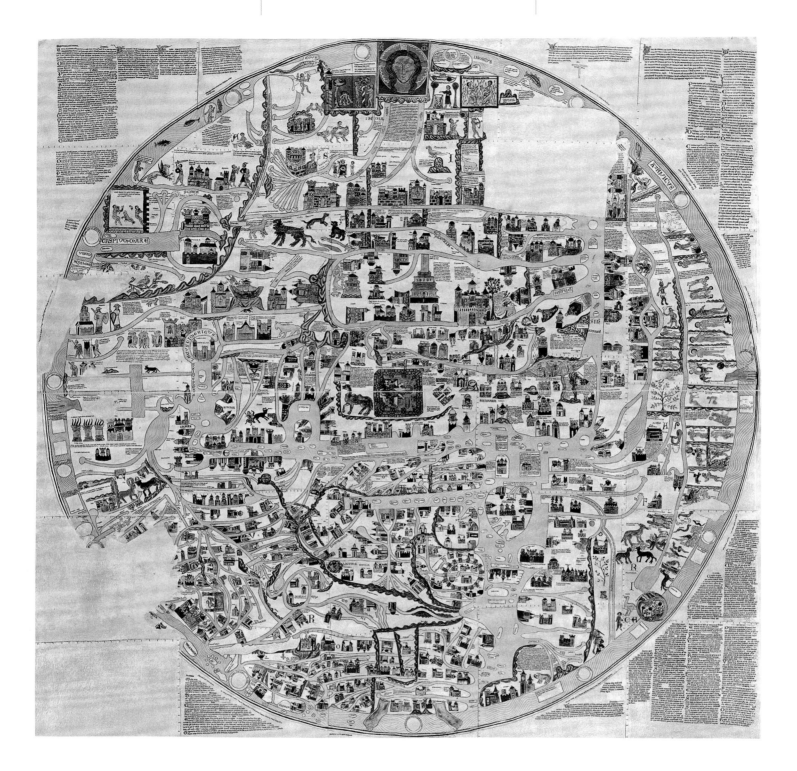

Ebstorf World Map | c.1300 | Unknown

Paint on goatskin. 3.58 × 3.56 m / 11 ft 9 in × 11 ft 9 in. Staatsbibliothek zu Berlin

Measuring just over 3.5 metres (11 feet 9 inches) square – it was painted on thirty goatskins that were stitched together – the Ebstorf World Map is the largest known mappa mundi. As the copious notes make clear, it was designed to convey not only geographical knowledge but also the world's unseen nature as created through God the Son. The map combines European geographical knowledge from the mid-thirteenth century – it details some 500 buildings, 160 seas, rivers and lakes and 60 islands, alongside people and animals – with the Christian belief that God became incarnate in the world. It shares features with maps based on the T–O tradition (see p.13), being centred on Jerusalem, with east at the top and Rome depicted as a lion. What is distinctive about the map is its presentation of Christ within the created sphere. The world revolves around him: his navel is the earth's navel (a biblical idea), he has been crucified to save it (note his hands on either side and his feet at the bottom) and it is in his care. This confession of faith was lost for centuries after its creation before it was rediscovered in Ebstorf Abbey in 1830. It was moved in 1834 to Hanover, but was destroyed there in an Allied air raid in 1943. Versions of the map like this facsimile are based on nineteenth-century copies.

World Map | c.1450 | Fra Mauro

Manuscript on vellum. 2.4 × 2.4 m / 7 ft 11 in × 7 ft 11 in. Biblioteca Nazionale Marciana, Venice

This monumental world map is one of the most important maps of the fifteenth century. Although it covers the entire known world, and was the first Western map to depict Japan, its most important feature is probably its depiction of the Indian Ocean. Four decades before Portuguese ships crossed the ocean, it presents a balanced view of the coasts and shows the ocean as being open to the Atlantic and Pacific. This vellum map made by the Venetian monk Fra Mauro is orientated with south at the top and was based on information from Marco Polo and another Venetian traveller, Niccolò de' Conti, who had returned to Venice a few years earlier. But it is more than a geographical map: it contains 3,000 inscriptions about the lands and seas it depicts, creating one of the most detailed contemporary accounts of Africa and Asia. Vignettes in each corner illustrate such scenes as the Garden of Eden and a diagram of the cosmos. The map was commissioned from Fra Mauro – then in the monastery of St Michele in Venice – by King Alfonso V of Portugal, who wanted to visualize the sea route to Asia, but there is some ambiguity about its history. It is not clear whether it is a copy of the commissioned map, or whether the 'Portuguese copy' was never sent and there was only ever one made.

Imperial Federation | 1886 | Walter Crane and Sir John C.R. Colomb

Lithograph. 63 × 86 cm / 24¾ × 34 in. Norman B. Leventhal Map Center, Boston Public Library, Massachusetts

This elaborate map is perhaps the most iconic cartographic representation of the British Empire (it established reddish pink as the colour of the empire on twentieth-century maps). It was drawn by Walter Crane – a prominent Arts and Crafts illustrator with strong socialist sympathies – for the naval strategist Sir John C.R. Colomb. Colomb was a leading member of the Imperial Federation League, which reacted to threats by some colonies to leave by proposing to reconfigure the empire as a federation based on shared interests rather than imperial domination. Britain's primacy is highlighted by the use of the Mercator projection, which is centred on the prime meridian established at Greenwich in 1851, pushing the colonies to the periphery. But the depicted geography – and Colomb's details of the sailing routes that stitched the empire together – is almost secondary to the lavish illustrations of the flora, fauna and inhabitants of the colonies, suggesting the exoticism of these distant lands. The dominant figure is Britannia, the very manifestation of imperialism, enthroned with her trident and shield, projecting the civilizing force of Great Britain while her subservient subjects, stereotypes of indigenous peoples, look to her for leadership.

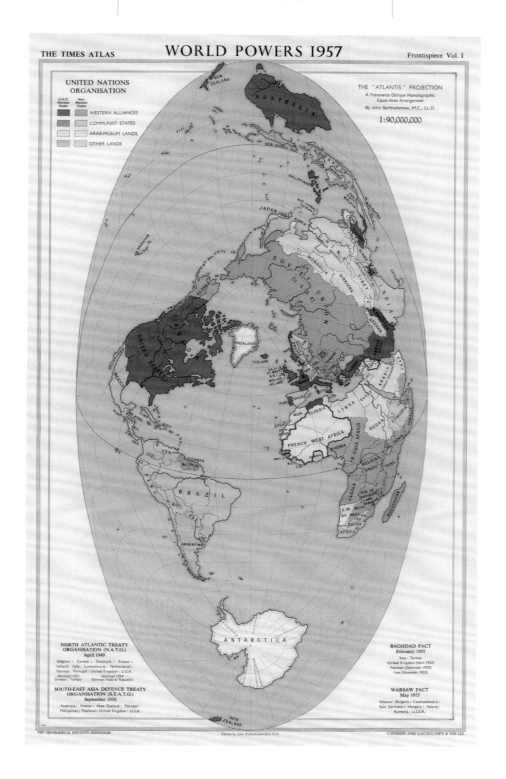

World Powers 1957 | 1958 | John Bartholomew

Printed in *The Times Atlas of the World, Mid-Century Edition* (1958). 49 × 31 cm / 19⅓ × 12¼ in. Private collection

The purples of the Western allies ring the oranges of the world's communist states in this summary of the global power struggle at the height of the Cold War. The map, which was included in *The Times Atlas of the World, Mid-Century Edition* (1958), abandons the convention of depicting the poles at the top and bottom of the map to show graphically the antagonism between the world's power blocs. The so-called Atlantis Projection was devised in 1948 by John Bartholomew of the Edinburgh-based family cartographic firm, based on an oblique view of the Earth centred on the coordinates of 30° W and 45° N, in order to put the focus on the Atlantic. In the ten years since the projection's creation, the world had seen the establishment of the North Atlantic Treaty Organization (NATO) in 1949 to limit the spread of world communism and of the Warsaw Pact in 1955 to defend communist states. US foreign policy had become based on the so-called Domino Theory, according to which any country turning communist might lead its neighbours to do the same: the theory had led the United States to war in Korea (1950–53) and would eventually lead it to defeat in Vietnam in 1973 – when Bartholomew's map would need updating again.

Carte Pisane | c.1290 | Unknown

Ink on vellum. 50 × 105 cm / 19½ × 41¼ in. Bibliothèque nationale de France, Paris

Although this chart of the Mediterranean, the Black Sea and part of the Atlantic coast was drawn shortly after the introduction of the magnetic compass into the Mediterranean in the twelfth century, it is unlikely to have been the first of its kind. But whatever chart set the initial pattern, the style and content were widely copied and the model remained fixed for 400 years. The development of portolans – along with the magnetic compass upon which they were based – represented a huge advance in navigation. Previously, sea voyages had taken place mainly along coastlines between ports. Now longer itineraries and winter sailing became routine. To create the map, two points were selected as the centres of tangent circles. From each of these circles radiate straight lines – rhumbs – that indicate the major cardinal points and intermediate directions. The cartographer drew the coastlines of landmasses and islands against this background network. The chart includes features that became standard on sea charts: the circle defining the rhumb lines, the scale bars, and the place names set on the land perpendicular to the coast. There is no detail within the landmasses: this map – the oldest surviving nautical chart – was intended for navigating at sea, so details of the interior would have been superfluous.

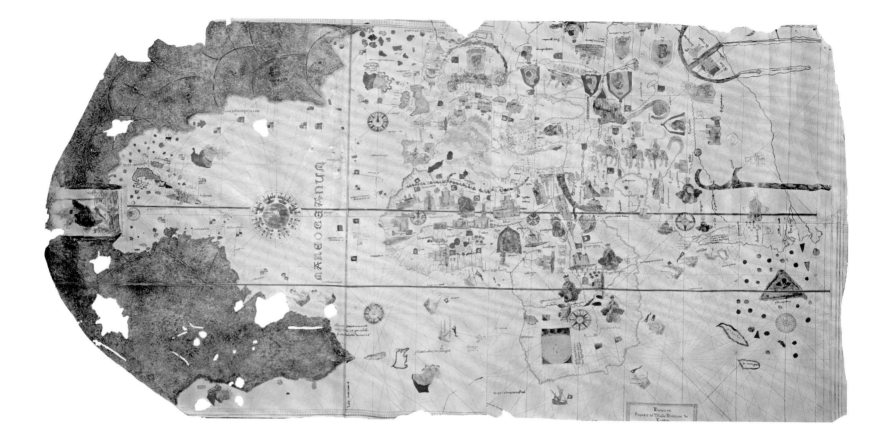

World Map | 1500 | Juan de la Cosa

Ink on parchment. 96 × 183 cm / 37¾ × 72 in. Museo Naval, Madrid

The earliest surviving world map to show America was drawn by one of the first few Europeans to visit the New World. An inscription on the map identifies its maker as Juan de la Cosa, a Basque navigator and cartographer who made seven voyages to the Americas, including Christopher Columbus's first voyage of discovery in 1492 (De la Cosa was owner and master of the *Santa Maria,* Columbus's flagship). The map depicts the world from India in the east to the new lands discovered by Columbus in the west. It is the first to show the West Indies and Venezuela, discovered by Columbus for Spain; Brazil, discovered by Pedro Álvares Cabral for Portugal in 1500; and Newfoundland, discovered by John Cabot for England in 1497. In Asia an inscription notes Vasco da Gama's first expedition to India in 1498–9. De la Cosa may have intended the face of St Christopher in the vignette at the far western edge of the map to represent Columbus. This precious document was probably made at the request of the Spanish monarchs Queen Isabella and King Ferdinand. It is the first world map in the style of the medieval portolan charts that were first drawn and used in the Mediterranean; the extended style continued to be used for world maps for two centuries.

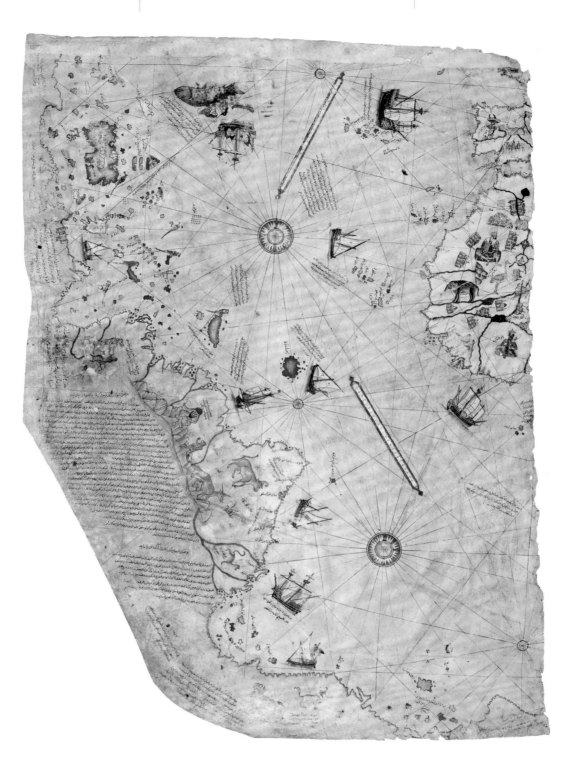

Map Fragment of the Atlantic | 1513 | Piri Reis

Ink and pigments on parchment. 90 × 65 cm / 35½ × 25½ in. Topkapı Sarayı Müzesi, Istanbul

This fragment is all that survives – the western third – of an Ottoman world map, but it has fascinated historians for its combining of Turkish and European geographical knowledge. It depicts the Iberian Peninsula and West Africa (top right), the West Indies (top left), South America (centre left) and the coastline of a conjectured Southern Continent (bottom left). Before Piri became an admiral (*reis* means 'admiral' or 'captain') in the

Ottoman navy, he was a corsair fighting Europeans in the Mediterranean, where he claimed to have captured a map of the West Indies drawn by Christopher Columbus. Piri based his own creation on that map – no evidence of which survives – and many others. Most of the geography on this fragment comes from contemporary Portuguese maps, although it also includes information from European mappa mundi. There are illustrations of

mythical creatures and legendary events, including the Irish saint Brendan mistaking a whale for an island (top, centre) and a humanlike figure in South America. Piri's map has twenty-four Turkish inscriptions describing the people, animals and mineral wealth of various regions and describing the voyages of Columbus, the 'Genoese infidel'. Some have thought the coastline of the South-ern Continent looks rather like Antarctica.

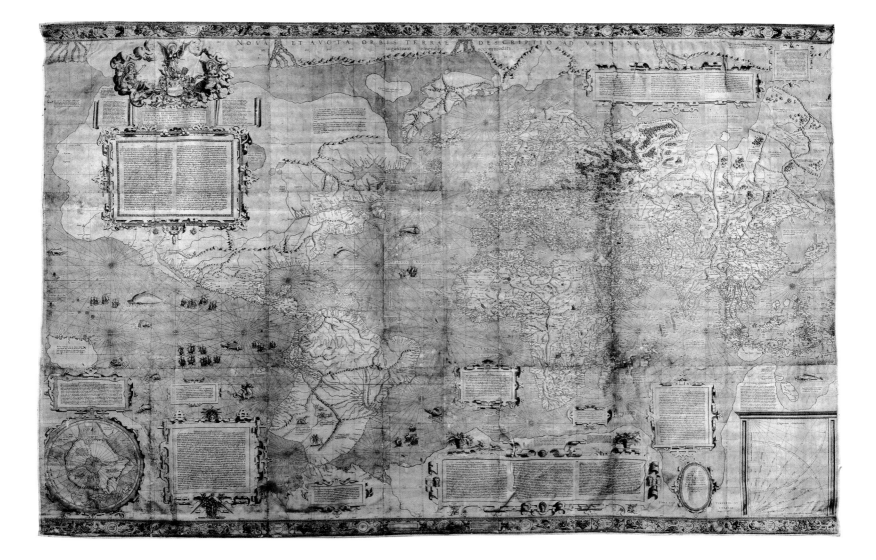

A New and Enlarged Description of the Earth | 1569 | Gerard Mercator

Engraving. 123.6 × 202.4 cm / 48⅝ × 79⅝ in. Bibliothèque nationale de France, Paris

Until 1569, navigators could plot a straight line on a globe that would allow them to sail in a straight course following lines of constant bearing – rhumbs – but not on a flat map. This was not a problem over small distances, but as European seafarers ventured farther afield, it became more difficult. It was solved by the Flemish map-maker Gerard Mercator, but how he accomplished his mathematical feat is still not fully understood. Mercator devised a projection that captured the curved surface of the globe on a map, so that a course plotted with a straight line crossed the parallels and lines of meridian at a consistent angle. Mercator's projection became the model for general-purpose world maps from the late nineteenth century – a task for which it was never designed – but its remarkable achievement was somewhat overshadowed by later criticism that it made the northern continents appear larger and more dominant than the southern, a bias corrected in, for example, the Peters projection (see p.156). Nevertheless, derivations of Mercator's projection were developed in the 1970s for satellites and adopted in 2005 by Google for its online maps (see p.310). By 2010 Web Mercator had been adopted by Microsoft Bing Maps, Google Maps and ESRI ArcGIS online, so Mercator's legacy endures.

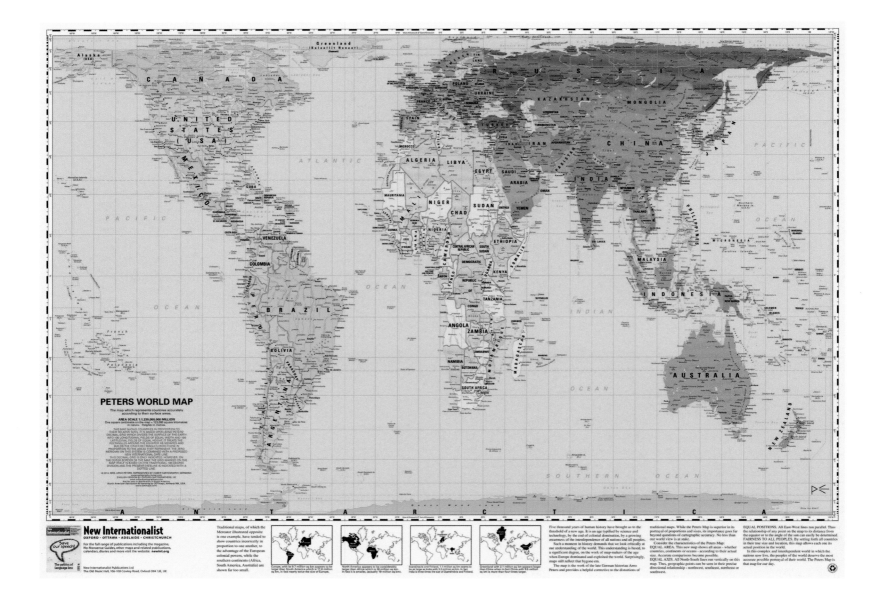

New Internationalist World Map on the Peters Projection | 1983 | Arno Peters

Offset lithograph. 52 cm × 81 cm / 20½ × 25½ in. Private collection

This map projection was created in an attempt to right the wrongs of the standard Mercator projection (see p.155) – namely that it makes the northern continents misleadingly larger than those of the south, particularly Africa. Although map-makers had long known that the Mercator projection was a poor choice for general world maps, it took an outsider – the German historian Arno Peters – to change things. Peters launched this equal-area world map – with a colour scheme chosen to emphasize regional connections rather than divisions – in 1973. It was later taken up by groups working in the developing world, such as Oxfam and UNICEF, and 80 million copies were distributed world wide; this wall poster was first published by *New Internationalist* magazine in 1983 with the insignia of the UN Development Programme. Several cartographers argued that, like all rectangular maps, the projection had distortions of its own and pointed out that it had actually been developed in 1855 by James Gall (it is often termed the Gall-Peters Projection). In 1989 the-then American Cartographic Association recommended that rectangular projections should not be used at all for general-purpose world maps, but Peters' contention that we should scrutinize the way we depict the world remains valid.

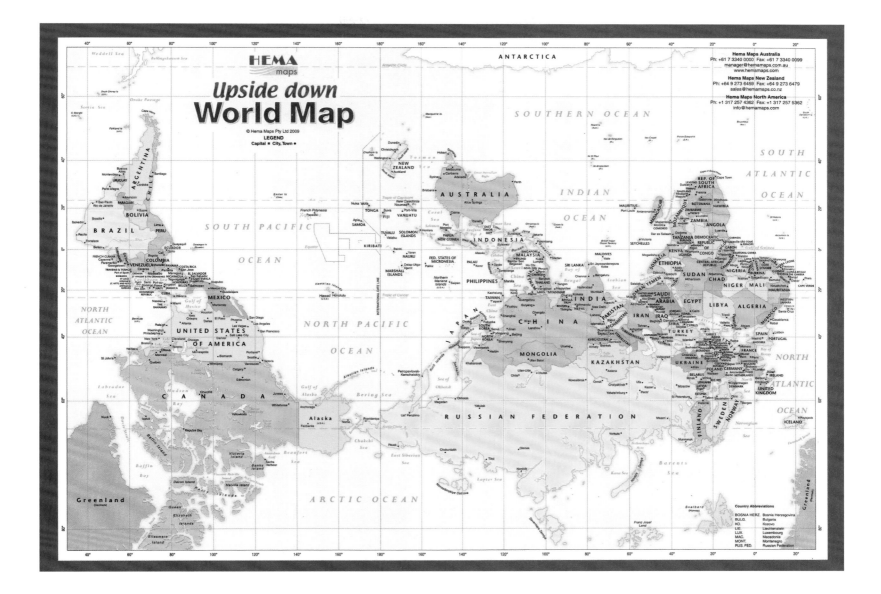

Upside Down World Map | 2009 | Hema Maps

Offset lithograph. 21 × 30 cm / 8¼ × 11¾ in. Private collection

World maps with south at the top are made and sold in Australia and New Zealand, largely aimed at the tourist market, many of whom come from the northern hemisphere. Both makers and their intended audience find this view of the world amusing, thumbing the nose at conventional representations that reinforce notions of the north 'on top' to those 'down under'. Of course, maps of the world didn't always show north at the top – medieval mappa mundi and many early portolan charts are orientated otherwise – but the convention is so long-standing that today it is disconcerting to invert the image. We are so used to seeing north on top – with all its symbolic associations – that it usually goes unquestioned. However, the notion of the world turned upside down harks back to an old tradition of misrule in European broadsheet imagery, in which the poor lord it over the rich, women over men, animals over humans, and so on. The use of a conventional, rectangular projection arguably adds to the sense of disruption. Henry and Margaret Boegheim set up Hema Maps in the 1980s, later making their own GPS-based route maps for travel in the outback.

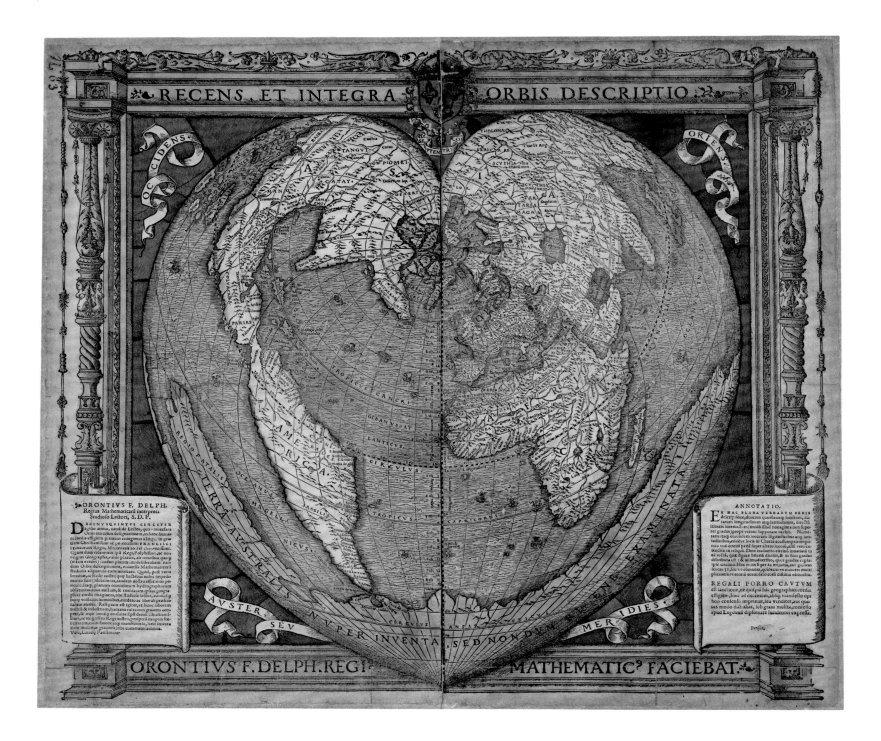

Current and Complete Description of the World | 1536 | Oronce Fine

Hand-coloured woodcut. 51 × 57 cm / 20 × 22½ in. Bibliothèque nationale de France, Paris

Oronce Fine's interest in geometry eventually ruined his reputation – a career as a royal mathematician to Francis I was overshadowed by his doubtful claim to have squared the circle, a popular problem for early modern thinkers – but is reflected in a notable cartographic output. Although the cordiform projection – from the Latin for heart, *cor* – was not Fine's invention, he was the first to make such a map, in 1519. That version no longer exists, but for this printed version Finé updated the geographical information to label the east coast of North America 'Terra Francesca' – French land – after the voyages of Giovanni da Verrazzano in the 1520s. In the late fifteenth and early sixteenth centuries, mathematicians and cartographers were developing the work of the second-century Egyptian-Greek Claudius Ptolemy. This map is derived from Ptolemy's second projection. It is an equal-area map, showing each landform in correct proportion to the others. These and related maps – such as the Waldseemüller map of 1507 (see p.228) – were attempts to find better ways to depict a world that now included the 'new' landmass of the Americas. The map projects a *concordia mundi* – a world in harmony – adding a deeper resonance to the image of the world in the age of exploration.

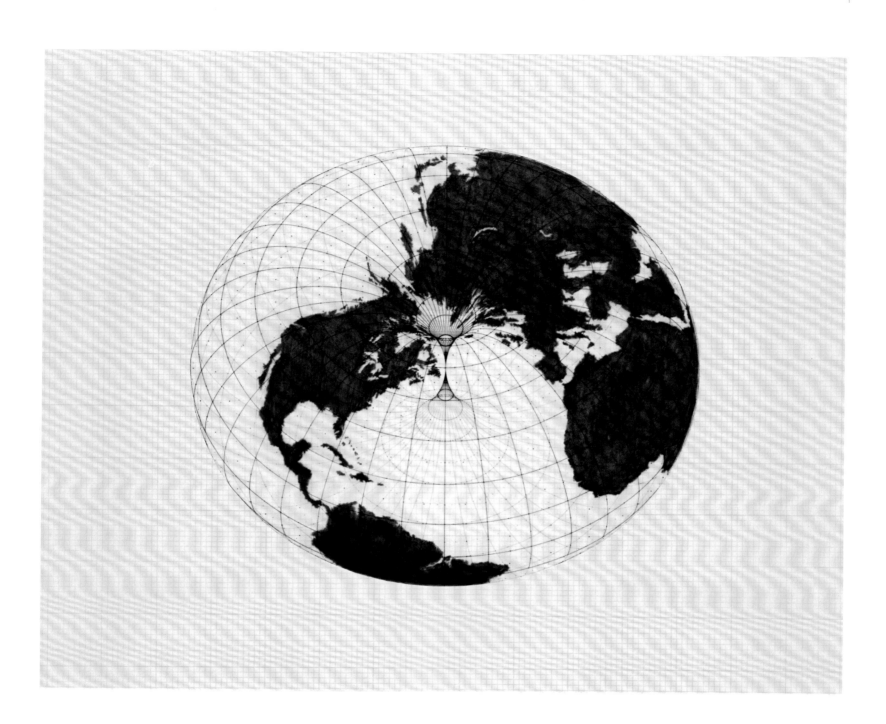

Isometric Systems in Isotropic Space – Map Projections: The Doughnut | 1974 | Agnes Denes

Ink and charcoal on graph paper and Mylar. 61 × 76.2 cm / 24 × 30 in. Whitney Museum of American Art, New York

In the late 1960s, the Hungarian-born American artist Agnes Denes begun an influential series of artworks using the principles of isometric projection – a method to represent three-dimensional objects on a two-dimensional surface. The works were made during the golden era of space exploration, soon after satellites had transmitted the first full-disk photographs of the Earth from space and confirmed its undeniably spherical shape. An advocate for human stewardship of and responsibility for the planet, Denes manipulated the highly familiar image of the globe to prompt viewers to see the world anew and contemplate their own place in it. The intriguing and delicate drawings saw the sphere abandoned in favour of other geometric forms such as cube, pyramid, cone and, in this case, the ring doughnut. In this projection, the North and South Poles met within the doughnut's 'hole'. In Denes's words, 'longitude and latitude lines were unravelled, points of intersection cut, continents allowed to drift, gravity tampered with, earth mass altered'. The series can also be seen in the context of post-colonialist thinking at the time, which rejected the accepted systems of representing the world in maps that served the political agendas of old world powers above geographical accuracy.

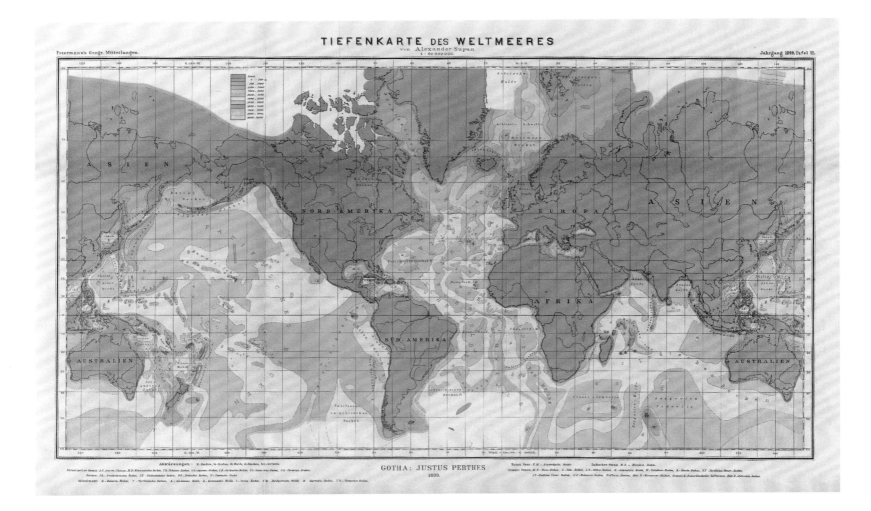

Depth Map of the World's Oceans | 1899 | Alexander Supan

Printed paper. 31 × 56 cm / 12¼ × 22 in. NOAA Central Library, Silver Spring, Maryland

Although this map was published at the very end of the nineteenth century, its origins lay at the century's start, in Alexander von Humboldt's conviction that there was only one world science to define the one world (see p.50). Humboldt helped to establish a geographical school of art in Potsdam, Germany, to train a new generation of cartographers. This included Augustus Petermann, who in 1854 established *Petermanns Geographische Mitteilungen*, a leading international geographic journal. Some years after Petermann's suicide in 1878, Supan – from the next generation of cartographers – became the journal's editor. Although geography was usually terrestially orientated, Supan had a great regard for the oceans, and under his editorship *Petermanns* investigated the structure of the ocean basins and the strata of ocean currents and temperatures, in articles enhanced by the chromolithographic maps that were the journal's speciality. The annotations along the bottom list scientists and ship's crews whose soundings helped to make the map. There is also a cartographic anomaly: the ocean depths are colour-coded in gradated hues, except for the very light band representing depths of 4,000–5,000 metres (13,123–16,404 feet), which Supan used to emphasize some point that is now hard to discern.

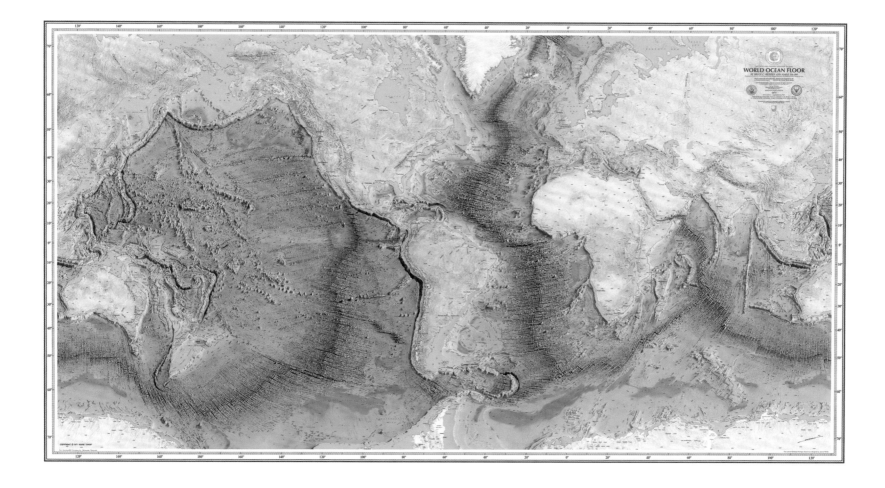

World Ocean Floor | 1977 | Marie Tharp, Bruce Heezen and Heinrich Berann

Printed paper. 106 × 189 cm / 41¾ × 74½ in. Private collection

When it was published in 1977, the Heezen-Tharp map of the ocean floor, hand-painted by the artist Heinrich Berann (see also p.197), revolutionized the understanding of the Earth by supporting the theory of plate tectonics. The map reflects decades of research by Bruce Heezen, a marine geologist, and the geologist and cartographer Marie Tharp. The pair started working together at Columbia University, where they researched ocean-floor data and produced diagrams of ocean-floor relief. Their first map, in 1959, defined the North Atlantic floor; then came the South Atlantic in 1961 and the Indian Ocean in 1964. They revised their maps as new technology provided data for more accurate cartography, revealing for the first time the varied landscapes of the ocean floor, such as the network of underwater mountains that form the volcanic Mid-Atlantic Ridge, Earth's longest mountain range at 65,000 kilometres (40,390 miles). Ridges appear in dark-blue, most often found in the central areas of ocean basins. Here the massive outpouring of lava creates new ocean-floor crust, pushing older oceanic crust – and the continents – outwards. After Heezen's death in 1977, Tharp completed the world map alone, and it was published by the Office of Naval Research later that year.

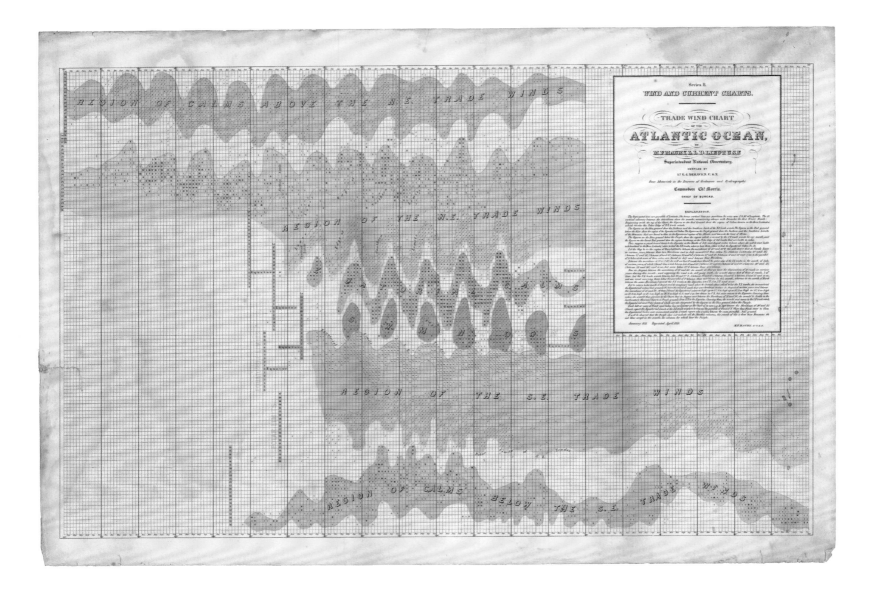

Trade Wind Chart of the Atlantic Ocean | 1851 | Matthew Fontaine Maury

Lithograph. 60 × 91 cm / 23⅝ × 35⅞ in. Private collection

Although ocean currents and the 'trade winds' – winds that blow steadily enough to be used by sailing ships – had been recorded for centuries, they were not mapped systematically until the mid-nineteenth century. After an injury, US Navy midshipman Matthew Fontaine Maury (see p.40) was given the shore-based task of drawing charts, eventually becoming Superintendent of the United States Naval Observatory. His study of hundreds of ships' logs from different years revealed consistent seasonal wind patterns, and he used the data to chart regular winds, significantly shortening travel times by directing ships to areas of reliable wind at particular times of the year. Maury's *Trade Wind Chart of the Atlantic Ocean of 1851* (this one is a reprint of 1858) is an unusual map that attempts to represent time and space in a single grid, omitting landmasses altogether. Parallels are presented vertically and meridians horizontally in much wider margins; the space between represents months of the year. Numbers in the grid note the number of ships that recorded particular conditions in those locations. Calms appear in Roman numerals, coloured blue; reliable trade winds in Arabic numerals, coloured red; and tropical monsoons appear in purple near the equator, interrupted because of their seasonal nature.

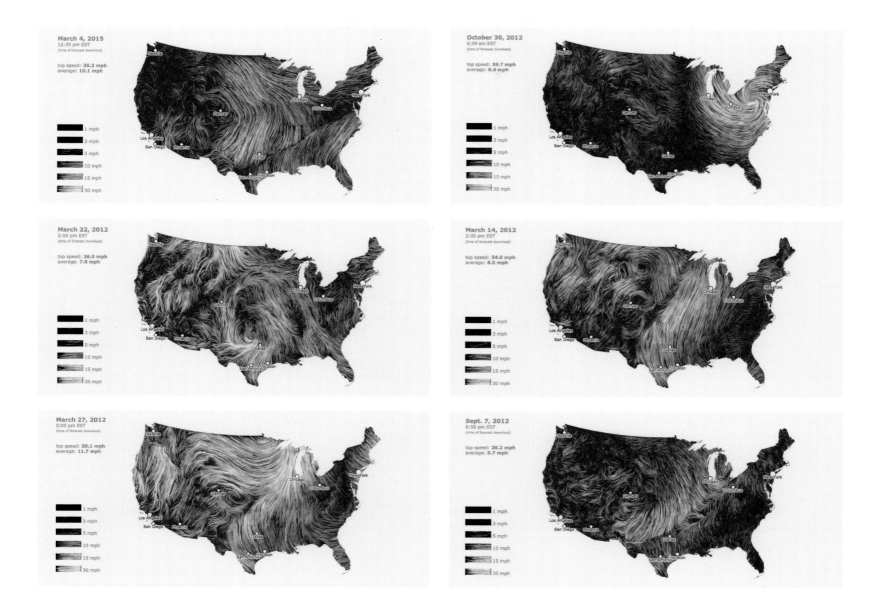

Wind Map | 2012 | Fernanda Bertini Viégas and Martin Wattenberg

Digital. Dimensions variable

Until relatively recently, weather maps were static – unlike the constant motion, flow and change of the weather itself. Digital technology changed that, and its potential was seized on by the Brazilian scientist Fernanda Bertini Viégas and her American counterpart Martin Wattenberg to display the strength and motion of the winds over the United States as a dynamic process. *Wind Map* is a flow animation based on data from the US National Weather Service's National Digital Forecast Database, which is updated every hour and comes in a variety of spatial resolutions. The map is, however, more than just a striking image, in that its creators are trying to draw attention to the potential of wind for energy generation by demonstrating the near-constant motion of the air masses above the United States. Taking inspiration from the maps of the astronomer Edmond Halley, who used trailing lines in many of his maps to show motion in the late seventeenth century (see p.282), Viégas and Wattenberg use thicker lines to represent higher wind speeds, rather than increasing the speed of the animation itself. This gives *Wind Map* – one of a number of geographic visualizations by the two scientists – visual density and contrast, unlike conventional weather maps.

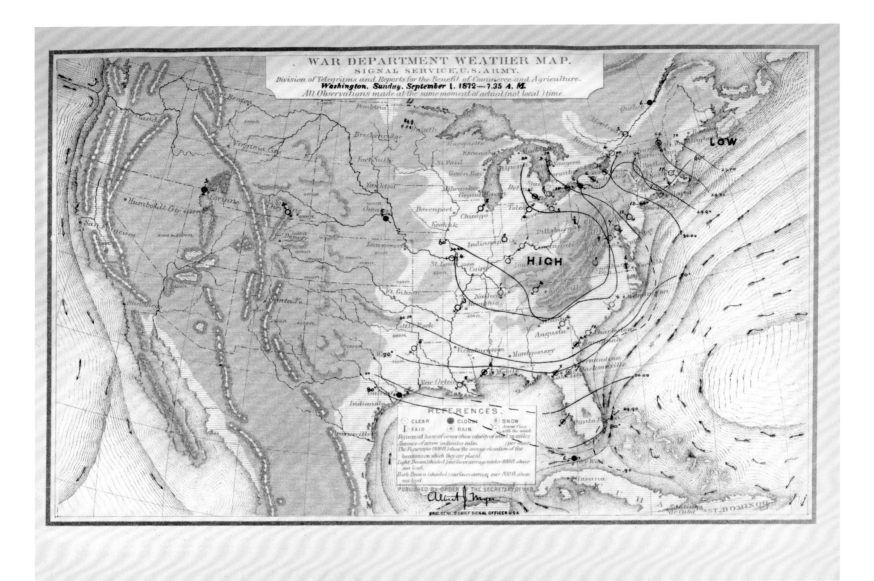

WAR DEPARTMENT WEATHER MAP.
SIGNAL SERVICE, U.S. ARMY.
Division of Telegrams and Reports for the Benefit of Commerce and Agriculture.
Washington, Sunday, September 1, 1872—7.35 A. M.
All Observations made at the same moment of actual (not local) time.

REFERENCES.

Weather Conditions at 7:35 a.m. on September 1, 1872 | 1872 | United States Army Signal Service

Printed paper. 22 × 30 cm / 8¼ × 11¾ in. NOAA Central Library, Silver Spring, Maryland

Today weather maps are part of everyday life, but when this map was drawn, in 1872, the study of weather had only recently developed from seasonal generalizations to day-to-day measurements of specific conditions. The key to such an advance was using isobars to connect points with the same atmospheric pressure in order to reveal observable patterns. High-pressure centres moving across continents were associated with clear, dry conditions and low-pressure centres with rain or snow. Both were mapped each day to show their movement, aiding weather forecasting. This early example includes isobars and symbols showing wind speed and precipitation, but is otherwise limited. In 1870, President Ulysses S. Grant had handed official forecasting duties to the Army Signal Service, which enhanced US military preparedness and ensured reliable funding and data collection, although this map also claims to be drawn 'for the benefit of commerce and agriculture'. When such duties were transferred to the new United States Weather Bureau in 1891, increasingly detailed measurements of air pressure, wind speed and direction, precipitation and temperature were represented and simplified, albeit at the expense of other details, such as topography and elevation.

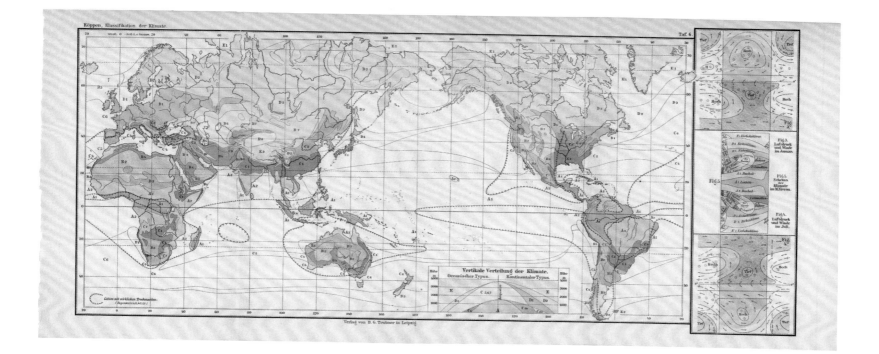

A Proposed System of Climate Classification | 1900 | Wladimir Köppen

Printed paper. 22.3 × 50.8 cm / 9 × 20 in. Herman B. Wells Map Collection, Indiana University, Bloomington

Representing climate effectively on a map has long been a challenge for geographers. Climate is visually elusive, so it can only be represented in terms of its measurable effects or conditions. While Alexander von Humboldt had mapped the world's general temperature or 'isothermal' zones in 1817 (see p.50), the Russian-born German geographer Wladimir Köppen of the Naval Observatory in Hamburg theorized a more precise climate classification system – still in use internationally today – over several decades. During a childhood of regular travel between St Petersburg and the Crimean Peninsula, Köppen studied differences in vegetation that corresponded to local conditions such as topography and elevation, proximity to the coast, and temperature and moisture. He went on to classify climate in terms of the distribution of plant species, using the theory that plant communities become established only in areas where local climatic conditions allow. This map, which accompanied an article in a geography journal, was Köppen's first published attempt to use an intuitive colour scheme to represent and classify distinct climates of the Earth: arid in yellows and reds, lush in shades of green. The diagrams on the right further illustrate relevant atmospheric patterns, such as air pressure and wind.

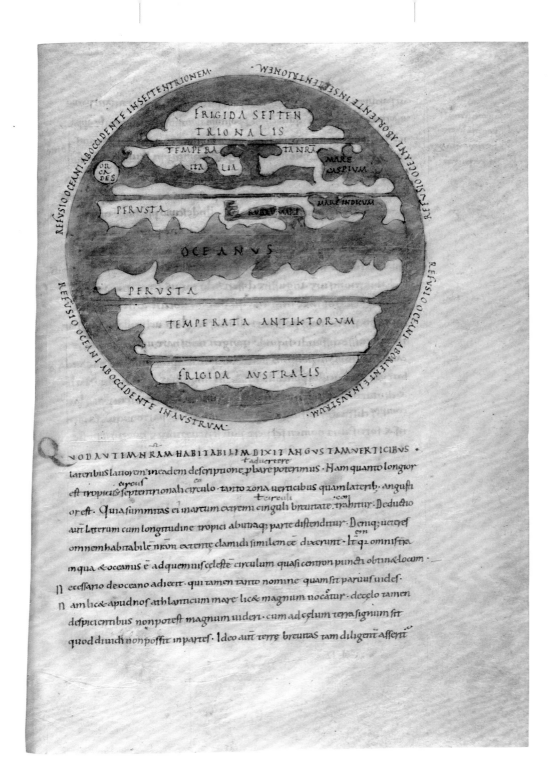

Circular Zonal Map | c.1000 | Macrobius

Ink on parchment. 25 × 17.7 cm / 9¾ × 7 in. Bodleian Library, Oxford

This map was one of the first to divide the Earth into climatic zones; beyond that, however, it poses key questions. Macrobius, a Neoplatonic thinker in the Roman empire, described the climatic zones in detail: near each pole, frigid uninhabitable regions; near the equator, an uninhabitable zone burned up (*perusta*) by the sun and divided by 'the ocean stream' (*oceanus*). Between these belts to north and south lie the 'temperate' climes. The

northern one runs from the Orkneys (*Orcades*) to the Caspian Sea, while in the southern hemisphere live 'the Antipodes' (*[zona] antiktorum* – an error for *antoecorum*), the existence of which was disputed by Christian theologians. The map raises a key problem: maps always reflect their creators' world views, but this drawing was produced in about 1000 to illustrate a text written some 600 years earlier. Given that there was a tradition

of copying drawings, are we looking at the state of knowledge in 400 or at the actual artist's understanding of the world? The many variations (and blunders) in the manuscripts – all produced centuries after Macrobius – suggest that there is rarely a straightforward answer. These 'Macrobian zonal maps' were among the first to locate north at the top, and we still show the equator, the tropics and arctic circles on maps and globes.

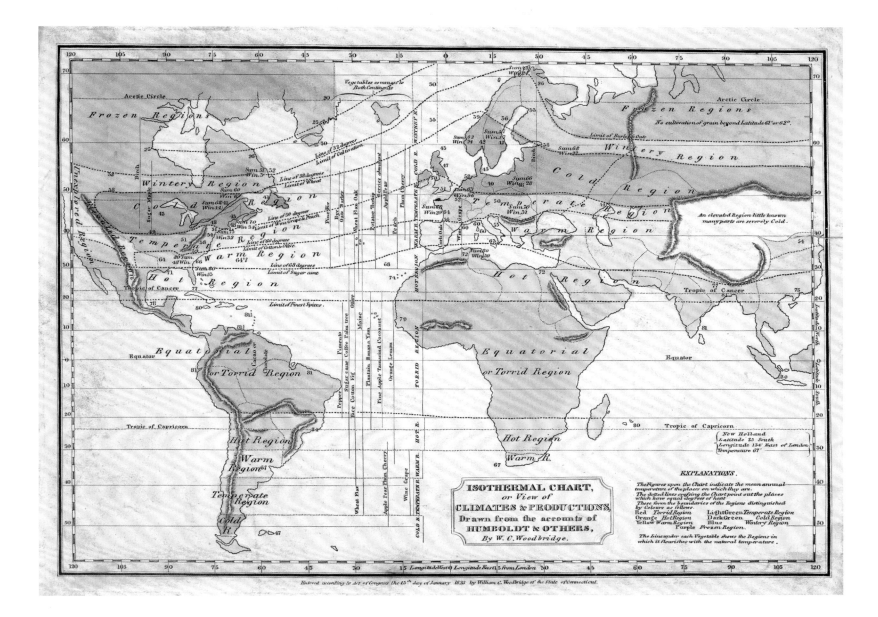

Isothermal Chart | 1823 | William C. Woodbridge

Hand-coloured engraving. 20.3 × 28.2 cm / 8 × 11⅛ in. Princeton University, New Jersey

Some 1,400 years after Macrobius (see opposite), it might come as a surprise to learn that the mapping of climate zones is relatively recent. This map is an early example of an isothermal map – drawn to link places with similar climates – from 1823. A world isothermal chart had recently been developed by the German botanist and explorer Alexander von Humboldt to show bands of cold and warm temperatures corresponding to latitude and surface conditions such as land elevation. Humboldt's first such chart, drawn in 1817, showed these bands without landforms. While Humboldt waited to fill out his charts with data from new weather stations around the world, educator William C. Woodbridge drew a simplified version for teaching. Woodbridge, who is known primarily for the school geography texts he wrote with fellow educational reformer Emma Willard, sought to make the theory accessible. Coloured climatic 'regions' would allow students to evaluate which agricultural commodities would grow where; some examples appear left of centre alongside vertical lines that suggest their potential ranges. Humboldt's own suggestions of climatic regions, versions of which appeared in Berghaus's *Atlas* in 1845 (see p.51), would employ Latin names derived from Carl Linnaeus's *System of Nature*.

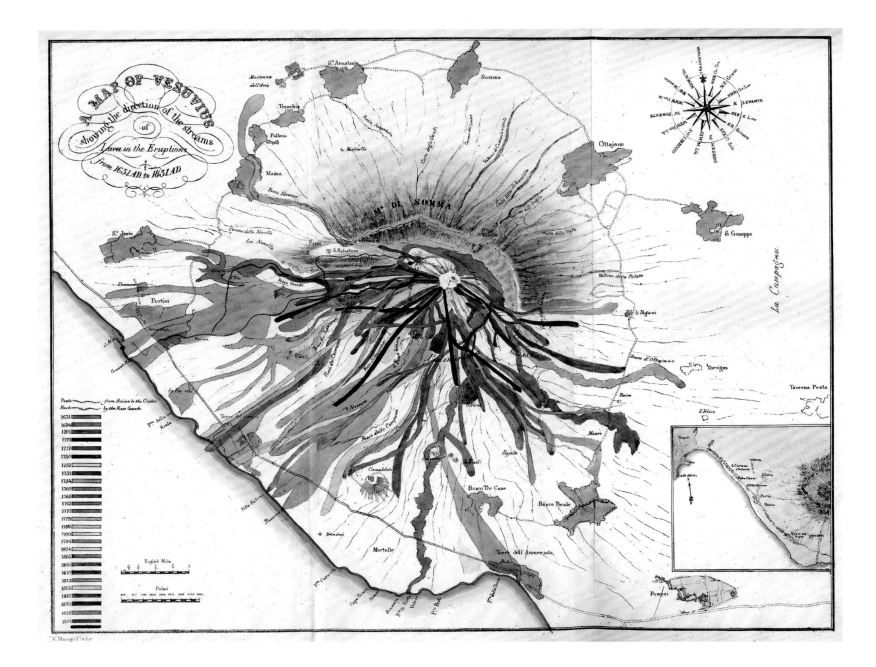

A Map of Vesuvius | 1832 | John Auldjo

Lithograph. 29 × 34 cm / 11⅜ × 13⅜ in. University of Otago, Dunedin

The beauty of this map disguises two centuries of geological violence. Its various colours, applied by printing, represent the direction and extension of lava flows from twenty-seven eruptions of Mount Vesuvius between 1631 and 1831, all clearly labelled. Although overcharged with too many colours, and thus not easy to read, the map is an accurate record of volcanic activity. The first eruption, in pink, seems to have been the largest and

became a reference by which to measure the impact of subsequent eruptions. The geologist John Auldjo – the first Briton to climb Mont Blanc – lived in nearby Naples and cimbed Vesuvius, collecting and dating rock samples on which to base a book of lithographs of the volcano. At the time, scientists were turning increasingly to drawings to explain the seismic causes of natural catastrophes, such as the earthquakes of Lisbon (1755) and Calabria

(1783), as well as other unseen geological activity. While these charts were used from the second half of the seventeenth century, the development of graphics, advances in techniques of colour printing, the lowering of the costs of printing and, in general, the deployment of new modes of visual communication encouraged the emergence of geology as an autonomous academic discipline during the nineteenth century.

Depth (ft.)

- 0 - 1
- 1 - 2
- 2 - 3
- 3 - 4
- 4 - 5
- 5 - 6
- 6 - 7
- 7 - 8
- 8 - 9
- 9 - 10
- 10 - 15
- 15 - 20
- > 20

USACE Flood
Status Zones

Zone ID

Hurricane Katrina Flooding
Estimated Depth and Extent
03 September 2005

Hurricane Katrina Flooding Estimated Depths and Extent | 2005 | NOAA/FEMA

Colour-coded satellite image. Dimensions variable

Maps have become part of the vocabulary of natural disasters. Enhanced satellite images like this one, made five days after Hurricane Katrina made landfall in Louisiana on 29 August 2005, are an essential tool in helping authorities – and the public – grasp the severity of an emergency. Katrina was one of the largest and costliest natural disasters in the history of the United States. The city of New Orleans, which lay in the storm's path, was protected by a series of levees and floodwalls intended to shield its inhabited areas from the storm surge that accompanies most large hurricanes in the Gulf of Mexico. The levees failed, however, and breaches in the floodwalls allowed seawater into neighbourhoods along the Mississippi River, overflowing Lake Pontchartrain. Much of the city lies near or only just above sea level, and it was inundated. This map was prepared by the National Oceanic and Atmospheric Administration (NOAA) and the Federal Emergency Management Agency (FEMA) to record the depth of floodwater on 3 September (yellow and green mark the deepest water). Although it is an estimate made from remote-sensing data, the map shows in stark detail that parts of the coast were still under as much as 3 metres (10 feet) of water almost a week after the storm had abated.

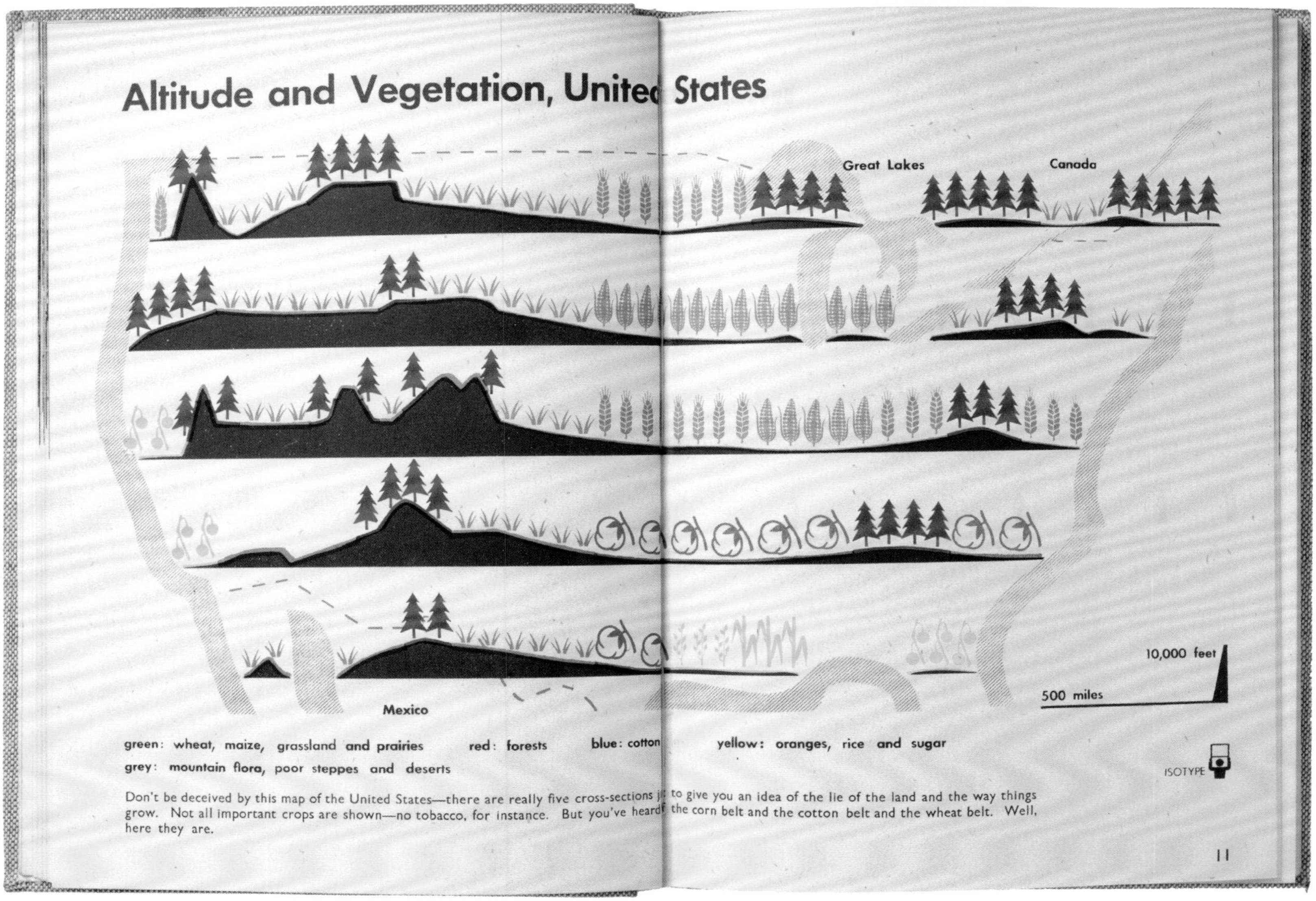
Altitude and Vegetation, United States
Great Lakes
Canada
Mexico
10,000 feet
500 miles
green: wheat, maize, grassland and prairies
red: forests
blue: cotton
yellow: oranges, rice and sugar
grey: mountain flora, poor steppes and deserts
ISOTYPE
Don't be deceived by this map of the United States—there are really five cross-sections just to give you an idea of the lie of the land and the way things grow. Not all important crops are shown—no tobacco, for instance. But you've heard of the corn belt and the cotton belt and the wheat belt. Well, here they are.
11

Altitude and Vegetation, United States | 1943 | P. Sargant Florence and Lella Secor Florence

Printed in *Only an Ocean Between* by P. Sargant Florence and Lella Secor Florence (1943). 23 × 34 cm / 9 × 13½ in. Private collection

Developed by Otto Neurath, Gerd Arntz and Marie Reidemeister during the interwar period in Vienna, Isotype (the International System of Typographic Picture Education) was an attempt to create a set of universal pictograms that could communicate clearly across all cultures. Isotype never met its lofty – possibly unattainable – goal, but the system influenced a number of works in the twentieth century and continues to resonate with some designers and map-makers today. This map uses Isotype pictograms to present a greatly simplified picture of American terrain and farm production. It sacrifices detail in favour of clarity, in keeping with the Isotype principle that it is more useful to tell a basic, memorable story than a complex, forgettable one. The pictograms are approachable, suitable for all ages and even fun. More importantly, the simplicity of the drawings gives the reader a clue about the data: that the story they tell is likewise simplified. This is not a wholly accurate image of the United States, but it does tell us, roughly, what grows where – the accompanying text mentions the Corn Belt, for example – and the pictograms remind us that we should not take it too seriously. It is a useful, albeit approximate, picture, designed not for detailed analysis, but to be memorable.

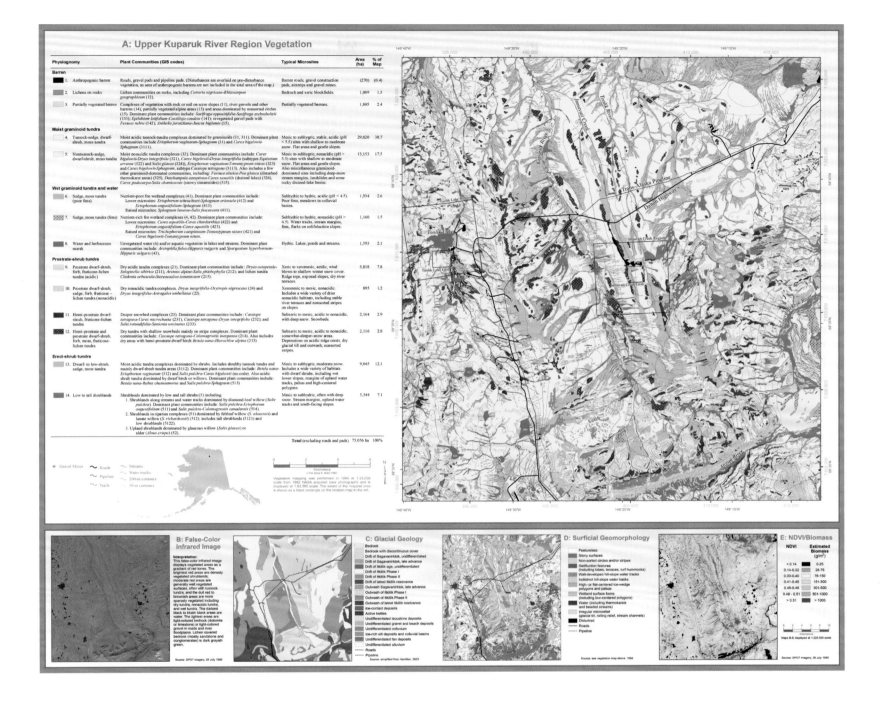

Vegetation in the Vicinity of the Toolik Field Station, Alaska | 2008 | Donald A. Walker and Hilmar A. Maier

Digital image. Dimensions variable

This striking map, produced by the Alaska Geobotany Center, has been put together using a Geographic Information System (GIS) from botanical and geological data to show vegetation around Toolik Lake, Alaska. Blacks and greys represent barren ground; yellows damp tundra (moss and sedge); blues wet tundra; pinks and purples dwarf shrubs; and greens taller shrubs and trees. Maps made using GIS technology are among the most common forms of cartography today: almost every university, city-planning department, government agency and construction company employs some form of GIS map-making. Because of its ability to combine a flexible range of data sources that can be layered, coloured and presented in striking ways, GIS-produced cartography is used both for analytic and scientific purposes – as here – and more generally by policy-makers wishing to put forward a particular point. Because most GIS maps are made of multiple layers of data, they are often designed to be striking so that the viewer can readily tell the different layers apart. The cartographers Donald A. Walker and Hilmar A. Maier made this map from SPOT constellation satellite imagery operated by the French Airbus Corporation, one of the largest providers of remote-sensing imagery.

The Landtafel of Rothenburg | 1537 | Wilhelm Ziegler

Ink and watercolour on linen. 161 × 163 cm / 63⅔ × 64 in. Germanisches Nationalmuseum, Nuremberg

In common with other art forms, cartography has its national types. While the English were by about 1600 drawing planimetrically accurate estate plans for individual landowners (see p.176), the German-speaking regions of Europe, from Oldenburg to Bavaria, had the *Landtafel* ('land table'). This tended to show a generalized bird's-eye view 'as if in a mirror' – that being how the viewer could most readily grasp the essentials of a scene. Its main characteristics were a large area shown from a high-angle view, with towns inserted roughly in their correct places. Wilhelm Ziegler's image of Rothenburg in Bavaria is a typical example, with the River Tauber in the foreground, wooded hills behind the town and lesser settlements that probably could not be confidently identified. By the early seventeenth century several manuals had been published in the German-speaking world explaining how to draw maps of the countryside, so it was not necessary to be a surveyor to make such a map. At the time there was little distinction between painters and map-makers. Many celebrated painters of the sixteenth century also made maps, and it was not until the seventeenth century that the two skills drew apart, as one calling came to be regarded as an art and the other as a science.

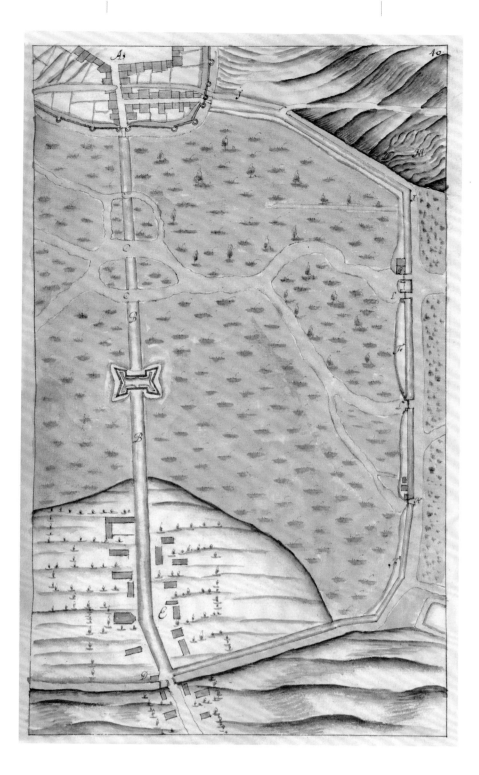

Map of Part of the River Somme | 1644 | The Sieur Lenin

Watercolour on paper. 33.5 × 20 cm / 13⅛ × 7⅞ in. Newberry Library, Chicago, Illinois

For all its beauty, this is a thoroughly functional map prepared by the French military. In the sixteenth century there were no large-scale maps of the French countryside comparable to English estate plans (see p.176). Such maps began to be drawn in about 1600 by two branches of the French army, the service of lodgings-officers (*maréchaux des logis*) and of the engineers (*ingénieurs du roi*). The former prepared a huge archive of manuscript maps showing potential routes for French troops and the places where lodgings might be found. These maps were far more detailed than printed maps of the time, but were known only to a small number of royal officials. Meanwhile, the engineers also drew detailed maps of particular areas. This one forms part of a set of forty-four such maps, showing the crossings of the River Somme from its mouth to its source. It was drawn in 1644 on the orders of Cardinal Richelieu, who wanted to avoid a debacle like that of 1636, when Spanish forces in the Netherlands had crossed the river easily during their invasion of France. The cartographer, the Sieur Lenin – one of a dozen or so engineers working in Picardy – takes care to show how the crossings may be defended. In the process, he also gives details of the towns, marshes, fields and houses alongside the river.

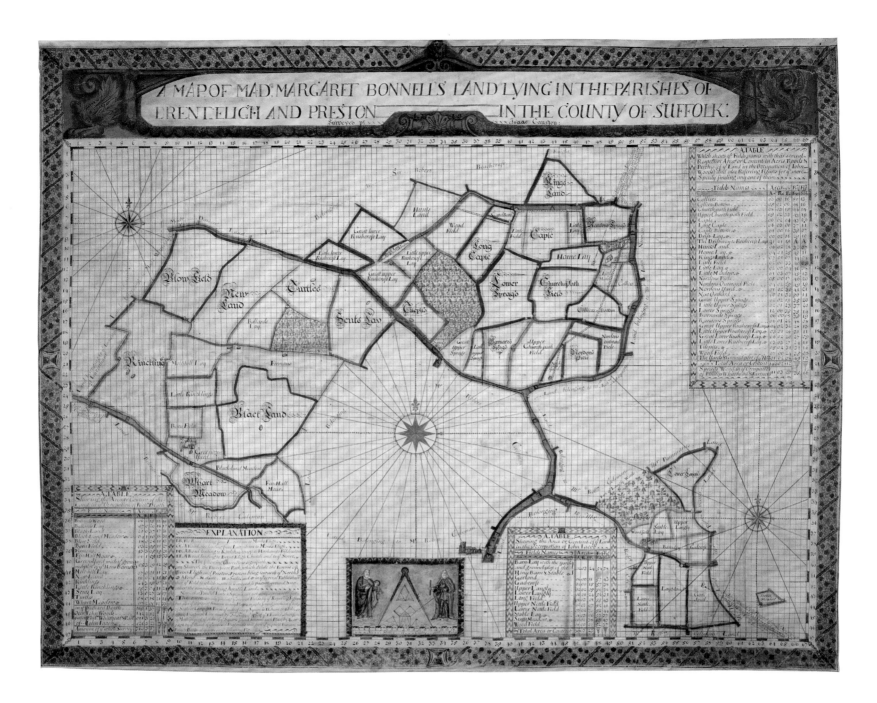

A Map of Madame Margaret Bonnell's Land | 1719 | Isaac Causton

Ink and watercolour on vellum. 76 × 91.5 cm / 30 × 36 in. British Library, London

An elegant estate map like this might have hung in some conspicuous place as a demonstration of the wealth of the landowner whose property it surveys. This is a relatively late example of such a map, showing the holdings of Margaret Bonnell in the Suffolk countryside in eastern England, a little way east of Lavenham. As is usual with such maps, the Bonnell holdings are set out in considerable detail. The surveyor, Isaac Causton, emphasizes the scientific nature of his work by including the two figures of Algebra and Geometry, separated by a large pair of dividers. A dense grid covers the map, and is geared to the figures running from top to bottom and from left to right. The three large tables set out the fields leased by three farmers: Richard Death, John Jacob and John Woods. The table for the last is in the top right, and begins with the field called 'Colliers'. It lists its size in 'acres, roods and perches', and gives its location at '50' (along the top) and '13' (along the side). Many of the fields have evocative names, such as 'Turtles', and here and there some buildings are shown. This map is remarkably elaborate in its presentation, and must be Causton's masterpiece. All the same, he no doubt made it in a thoroughly traditional way, using a compass and chains, and perhaps a plane table.

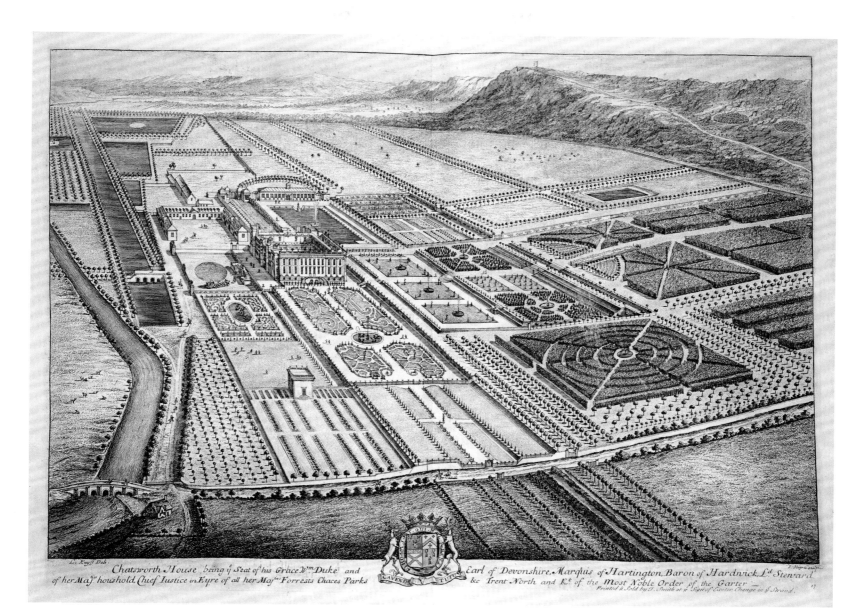

Chatsworth House being y Seat of his Grace W.m Duke and ... Earl of Devonshire, Marquis of Hartington, Baron of Hardwick, L.d Steward of her Maj.ys houshold, Chief Iustice in Eyre of all her Maj.ties Forrests Chaces Parks &c. Trent North and K.t of the Most Noble Order of the Garter

Chatsworth House | 1699 | Leonard Knyff and Johannes Kip

Engraving. 46.3 × 57.8 cm / 18¼ × 22¾ in. Private collection

This bird's-eye view of the garden at Chatsworth in Derbyshire, the seat of the Cavendish family (the dukes of Devonshire), captures the zenith of baroque formality in England from the Continent. The first duke of Devonshire enlarged the house in the neo-classical style near the end of the seventeenth century, and called in the most fashionable garden designers of the day – George London and Henry Wise of the Brompton Park Nursery

in London – to enlarge and restyle the garden. The new gardens were laid out in a Dutch baroque style with *parterres de broderie* - patterned ornamental flower beds - in front of the house and climbing the hillside above the house geometric compartments containing water features, statues and topiary, a bowling green, and ornamental 'wilderness' groves of trees and avenues leading out into the surrounding countryside. This plate showing

the still-unfinished house and garden was published in 1707 by a Dutch pair – the artist Leonard Knyff and the engraver Johannes Kip – in *Britannia Illustrata: Or Views of Several of the Queens Palaces, as Also of the Principal seats of the Nobility and Gentry of Great Britain, Curiously Engraven on 80 Copper Plates*, which is arguably the most significant English topographical publication of the eighteenth century.

A Map of the Coast of Cornwall and Devon | 1539–40 | Unknown

Pigments on vellum. Four sheets, overall 79.4 × 334 cm / 31¼ × 131½ in. British Library, London

Few rulers have had as much reason to fear their enemies as King Henry VIII, whose chief minister Thomas Cromwell commissioned local people to survey the defences along England's south coast. In London, their sketches and letters were used to create the roll map of the coast from Land's End to Exeter of which this is a detail. Henry's territorial ambitions in France, his suspicion of the Low Countries and his worsening relations with Scotland laid his country open to attack or invasion. His declaration in 1543 allowing unrestricted private warfare at sea further provoked the French, who in 1545 landed troops on the Isle of Wight and brought a fleet into the Solent. The Holy Roman Emperor Charles V also threatened to invade from France. The map, which includes the important naval base of Plymouth, home to such English sea heroes as Sir Francis Drake, is one of the earliest existing charts made for both navigational and defence use. It shows from an invader's point of view possible landing sites, with practical information about the state of existing sea-forts and weak spots where additional forts should be built. The features for which a seaman would need to keep a lookout have been exaggerated, widened and foreshortened to make them more easily identifiable, giving the view its charm.

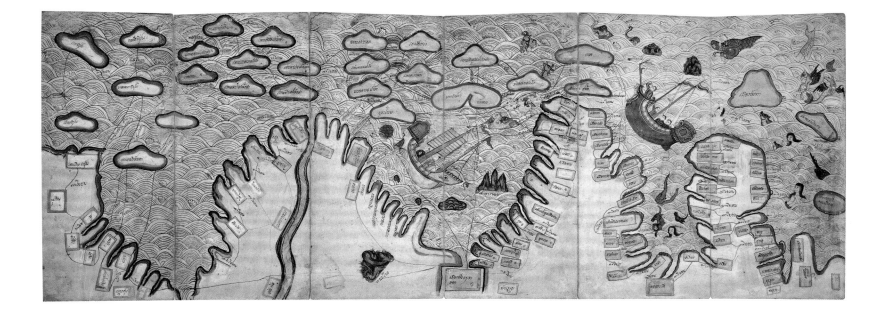

Asia from the Arabian Sea to Korea and Japan | 1776 | Unknown

Manuscript on paper. 51.8 × 320 cm / 20⅓ in × 10 ft 6 in. Museum für Islamische Kunst, Berlin

This beautiful map covers six panels of the *Trai phum* (Story of Three Worlds), a Thai treatise on the shape of the universe. The billowing shapes with blue-green outlines that rise from the bottom of the map are the peninsulas of Asia – the map is orientated broadly with south at the top and east to the right, although the orientation varies in different places – from India on the right and Korea on the left. Above and to the left are the island groups of the Indian and South China Sea. While the mainland has some detail – cities and provinces are named along the coasts and within Thailand – many of the islands are absolutely identical. They are also coloured yellow, reflecting the fact that the islands of Southeast Asia were known in ancient India as the islands of gold. Although the map shows places linked by thin ochre lines marked with distances, there is no suggestion that it was actually intended for navigation (its size alone would make it impractical). Instead, it probably reflects a Chinese or other Asian original, although the appearance of a European sailing ship and a Chinese junk – the map is also decorated with mermaids and sea creatures – is a symbolic representation of the contacts with both east and west that were altering Thai views of the world at the time.

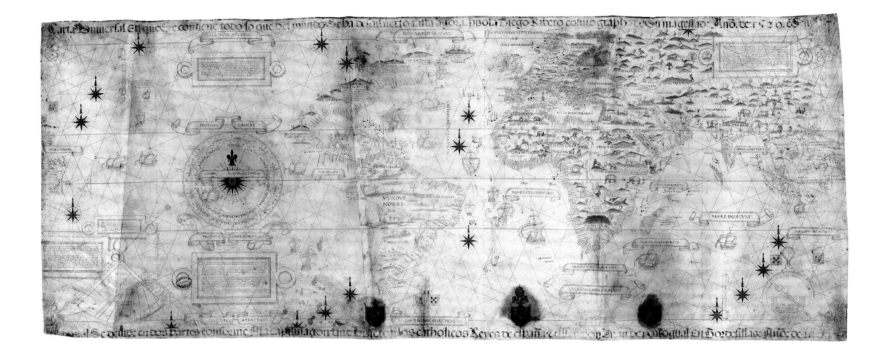

Universal Chart | 1529 | Diogo Ribeiro

Ink and pigments on parchment. 85 × 205 cm / 33 × 81 in. Biblioteca Apostolica Vaticana, Vatican City

This map, drawn in 1529 by the Portuguese-born Diogo Ribeiro (known in Spain as Diego Ribero), depicts a Spanish empire that might have been. After Christopher Columbus's discoveries in 1492, Spain and Portugal divided the 'New World' between them in the Treaty of Tordesillas (1494). The arrangement lasted until the 1520s, when both nations reached the valuable Spice Islands, or Moluccas, of Indonesia. Emperor Charles V,

needing money for his European wars, gave up Spain's claim in return for cash, and in April 1529 the Treaty of Zaragoza placed the Spice Islands in the Portuguese half of the world. Ribeiro's world map, made the same year, shows the Moluccas still in the Spanish sphere of influence, and may have been made before the treaty. As royal cosmographer, Ribeiro was responsible for updating the *Padrón Real* (or *Padrón General*), the standard

world map. He was also an instrument-maker, and the map depicts an astrolabe and a quadrant with notes on navigational methods. It is richly decorated with mountains, trees, cities, native peoples, birds and animals. The seventeen ships sailing around the world evoke the Magellan-Elcano circumnavigation of 1519–22, reports from which influenced the realistic width of the Pacific Ocean that Ribeiro shows.

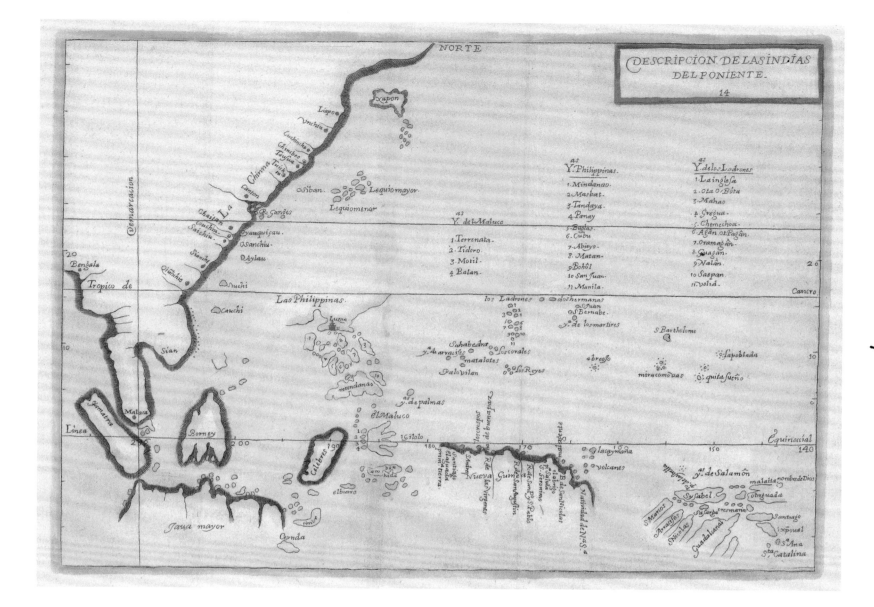

Description of the East Indies | 1601 | Antonio de Herrera y Tordesillas

Hand-coloured engraving. 20 × 28 cm / 7¾ × 11 in. Princeton University, New Jersey

This is the earliest map to name all the principal islands of the Philippine archipelago, first visited by Ferdinand Magellan in 1521 (he was killed there). But the map's main interest is probably not the islands but the ruled vertical line on the left, labelled 'Demarcacion'. It indicates the division agreed by Spain and Portugal in order to apportion the new lands being discovered by their respective explorers. The Treaty of Tordesillas of 1494 drew a line

of demarcation along a meridian 370 leagues (1907 kilometres / 1,185 miles) west of the Cape Verde islands. Any lands falling to the east of the line belonged to Portugal; those to the west were Spain's. The agreement held until both the Portuguese and the Spanish reached the Spice Islands. It was then that a second line of demarcation was negotiated (the anti-meridian) in the Treaty of Zaragoza of 1529, some 1,653 kilometres (1,027 miles)

east of the Moluccas. The vertical line on the map should have been much further to the east – near the eastern tip of Hokkaido, Japan's northernmost island. But the geographers who drew up maps like this one – based on a 1575 map by the Spanish court geographer Juan López de Velasco – moved the line to support the claim of their monarch, in this case the king of Spain, to the detriment of the Portuguese ruler.

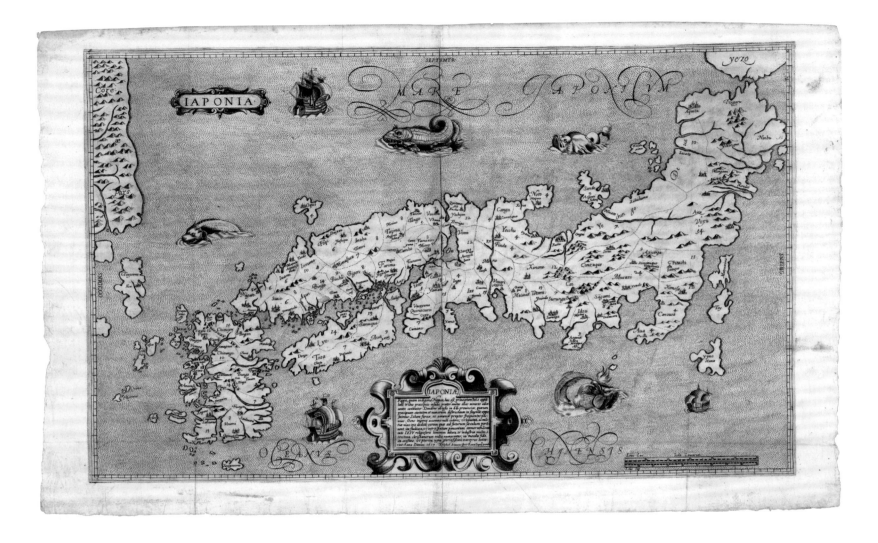

Iaponia (map of Japan) | 1617 | Ignacio Moreira and Christophoro Blancus

Engraving. 42 × 66.5 cm / 16½ × 26⅛ in. Private collection

When it was created, this beautifully engraved map was the most accurate Western cartographic representation of Japan. In terms of the orientation of the Japanese mainland, the placement and proportions of the islands of Kyushu and Shikoku in relation to it and the inclusion of the island of Yezo (Hokkaido) for the first time, the map represented significant improvements on earlier maps. It was also the first map to name the sixty-six provinces of Japan, and contains twice as many place names as previous maps; but it appears to be a proof copy, as the latitude and longitude numbers are absent. The map may have been intended for inclusion in a Jesuit history of Christianity in Japan, but by the time it was ready the Japanese authorities were expelling Christians from the country and the Jesuit influence was collapsing. The map seems to have been put aside, and remained lost until it was rediscovered in 1985. Only one copy is known to exist. The map's cartography has been traced to Ignacio Moreira, a Portuguese map-maker who visited Japan in 1590–92, but it was engraved by Christophoro Blancus (Christophe Blanc), a French artist active in Milan and Rome at the end of the sixteenth century who was known for his works on religious themes rather than for his cartography.

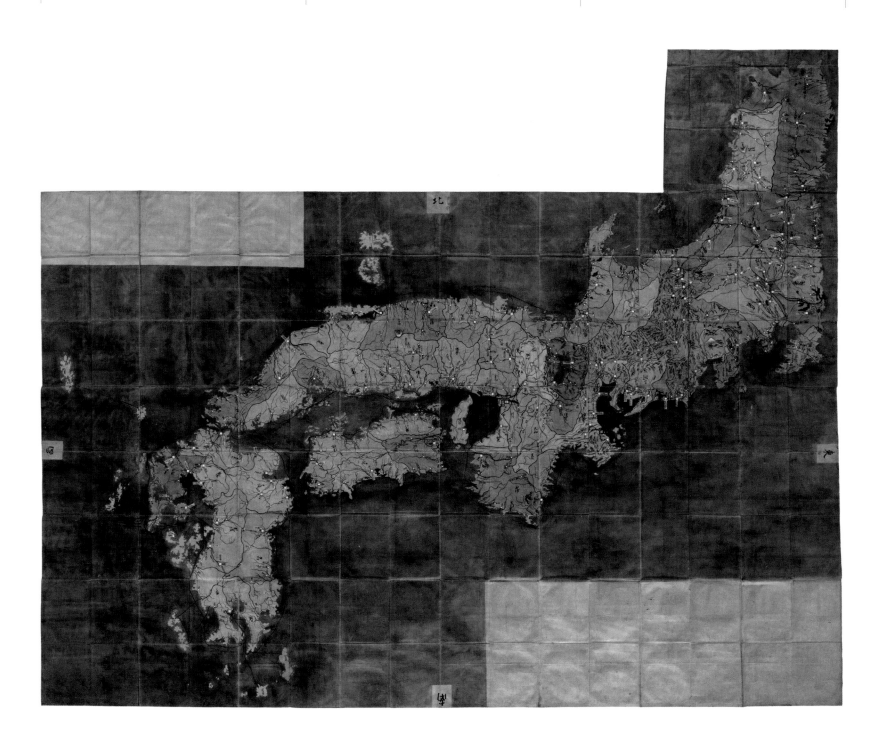

Keicho Map of Japan | c.1653 | Unknown

Manuscript map. 370 × 434 cm / 145⅝ × 170⅞ in. National Diet Library, Tokyo

In early seventeenth-century Japan, this massive map would have been a novelty, since there were few representations of the whole nation. Users would unfold the map on the floor and kneel around it, rotating it to gain new viewpoints. The map's scope – it depicts three of the four main Japanese islands (Honshu, Shikoku and Kyushu) – reflected both a shift in cartographic strategy and the politics of the newly established Tokugawa shogunate.

The Edo Period (1603–1868) established by the shogunate was a time of stability, contact with Europe and the application of Western mapping techniques. The shoguns sought accurately to define the shape of the Japanese archipelago and ordered the first official map of Japan in 1605, a feat that was completed in 1639. This earlier version reflects the shogunate's portrayal of a holistic country that in reality was divided by differences of region,

administration, class and status. Rather than abundant village and town names, the colour scheme makes the provinces dominant, followed by the roads connecting the castle towns (white rectangles) and post stations (white circles). This portrayal of Japan – impressive in its size, scope and representational simplicity – was widely copied in commercial publications, helping to spread the shogunate's vision of national unity.

King Njoya's Survey Map of Bamum | *c.*1920 | Ibrahim Mbouombouo Njoya

Ink and crayon on paper. 96 × 87.5 cm / 3 ft 1¾ × 2 ft 10½ in. Musée d'Ethnographie, Geneva

There is no point in trying to read the labels of this map of the Kingdom of Bamum, a precolonial state based in what is now northwestern Cameroon. They are written in the Bamum script, invented by King Ibrahim Mbouombouo Njoya at the end of the nineteenth century, initially as a series of pictographs but later modified to become a partially alphabetic writing system. The first books and documents to use the script were printed in 1918 but it fell into disuse during the king's life and disappeared shortly after his death in 1933. This map comes from a survey of his kingdom that Njoya produced largely in an attempt to legitimize his kingdom as an actual geographic entity and to confirm his claim to sovereignty in the face of European colonial rule in the region (Bamum had become part of German Cameroon since 1884). The map combines Bamum script, symbolism and iconography with traditional European forms of cartography and surveying methods, but differs from European maps in being orientated with south at the top and in lacking any system of latitude and longitude that would allow it to be placed into a larger geographical context. Njoya's royal ambitions were untimately as unsuccessful as his script. Bamum passed to France in 1918 and the king was deposed in 1923.

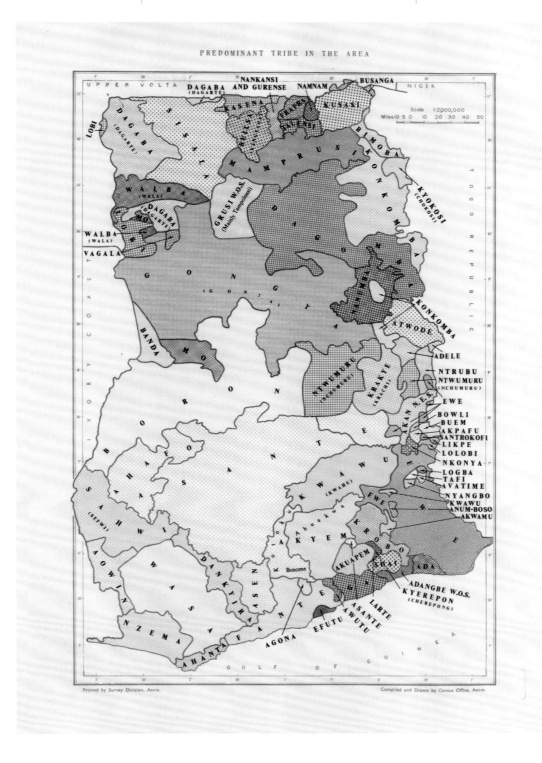

Printed by Survey Division, Accra.   Compiled and Drawn by Census Office, Accra.

Predominent Tribe in the Area (Ghana) | 1966 | Ghana Census Office

Printed paper. 36 × 24 cm 14 × 9½ in. Library of Congress, Washington, DC

One of the most common governmental uses of cartography is to chart population distribution. The task took on a certain urgency during the decolonization of Africa from the 1950s onwards, as independent states were created that sometimes cut across traditional tribal homelands or incorporated citizens from many tribal groups. This map was produced by the Ghana Census Office nearly a decade after Ghana became an independent country in 1957 – the first in Africa – to show the dominant tribes in different regions, although the divisions were never quite as clear-cut as the map's lines suggest. The map draws on information from the new country's first official census, in 1960, and colour-codes peoples according to Ghana's three main language families: Kwa (greens), Mande (blues) and Gur (browns). Like many other African states, Ghana has numerous different languages – up to sixty-nine – of which the most widely spoken is Akan, from the Kwa family. The greatest linguistic diversity appears around Lake Volta and near the border with Togo in the east. In the same year the map was drawn a military coup overthrew Ghana's first prime minister, Kwame Nkrumah, and began a long period of military rule.

Carta Marina | 1539 | Olaus Magnus

Woodcut. 125 × 170 cm / 49¼ × 67 in. Uppsala University Library

The Swedish clergyman and historian Olaus Magnus clearly had an active imagination. Although the importance of his Carta Marina – Latin for 'sea chart' – rests on the fact that it is the first detailed map of Scandinavia to feature place names, it is equally remarkable for its decoration. More than one hundred illustrations summarize the culture, ethnography and myth of northern Europe. Each kingdom is marked by a seated monarch holding a sceptre and orb, together with his coats of arms. The sea is populated by monsters harrying galleons, a reminder of a lingering European belief not only in the perils of sea travel but also in mythical creatures such as dragons and unicorns. Magnus identifies the monsters in the key as if they were real. One monster has been caught and is being dismembered by Faroe Islanders. Much of the southern coast of the Baltic Sea and the gulfs of Finland and Bothnia are frozen and covered with horses pulling sleighs, men skiing and Finns fighting Russians. On land, reindeers pull sleighs and are milked, knights battle with bulls and three men throw snowballs. Natural resources are shown, with a circle denoting iron deposits, a square copper and a rectangle silver. Such remarkable detail took Magnus nearly twelve years: he completed his map in Rome in 1539.

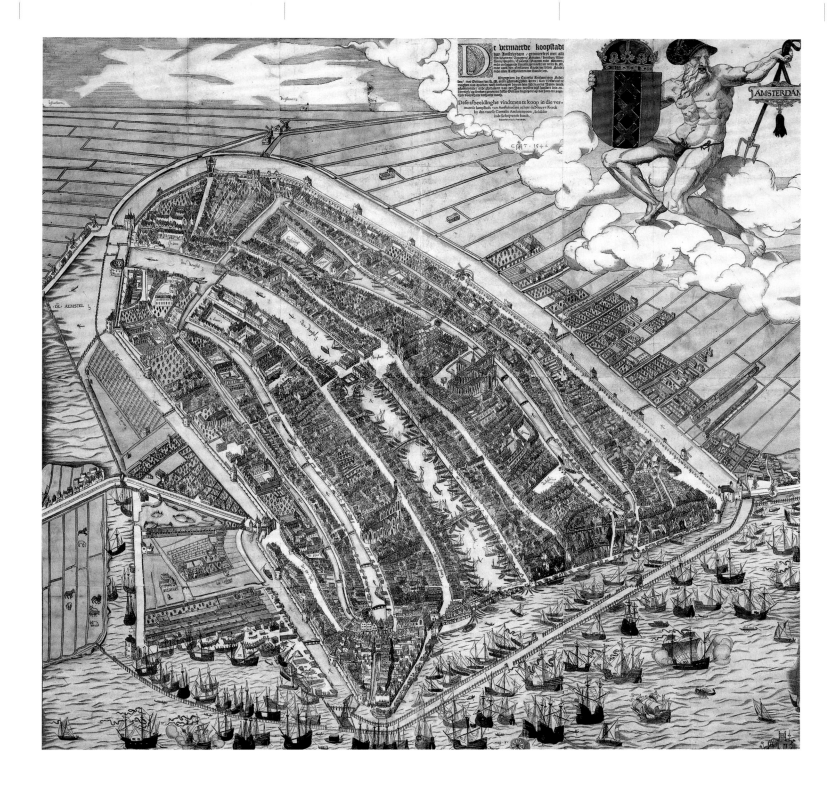

Map of Amsterdam | 1544 | Cornelis Anthonisz

Hand-coloured woodcut. 100.7 × 109.3 cm / 39⅝ × 43 in. Rijksmuseum, Amsterdam

When this map of Amsterdam was drawn, the Dutch were embarking on a golden age that would take their explorers to the far side of the Earth, create lucrative trade monopolies with Asia and make them dominant in the European economy. Dutch expansion was based on hard work and order at home and maritime power abroad, and both are evident in this first printed plan of Amsterdam. The city and its surrounding fields are laid out with geometrical precision, while vessels are shown being unloaded in the central canal – now an avenue named the Damrak – and a large flotilla sails in calm waters in the foreground. The city's close connection with the ocean is underlined by a large figure of Neptune, god of the sea, bearing a trident and with the arms of Amsterdam resting on his leg. Drawn from an imaginary vantage point high above the harbour, looking south, the map shows the city as it was in 1544, before the construction of an outer semicircle of canals. Cornelis Anthonisz. depicts Amsterdam as a city of canals – the 'Venice of the North' – in a conscious echo of the famous plan of the Italian city by Jacopo de' Barbari in 1500 (see p.36), a fact that would undoubtedly have pleased the council of Amsterdam, which commissioned it as an expression of civic pride.

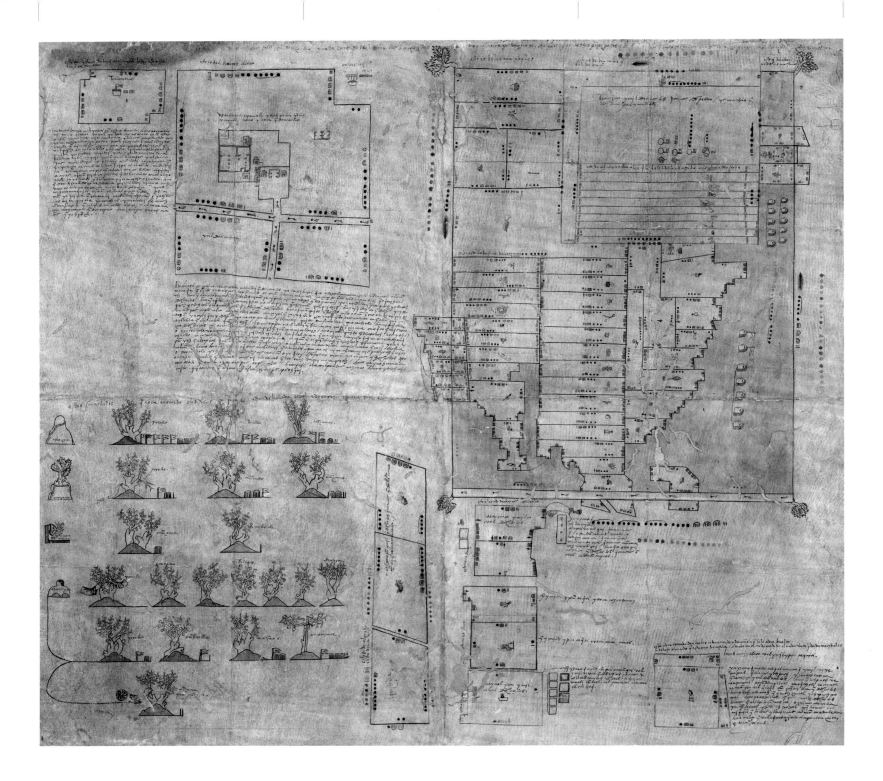

The Oztoticpac Lands Map | c.1540 | Unknown

Red and black ink on amatl paper. 76 × 84 cm / 30 × 33 in. Library of Congress, Washington, DC

This is one of the earliest-surviving indigenous pictorial documents created after the Spanish conquest of Mexico in 1521, and incorporates maps, plans, views, glyphs – pictorial symbols – and texts in both Spanish and the Aztec language, Nahuatl. It relates to a lawsuit concerning the estate of Don Carlos Ometochtzin Chichimecatecatl, an Aztec lord, who was executed by the Spanish for heresy in 1539. The document was commissioned by

Don Carlos's half-brother, Antonio Pimentel Tlahuilotzin, governor of Texcoco, to support the claim that the lands belonged to Don Carlos's family rather than to him personally. The document is arranged in four quadrants. The map portions are cadastral maps showing the locations, boundaries and owners of plots of land, including a plan of several houses and maps of more than seventy-five plots and fields differentiated between private, rented,

common, peasant and temple land. Twenty trees show the grafting of European pears, pomegranates, apricots, quinces, peaches and apples from Spain onto local apple and cherry trees. Although the map seems simple, it uses a complex scheme of indigenous features, such as two local measurement systems alongside the Spanish system, glyphs for place names, former and present ownerships and dynastic genealogies.

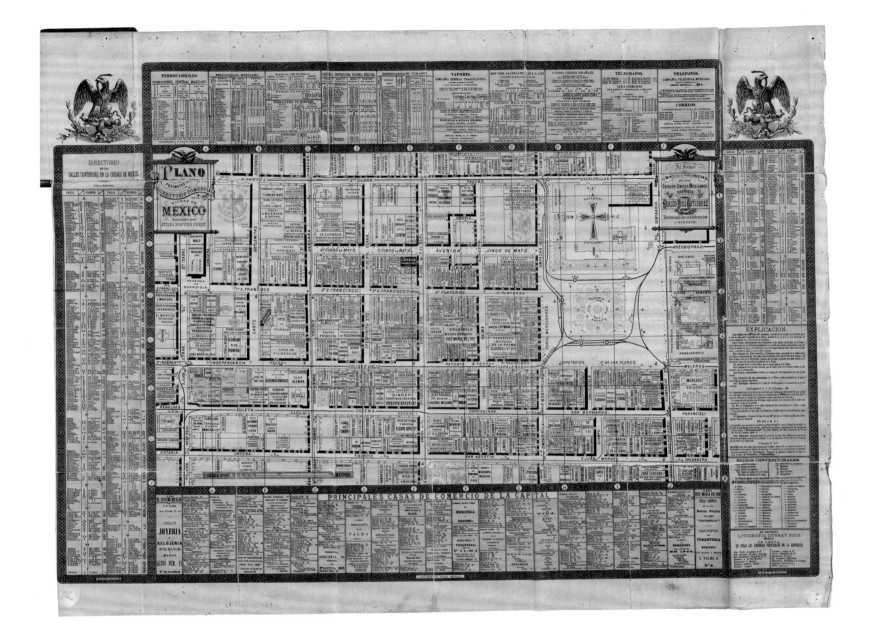

Map and Commercial Directory of Central Mexico City | 1883 | Julio Popper Ferry

Lithograph. 61 × 85 cm / 24 × 33½ in. Private collection

The publisher Julio Popper Ferry was a businessman, and his monetary focus is evident in the practical information he provides in the margins of his maps for businesses (he produced a similar map of New Orleans): railway timetables, street indexes and information about markets. The map itself depicts in detail the commercial occupants of buildings to the west of the heart of Mexico City's cultural life, its main plaza, the Zócalo. The space was once the ceremonial centre of the Aztec city of Tenochtitlán (see p.77). By 1883 the area had been partially converted to a streetcar station but only eight years later the tramlines of the area were paved over. The image is overlaid with a red grid that makes it easy to find information. It was smartly folded into brown leather covers that allowed it to fit into a pocket. Popper Ferry was a Jewish Romanian engineer who travelled extensively, usually in search of gold. He found it, shortly after making this map, in Tierra del Fuego. The discovery turned out to be the beginning of the end of his brief thirty-five year life. Once he found gold, he raised his own army to protect it and was partly responsible for the genocide of the local indigenous people, the Selk'nam. Popper made many enemies – one of whom allegedly fatally poisoned him in 1893.

Forma Urbis Romae | 203–211 AD | Unknown

Marble. 72 × 73 × 7 cm / 28⅓ × 28⅔ × 2¾ in. Musei Capitolini, Rome

During the reign of the Emperor Septimus Severus, Roman carvers worked for eight years to create the *Forma Urbis Romae* ('Map of the City of Rome'). Carved on 150 slabs of marble, the detailed plan – which included every public and private building in the city, plus fountains, gardens, columns and memorials – was mounted on the outer wall of a library attached to the Temple of Peace (Templum Pacis). It is not clear how common such expressions of civic pride were in Roman cities, although other large town plans have been identified. What makes this map special is its remarkable size and the skill of the surveyors (*agrimensores*) who compiled the information (the city also had similar paper or papyrus charts). Important buildings are shown somewhat larger than they should be, marked with double outlines and originally highlighted with paint. The first fragments of the map – originally about 18 by 13 metres (59 ft by 42 ft 6 in) – were discovered in 1562 during excavations. About 10–15 per cent of the map has now been recovered in more than 1,186 fragments; the rest may have been used as building material or burned to make lime mortar during the Middle Ages. Although only fragmentary, the map has been important in attempts to reconstruct the layout of ancient Rome.

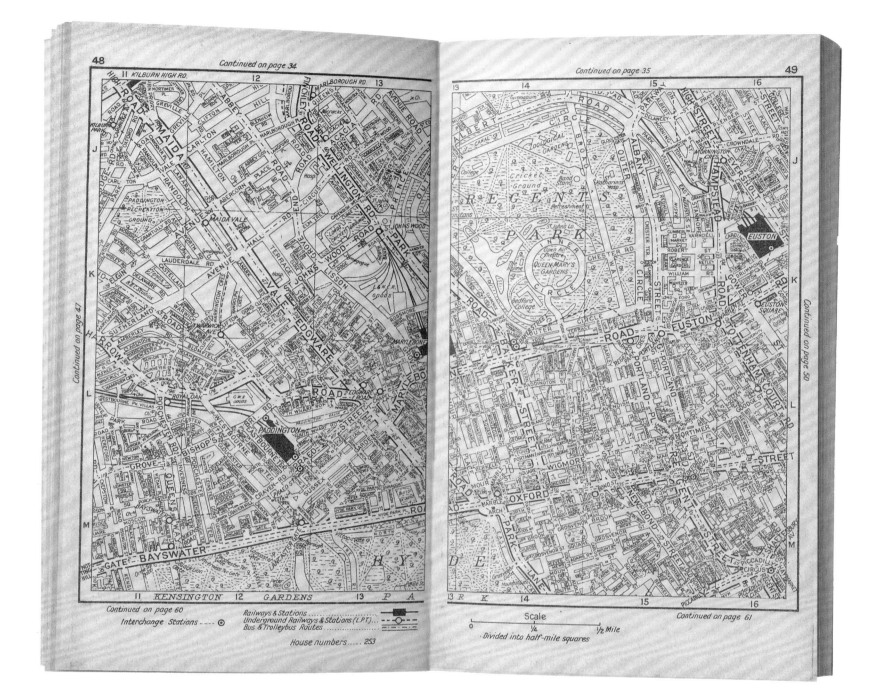

48 Continued on page 34 12 MARLBOROUGH RD. 13 Continued on page 35 14 15 16 49

Continued on page 47

Continued on page 50

Railways & Stations ....
Underground Railways & Stations (L.P.T.) ...
Bus & Trolleybus Routes ....
Interchange Stations ---- ⊙

House numbers..... 253

Continued on page 60

Scale

0   ¼   ½ Mile
Divided into half-mile squares

Continued on page 61

A–Z Atlas and Guide to London and Suburbs | 1936 | Phyllis Pearsall

Printed paper. 18.4 × 10.7 cm / 7¼ × 4¼ in. Private collection

The A to Z is such an institution that it may come as a shock to learn that it was the result of one woman's efforts. Phyllis Pearsall, a painter and writer, created it in 1936 after becoming lost while using an Ordnance Survey map to get to a party. Her subsequent endeavours are possibly the first attempt to generate a citizen-sourced map, and might even be seen as a forerunner of the OpenStreetmap movement. Pearsall decided to map London, an undertaking that involved walking more than 4,830 kilometres (3,000 miles), mapping over 23,000 streets as she went. When established publishers rejected her new atlas, she founded the Geographer's Map Company to publish it herself. Pearsall designed, drew and proofread the map with the help of a single draughtsman. Although the map contained hundreds of combinations of type – bold, italics, spacing of characters, sans serif, reversed type, size, rotation, upper and lower case – the design of the typography is meticulous. The modern version uses orange for primary routes, yellow for secondary and white for local. The pocket size of the original book was perfect for navigation – this is a facsimile – and, despite being crammed with detail, the atlas is extremely well structured in graphical terms.

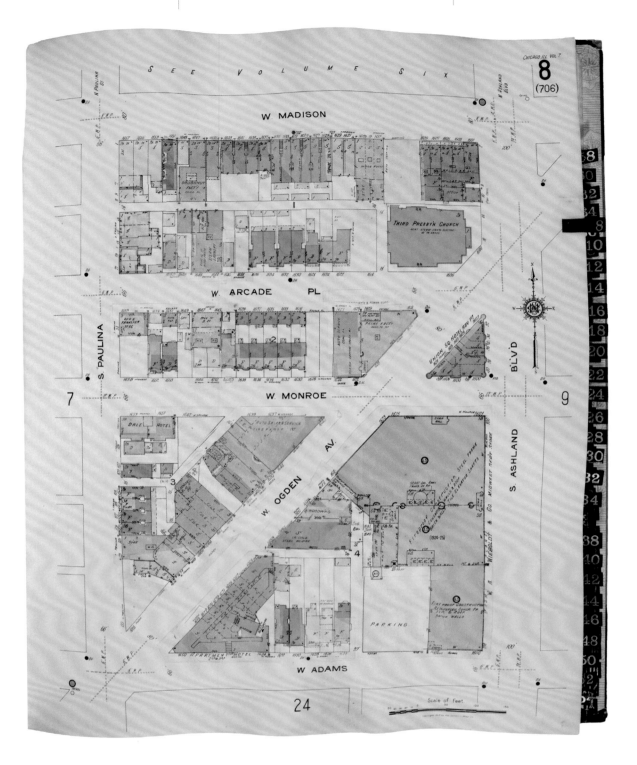

W. MADISON

W. ARCADE PL.

W. MONROE

W. ADAPTS

W. OGDEN AV.

S. PAULINA

BLV'D

S. ASHLAND

THIRD PRESBYN CHURCH

PARKING

DALE HOTEL

Insurance Map of Chicago, Illinois | 1916 | Sanborn Map Company

Printed paper. 64 × 53 cm / 25 × 21 in. Newberry Library, Chicago, Illinois

The Great Chicago Fire in 1871 gave additional impetus to a project that had begun several years earlier: the mapping of American cities for insurance purposes. Over nearly a century and a half, the Sanborn Map Company eventually mapped some 12,000 towns and cities in the United States, Canada and Mexico – including Chicago itself. Construction material, building use and type of heat and energy source were all relevant to assessing the

risk of fire. This older section of Chicago – near where the Great Fire began – included many brick residences (pink), some with stone façades (blue), wood-framed houses and outbuildings (yellow), a stone church (blue) and a 'fireproof' concrete-and-steel department store topped by a water tank. The map also identifies industries including a paint factory, a steam laundry and a 'doughnut factory'. Atlases were purchased by

subscription for a set number of years, during which the publisher supplied updates to be pasted into each page as buildings were built, removed or altered: paste-overs and evidence of former buildings are still visible. It took fifty such volumes to cover the whole of Chicago, where new building codes after the fire mandated brick construction in many areas. This volume, published in 1916, was owned by a real-estate firm.

Chicago, USA | 1931 | Charles Turzak and Henry T. Chapman

Colour lithograph. 58 × 96 cm / 22⅞ × 37¾ in. Private collection

Unlike many maps, this busy and colourful bird's-eye view of Chicago is aimed at people who already know their way around the city. There is no label to indicate the Wrigley Building, for example – just a cartoonish puff claiming, 'Built of 5¢ chewing gum'. As with many of the labels on the map, the reader needs to know the reference already. At the time the map was published, the effects of the Great Depression were already starting to bite – and would grow worse – but the language of the map is defiant and exuberant. An optimistic tone permeates the whole image, from the frequent use of boastful words – 'best', 'largest' and 'fastest' – and the fisherman bragging 'it was that big', to the Carl Sand-burg poem that launched the nickname 'City of the Big Shoulders', which is lettered around the perimeter. Even the convicts approach prison with a spring in their steps – in the same year the notorious Windy City gangster Al Capone was convicted of tax evasion. Despite being so busy, the map is stylistically tidy - the wakes of the boats mirror the grid of the boulevards. Drawings of the major sights are magnified on the map and listed in the legend. The maps features the approaching 1933 Chicago World's Fair, where illustrator Charles Turzak ultimately had a booth selling his woodcuts and watercolours.

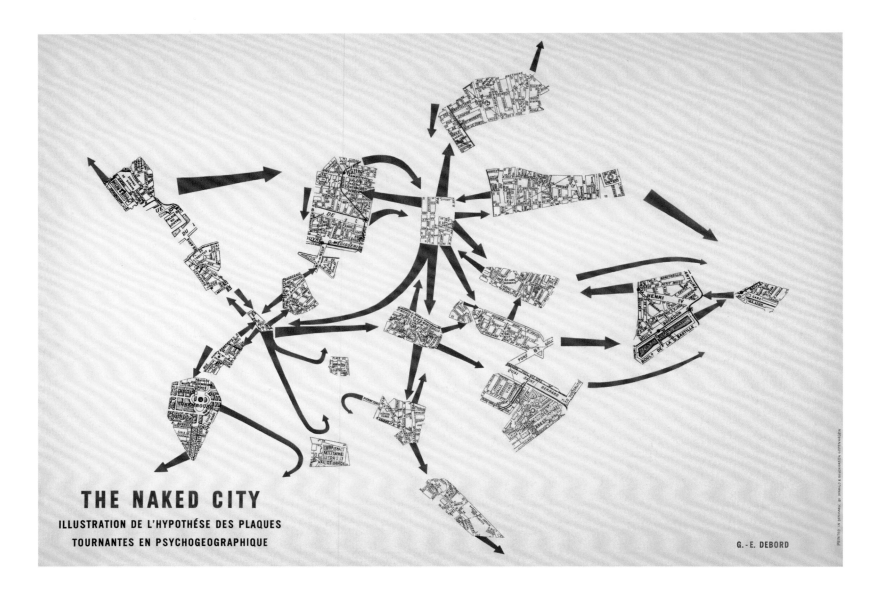

THE NAKED CITY

ILLUSTRATION DE L'HYPOTHÉSE DES PLAQUES
TOURNANTES EN PSYCHOGEOGRAPHIQUE

G.-E. DEBORD

The Naked City | c.1957 | Guy Debord

Printed paper. 33 × 48 cm / 13 × 18⅞ in. Beinecke Rare Book and Manuscript Library, Yale University, New Haven, Connecticut

Guy Debord, the French Marxist theorist and filmmaker, introduced the concept of psychogeography in the 1950s to describe the effects a particular geographic environment had on the emotions, behaviour and well-being of individuals who lived and worked in the spaces from which it was composed. For this map – conceived by Debord and the artist Asger Jorn and named after its inspiration, the US detective film *The* *Naked City* (1948) – Debord cut a tourist map of Paris into nineteen fragments and reassembled it in order to transform the cartographic topography of the city into a social landscape. The spaces between the map sections are filled with red arrows and are meant to reflect the 'mental' or 'emotional' distance between parts of the city. This experiential – as opposed to wayfinding – map was created to emphasize how different it 'felt' to cross the boundaries of each area of the city and to transcend geometric 'distance', which Debord believed was not how a pedestrian experienced urban spaces. Many of the architects and urban planners working in France during the 1950s and 1960s shared Debord's theories about the psychological effects induced by the built and planned environment, and their radical ideas later greatly influenced the design of urban living spaces.

Signs for Strangers | 1982 | Denis Wood

Printed in *Everything Sings: Maps for a Narrative Atlas* by Denis Wood. 76.2 × 76.2 cm / 30 × 30 in. Private collection

Any given place holds an infinite number of things that can be mapped. An individual neighbourhood has streets and houses and parks – all of which we might expect to see on a map. But it also has power lines and Christmas lights and sounds and graffiti and people with their own aspirations, and all this can also be shown cartographically if we simply take the trouble to collect the information. Here, the US artist and academic Denis Wood shows the many street signs that can be found in his neighbourhood of Boylan Heights in Raleigh, North Carolina. As Wood points out, the signs are mostly for outsiders passing through, and the patterns reveal the interface between locals and strangers. This map is published alongside many other views of Boylan Heights in an atlas by Wood, *Everything Sings: Maps for a Narrative Atlas.* He portrays everything from where jack-o-lanterns are found on Halloween to the route the postman takes through the neighbourhood. Wood shows us a place with a depth and humanity that map-makers rarely try to achieve. Maps need not be sterile records of land ownership and transportation; they can help us understand life in places to which we've never been.

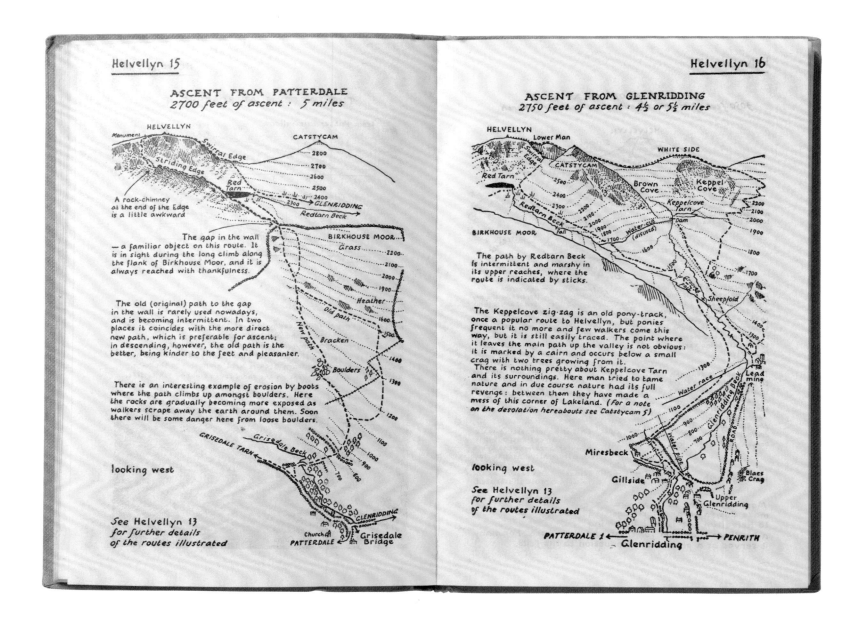

Helvellyn | 1966 | Alfred Wainwright

Printed in *A Pictorial Guide to the Lakeland Fells*, volume 7, *The Western Fells* (1966) by Alfred Wainwright. 17.7 × 12 cm / 7 × 4¾ in (each page). Private collection

It took the British writer and walker Alfred Wainwright thirteen years to complete the seven volumes of the *Pictorial Guide to the Lakeland Fells*, his most renowned work. The books all included Wainwright's handwritten manuscripts, hand-drawn maps and original illustrations, and their unique marriage of art, cartography and the written word lends a sense of romance to the long-distance footpaths Wainwright walked and recorded in such an intensely personal way. The maps bring to life both the beauty of the Lakeland landscape of northern England and its remoteness. They appear simple, yet contain a depth of information that could be acquired only by someone who had walked every mile of the paths. The ascent maps are planimetric in the foreground and morph to become perspective in the distance, showing natural features and the climb ahead. Contours both provide useful information and add to the depth of illustration. The hand-drawn approach helps create a sense of authenticity that makes the maps far more than a personal perspective – these are maps that can be relied upon for navigation halfway up a fell. Planimetric detail is marked and pictorial symbols such as trees are also used to good effect, while small inset maps bring clarity to specific parts of a route.

A SIX DAY WALK OVER ALL ROADS, LANES AND DOUBLE TRACKS INSIDE
A SIX MILE WIDE CIRCLE CENTRED ON THE GIANT OF CERNE ABBAS.

DORSET 1975

Cerne Abbas Walk | 1975 | Richard Long

Ink, photograph and printed map. 68.7 × 69.7 cm / 27 × 27½ in. Tate, London

In 1975 the British Land Art pioneer Richard Long set out to walk along all the roads, lanes and cart tracks within a 4.83-kilometre (3-mile) radius of the Cerne Giant, a 55-metre (180-foot) male figure carved into a chalk hillside in Dorset in southern England. Long traced his route in ink on a standard road map, creating a distinct circle that echoes the importance of circles in the rituals and cosmology of such prehistoric societies thought to have created the chalk figure or constructed Britain's many standing stone circles. Long accompanied the map with a photograph of the area's verdant trees and gently rolling hills. The archetypally picturesque vista might seem to be little changed since ancient times, yet the map reveals a different picture: a tight and tangled web of human interventions carved into the natural landscape in the form of roads and paths dissecting the countryside in all directions. The six-day walk around the figure – particularly famous as a fertility symbol – took Long six days and was one of a number of carefully planned rural walks he made in Britain and abroad in the early 1970s, about which he produced sculptures and works-on-paper.

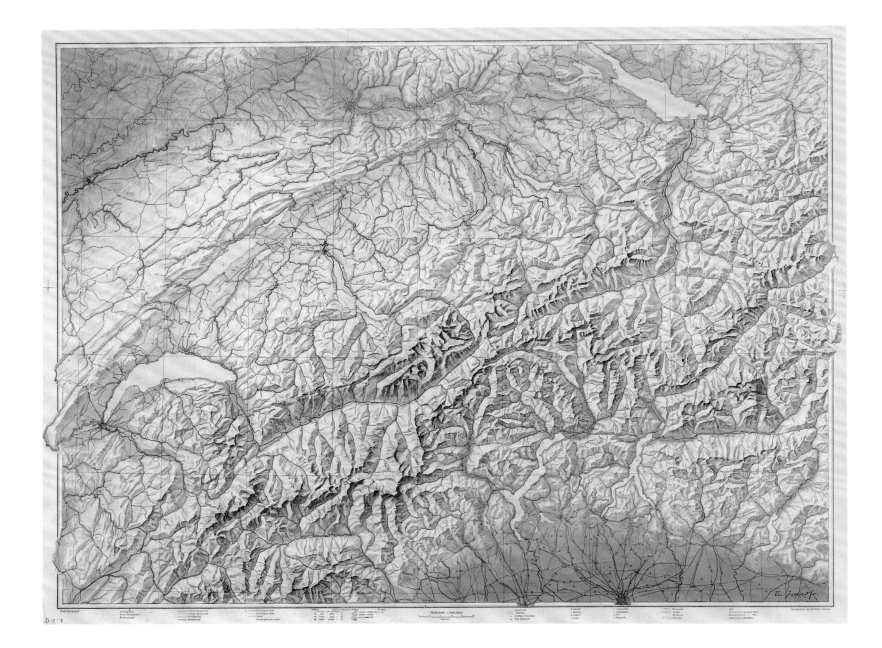

School Map of Switzerland | 1924 | Eduard Imhof

Print with watercolour. 55 × 73 cm / 21½ × 28¾ in. ETH-Bibliothek, Zurich

It should probably come as no surprise that Swiss cartographers have long been at the forefront of terrain representation, given the mountainous nature of their country. The peak of their art in the twentieth century was represented by the work of Eduard Imhof. Imhof was a master of shaded relief, a way of painting or drawing light and dark areas on a map in order to convey a sense of depth. Imhof's skillful shading gives a sense that the mountains are popping up out of the page, as though we were floating a few miles above the surface, looking down. There is no need to interpret contour lines or elevation tints; the mountains are simply *there*. Using shaded relief requires an artist's sensibilities. Decisions must be made about which details to illustrate and which to smooth, which to emphasize and which to leave in the background. Today, shaded relief is frequently carried out by automated algorithms, but these decisions are difficult for computers and the results often lack the clarity that Imhof and other artists brought to their maps. It may be possible to create shaded relief much faster with computers, but works such as Imhof's remain the gold standard.

Greater Yellowstone, Mammoth Hot Springs, Old Faithful, Yellowstone Lake, Grand Teton — the far-reaching Greater Yellowstone area reverberates with places symbolizing the American West. Today federal land agencies and other groups work together to protect this magnificent natural habitat of the grizzly bear, elk, bison, trumpeter swan, and other wildlife.

Yellowstone National Park / Wyoming, Montana, and Idaho
Grand Teton National Park / Wyoming

National Park Service
U.S. Department of the Interior

Greater Yellowstone | 1962 | Heinrich C. Berann

Printed paper. 74 × 100 cm / 29 × 39½ in. Private collection

This remarkable view of one of North America's natural treasures was created by the Austrian Heinrich C. Berann, who has a reasonable claim to be seen as the father of panoramic mapping. Berann applied his training as an artist to maps after winning a competition for a panorama of a new mountain pass road in Austria in 1934. The map of Yellowstone – one of four such works for the United States National Park Service – represents Berann at the height of his abilities in its meticulous attention to detail, saturated colours and curved projection, which mimics an exaggerated view from an aeroplane. The almost planimetric foreground curves away to a horizon depicting mountains in profile. This creates a sense of place well-suited to a tourist map, which is designed to encourage visitors. Berann also developed a trademark way of rendering cloudscapes, which is also unlikely to be seen in nature. In this way, Berann's panoramas can be seen as being hideously distorted in scale and representation, but if the art of cartography is to capture a landscape and communicate something of its beauty, the distortions do their job well. This may not be a map in a traditional sense, but it is an expert way of laying out the features of a landscape, with rich colours and a sense of drama that mimics the landscape itself.

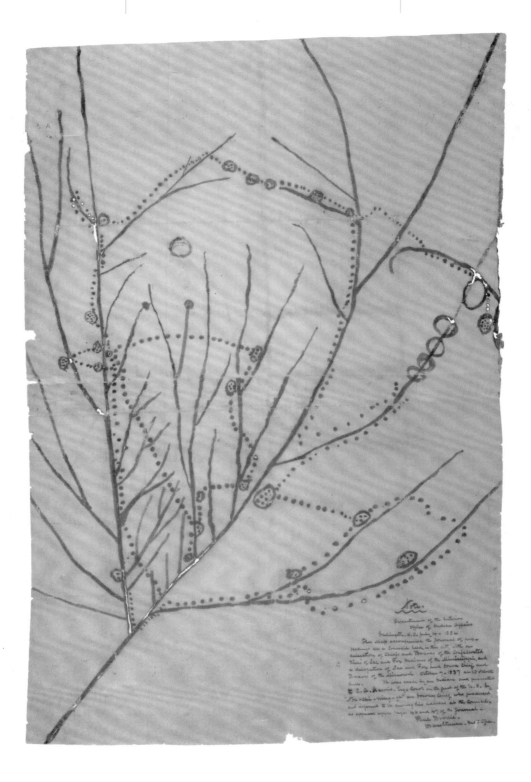

Territory of the Ioway Nation | 1837 | Unknown

Ink on paper. 104.1 × 68.6 cm / 41 × 27 in. National Archives, Washington, DC

Native Americans had their own mapping traditions long before they encountered Europeans, but the westward expansion of the United States in the early nineteenth century made it more urgent for Indigenous Peoples to define their own territory. As the United States spread beyond the Appalachian Mountains and Ohio Valley, government and settlers attempted to persuade Native People to cede tracts of land. This map of the area between the Upper Mississippi and Missouri rivers, which the Ioway people have long known as their homeland - now also known as the US state of Iowa - was drawn to clarify Ioway Nation territory, and to prevent members of nearby Sac and Fox Nations from negotiating away the lands the Ioway claimed as their own. This map was presented by Chief No-Heart - Na'je Ninge in the Ioway Language - to the US Indian Commissioner in Washington DC in 1837. It is orientated with west at the top, rather than north, as was the European convention, and shows many smaller rivers, lakes, Ioway towns, and travel routes. The linear presentation of the rivers and routes reflects the geometric style characteristic of Native American cartography, yet the distances and locations were precise and correspond well to contemporary maps.

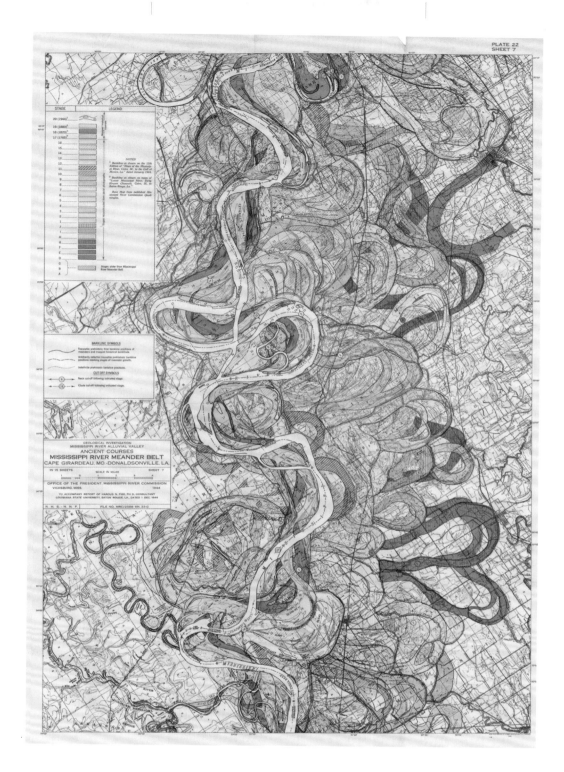

Geological Investigation of the Alluvial Valley of the Lower Mississippi River | 1944 | Harold N. Fisk

Lithograph. 103 × 73.4 cm / 40½ × 28½ in. United States Army Corps of Engineers

The bloom of colours on this map charts the meanders of the Mississippi River, as traced through a legacy of lakes, marshes and layers of silt. Remarkably, the task of tracking the river's history through aerial views and thousands of soil samples and assembling it into a map took Harold Fisk and a small team from the Louisiana Geological Society only three years to complete. The impetus behind such an effort came from the Great Mississippi River Floods of 1927, which devastated much of the Lower Mississippi Valley. Fisk's map was the first step in maintaining a safe and reliable commercial waterway by studying the river's past in order to predict how the force of water might shape its course in the future. Without intervention, the river's course might permanently abandon the dredged channels that took it past cities and ports to the south-east, including New Orleans and Baton Rouge, into a distributary called the Atchafalaya. The United States Army Corps of Engineers eventually used Fisk's map to construct a series of dams, floodways and 'control structures' to prevent a repeat of the floods of 1927. This sheet – one of fifteen – shows one of the wider sections of the river's 'meander belt', colouring centuries of former bends and meanders by estimated date.

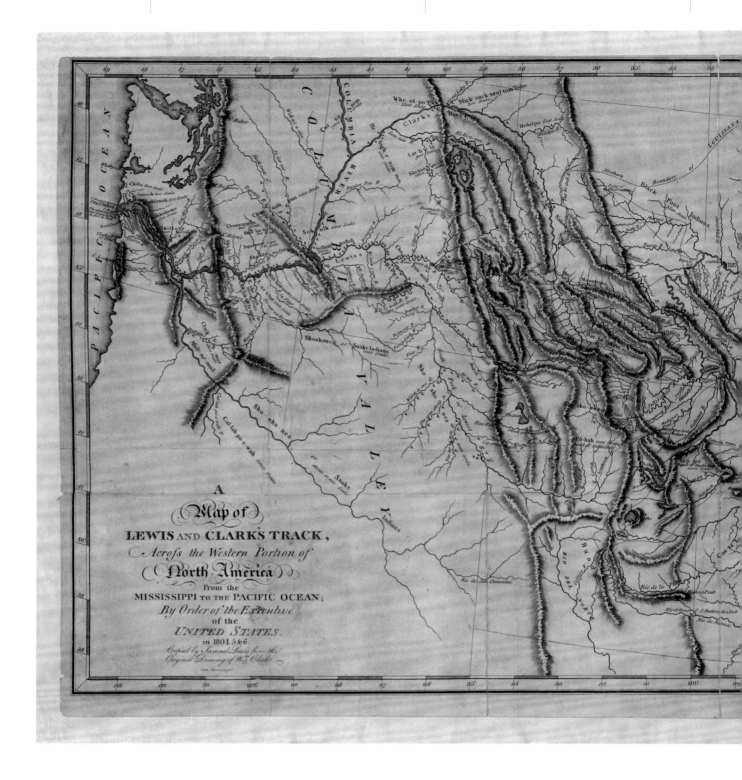

A
Map of
LEWIS AND CLARK'S TRACK,
Across the Western Portion of
North America
From the
MISSISSIPPI TO THE PACIFIC OCEAN;
By Order of the Executive
of the
UNITED STATES,
in 1804. 5. & 6.
Copied by Samuel Lewis from the
Original Drawing of W.ᵐ Clark.

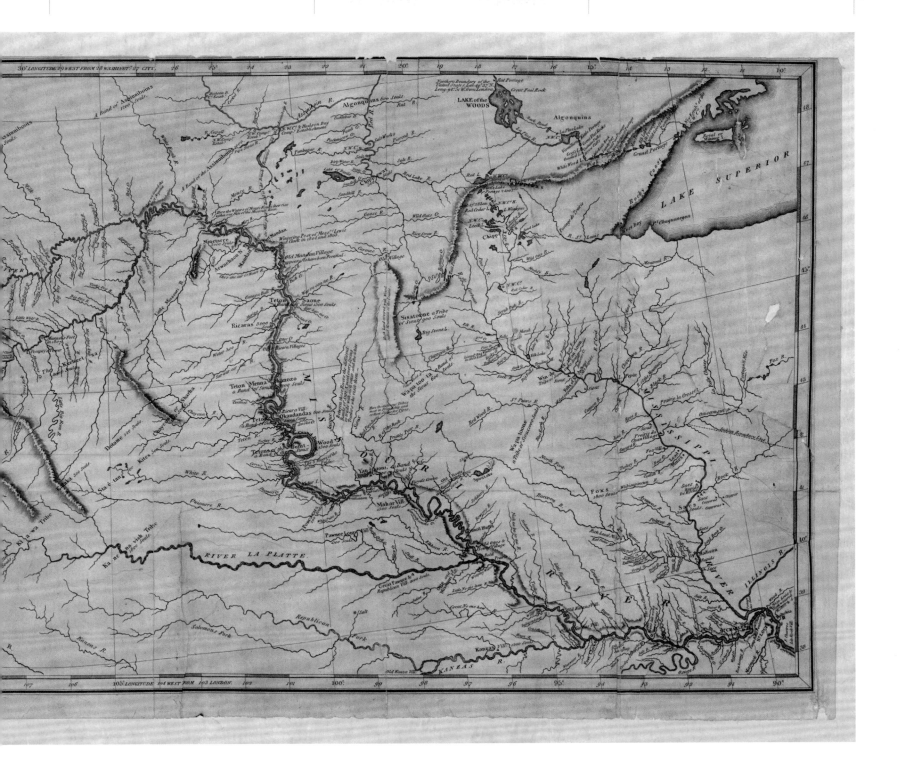

A Map of Lewis and Clark's Track | 1814 | Samuel Lewis

Engraving. 30 × 70 cm / 11¾ × 27½ in. Library of Congress, Washington, DC

When the new president Thomas Jefferson sent his former private secretary Meriwether Lewis and William Clark to explore west of the Mississippi River in 1804, he mused that the uncharted land beyond might be home to volcanoes (which it was) and woolly mammoths (which it was not). This map, drawn by the Philadelphia cartographer Samuel Lewis from Clark's master chart – Clark made more than 137 sketch maps of the expedition that he later incorporated into a map of the whole West – shows the route of the so-called Corps of Discovery along the Missouri River, across the Continental Divide, through the Rocky Mountains and down the Clearwater, Snake and Columbia Rivers to the Pacific coast. The expedition took from May 1804 to November 1805 to reach the Pacific, guided in part by Sacagawea, the Shoshone wife of one of the Corps. While the Corps did not find the hoped-for navigable route across the continent, it helped fill in details of the Rockies and the Columbia River, which was important at a time when the Oregon Territory was disputed by British Canada. The expedition encouraged the creation of the Corps of Topographical Engineers in the US Army, which went on to sponsor regular mapping expeditions to the West, such as those by John C. Frémont (see p.241).

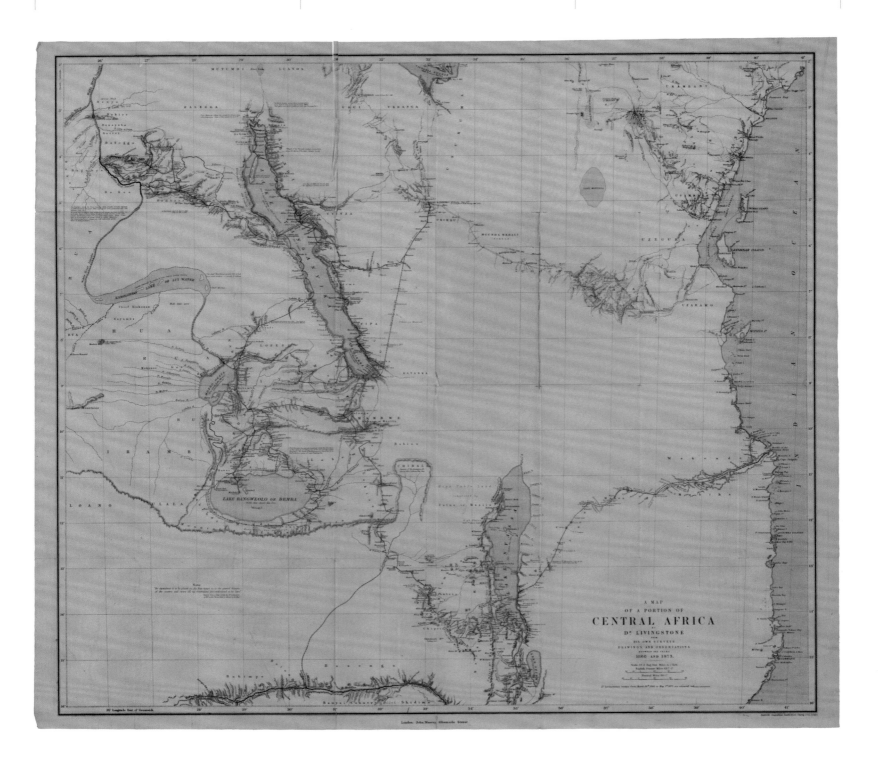

A Map of a Portion of Central Africa | 1866–73 | David Livingstone

Coloured map, mounted on cloth. 72 × 80 cm / 28⅜ × 31½ in. National Library of Scotland, Edinburgh

The Scottish missionary David Livingstone was possibly the most famous of all nineteenth-century explorers, and this map represents the route of his most famous expedition in 1866–73, when he explored the Great Lakes region of Central Africa. When little to nothing was heard from or about Livingstone for years, both the Royal Geographical Society and the *New York Herald* organized expeditions to find him, the latter led by Henry M. Stanley. When Stanley eventually found Livingstone, in 1871 in Ujiji, a remote village on the shore of Lake Tanganyika, he greeted him with the celebrated words: 'Dr Livingstone, I presume?' This map, published by John Murray to accompany Livingstone's diaries, shows many geographical features first recorded by Livingstone, including lakes Tanganyika and Malawi, the Chambeshi River, the headstream of the Congo, the Lualaba River (which Livingstone wrongly took to be the source of the Nile) and lakes Mweru and Bangweulu. When Livingstone died of malaria in 1873, his body and journal were carried over 1,600 kilometres (1,000 miles) by his African attendants, Chuma and Susi, and returned to Britain. The knowledge of his last expedition was thus preserved, and his posthumously published journal – including this map – caused a worldwide sensation.

Kingdom of Ethiopia | 1923 | Unknown

Ink and watercolour on paper. 151 × 136 cm / 59½ × 53½ in. Library of Congress, Washington, DC

This map of Ethiopia, commissioned from the court geographer by the Prince Regent Haile Selassie, is evidence of Selassie's ambitions – for himself and for his country. On 28 September 1923 Selassie secured Ethiopia's entry into the League of Nations, the international body set up after World War I (1914–18). Selassie – a modernizer – needed a new map to reflect his country's new-found international position. Without explicitly citing a source, the court geographer appears to have based the map on the British War Office map of Abyssinia, as Ethiopia was formerly known, of 1918. Selassie's map thus expressed his state's unity and identity by recasting a foreign map in the Ethiopian language, Amharic, and his personal ambitions by placing his own portrait in the map's upper portions, together with that of his consort, Menen Asfaw. At the time of the map's creation, Selassie was effectively the country's administrative ruler while Empress Zewditu actually held the throne. On her death in 1930, however, he would become emperor of Ethiopia – officially 'His Imperial Majesty Haile Selassie I, Conquering Lion of the Tribe of Judah, King of Kings of Ethiopia and Elect of God' – and one of the most influential figures in African history.

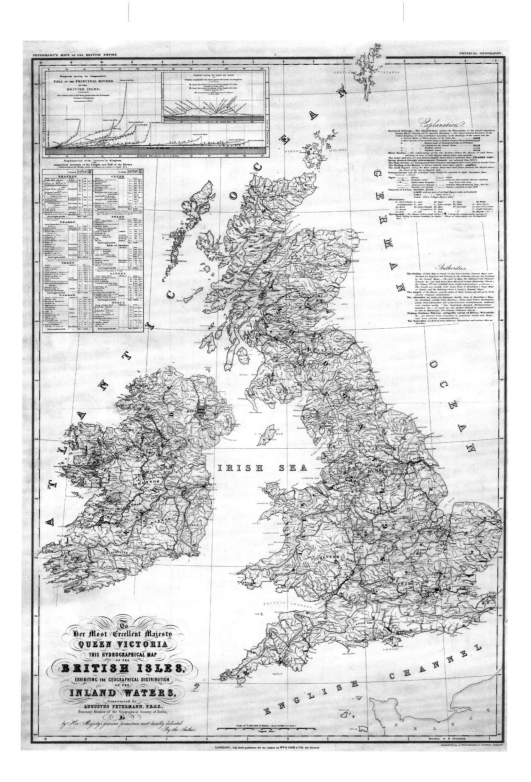

Hydrographical Map of the British Isles | 1849 | Augustus Petermann

Hand-coloured engraving. 81 x 53 cm / 31⅞ x 20⅞ in. Princeton University, New Jersey

This mid-nineteenth-century hydrological map of Britain captures the country at the height of the Industrial Revolution, when its rivers powered factories and mills and, with canals, provided highways for moving manufactured goods. The map presents a remarkable amount of information on rivers, lakes and even ponds; the great watershed boundaries are indicated by different colours and their numbered subdivisions by thinner lines of the

same colour. A table organizes statistical data on each river; a novel diagram displays the comparative falls of the principal rivers, shown in profile; and yet another diagram shows 'Canals remarkable for their great elevation or steepness'. The creator of this tour de force, Augustus Petermann, is part of a great cartographic arc that reached from Alexander von Humboldt (see p.50), through Heinrich Berghaus (see p.51), who created his

Geographical School of Art in Potsdam, Germany, with Humboldt's support, to Petermann, who was a student of Berghaus. From 1845 to 1854 Petermann lived and worked in Edinburgh and London, and in 1857 he became a fellow of the Royal Geographical Society. This map is one of two he completed for a planned Geographical and Statistical Atlas of the British Empire.

Great Britain: Her Natural & Industrial Resources | 1939–45 | British Information Services

Printed paper. 93 × 77 cm / 36½ × 30¼ in. Boston Public Library, Massachusetts

This image lies somewhere between a map and an infographic. It is beautifully executed, but belongs as firmly in the tradition of wartime propaganda as far cruder images (see pp.264–5). The map takes a stylized approach to the topography and coastline of the United Kingdom in order to deliver a vivid measure of the nation's industrial production at the height of World War II (1939–45). The map was sponsored by the British

Information Services, a British government agency set up in the United States in 1942 to strengthen the Anglo-American alliance through positive portrayals of Britain in US newspapers, radio shows and posters such as this. The map was distributed in New York as part of a large public information campaign that included an extensive run of propaganda about British culture and the legitimacy of the US support for the Allies. This example

focuses on British domestic agriculture and industrial production, and uses a graphic style that gives it a kind of whimsical, commercial air, almost like an advertisement for British tourism. Yet its purpose is altogether more serious: promoting the British cause to Americans who might be sceptical about the Allied cause and, more generally, the nation's new role of steward of the post-war world.

Diwali Celebrations at the Royal Palace at Kotah, Rajasthan | c.1690 | Unknown

Opaque watercolour on paper. 48.5 × 43.4 cm / 19 × 17 in. National Gallery of Victoria, Melbourne

An anonymous north Indian craftsman painted this map of the celebration of Diwali – the Hindu autumn festival that celebrates light's victory over darkness – in the palace of the maharana of Kotah, Rajasthan, for whom it was presumably commissioned. As musicians, animal trainers, acrobats and other entertainers gather outside the orange main gates of the palace, the maharana and his harem sit inside a courtyard filled with Diwali can-

dles, where a priest prays. The map is an example of a style known as *tamasha* – richly detailed panoramas of courtly life in an architectural and geographical setting – that emerged around the start of the eighteenth century in Mewar, a princely state in north-western India. In common with other *tamasha*, the painting uses multiple viewpoints and oblique perspective in order to show both the main parts of the palace and its surrounding

buildings in detail, as well as the hills rising in the distance – complete with an elephant – but it also reflects the influence of Muslim and Hindu miniature painters from other parts of India.

Mecca | c.1650–1750 | Unknown

Opaque watercolour, gold, silver and ink on paper. 65 × 48 cm / 25⅝ × 18⅞ in. Nasser D. Khalili Collection of Islamic Art

This colourful plan represents the most sacred site in Islam, the courtyard of the mosque of the Prophet Mohammad in Mecca. It shows the *kabah*, a cube-shaped pavilion draped in a black cloth that contains fragments of the Black Stone, said to have been given to Adam as a token of forgiveness for the sins of humankind. This image is a detail from a scroll created as a certificate to show that a Muslim pilgrim had either completed the Hajj (pilgrimage to Mecca, which all Muslims who can afford to must make at least once in their lives) or had had someone complete the prescribed rites in Mecca on his or her behalf. Stylistic details suggest that this drawing was made in Mecca by an Indian artist, whose bird's-eye view drew on the established practice of folding the walls of the mosque outwards to reveal the arcading within, typically coloured red and green. The map itself – like its accompanying image of the Mosque of the Prophet in Medina – is two-dimensional, but its varied perspective creates an impression of depth. Illustrated Hajj certificates first appeared in the twelfth century, and the trade in such images reached its peak in the fifteenth and sixteenth centuries.

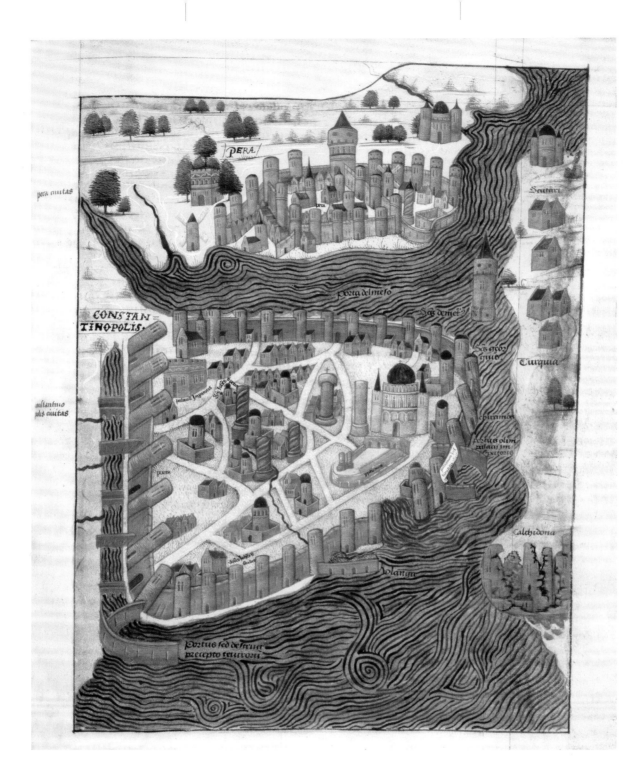

Constantinople and Pera | 1422 | Christoforo Buondelmonti

Coloured ink and wash on vellum. 27 × 17 cm / 10¾ × 6¾ in. British Library, London

This is a copy of the oldest surviving map of Constantinople (now Istanbul) and the only map to depict the Byzantine capital before its conquest by the Ottoman Turks in 1453. The illustration is drawn from the first *isolario* (book of islands), in which maps of the islands were integrated with descriptive text. In the early fifteenth century, the Florentine monk Christoforo Buondelmonti visited the islands of the Aegean Sea, and these islands dominate the resulting manuscript, *Liber Insularum Archipelagi*, which contained seventy-nine maps and bird's-eye views. The book was widely copied, expanded and translated, making the *isolario* a popular genre of the fifteenth, sixteenth and seventeenth centuries. Buondelmonti's map shows the Golden Horn and Bosporus waterways, along with many identifiable monuments and architectural features, some of which survive today. The large white building with the blue dome is Hagia Sophia, then a Greek Orthodox church but later converted by the Ottomans into a mosque. The fifth-century walls built by the Emperor Theodosius surround the city, with various gates on both the landward and seaward sides. In the siege of 1453 the Ottomans used huge cannon to breach these formidable defences in one of the first decisive uses of artillery in warfare.

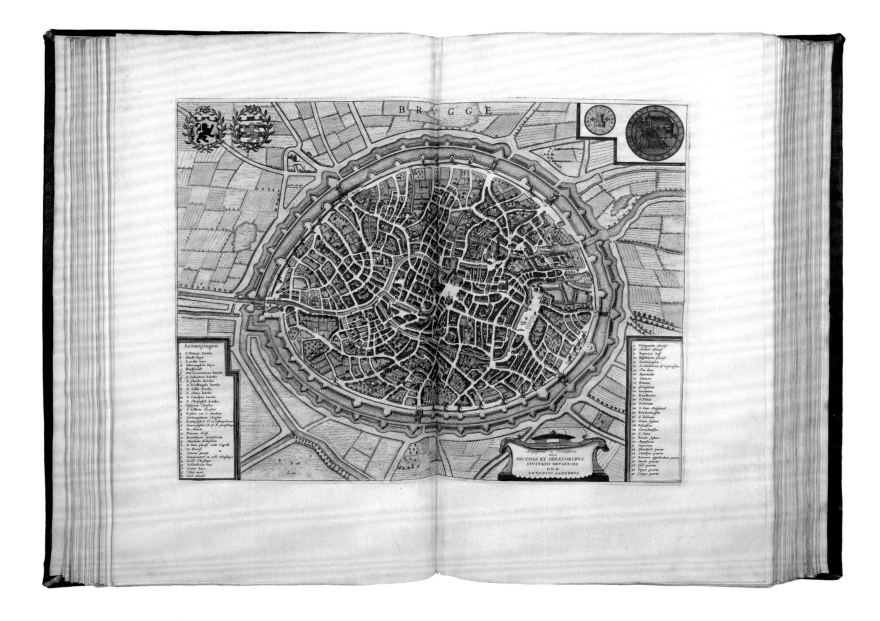

Brugge | 1649 | Johannes Blaeu

Hand-coloured engraving. 38.5 × 50 cm / 15⅛ × 19⅝ in. Collection Daniel Crouch Rare Books, London

City plans were an important expression of civic pride throughout the Dutch Golden Age (see p.185), but this plan of Bruges – today in Belgium but then part of the Spanish Netherlands – is also an embodiment of national pride. It was drawn towards the end of the Eighty Years' War, the long Dutch revolt against Spanish rule (1568–1648) that culminated in the creation of an independent Dutch Republic. The Amsterdam cartographer Joan Blaeu – son of the renowned Willem Janszoon Blaeu – originally planned two volumes of *Tooneel der steden*, or 'theatre of towns', one each for the Dutch Republic and the Spanish Netherlands. In the first edition, the 220 or so maps were distributed more or less evenly between the books. As the atlas was being prepared, however, the army of the Republic captured more of the 'Spanish' towns, so in later editions a number of maps moved between volumes, making the books uneven. Bruges itself remained under Spanish control. Blaeu's map shows the city orientated with east at the top, and with the tower of the Onze Lieve Vrouwekerk (Church of Our Lady) visible at the centre of the city. Under Joan and his brother Cornelis, the family firm was the most productive cartographic business in the Netherlands until its premises were destroyed by fire in 1672.

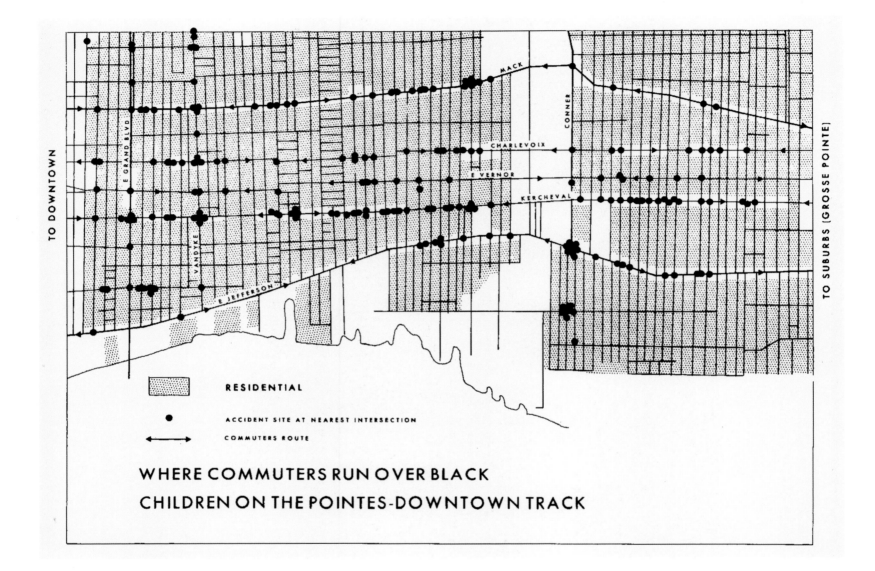

RESIDENTIAL

● ACCIDENT SITE AT NEAREST INTERSECTION

◄——► COMMUTERS ROUTE

WHERE COMMUTERS RUN OVER BLACK
CHILDREN ON THE POINTES-DOWNTOWN TRACK

Where Commuters Run Over Black Children on the Pointes-Downtown Track | 1971 | William Bunge

Printed in *Field Notes* (1971). 21.4 × 25.4 cm / 8½ × 10 in. Private collection

For most of human history, mapping has been undertaken mainly by people with wealth or power, and so many maps depict subjects that are of interest to those types of people: who owns what land, where colonies can be sited, how business can move by road or rail and so on. Those who made the maps had the power to show the world as they liked. The US geographer William Bunge instead used his cartographic training to empower people who normally did not have the opportunity to make maps. Bunge told stories about Detroit that no one else would have dared to put on a map: where rich suburbanites run over schoolchildren, where rats bite babies, how the rich suburbs pull money from the poor inner city, where people can afford to buy toys, and similar subjects. The maps are based on real statistics, but none that any government or corporation would ever have paid to map. Bunge articulated societal problems in Detroit in a familiar, respectable cartographic language – and one that was usually inaccessible to the people who suffered their ills. Today, changes in technology have allowed a boom in citizen-mapping that builds on the legacy of Bunge's work and gives more people a chance to share stories that no one else will map.

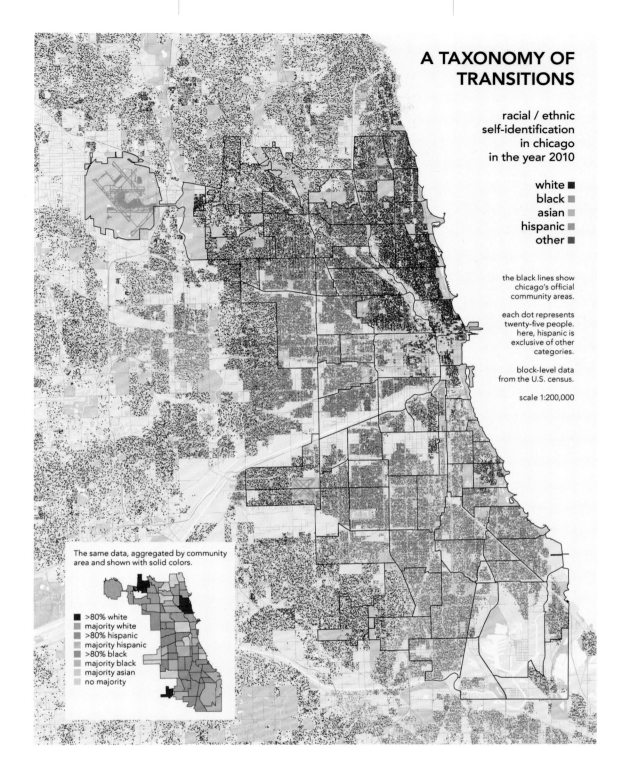

A TAXONOMY OF TRANSITIONS

racial / ethnic
self-identification
in chicago
in the year 2010

white ■
black ■
asian ■
hispanic ■
other ■

the black lines show
chicago's official
community areas.

each dot represents
twenty-five people.
here, hispanic is
exclusive of other
categories.

block-level data
from the U.S. census.

scale 1:200,000

The same data, aggregated by community
area and shown with solid colors.

■ >80% white
majority white
>80% hispanic
majority hispanic
>80% black
majority black
majority asian
no majority

A Taxonomy of Transitions | 2009 | Bill Rankin

Digital. Dimensions variable

The way data is portrayed in a map affects its message, a point well made in this piece on race and ethnicity in Chicago by Bill Rankin. Rankin – an assistant professor in the History of Science at Yale and a cartographer fascinated by the potential of cutting-edge digital mapping – uses in his main map a technique called dot density to indicate where people of different race or ethnicity live, and how closely spaced they are. In the smaller map at lower left, he shows the same data using a choropleth map, colouring in each region based on the predominant race or ethnicity (see p.91). The city's segregation is apparent in both maps, but the dot map also shows occasional interminglings, while the choropleth presents a false sense of uniformity and hides not only areas of intermixing but whole groups with small numbers (such as Asians). It also gives the sense of the city being uniformly inhabited, while the dot map reveals areas of public and industrial land. Had Rankin made only the choropleth, most readers might not have given a second thought to what lay beneath the uniformly painted spaces. No mapping technique is perfect, and choropleths work well in many situations, but this work points out that we as map readers should think critically about how information is presented to us.

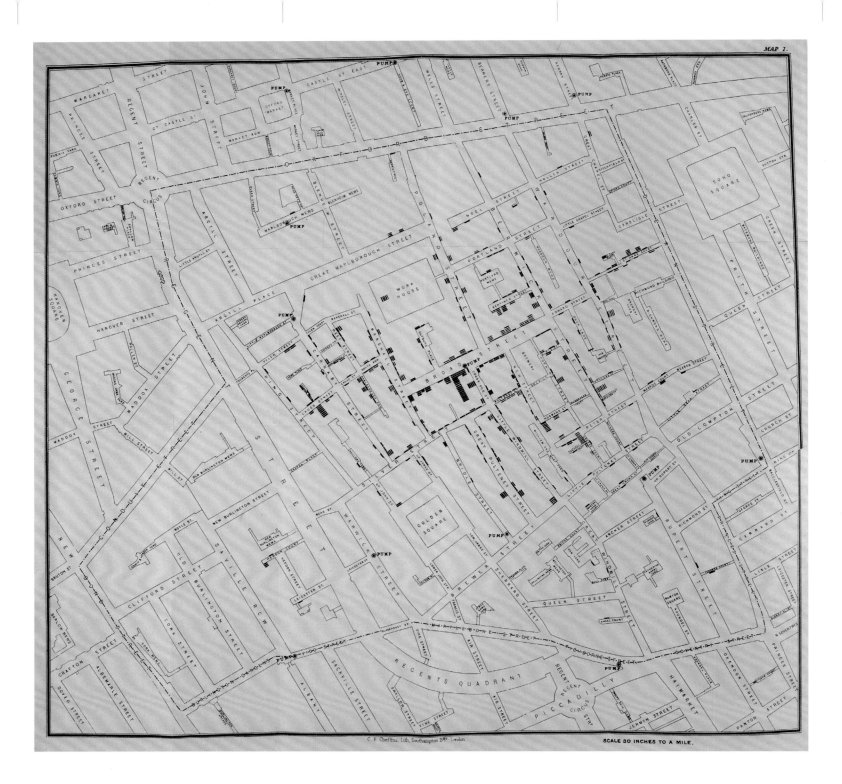

MAP 1.

SCALE 30 INCHES TO A MILE.

C. F. Cheffins, Lith, Southampton B[d]. London.

Deaths from Cholera in Soho | 1855 | John Snow

Printed paper, from *On the Mode of Communication of Cholera* (1855). 28.5 × 30 cm / 11¼ × 11¾ in. British Library, London

More than any other map in the history of cartography, this map of Soho in London has become the stand-ard-bearer for demonstrating the power of maps to reveal patterns in data. All cartographers are familiar with the story of John Snow. An English physician, epi-demiologist and pioneer of anaesthesia, Snow set out to make sense of an outbreak of cholera in Soho in 1854 by plotting all known deaths on a map. He indicated 578

cholera deaths as black bars stacked next to the street at the relevant address. At the time, many physicians believed the disease was spread through the air by a 'miasma', but Snow's map showed a cluster of deaths around a particular water pump – one of thirteen water sources on the map – on Broad Street. He therefore concluded, correctly, that cholera was a water-borne disease, and the pump was disabled (although by then

the outbreak was slowing down). Spatial epidemiology, the study of the spread of disease, was born; more generally, Snow brought thematic cartography to the fore. His plotting of data threw new light on previously known information. It seems remarkable that such a technique was not more widely used before Snow's efforts: the street network and the bars plotting each death could not have been simpler.

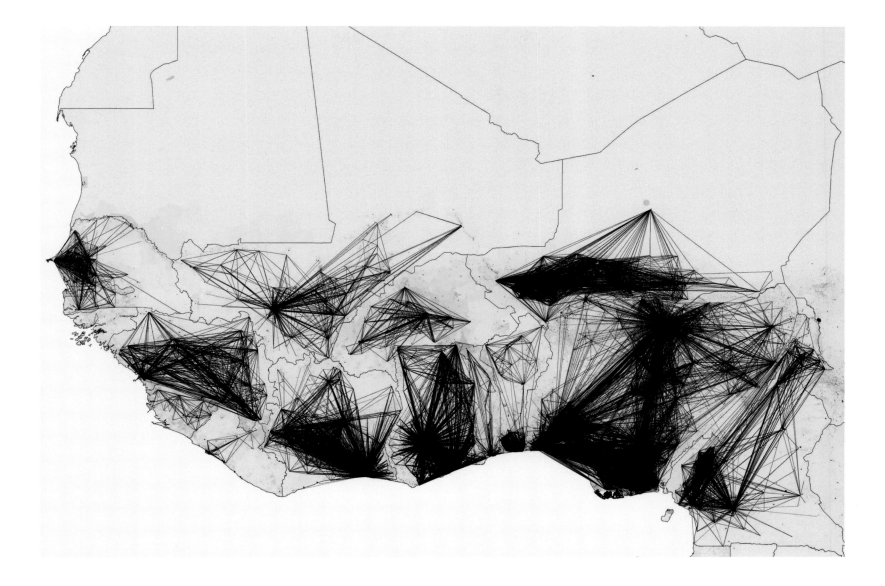

Human Mobility and the Spread of Ebola in West Africa | 2014 | Flowminder Foundation

Digital. Dimensions variable.

This map of West Africa – both strangely beautiful and oddly menacing – attempts to chart possible routes by which the Ebola outbreak of 2014 spread. There has been crisis mapping before (see opposite), but this map represents one of the more amazing cartographic developments since the advent of the World Wide Web and the widespread use of mobile phones. Increasingly, large amounts of spatial data taken from the Web and from mobile-phone networks are being use to track, analyse, predict and respond to natural disasters, revolutions and wars. Flowminder – a Sweden-based not-for-profit foundation whose mission is to improve public health by analysing data collected from mobile phones and satellites – created this map from information provided by Orange Telecom in Senegal. The data was gathered in 2013 from 150,000 mobile phones and modelled to build a network of the travel patterns of people across a region encompassing Senegal, Guinea and Liberia. The models were later used in an attempt to understand the spread of the Ebola epidemic by looking closely at typical journeys in the region. Because the map was based on historical movements before the Ebola crisis took firm hold, it may not reflect how those movements changed or developed as the crisis unfolded in 2014.

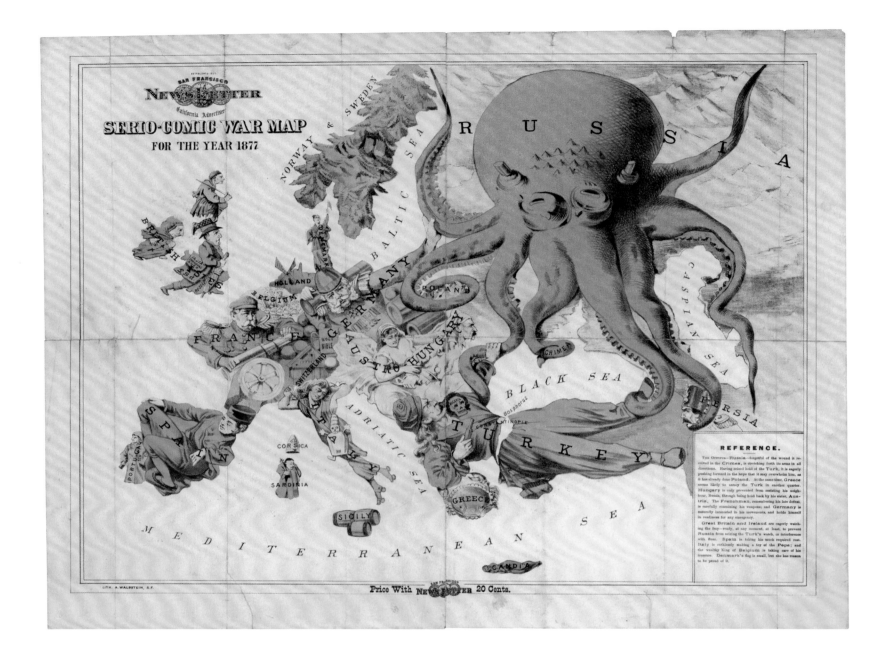

Serio-Comic War Map for the Year 1877 | 1877 | Frederick W. Rose

Printed paper. 45 × 61 cm / 17¾ × 24 in. Library of Congress, Washington, DC

The English draftsman and illustrator Frederick W. Rose's decision to describe his map of 1877 as 'serio-comic' was highly appropriate. The satire of portraying Russia as a giant octopus with threatening tentacles reaching into Europe reflects real – and deadly – tension. One tentacle envelops Poland, which had become a restive part of the Russian Empire. Two more attack Turkey: in 1877 Russia went to war to avenge Bulgarians killed by Turks – signified by the skull on Turkey's shoulder – and to regain lands lost in the Crimean War (1853–56), marked by a wounded tentacle. One tentacle curls around the neck of Persia, while Germany pushes another away and Austria restrains Hungary from fighting. The British look on anxiously, while Italy and Spain show no interest in the Russian menace. Rose, who lived in London but travelled widely in Europe, designed comical maps intended to make the continent's complex geopolitical situation easily understandable. The national rivalries he caricatured ultimately led to World War I (1914–18), when Austria-Hungary and Germany fought Serbia, Russia, France, Belgium and Britain. Rose lost two sons on the Western Front in the first weeks of the war, and he died the following year. The comical interaction of nations on Rose's maps had truly tragic consequences.

German Annexations | 1938 | Reich Ministry of Public Enlightenment and Propaganda

Colour lithograph. 10.5 × 14.9 cm / 4⅛ × 5⅞. Private collection

This map of German territorial annexations was issued by Joseph Goebbels's Reich Ministry of Public Enlightenment and Propaganda to encourage German support for the Nazi regime. For other Europeans, now growing uneasy about the ambitions of Adolf Hitler, the map's dark background reflected a gathering storm. The power of the image relies on simplicity: the growing shape of 'Greater Germany' appears as a mouth hungry for the Sudetenland. The slogan is brief and comprehensive: *Ein Volk – Ein Reich – Ein Führer* ('One People – One Nation – One Leader'). Nazi Germany had taken back Saarland from France in 1935 and had forced the annexation of Austria (*Österreich*) in March 1938. Hitler's next target was the Sudetenland, a region of Czechoslovakia that was home to three million ethnic Germans. Britain and France appeased Hitler by forcing Czechoslovakia to relinquish the Sudetenland to Germany in the infamous Munich Agreement of 30 September, 1938. German troops occupied the rest of Czechoslovakia in March 1939. The next time Hitler made a grab for land in Europe, however – this time Poland, (Polen on the map) – Britain and France had learned their lesson. Two days after the German invasion of Poland on 1 September 1939, they declared war on Germany, starting World War II.

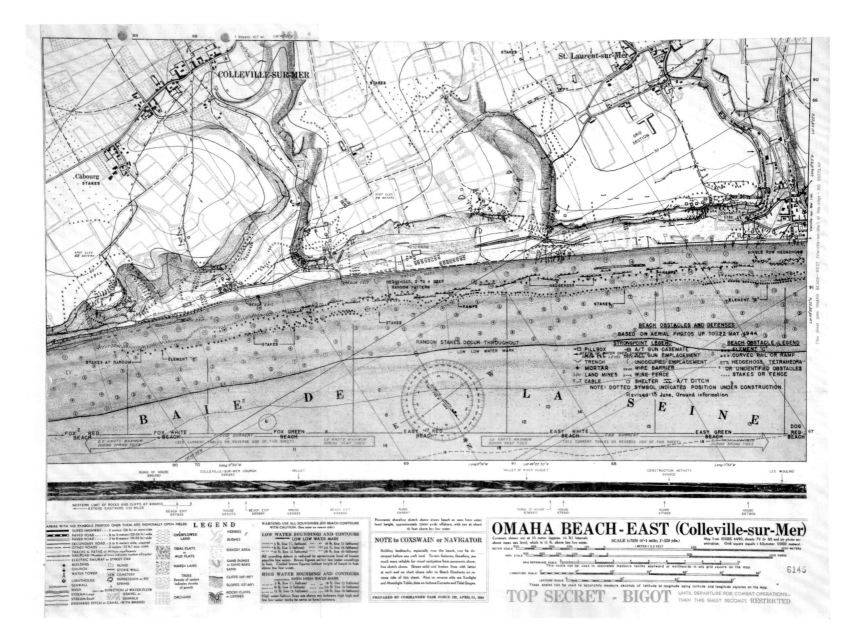

OMAHA BEACH-EAST (Colleville-sur-Mer)

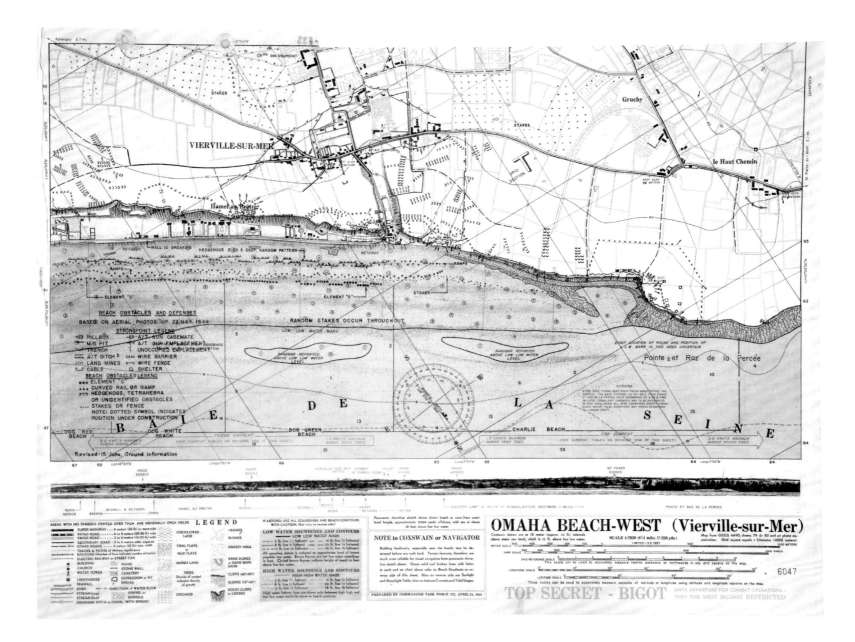

Operation Overlord: Omaha Beach – West and East | 1944 | Admiral Alan Goodrich Kirk

Printed paper. 34 × 53 cm / 13¼ × 20¾ in (each map). National Archives, London

The Allied invasion of Normandy on D–Day, 6 June 1944, was the largest amphibious operation ever undertaken. In two years of planning, the Allies drew an estimated 170 million maps. These US maps of Omaha Beach – the target for the 1st and 29th Infantry Divisions – were prepared to guide landing-craft crew, and are orientated with south-west at the top so that they would be the right way up on the approach, helping the crew to identify their objectives. For the same reason, the map includes a profile of the coastline as it appeared from water level 1,800 metres (6,000 feet) offshore. Allied aircraft took photographs of German defences, such as pillboxes and fences, and combat swimmers reconnoitred beach obstacles including stakes and anti-tank 'hedgehogs' until late in May. Such defences are detailed in red, although the maps warn that they might have changed. The map is classified at the highest level of secrecy –'BIGOT' – to prevent word of the location of the landings leaking out. As it was, a combination of bad luck and unforeseen problems turned Omaha Beach into a death trap. The first waves of soldiers to come ashore suffered some 10,000 casualties, and the operation was nearly abandoned. By the end of the day, however, US forces had established a defensible toehold.

A Description of the Coasts, Bridges, Harbours, Islands of New France | 1607 | Samuel de Champlain

Ink and wash on vellum. 37 × 55 cm / 14½ × 21½ in. Library of Congress, Washington, DC

The French explorer Samuel de Champlain is celebrated as the father of New France (Canada), founding colonies in Acadia and Quebec in 1608. Hand-drawn by Champlain in pen and ink with a green wash, with Native American contributions, this map records the surveys he had carried out the previous year as part of his expedition to found a settlement as the French king Henri IV's agent for the fur trade. The map covers the south-west part of Nova Scotia, the Bay of Fundy ('La Baye François') to Cape Cod ('Cape Blanc'). The site of Boston is shown at Baye Longue, and in the middle of the coast are present-day Bangor and Penobscot Bay. At the top right of the chart is a table of Champlain's longitude calculations, while the cartouche headlines the chart's salient features. The scale is probably in French leagues, which equated roughly to the English and French league of three nautical miles, although during the Ancien Régime there was wide variation in French standard units (to the extent that the *lieue* or league, originally the distance someone could walk in an hour, varied from 3.2 to 5.9 kilometres/2 to 3⅝ miles). Champlain's exploratory achievements were recognized when he was made lieutenant governor of New France in 1612.

A Map of Virginia Discovered to the Hills | 1651 | John Farrer

Hand-coloured engraving. 27 × 36 cm / 10⅝ × 14¼ in. Library of Congress, Washington, DC

This map by John Farrer might give the impression that England dominated the entire North American continent. Farrer's map – orientated with west at the top – stretches from North Carolina in the south to Massachusetts in the north. The modern reader will recognize place names along the Atlantic coast – Cape Hatteras, Long Island, Cape Cod – but in the west, towards the Appalachian Mountains, the familiarity disappears. The Hudson River

flows through a territory named New Albion (where Dutch plantations will later become New York) until it reaches New France in the top right-hand corner of the map and flows into 'A Mighty great Lake'. French explorers had already identified what would later be named the Great Lakes, but Farrer allows the lake to empty into the Pacific Ocean. Beyond this swathe of territory, he also eliminates Spanish land to the south and west. A textual

explanation indicates that Francis Drake's discovery of New Albion (California) lay only ten days' walk beyond the Appalachians; it concludes that a little more effort may discover additional territory 'to the exceeding benefit of Great Brittain'. The conflation of the Appalachian range with one in California, and the placement of New Albion to the east as well as the west, helps to explain this unique configuration.

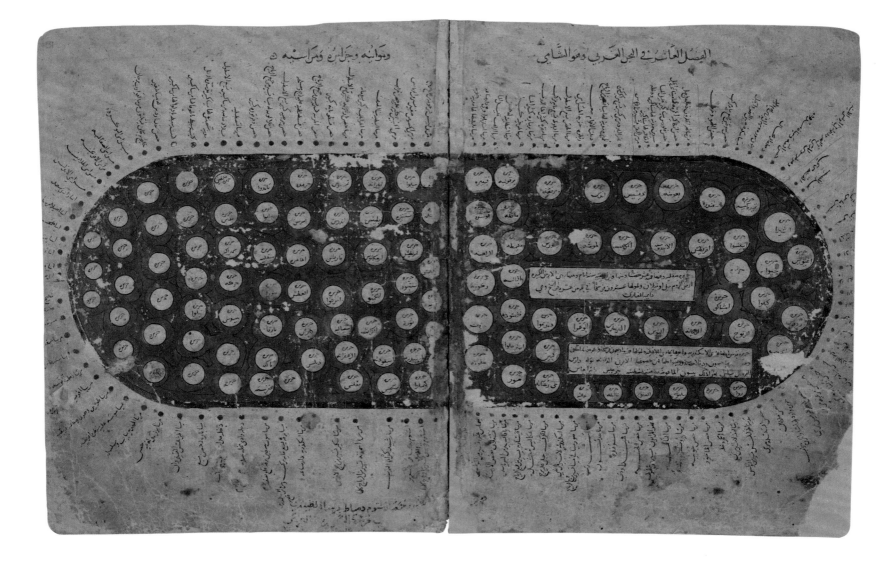

The Mediterranean | c.1021–50 | Unknown

Ink on paper. 64.8 × 49 cm / 25½ × 19⅓ in. Bodleian Library, Oxford

One of the oldest sea charts of the Mediterranean, this map was probably created in Cairo in the mid-eleventh century; it appears in the Egyptian cosmography *The Book of Curiosities*. It shows the entire Mediterranean, with the eastern half disproportionately large, its edges inscribed with the names of ports between Cairo and Constantinople (modern Istanbul). Each is marked by a red dot followed by the name of the place in Arabic script written perpendicular to the water – a style that later became the Mediterranean and European standard of writing port names. While later maps illustrated irregular, geographically accurate coastlines, this map follows the Islamic style of using geometric shapes: the Mediterranean appears elliptical, while islands remain circular. Although the placement of names follows their actual sequence along the coast – making even this minimalist map practical for navigators who rarely moved out of sight of the coast – the labels of islands are far more dispersed. Islands from the Aegean, Ligurian and Mediterranean seas appear next to one another, even though they are actually a considerable distance apart. Cyprus and Sicily, the two most important stopping places between North Africa and Europe, appear as long rectangles, although Sicily is far from its actual location.

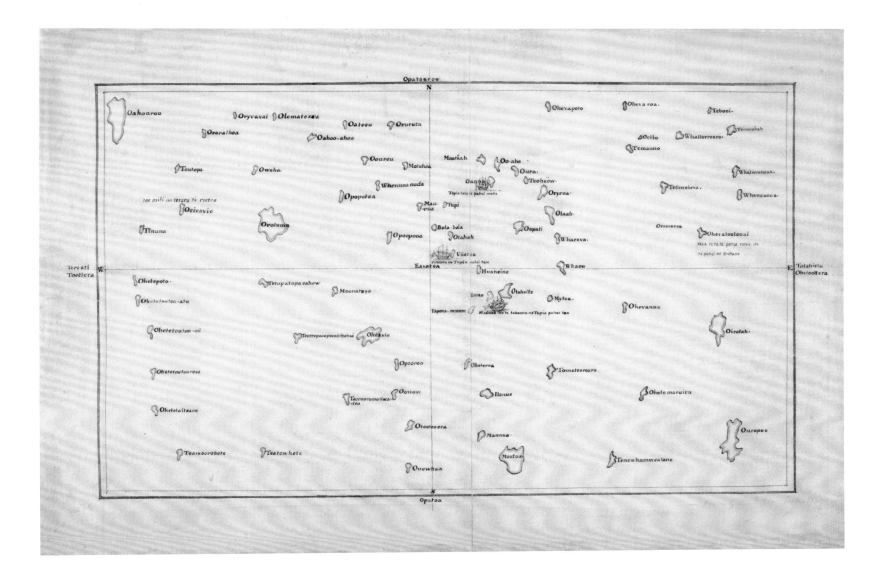

Chart of the Society Islands, with Otaheite [Tahiti] in the Centre | 1769 | Tupaia

Ink and colour on paper. 20.2 × 33.6 cm / 8 × 13¼ in. British Library, London

It has taken many years to recognize that Captain James Cook may not have been the greatest navigator on board the *Endeavour*, which he commanded on his second voyage to the Pacific (see p.257). When Cook went to Tahiti in 1769, he took on board a local mariner named Tupaia. Tupaia joined *Endeavour* in the hope of visiting England, but Cook's orders sent the ship south in search of *Terra Australis Incognita* (the supposed Southern Continent). The Europeans showed little curiosity about Tupaia's methods of navigation, beyond noting that, at any time, anywhere, he could point in the direction of Tahiti. They gave him paper on which he sketched the Polynesians and Australian Aborigines they met; those drawings were so talented that for 200 years they were attributed to the botanist Joseph Banks. Tupaia made this map of much of the South Pacific; annotations and island names are written at his dictation. It is either his original or Cook's copy of it (Tupaia, along with many of Cook's men, died of disease in what is now Indonesia). Tupaia's geographic knowledge spanned most of the southern Pacific ocean. His complex graphic cannot be readily interpreted according to Western map standards, and the map has only recently received the regard it deserves.

Chart of the Mediterranean Sea | 1489 | Albino de Canepa

Ink and pigments on vellum. 80 × 120 cm / 31½ × 47¼ in. James Ford Bell Library, University of Minnesota, Minneapolis

Although portolan charts follow a specific style, this late fifteenth-century Genoese chart is a reminder that they varied significantly in their decorative elements. One of the most elaborate portolans, it depicts inland features such as the Atlas Mountains, the Alps, the Pyrenees, the Red Sea and the Danube River with its river ports, as well as flags, town vignettes and rulers' tents. The flags are of particular interest. The Genoese flag flies over Genoa but also throughout the Black Sea. While the Genoese had interests in the area, the chart overstates their dominance, reflecting its origin. Another flag of note is the Moorish flag over Granada in southern Spain. Three years later Granada would fall to Spain's Catholic monarchs, Ferdinand and Isabella, during the Reconquista, ending the Arab presence in Iberia. In common with other contemporary charts, the map shows the large, fictitious islands of Antillia and Satanazes in the middle of the Atlantic, which may have reflected a legend about a Portuguese bishop founding cities on an island to the west. These islands persisted on European charts for 100 years, even after transatlantic travel proved they were fictional. We know little about Albino de Canepa, the author of this map, but one more of his charts survives, dated to 1480.

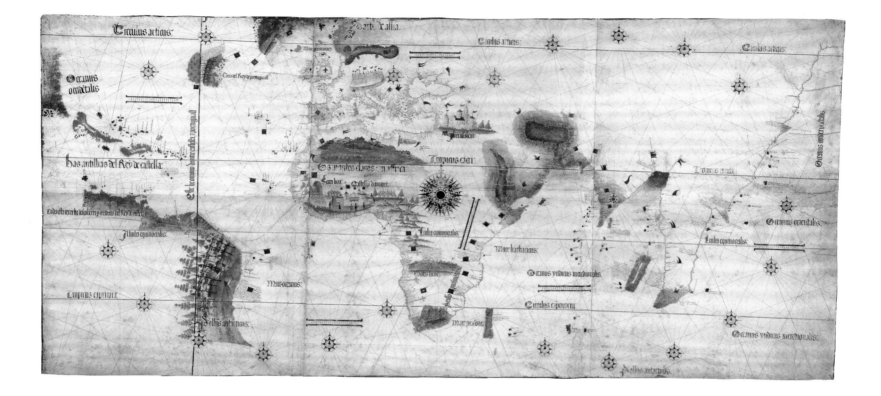

Cantino Planisphere | 1502 | Unknown

Ink and pigment on vellum. 105 × 220 cm / 41⅜ × 86⅝ in. Biblioteca Estense Universitaria, Modena

This magnificent chart brings together cartography, exploration and espionage. When it was drawn at the start of the sixteenth century, the Portuguese had the most accurate idea of the world beyond Europe – and they were determined to keep it that way. Two generations of Portuguese mariners had clawed their way down the west coast of Africa; Bartolomeu Dias had rounded the Cape of Good Hope; Vasco da Gama had opened the sea route to India; Pedro Álvares Cabral had landed in Brazil; and Portuguese explorers had even visited the north-east coast of North America. New discoveries were recorded systematically on the standard map (or *padrão real*) maintained in Lisbon. Other European powers coveted these secrets, and Ercole I d'Este, Duke of Ferrara, sent his agent, Alberto Cantino, to Portugal with orders to obtain a copy of the *padrão* by whatever means necessary. No one knows how much money changed hands, but Cantino returned home with this chart. Besides depicting coasts and islands, the map includes another important feature: the Line of Demarcation adjudicated by Pope Alexander VI to divide the world into Spanish and Portuguese spheres of influence. The original *padrão* has not survived, so this purloined copy is our best picture of how the Portuguese saw the world in 1502.

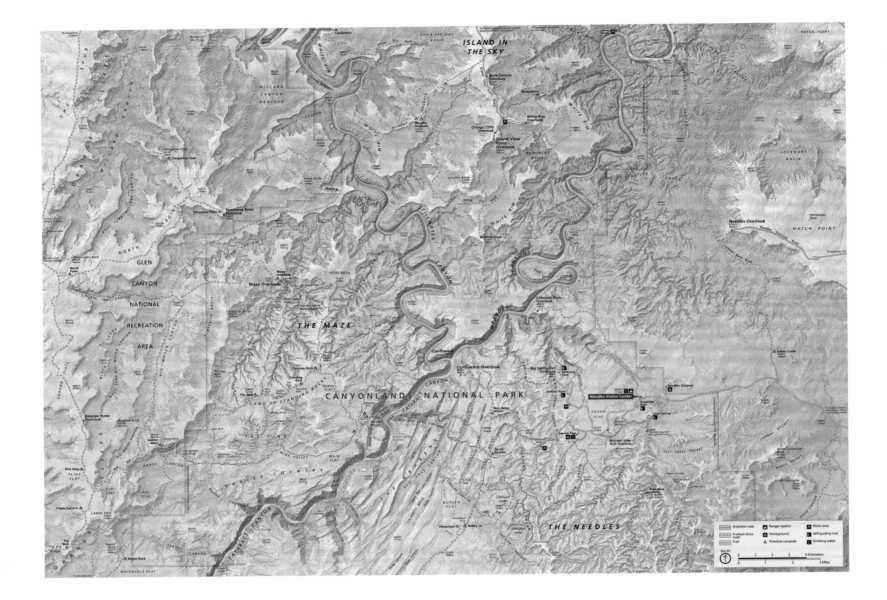

The Heart of Canyonlands National Park | 2014 | Tom Patterson

Printed paper. 91 × 60 cm / 35⅞ × 23⅝ in. National Park Service, Washington, DC

Tom Patterson's map of 2014 is evidence that beautiful maps are not the preserve of a bygone era. Modern techniques are no less capable of producing impressive work. Here Patterson, inspired by the map of *The Heart of the Grand Canyon* (1978) by Bradford Washburn, uses modern data, software and processing systems to create an exquisite depiction of the terrain morphology and colours of the landscape. He uses a range of techniques

to build a realistic rendering of the terrain that captures not only the land's relief but also some of its horizontal structure, revealed by the hill-shading techniques. In particular, his techniques give an impression of rock texturing synonymous of historic, manually drawn relief and rock shading typical of the Swiss school of cartography (see p.196). Patterson creates a realistic and engaging three-dimensional landscape. The colours are derived

from a process that combines aerial photography with relief renderings and allows natural hues to play a part in the map (with additional exaggeration of colours, such as blue for water). Overall, Patterson's map combines advanced digital terrain model processing, some clever compositing with aerial photography and an artist's eye to adjust colour manually.

Ecological Land Units | 2014 | United States Geological Survey and Environmental Systems Research Unit

Digital. Dimensions variable

This view of the western end of the Himalaya – a politically volatile region, which encompasses a disputed border between India and Pakistan and the mountainous region between Pakistan and Afghanistan, said to shelter Taliban and other terrorists – is a detail from one of the most ambitious maps ever created. Its makers set out to create a current, Web-based global database and map that could be easily used by the public, scientists and conservationists to help increase our understanding of Earth's changing ecology. Global in its extent, the map shows the diversity of the world's ecosystems and natural resources in unprecedented detail. In order to make this dynamic, multilayered map, the globe was divided into cells with a scale resolution of 250 metres (820 feet). The content of each cell is made up by layering various data, a technique typical of cartography made using Geographic Information System technology (see p.171). Each cell contains information about variables that drive ecological processes, including climate, types of landform, soil and land cover. The vast amount of data in the map has produced a geospatial database that contains 47,650 unique combinations of the input data layers, which have been further aggregated into what the mapmakers call Ecological Land Units.

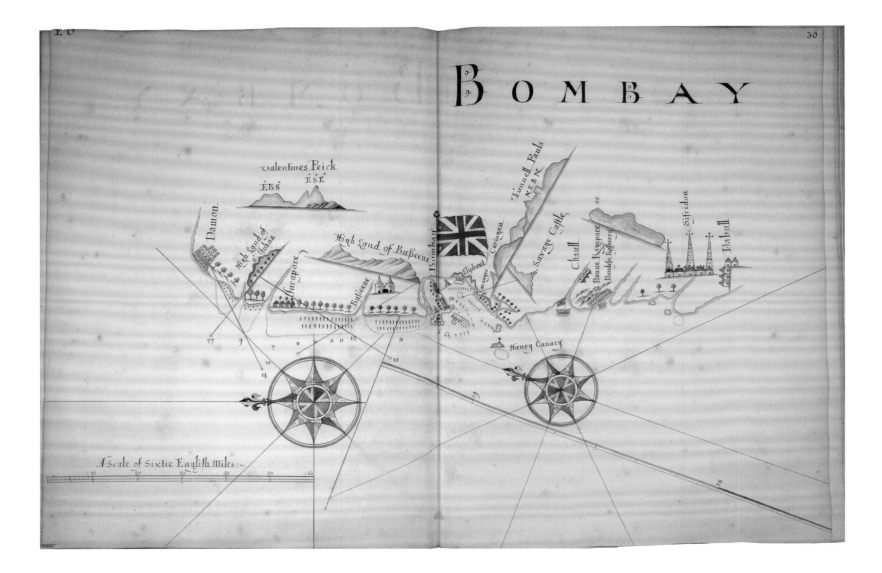

A Chart of the Coast around Bombay | *c.*1680 | William Hacke

Ink and watercolour on vellum. 66 x 46 cm / 26 x 18 in. British Library, London

The Union Jack that flies at the centre of this map of the coastline around Mumbai – formerly Bombay – marks both the actual possession of the port by the English and its future importance as a seat of the empire in India. Originally a group of seven islands surrounded by swampy shallows with a natural deep-water harbour named Bom Bahia ('good bay') by the Portuguese, Bombay was ceded by Portugal to England as part of

Catherine of Braganza's dowry when she married Charles II of England in 1661. Seven years later, the Crown leased the port to the East India Company, which built a dock, a custom house and fortifications. Despite attacks by local rulers and the Dutch, the port grew rapidly, and in 1867 the Company made Bombay its headquarters. This map of a stretch of the Indian coast 370 kilometres (230 miles) long was drawn some two decades later

by William Hacke, one of the most prolific members of the Thames School, a group of chart-makers within the Drapers' Company in London that produced nautical charts for overseas commercial activities. Hacke's chart uses compass roses and rhumb lines to guide mariners towards Bombay, marked with a prominent Union Jack. There are indications of water depths, and views of inland hills that could be useful for navigation.

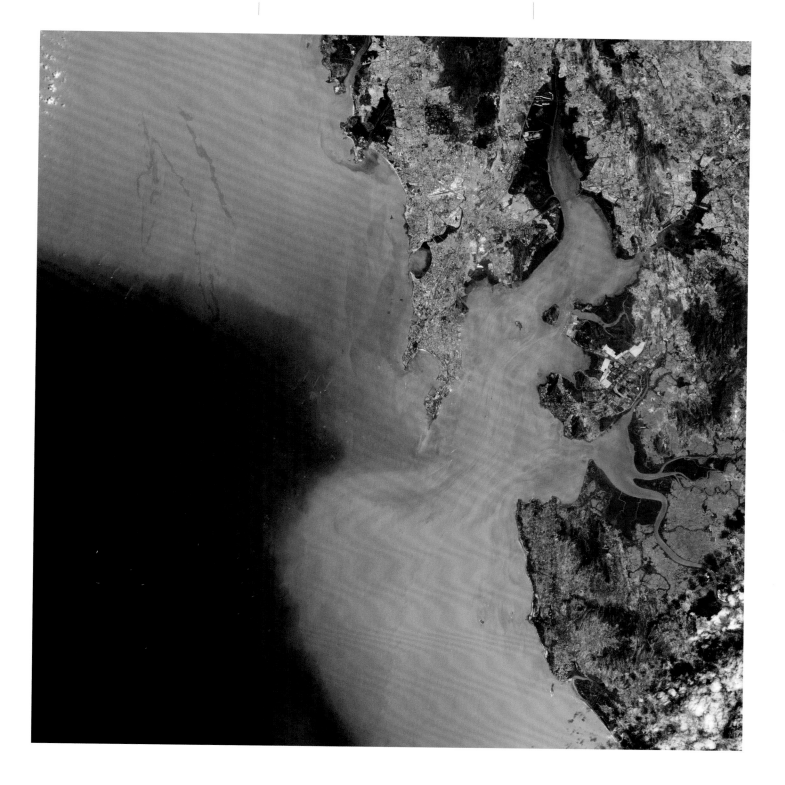

Mumbai | 2011 | European Space Agency

Digital. Dimensions variable

This striking satellite image of Mumbai, India, is actually a record of what was in some ways a technological failure. It was produced by the Advanced Land Observing Satellite (ALOS) shortly before it lost power in April 2011. ALOS had been launched five years earlier as a cartographic and disaster-monitoring satellite, but the images it produced were too blurred to be useful for accurate mapping. Nevertheless, it had its uses, such as monitoring the rapid growth of cities in developing countries where existing mapping is rarely up-to-date and is of little use for making planning decisions (the problem is particularly bad in India, where the distribution of accurate medium- or large-scale maps is limited by concerns over security). ALOS had three separate imaging systems: a high-resolution panchromatic (black-and-white) scanner, a multispectral scanner producing 10-metre (33-foot) pixels, and a radar scanner. The image of Mumbai was produced by the multispectral scanner, with different bands combined to produce a near-natural colour image. Urban areas stand out in white or grey, with bare ground in various shades of brown and coastal mangrove swamps in green. There are few green areas inland, as the image was taken in the dry season, when vegetation had died back.

Map of the World (Universalis cosmographia) | 1507 | Martin Waldseemüller

Woodcut on twelve sheets. 128 cm × 233 cm / 50⅜ × 91¾ in. Library of Congress, Washington, DC

The most significant thing about Martin Waldseemüller's depiction of the 'New World' – on the left of this map – is not its elongated shape, but the label he gives it: America. It was the first known use of the name on a map. Waldseemüller based the name on that of the Italian explorer Amerigo Vespucci, who had recently visited South America, and chose the name partly because both Europe and Asia had been named after women.

Waldseemüller later had second thoughts, but by then the map had been widely distributed and the name of the continent had spread. Waldseemüller and his collaborator, Matthias Ringmann, translated the writings of the second-century Greek-Egyptian Claudius Ptolemy, and mapped recent discoveries. Made from twelve separate sheets, the complete map is some 2.3 metres (7½ feet) wide. Its unusual shape comes from its pro-

jection, an experiment based on Ptolemy's texts (see p.138). Long known to exist, this map was thought lost until this example was found in 1901 in Germany. After long negotiations, the Library of Congress confirmed its acquisition for a reported $10 million in 2003.

Theatrum Orbis Terrarum | 1570 | Abraham Ortelius

Hand-coloured engraving. 33.7 × 49.3 cm / 13¼ × 19½ in. Library of Congress, Washington, DC

The Flemish geographer Abraham Ortelius created the first modern atlas, the *Theatrum Orbis Terrarum* (Theatre of the World), in 1570. This was the first time maps made to a common scale, with explanatory text, had been published in book form. Ortelius's world map follows that of his friend Gerard Mercator, published the previous year (see p.155). The map is dominated by '*Terra Australis Nondum Cognita*' ('the Southern Land

Not Yet Known'), echoing the belief held by geographers since the time of the ancient Greeks that a large landmass must exist around the South Pole in order to balance the landmasses in the northern hemisphere. Ortelius shows Tierra Del Fuego as being attached to the Southern Continent, while an inscription next to New Guinea explains that it is uncertain whether or not it is part of the Southern Continent. The potato-shaped

South America was revised a few years later. Around the North Pole are four mythical islands derived from the *Inventio Fortunata*, a lost fourteenth-century travel narrative. Ortelius's modern-looking continents, the Southern Continent and the circumpolar islands formed the basic image of the world for cartographers for many years. Later editions of the atlas included more maps and were translated into several languages.

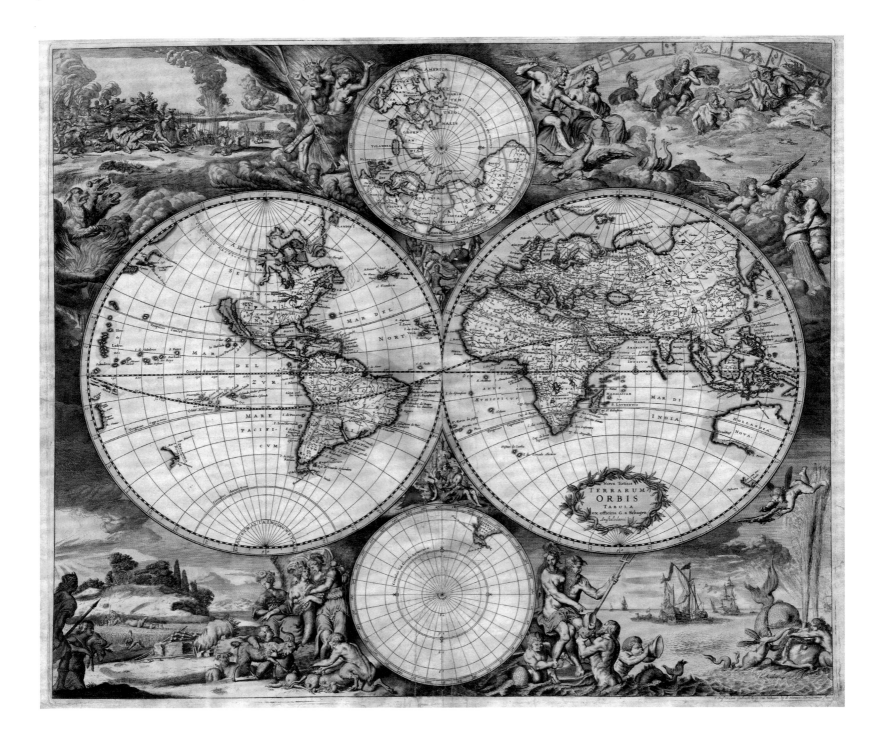

World Map | 1689 | Gerard van Schagen

Hand-coloured engraving. 48.3 × 56 cm / 19 × 22 in. Amsterdam University Library, Amsterdam

This imposing quadruple-hemisphere map of the world by Gerard (or Gerrit) Lucaszoon van Schagen is eloquent testimony to the wealth of Dutch society in the late seventeenth century. The gorgeously embellished maps of the period mark a golden age of Dutch cartography that accompanied the rise of Dutch international commerce. The Netherlands became the first global maritime power, the most prosperous nation in Europe and the leading European centre for trade, science and art, and its wealth allowed all levels of Dutch and Flemish society to engage in mass consumption of a wide variety of cultural goods, including maps. Van Schagen's map is not entirely accurate – the Pacific Ocean is undersized, California is presented as a large island and the hypothetical Southern Continent is omitted altogether – although the coastlines of Australia and New Zealand reflect the voyages of Abel Tasman in the 1640s. Four striking baroque scenes embellished with mythological figures signify the ancient elements. Fire is represented by a battle watched by Hades, god of the Underworld, with Cerberus, the three-headed dog. Zeus rules the Air, the realm of clouds, birds and the Zodiac. The bountiful Earth yields fruits, grains and meats, while Poseidon scans a sea dominated by Dutch merchant ships.

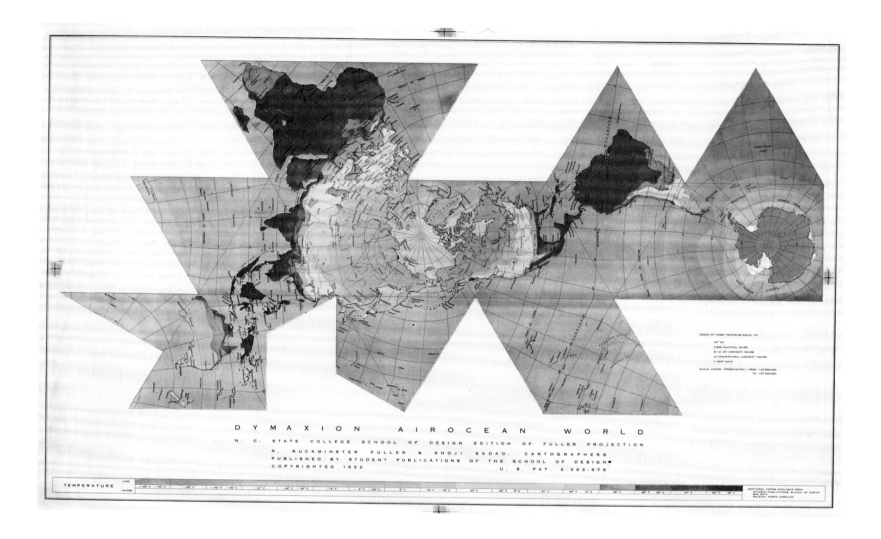

Dymaxion Airocean World Map | 1954 | R. Buckminster Fuller

Printed paper. 24 × 39 cm / 9½ × 15⅓ in. Buckminster Fuller Institute, Brooklyn, New York

There are many possible ways to project Earth onto a flat surface or a solid (see pp.19 and 155). The American designer, architect and polymath R. Buckminster Fuller – best known for his use of the geodesic dome – first published a dymaxion map in 1943. The several different versions of the map – coloured to represent temperature zones – all project the surface of the Earth onto the sides of an icosahedron, a regular polyhedron with twenty sides. When the icosahedron is unfolded, as here, Earth's landmasses form an almost continuous island, highlighting their closeness. Fuller favoured this projection for several reasons. Its proportions are more accurate than those of a regular rectangular map. The map has no right way up, and thus has no bias towards the typical north-at-the-top orientation. It also has no preferred centre to bias it towards the visualization of First World countries. The map can be orientated in different ways, one that shows the landmasses as an island and another that shows the oceans as all being connected in much the same way. Fuller saw design as a way to improve the lives of everyone on the planet. In the 1960s he invented the World Game, which used a version of the map as a tool to facilitate a design approach to solve the world's most pressing problems.

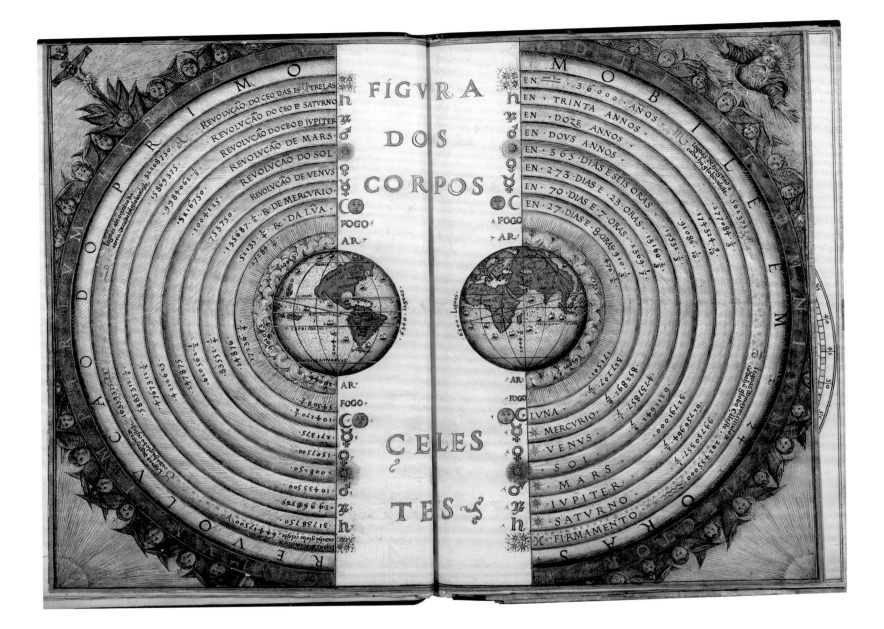

Figura dos Corpos Celestes | 1568 | Bartolomeo Velho

Illuminated manuscript on vellum. 34.3 x 47 cm / 13½ x 18½ in. Bibliothèque nationale de France, Paris

Although the image of Earth at its centre shows details of landmasses that had only recently been mapped, this map of the universe was already out of date when it was published. Twenty-five years earlier, in 1543, the Polish astronomer Nicolaus Copernicus had published his theory that the Earth revolved around the sun. For well over 1,000 years, European and Islamic stargazers had believed that Earth was the centre of the universe and that the sun and stars revolved around it. In classical Greece, Plato and Aristotle devised equations to confirm Earth's perceived position and define the arrangement of the circling bodies. Their teachings were followed by the second-century Greek–Egyptian geographer Claudius Ptolemy (see p.138), whose view was illustrated by the Portuguese cosmographer Bartolomeo Velho in this decorative map of the 'celestial bodies'. The two hemi-spheres are ringed by parallel bands representing the distances of stars, moons and planets from Earth, and the length of their orbits. The religious symbols in the upper corners of the map are a nod to the Church's promotion of the Earth-centred universe, which would galvanize church authorities to contrive against the Copernican sun-centred model of the universe and to continue to deny Earth's true position among celestial bodies.

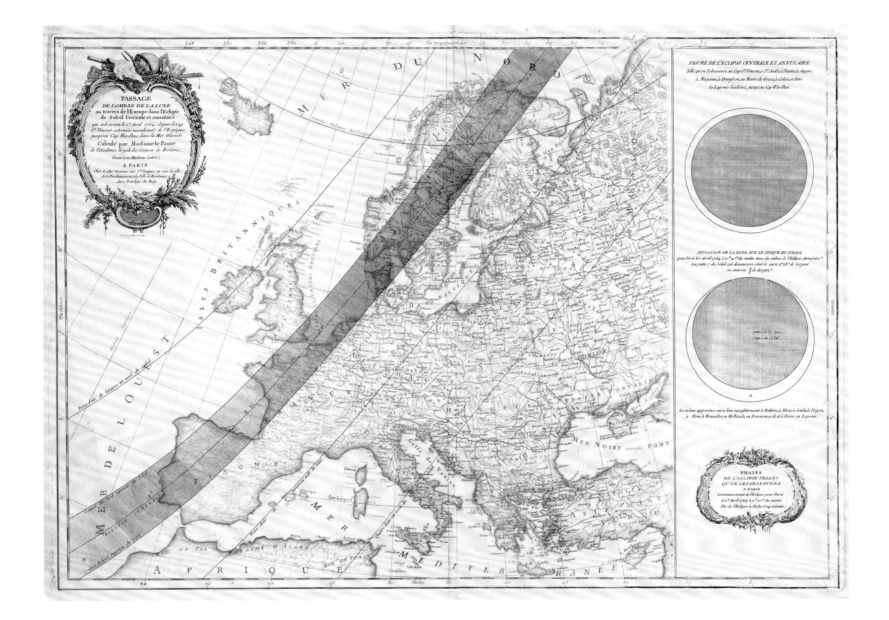

Passage of the Moon's Shadow across Europe | 1764 | Nicole-Reine Lepaute

Engraving. 46 × 51 cm / 18 × 20 in. Library of Congress, Washington, DC

This French map predicting the track of a solar eclipse across Europe is unique for the mid-eighteenth century in that it was both created and engraved by women. In 1762 Nicole-Reine Lepaute calculated the exact timing of an eclipse due on 1 April 1764, in fifteen-minute intervals across the continent, from Portugal to Lapland. Two years later she published this map to accompany an article about the event. The map was engraved by one Mme Lattré, the wife of the royal engraver, Jean Lattre. Both women had emerged from the circle of scientists encouraged by the French crown in Paris during the eighteenth century. Lepaute's husband was the renowned royal clockmaker Jean-André Lepaute, with whom she had constructed a clock with an astronomical function and – after a variety of astronomical calculations – collaborated on an annual guide for astronomers and navigators. The idea of using maps to plot natural phenomena had emerged in Europe during the seventeenth century. In 1701 Edmond Halley (of comet fame) set out the magnetic declination of the Atlantic Ocean on a map (see p.282), and in 1715 he published a map of the path across England of that year's solar eclipse. Later examples include the map of the Gulf Stream published by Benjamin Franklin in 1786 (see p.283).

Tabula Selenographica | 1707–42 | Johann Gabriel Doppelmayr and Johann Baptist Homann

Hand-coloured engraving. 57 × 48.2 cm / 22½ × 19 in. Private collection

What might appear to be a double-hemisphere map of the moon (the word 'selenography' comes from the Greek lunar goddess, Selene) is in fact two versions of the same map. The invention of the telescope early in the seventeenth century revealed mountains, craters and other topographical features on the lunar surface, but two systems for naming those features emerged. The astronomer Johann Gabriel Doppelmayr and the cartographer Johann Baptist Homann – published this map to illustrate the two rivals. On the left is the moon according to Johannes Hevelius, the father of lunar cartography, who in 1647 published a map devoted entirely to the moon. On the right is the system used by the Giovanni Battista Riccioli and Francesco Grimaldi four years later. Hevelius's names associate lunar features with locations on Earth, including 'Mare Mediterraneum' and 'Asia Minor'. Riccioli and Grimaldi named features after philosophers, astronomers and scientists, and their system forms the basis of today's nomenclature. Riccioli named the best-known lunar feature: the Sea of Tranquillity (Mare Tranquillitatis), the site of the moon landing in 1969. In the upper corners of the map are cherubs looking through a telescope and Diana, the Roman goddess of the moon.

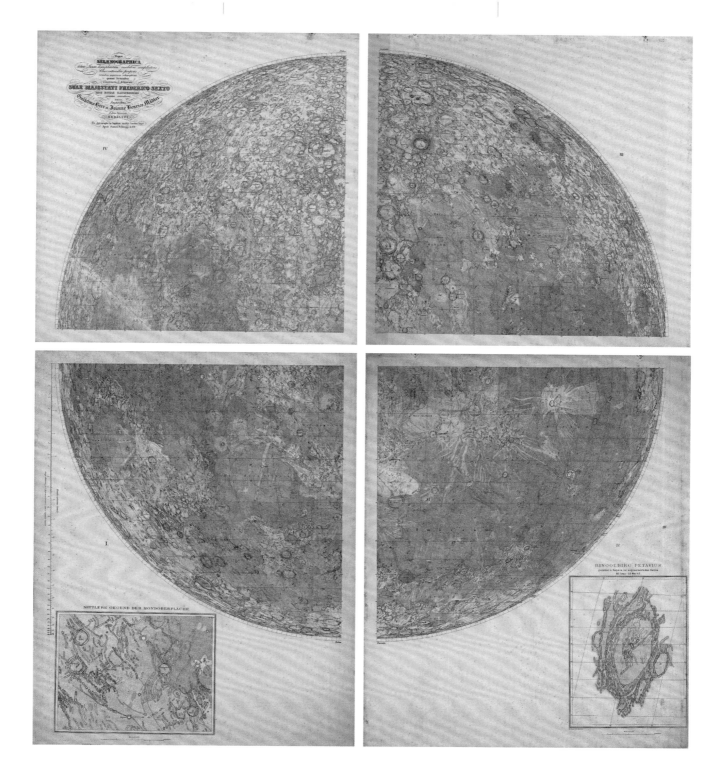

Mappa Selenographica | 1834–36 | Johann Heinrich von Mädler and Wilhelm Beer

Engraving on four sheets. Private collection

When it appeared in 1834, the first quadrant of this map was the most detailed image ever produced of the surface of the moon. The completed map – published in *Der Mond* (The Moon), four years later – was the creation of the German astronomers Wilhelm Beer and Johann Heinrich von Mädler. Using a 3.75-inch refracting telescope (Beer was a Berlin banker with his own observatory), Mädler not only spent 600 nights accurately mapping previously unknown craters, mountains and other surface features; he also used stippling to render the dark and light shading of the moon as visible from Earth. Beer and Mädler named more than a hundred new features, adopting the conventions introduced by the Italian Giovanni Battista Riccioli, who in the seventeeth century had named features after weather conditions and eminent astronomers. Beer and Mädler introduced a system of letters to indicate secondary craters, with Greek letters for high points and rilles, that is still used today. This map (it is orientated with south at the top) was probably the most influential lunar map of the nineteenth century. Even though *Der Mond* was never translated into English, most astronomers are familiar with Mädler's blunt assessment of what he had discovered: 'The moon is no copy of the Earth'.

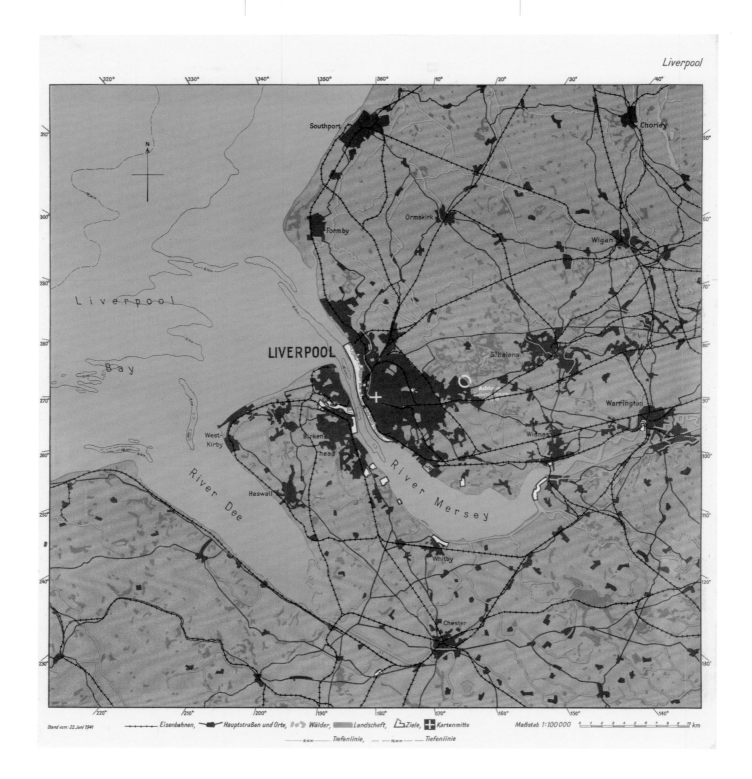

German Bombing Map of Liverpool | 1941 | Luftwaffe General Staff

Printed paper. 60 × 61 cm / 23½ × 24 in. British Library, London

Wars are crucibles of technological innovation, from brand-new weapons to small adaptations such as this luminous map of Liverpool, used by German aircrew on night-time bombing raids during the Blitz in World War II (1939–45). Early in the conflict, pilots on both sides navigated with small-scale topographic maps marked with such useful information as the position of landing fields or anti-aircraft batteries. When improved air defences made daylight raids more hazardous, air forces on both sides resorted to bombing at night. Navigating at night was made difficult by the use of blackouts in target areas, and by problems reading air charts in the red or amber lighting used in aircraft so as not to interfere with night vision. To overcome these problems, the Luftwaffe adopted a new colour scheme for maps, using browns, greens and yellow overprinted in black and blue to overprint such detail as rail lines and rivers by which a pilot might navigate. The targets (*Ziele*) are luminous yellow outlined in red. The edge of the map is marked with the bearings to the centre of Liverpool. The United States Army Air Force also used luminous maps, while Britain's Royal Air Force preferred charts that showed relief in various shades of purple, which could be seen under the amber lights used in their aircraft.

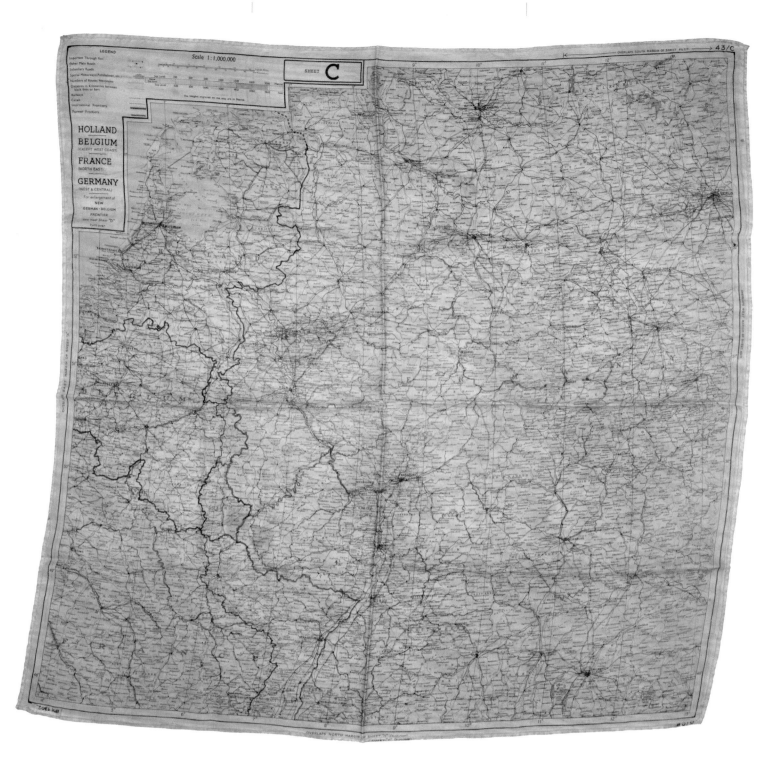

Silk Escape Map | 1939–45 | Christopher Clayton Hutton

Ink on silk. 68.5 × 71 cm / 30 × 28 in. Imperial War Museum, London

Who better than someone who had tried to outsmart the escape artist Harry Houdini to come up with an escape map for soldiers to use in World War II (1939–45)? In 1913 the British businessman Clayton Hutton, who was then working in a sawmill, accepted Houdini's challenge to construct a box from which he could not escape. Houdini won, but only because he bribed the carpenter who made the box. When Hutton told this story during his job inter-

view with the British military intelligence organization MI9 in 1939, he was hired to help its mission to get Allied soldiers out of enemy territory. Hutton came up with the idea of sending soldiers and prisoners of war escape maps on a lightweight material – originally parachute silk, later rayon – that would not draw attention by rustling, would not disintegrate in water and would not tear. (The maps could also serve as a bandage, a sling, a clothing patch or

a water filter during an escape.) The maps went through several series, covering parts of Germany, Norway, France, Belgium and most other areas where there was fighting. Some, like this one, were double-sided. Hutton used creative methods to smuggle the maps to POWs: he enclosed them in money purses (along with a compass and a small hacksaw), sewed them into jacket linings and even hid them inside the boards of Monopoly games.

Scott's Great Snake | 1861 | J.B. Elliott

Printed paper. 35 x 44 cm / 13¾ x 17¼ in. Library of Congress, Washington, DC

This cartoon from the beginning of the American Civil War in 1861 sums up in a simple image the war strategy of the Union: to starve the South into surrender. The 'great snake' was the brainchild of General Winfield Scott, the US commander-in-chief who was already the longest-serving general in US history. 'Old Fuss and Feathers' was widely seen as being too old to command a war – he eventually resigned in November 1861 – but

he realized that battles on land should be backed up by what came to be named the Anaconda Plan, after the South American snake that squeezes its victims to death. Scott proposed a naval blockade of the Confederacy and the Mississippi River to strangle Southern exports of cotton and sugar to finance their rebellion. J.B. Elliott – a publisher in Cincinnati, Ohio, on the frontier between North and South – took great pains to copyright his

map, rightly considering it a masterpiece thanks to its telling vignettes, which represent the disparate states and their approaches to the war. The map is often seen as deriding the Union plan, but it represents the blockade strategy very accurately, including the securing of the upper Mississippi as well as its mouth. Scott's anaconda was critical to the Union victory, and Elliott's map has made the reptile immortal.

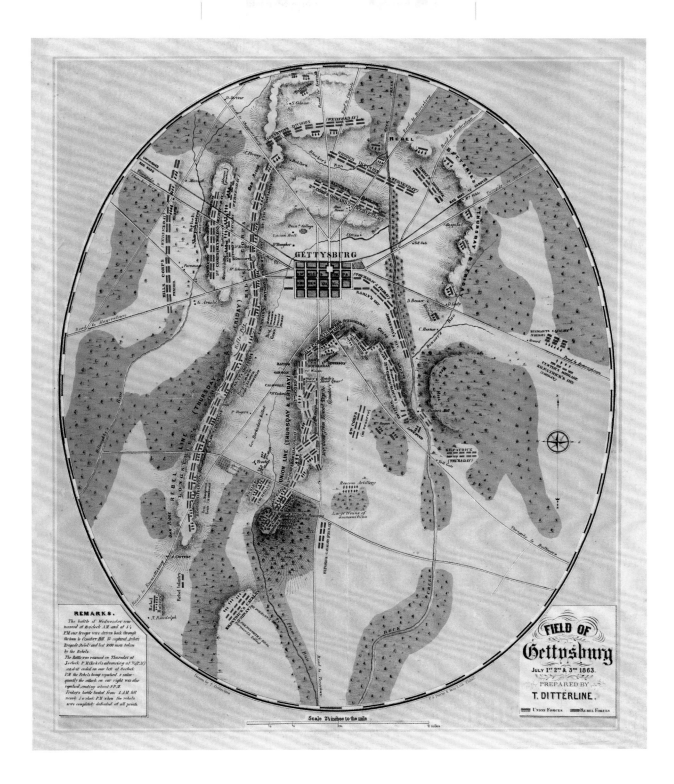

Field of Gettysburg, July 1st, 2nd & 3rd, 1863 | 1863 | Theodore R. Ditterline

Hand-coloured lithograph. 49 × 40 cm / 19¼ × 15¾ in. Library of Congress, Washington, DC

The mapmaker Theodore Ditterline was a resident of the quiet Pennsylvania town of Gettysburg when a chance encounter between Union and Confederate foraging parties on 1 July 1863 led to the bloodiest battle of the American Civil War (1861–5). He drew on local knowledge – at a premium when battles were fought, as they often were, on unsurveyed ground – and eyewitness stories to draw the first published map of the 'high-water mark of the Confederacy' at a time when readers on both sides were hungry for news of the conflict. The Confederate Army of Northern Virginia (in red on the map), led by General Robert E. Lee, met the Union Army of the Potomac (blue) under General George Meade. Ditterline's unusual oval map shows topography, roads and railways, and the troop movements over the three-day battle, from the initial confrontation on 1 July to the Confederate attack on the Union flanks the next day, and the final, doomed Confederate charge against the Union centre on 3 July. The killed, wounded and missing exceeded 45,000 men, and never again did the Confederates threaten the Union. A few months later, in dedicating a military cemetery nearby, President Abraham Lincoln recast the conflict as a fight for 'a new birth of freedom' in his renowned Gettysburg Address.

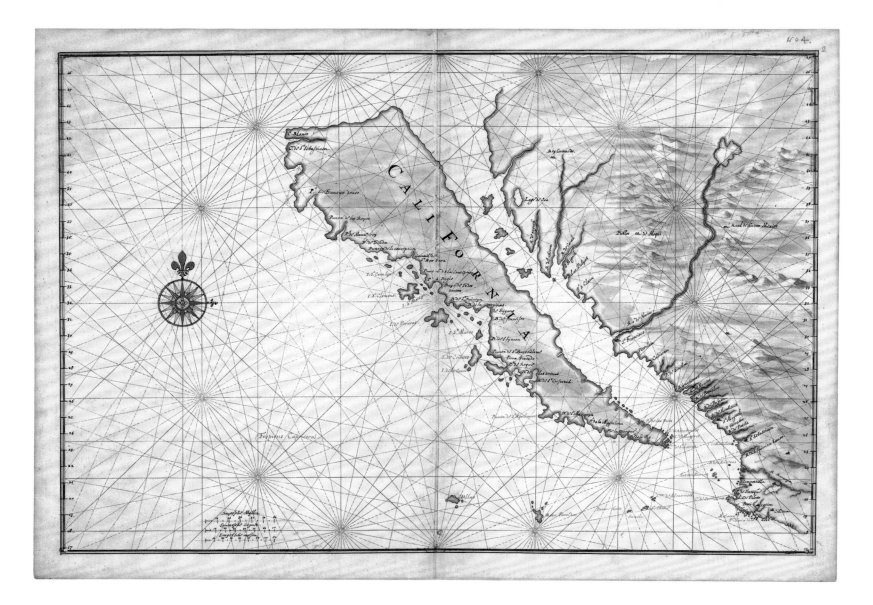

Map of Baja California Shown as an Island | 1639 | Johannes Vingboons

Pen-and-ink and watercolour on paper. 48 × 69 cm / 18⅞ × 27¼ in. Library of Congress, Washington, DC

Since the arrival of Hernán Cortés in Mexico, geographers had been uncertain about the form of California. Cortés had believed it to be an island, but sixteenth-century Spanish cartographers intermittently illustrated it as both an island and a peninsula. It was not until Francis Drake claimed to have landed there in 1579 that the debate about the size and extent of the territory and its attachment to the continent intensified. This map – one of hundreds of watercolour and sketch maps by the Flemish cartographer Johannes Vingboons, a collaborator with the renowned Johannes Blaeu – reflects the debate and includes, near the north of the island, the 'Puerto [de] Sir Francisco Draco'. Of equal importance are the place names on the mainland facing the island, which reflect recent Spanish efforts to colonize the area. Emptying into the gulf is a river labelled Rio de' Norta, which was rumoured to extend northwards as far as New France. At the time, the existence of a transcontinental river was hotly pursued, and in the latter part of the seventeenth century it would result in various expeditions along the Mississippi River. Vingboons carefully left the uppermost region of the map undefined and the coastline undrawn, suggesting that what lay beyond this point was unknown and in need of exploration.

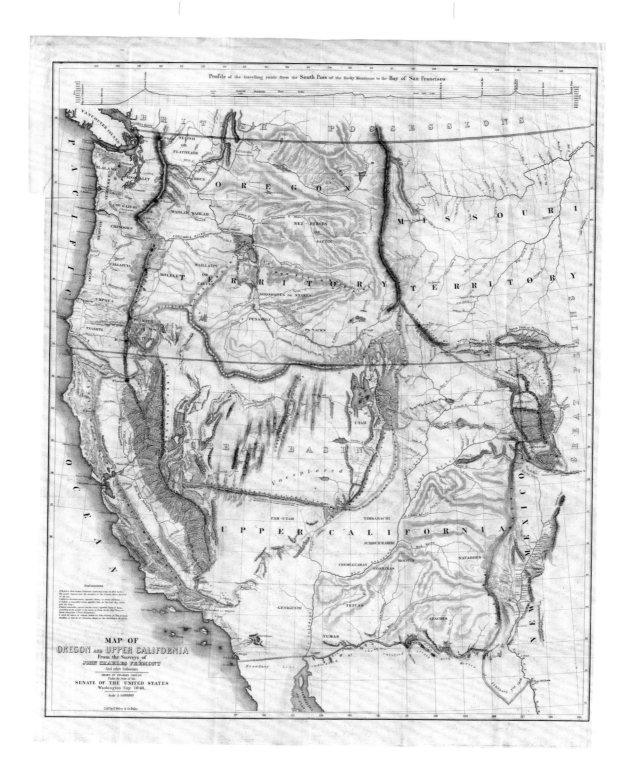

Map of Oregon and Upper California | 1848 | John Charles Frémont and Charles Preuss

Lithograph. 86 × 69 cm / 34 × 27 in. Library of Congress, Washington, DC

This map of the Great Basin in the western United States is one of the earliest cartographic representations of three events in 1848 that changed the American West forever: the ceding of 1,300,000 square kilometres (500,000 square miles) of land in California and New Mexico to the United States by Mexico at the end of the Mexican War; the establishment by Congress of the Oregon Territory; and the discovery of gold in California.

The map also includes the most accurate geographical information of the West available at the time. It was created after the mapmaker Charles Preuss joined the military surveyor John Charles Frémont on two expeditions. It is not a particularly attractive map – with its brown-on-brown image and a clashing green line denoting new boundaries between Oregon and California, and the eastern edge of the Rocky Mountains – but the

Forty-Niners joining the Gold Rush did not care. Seeing the label 'El Dorado or Gold Region' on a map for the first time, they rushed west to stake their claims and strike it rich. To that extent the map had done its job. It was not made to decorate a wall; it was a government-issued document intended to inspire pioneers to settle the West and further integrate the vast region with the rest of the United States.

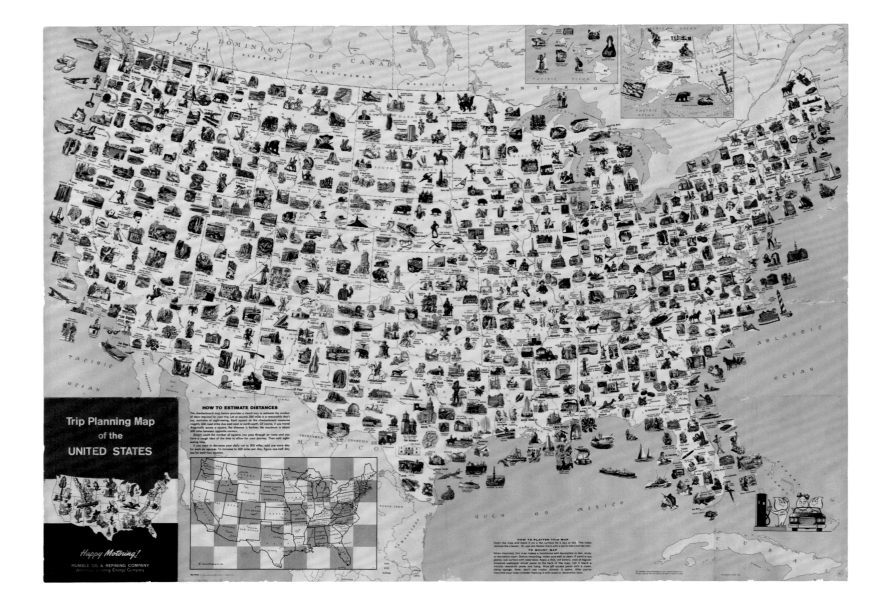

Trip Planning Map of the United States | 1962 | Humble Oil & Refining Company

Printed paper. 61 × 85 cm / 24 × 33½ in. Private collection

The most curious feature of this trip-planning map is its lack of roads (they appear on the back). Just as the tyre company Michelin began publishing road maps in France in 1900 to encourage automobile travel, so the idea caught on with oil companies in the United States at about the same time. It was not until 1956 that a national highway system was built and uniformly numbered across the United States, when so many gasoline com-panies got in on the map-giveaway promotion that a more creative strategy was needed to stand out among the competition. The hundreds of vignettes of activities or landmarks – bucking broncos in Montana, alligators in the Florida Keys, Yosemite in California – were meant to motivate families to plan motoring vacations around historic and patriotic sites. This map was made to be admired: at the bottom are mounting instructions that suggest ironing it and sticking it to the wall. A nation-wide trip could be planned using the yellow-and-orange checkerboard in the lower left corner to help estimate how many days it would take to travel from one place to the next. Humble Oil & Refining Company was rebranded several times (briefly being called Enco, which had to be changed because it means 'engine failure' in Japanese) until ultimately becoming part of Exxon in 1972.

Map | 1961 | Jasper Johns

Oil on canvas. 198.2 × 314.7 cm / 6 ft 6 in × 10 ft 3⅛ in. Museum of Modern Art, New York

Maps have always been used for artistic purposes because the shapes of the familiar lend themselves well to artistic expression and reimagination. Jasper Johns puts the art squarely into cartography with *Map*, which develops his use of easily recognizable images by using the map of the United States in a colourful celebration of both the country and the map itself. Johns wanted to use an image that viewers knew so well that they simply 'saw' it without having to look at or examine it in depth. This is also one of the fundamental aspects of map design – to create a product whose design is implicit rather than explicit, allowing the reader to understand the meaning without having to work hard – so Johns' painting can be seen as linking fine art and cartography together. It is an imaginative piece that provides a meta-phor for the abstract nature of mapping itself. Colourful and playful, interesting and immersive, it riffs on the Pop art painting of the time by such contemporaries of Johns as Andy Warhol, who also experimented with the use of maps. Johns' use of paint is somewhat abstract in application and does not conform to cartographic conventions. He labels places many times in the wrong location, so *Map* challenges convention as much as it reflects the uniformity of the map's familiar shape.

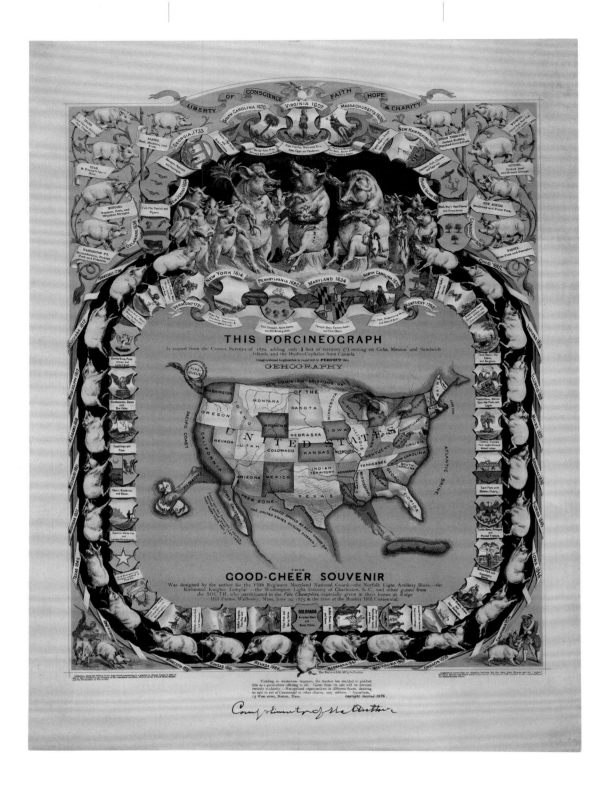

This Porcineograph | *c.*1875 | Forbes Lithograph Manufacturing Company and William Emerson Baker

Colour lithograph. 41 × 66 cm / 16 ⅛ × 26 in. Library of Congress, Washington, DC

This celebration of all things pork – complete with a map of the United States in the shape of a pig – promoted a campaign for agricultural reform by William Emerson Baker. Having made a fortune in business by the age of forty, Baker wanted a new challenge. He purchased a huge piece of land in Needham, Massachusetts, to pursue his quest to reduce the spread of food-borne illnesses through improved farming practices. Boston had long been a centre for social reform, so Baker was in his element. In June 1875 he hosted a party to commemorate the construction of his new 'Sanitary Piggery', which he hoped would revolutionize pork production. Each of the 2,500 guests – including the state governor and the mayor of Boston – received a copy of this 'good-cheer souvenir'. Baker's sense of humour – and hope – is evident everywhere, from the anthropomorphized pigs in the border to the vignettes celebrating the role of pigs in US history. To commemorate the nation's centennial in 1876, the states and territories are marked with their local pork dishes. The Porcineograph celebrates an enduring love of pork, but its graphic style also anticipates the advent of advertising as the nation began to mass-produce everything from clothing to food, with Chicago as the capital of pork production.

Tacografía | 2013 | Déborah Holtz, Juan Carlos Mena and Kitzia Sámano

Printed in *La Tacopedia: Enciclopedia del taco* (2013). 21 × 26.9 cm / 8½ × 10½ in. Private collection

Food and geography have long histories – and so, therefore, do food and maps. Many people know where Kentucky and Champagne are on the map simply because of the drinks they export to the world: bourbon and champagne, respectively. Food is highly regional. Germany and France have their mustards, Vermont and France have their cheeses, Italy and France have their wines. As befits the country that gave the world *haute cuisine*, France is particularly obsessed with anchoring food to regions, which is why the word used to define the connection of edible ingredients to specific geological and geographical determinants is French: *terroir*. This playful Mexican map identifies a variety of tacos from the country's thirty-one states and the capital city. Tacos are deceptively simple – a hand-held tortilla envelope filled with any ingredient – but the distinctions are in the assembled local ingredients, giving rise to territorial differences. According to *Tacografía*, pig-skin tacos (*tacos de chicharron*) are from Querétaro, brain tacos (*tacos de sesos*) can be found in Colima and grilled fish tacos (*tacos de pescado zarandesdo*) are from Nayarit. Lively pictures help readers rapidly identify their favourite fillings.

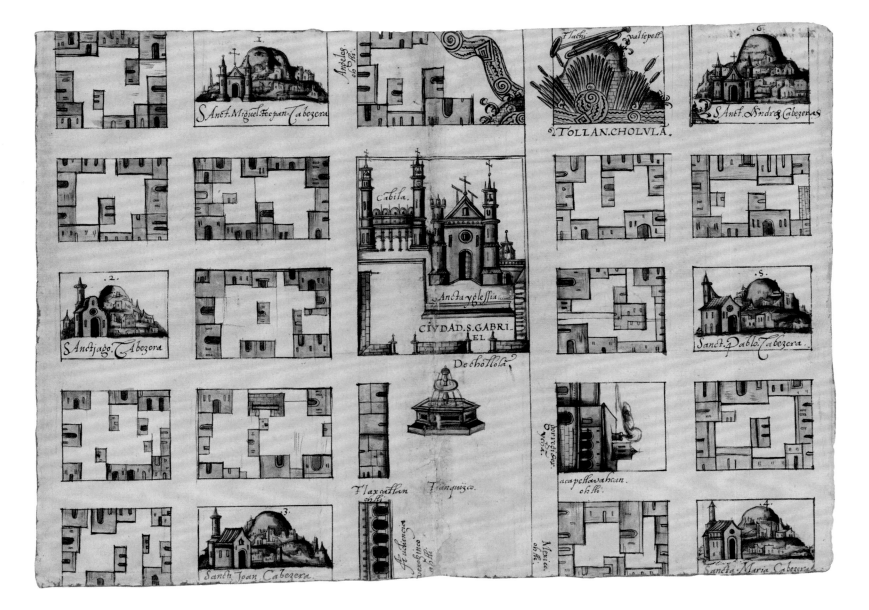

Cholula, Puebla, Mexico | 1581 | Unknown

Watercolour and ink on paper. 31 × 44 cm / 12¼ × 17⅜ in. University of Texas, Austin, Texas

This map of Cholula in Mexico portrays the development of the city nearly six decades after the Spanish had settled there. It was drawn, possibly by an indigenous artist working with the colonial authorities, as part of the *relaciones geográficas*, the series of imperial surveys carried out in response to requests from the Spanish king Phillip II to understand the nature of his empire in the 1570s and 1580s. The construction of San Gabriel,

the church and monastery on the main plaza in the heart of the town, commenced in 1549 and – as with most cities of the time – became emblematic of its administration. The hybrid Nahuatl-Spanish street names on this part of the map (*Tlaxcallan ohlli*, 'Tlaxcallan Street', and *Mexico ohlli*, 'Mexico Street'), together with the Nahuatl word for the market located in the main plaza, *tianquiz-co*, show that the map was intended for both native

and Spanish readers. Built on a grid pattern, like most colonial cities, Cholula is divided into blocks separated by rectilinear streets containing single and multi-storey houses. The parish churches that dot the city are portrayed with vignettes featuring the pastoral landscape around them, providing some rare geographical context for the location of the town.

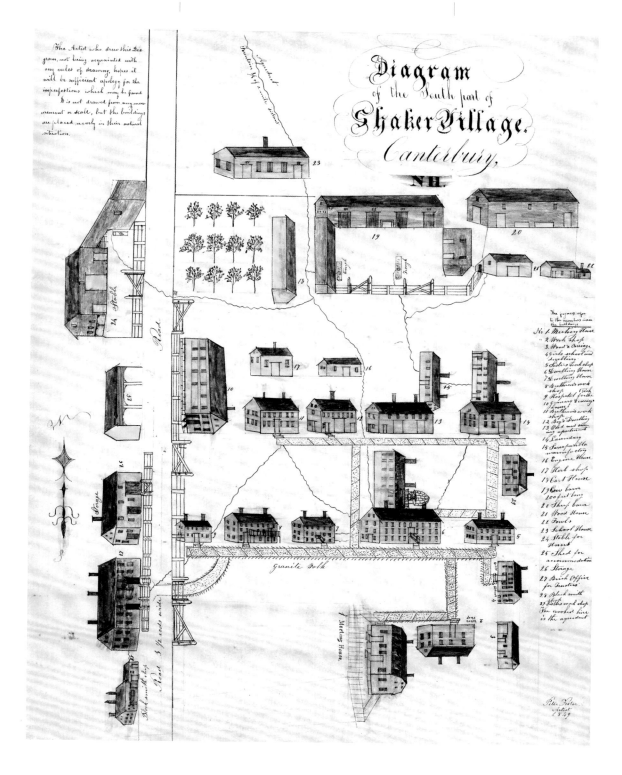

Diagram of the South Part of Shaker Village, Canterbury, New Hampshire | 1849 | Peter Foster

Pen and ink on paper. 42 × 32 cm / 16½ × 12½ in. Library of Congress, Washington, DC

The Shakers – a small sect properly known as the United Society of Believers in Christ's Second Appearing – arrived in North America from England in 1774 and are best known for their elegant and practical designs for furniture and architecture. Shaker philosophy discouraged decorative paintings, but maps were permitted because they had a functional value, which is why this view of the village of Canterbury, New Hampshire, sur-

vives. Peter Foster's map reflects Shaker aesthetics in its simple layout, although it also echoes the grid pattern of more sophisticated cities in the United States. The key identifies buildings by their use, including three types of barn (three-way, bank and gable-entranced) – for cows, sheep and fowl – plus a stable for horses and the sisters' workshop, for tailoring and basket-making. Foster, as befits Shaker humility, apologizes on the map

for his lack of ability to make it to scale, but promises that the placement of buildings is reliable. Other Shaker maps emphasize similar features: the placement and number of windows, entrances and chimneys; the location and types of fences; crops, orchards and landmark trees. There is no perspective, ornamentation or attempt at scale – just enough information to know where to go to get things done.

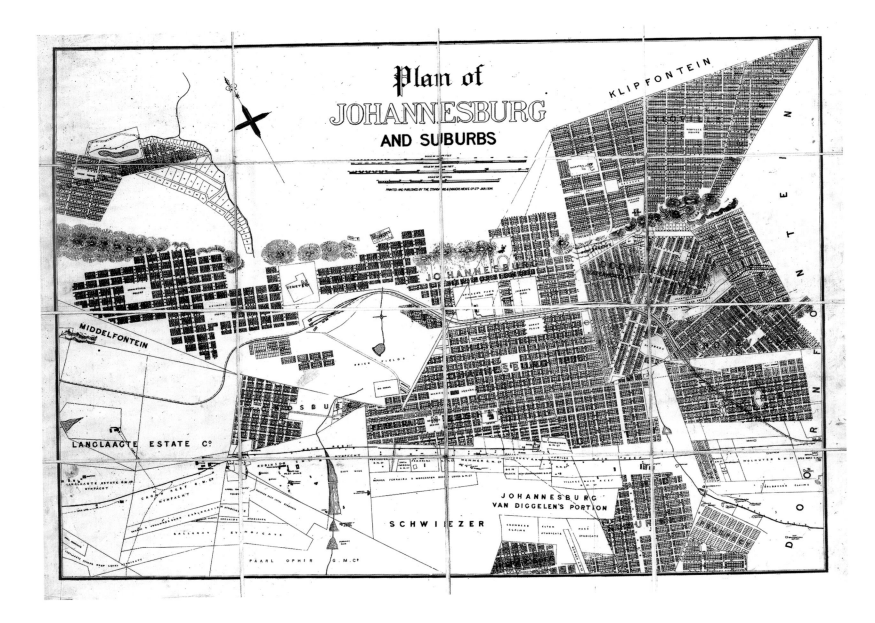

Plan of Johannesburg and Suburbs | 1894 | Unknown

Printed in *The Standards and Diggers' News* (1894). 71 x 97 cm / 28 x 38 in. Museum Africa, Johannesburg

This map gives the 'city' of Johannesburg on the Cape – then no more than a decade old – more of an appearance of permanence and order than it deserved at the time. It was little more than a glorified campsite crammed into a tiny area. The settlement had been a miner's camp named Ferreirasdorp until 1886, when the discovery of the largest gold vein then known in the nearby hills sparked the Witswaterand ('White Water Ridge') Gold Rush. Diggers poured in from around the world, mainly from Britain – this map was published eight years later in a newspaper set up for miners. The oldest parts of the city are marked by their narrow streets, created by the local government trying to cram as many settlers as possible into a small area. The newcomers soon outnumbered the local Boer (Dutch) farmers, who fought a second unsuccessful war against the British (1899–1902), spurred in part by British attempts to control the gold fields. Patterns of discrimination were apparent in the city's earliest history. Streets were carefully drawn in the areas where white (i.e. European-descended) peoples resided. In contrast, the zones where the largely African labourers lived are blank spaces inscribed with the word 'blacks'. As if to underline the difference, a double line surrounds these blanked-out areas.

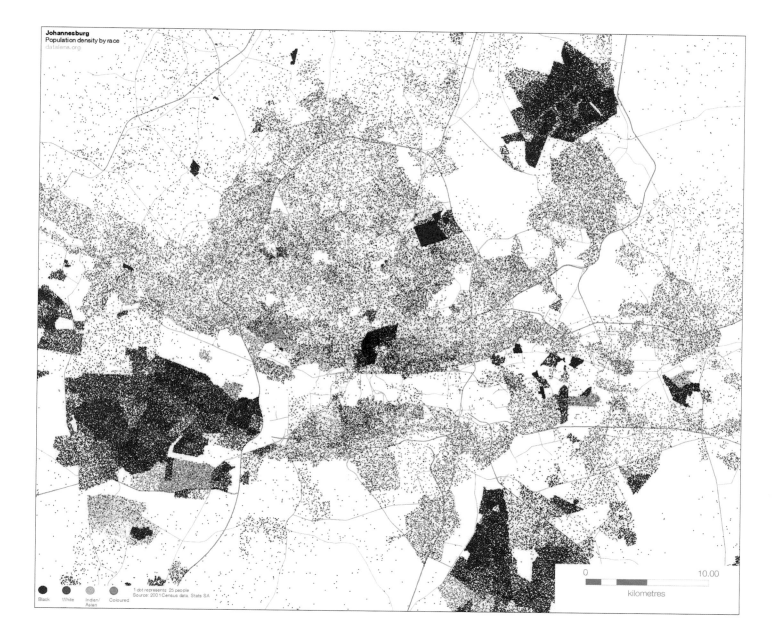

Johannesburg: Population Density by Race | 2012 | David Wilson

Digital. Dimensions variable.

This map of Johannesburg is an illustration of continuing separation in a society that was ostensibly becoming more united. After forty-six years of the official separation of its races, South Africa abandoned its policy of apartheid, 'the state of being apart', and held its first multiracial elections in 1994 in an atmosphere of great optimism. As the patterns of dots on the map indicate, however, the removal of laws on racial segregation was not the same thing as integration. The central area of the city appears predominantly blue (Caucasian) while the large red (Black) area in the lower left depicts Soweto (short for South Western Township), created in 1963 to resettle blacks outside the city of Johannesburg. Although the most striking aspect of the map is the continued racial segregation, the dot-density technique David Wilson uses reveals that the centre does contain a few red dots, signalling a small degree of integration. The other two colours on the map indicate the presence of South Africa's two other former racial categories: 'coloured', meaning of mixed racial origin (green dots) and 'Indian', which referred to descendants of immigrants from India, Pakistan, Bangladesh, Sri Lanka, China and Malaysia (yellow dots).

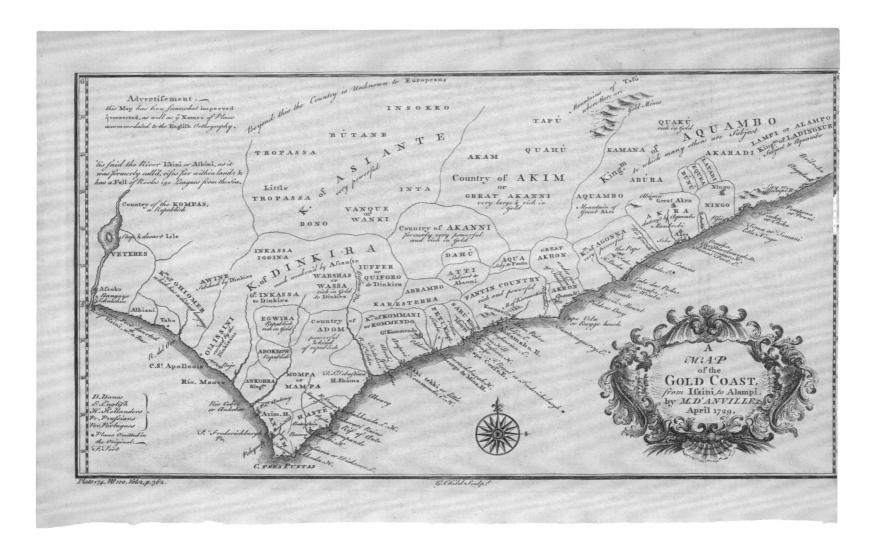

A Map of the Gold Coast from Issini to Alampi | 1729 | Jean Baptiste Bourguignon d'Anville

Engraving. 19 × 35 cm / 7½ × 13⅓ in. Stanford University Libraries, California

For 300 years, from the sixteenth to the nineteenth century, Europeans exploited the west coast of Africa. The region's various resources are made clear in its alternative names: the Slave Coast, the Gold Coast, the Grain Coast, the Ivory Coast and the Pepper Coast. This early eighteenth-century map of what are now Ghana, Togo and Benin by the French cartographer Jean Baptiste Bourguignon d'Anville – a prodigy who made his first map aged fifteen and became a royal geographer at twenty-two – focuses on the most densely rich areas of gold (labelled clearly in script, such as 'Mountains of Tafu where there are gold mines' and 'Republick rich in gold' of Egwira) and of slaves (more discreetly indicated by the euphemism 'forts' along the coastline). An estimated 12 million Africans survived the trip on slave ships across the Atlantic known as the Middle Passage, but many more died during the crossing. D'Anville was able to resist what most of his contemporary cartographers could not: when he did not know what was in a particular place, he did not fill it with drawings of monsters, extra cartouches or speculative information; nor did he copy maps by others whose information was unreliable. He simply left blank space. At the top of this map he notes: 'Beyond this the Country is unknown to Europeans'.

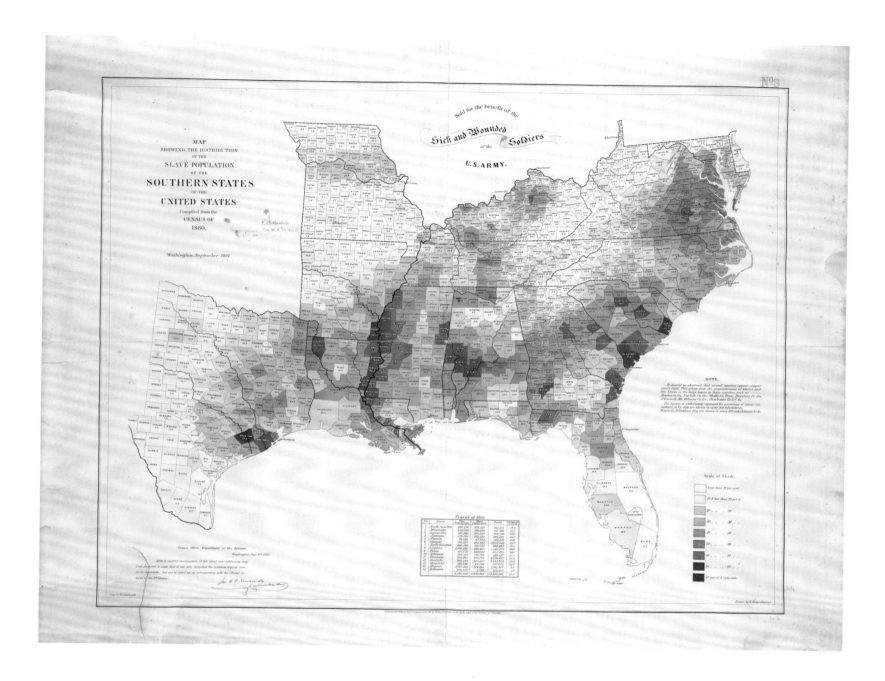

Distribution of the Slave Population of the Southern States | 1861 | Edwin Hergesheimer

Engraving. 66 × 84 cm / 26 × 33 in. Norman B. Leventhal Map Center, Boston Public Library, Boston, Massachusetts

Just prior to the Civil War (1861–65), the United States Coast Survey began to experiment with shading as a way to represent statistical data on a map. That technique was used to powerful effect once the election of Abraham Lincoln as president led eleven slave states to leave the Union. The first experiment was a map representing the distribution of the slave population in Virginia, issued just as the secession crisis turned to war in the summer of 1861. The map met with wide approval in Washington, DC, and in September the Coast Survey issued this similar map covering the entire South. Both maps identify the ratio of slaves to the total population based on the advance returns of the yet-unpublished census of 1860, which counted nearly four million slaves in the nation's total population of more than 31 million. The result was the first American attempt to map statistics. The map had a robust life, widely imitated in the popular press, and was a favorite of Lincoln. The painter Francis Bicknell Carpenter saw Lincoln consulting the map so often that he took pains to include it in his iconic portrait, *First Reading of the Emancipation Proclamation* (1864). The map revealed what thousands of wartime reconnaissance and topographic maps could not: the Confederacy's most valuable asset, its labour system.

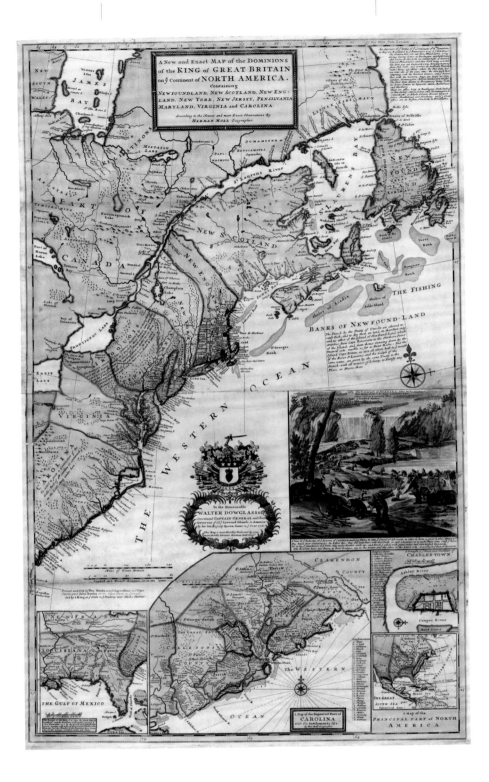

A New and Exact Map of the Dominions of the King of Great Britain | 1715 | Herman Moll

Hand-coloured engraving. 101 × 61 cm / 40 × 24 in. Private collection

Herman Moll's famed copperplate map of British North America from his folio atlas *The World Described*, published in editions from 1709 to 1754, is universally known as the 'Beaver Map' owing to its inset image of beavers labouring industriously downriver from Niagara Falls. The map reflects the addition to Britain's growing empire of Newfoundland and its valuable cod fisheries, which were obtained from France at the end of Queen Anne's War in 1713. In insets along the bottom of the map, Moll also stakes Britain's claim along the fluid border between Carolina and Spanish Florida. Within the British colonies, he illustrates the development of transportation and communications networks by showing rivers and a growing system of roads. All signs of Native Americans are passive. The map's positive view of British North America and its potential shows Moll to be an unabashed enthusiast for empire, although he had originally probably emigrated from Germany in the late 1670s. His skill as a fine engraver on metal brought him to the attention of London publishers and eventually gained him entry to the map trade at the heart of the emerging British Empire. In due course, Moll gained a reputation as one of the pre-eminent British mapmakers of the first half of the eighteenth century.

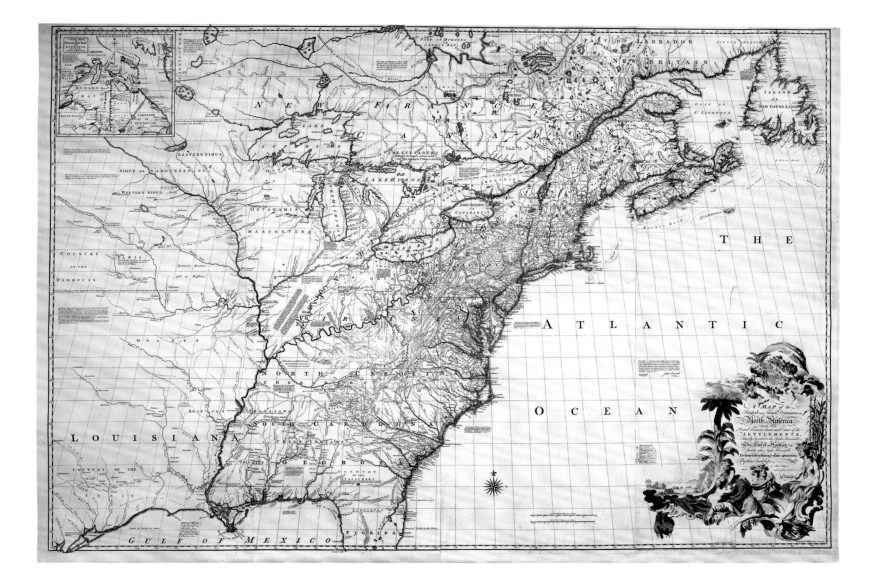

A Map of the British and French Dominions in North America | 1755 | John Mitchell

Hand-coloured engraving. 136 × 195 cm / 53½ × 76¾ in. Private collection

John Mitchell's map of the North American colonies has been described as the most important map in the continent's history. It played a role in encouraging one war and in concluding another. By the time Mitchell showed the territorial claims of Virginia and other colonies extending westwards beyond the Mississippi River, British troops were already at war to defend those claims. The French had built forts along the Ohio River, threatening British dreams of westward expansion, and Mitchell's map of the offending forts became a propaganda tool to rally the British in the French and Indian War, or Seven Years' War (1754–63). In the first battle in 1754, a Virginia militia commanded by the young George Washington attacked French forces near 'The Great Meadows' (on the map where the boundaries of Maryland, Pennsylvania and Virginia meet). Mitchell was born in Virginia in 1711 and moved in 1746 to London, where he met the Earl of Halifax (named in the cartouche), who commissioned a map showing the French threat. The large eight-sheet map was published seven times between 1755 and 1775. At the end of the American Revolution (1775–83), it was used to define the boundaries of the new United States during the peace negotiations in Paris, sealing its historical importance.

Sir Francis Drake's Raid on St Augustine | 1589 | Baptista Boazio

Hand-coloured engraving. 40 × 54 cm / 15 ¾ × 21 ¼ in. Library of Congress, Washington, DC

This map, drawn in 1589 by the London-based Italian artist Baptista Boazio, celebrates an English victory over Spain in Florida and is the first known map of part of what is now the United States. Spain claimed a region that stretched north to the Chesapeake Bay and west to the Appalachians, and St Augustine, founded in 1565, was Spanish Florida's main settlement – until it was raided by an English fleet commanded by Sir Francis Drake in May

1586. In this bird's-eye view, created to accompany a description of Drake's voyage to the West Indies, English ships (white flags with St George's cross) blockade the harbour and land soldiers to attack the town and fort (flying the diagonal Burgundy cross). Drake's destruction of St Augustine and other Spanish colonial cities enraged King Philip II, who in 1588 sent the Spanish Armada to invade England – where it was defeated by another fleet

commanded by Drake. The raid on St Augustine led ultimately to England's naval supremacy and colonization of North America. Boazio, who lived in London from about 1585 to 1603, painted many maps of English military victories, including Drake's raids on the Spanish Caribbean cities of Cartagena and Santo Domingo. The detail of the wooden fort and walled city is an invaluable historical record of early European settlement in North America.

Sea Chart of the Pacific | 1622 | Hessel Gerritsz

Ink on vellum. 107 × 141 cm / 42 × 55½ in. Bibliothèque nationale de France, Paris

The beauty of these galleons, shown under full sail, belies the importance of this secret 1622 chart of the South Pacific by the Dutch cartographer Hessel Gerritsz, which outlines early discoveries in Australia. After the Republic of the Seven United Netherlands achieved independence from Habsburg Spain in 1581, they created an aggressive trading company – the Dutch East India Company, or VOC – to rival that of England, to expand trade east to the Spice Islands and China, and to look for new territory in Australasia. In 1617 Gerritsz was appointed the first exclusive cartographer of the VOC, probably then the most important position for any mapmaker. All charts and logs from returning VOC captains were submitted to him, and he used the information to create charts to accompany later voyages. This chart shows the currents and winds of the ocean and incorporates a sighting of western Australia by the Spanish explorer Luis Váez de Torres in 1605 and the Dutch navigator Willem Janszoon's landing on Cape York the following year (the first European landing in Australia). Gerritsz named Australia Dove Land after Janszoon's ship, the *Duyfken* ('Dove'). Abel Tasman consulted Gerrtisz's maps extensively on his voyage around Australia and to New Zealand in 1642.

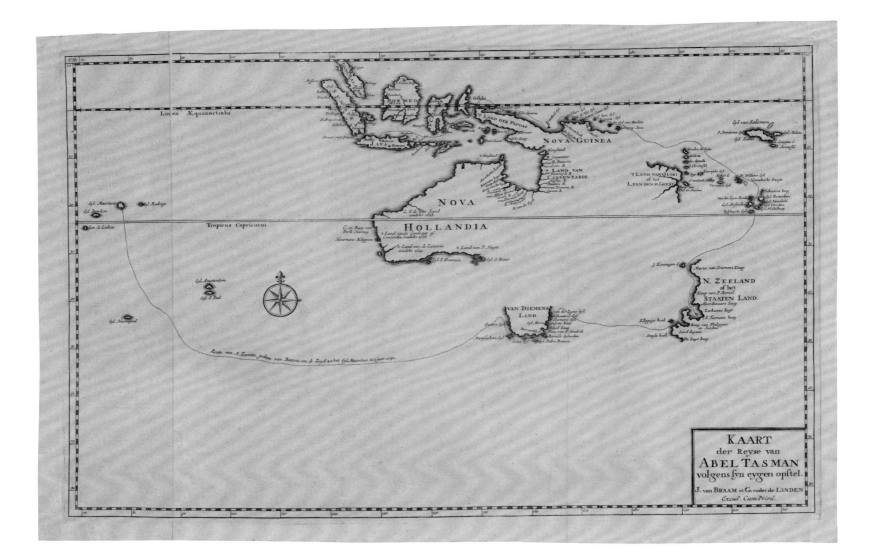

Abel Tasman's Discoveries in Australasia | 1726 | François Valentijn

Engraving. 29.2 × 45.4 cm / 11½ × 18 in. Mitchell Library, State Library of New South Wales, Sydney

The incomplete coastlines of this map reflect the gradual process by which Europeans learned about Australasia in the seventeenth century. The map actually charts a journey made more than eighty years before it was drawn: the voyage by the navigator Abel Tasman in 1642 from the capital of the Dutch East Indies in Batavia – now Jakarta in Indonesia – in search of the legendary land of Boeach. In the late thirteenth century the

Venetian traveller Marco Polo had returned from China with reports of this wealthy land far to the south of Java and Guinea, and cartographers such as Abraham Ortelius had incorporated this information into maps as part of the Great Southern Continent Europeans supposed existed (see p.229). This map covers Tasman's route from Batavia to Mauritius and Australasia, where he discovered Tasmania and New Zealand and showed

that Australia was not part of a southern continent. The map also includes discoveries Tasman made in northern Australia on his second voyage, in 1644. The outlines of Australia and New Zealand were superseded only by the charts of James Cook in 1770 (see opposite). The creator of this chart, François Valentijn, used the formerly secret archives of the Dutch East India Company to publish the first accurate account of Tasman's voyages.

A Chart of New Zealand | 1769–70 | James Cook

Ink on paper. 183 x 128 cm / 72 x 50½ in. British Library, London

The British naval captain James Cook explored more of the planet than any other individual. This chart of New Zealand, from the first of his three voyages to the Pacific (1768–71), marks one of the most remarkable feats of surveying in history. Cook circumnavigated the two islands – then unknown to Europeans – in monotonously rough weather and perilously stormy seas that prevented him from being able to land a boat to set up the shore points that would have enabled him to chart the coast using triangulation. Instead, he carried out his running survey with remarkably accurate dead reckoning, deducing his position based on astronomical observations with horizontal sextant angles. Such was Cook's accuracy that the Royal New Zealand Navy replaced his charts of the straits between North and South islands only at the end of the twentieth century. A version of the chart was later engraved from Cook's original by Charles Praval, a Frenchman who was among the artists recruited by the botanist Joseph Banks – who accompanied Cook on his voyage – mainly to complete the sketches made by the expedition artist, Sydney Parkinson, who died on the voyage home. Having confirmed that New Zealand was not the legendary unknown Southern Continent, Cook sailed on to explore Australia.

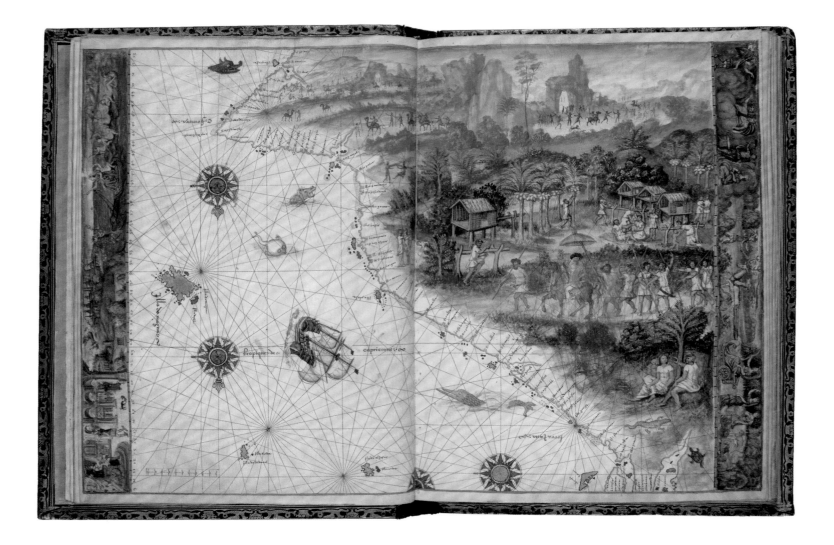

Java le Grande, from the Vallard Atlas | 1547 | Unknown

Manuscript with pigments and gold highlights on parchment. 37 × 48 cm / 14½ × 19 in. Huntington Library, San Marino, California

This portolan chart of the coast of 'Java le Grande' – a fictional representation of an unknown Southern Continent – comes from the beautiful sixteenth-century *Vallard Atlas*. Although the atlas is inscribed with the name of Nicholas Vallard, he was probably its first owner rather than its creator, who is unknown. The atlas was probably made in Dieppe, at the time a major map-making centre, the artistic productions of which usually relied on Portuguese maps for their content. The atlas contains fifteen double-page charts of different parts of the world, including the theoretical Southern Continent, thought by geographers to be necessary to balance the landmasses in the northern hemisphere. Terra Java and Jave le Grande, the names used in the *Atlas* for the conjectured Southern Continent, have their origin in *The Travels of Marco Polo*, written in about 1298. Through a later transcription error, Polo's island of Java was misunderstood as being part of the hypothetical continent. The superficial similarity of this coastline to part of the Australian coast has led to – somewhat tenuous – speculation about an unknown Portuguese discovery of Australia. The atlas is lavishly illustrated with scenes of warriors, camels, sea monsters, ships, horses, exotic animals and so on. It is orientated with south at the top.

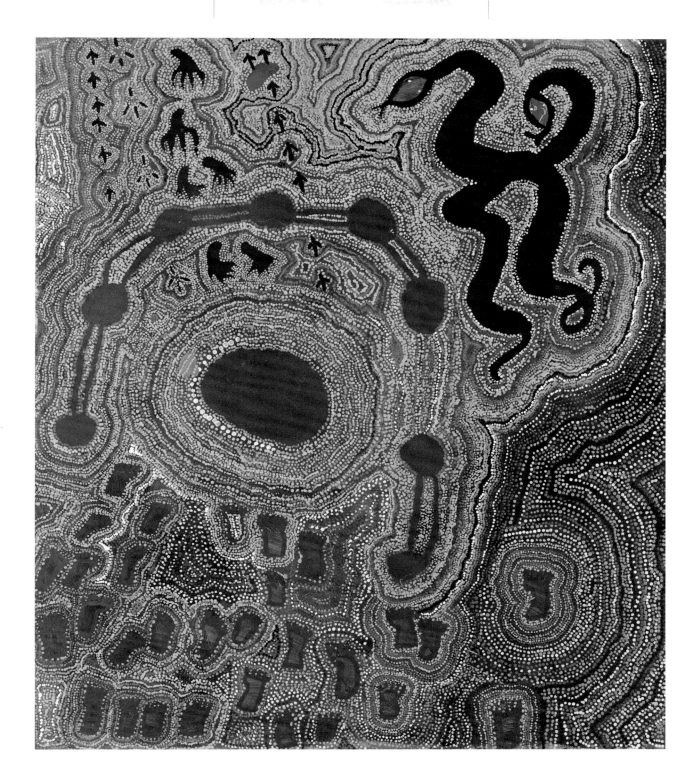

Baltaltjara | 1997–9 | Estelle Hogan

Synthetic polymer paint on canvas. 134.5 × 120.5 cm / 53 × 47½ in. National Gallery of Victoria, Melbourne

The aboriginal artist Estelle Hogan was born at Tjintirrkara near the border of Western and South Australia in about 1937, and this symbolic map shows an area near her birthplace. It shows the sacred site of Baltaljtjara, where the Seven Sisters – who eventually became the star constellation of the Pleiades – came to drink and camp. Their footprints can be seen towards the top left-hand corner of the image. The area of Baltaljtjara was sacred to aboriginal peoples – mirri-mirri – and so can only be discussed in general terms, but the complex patterns and rich colours indicate its spirituality. Unusually for traditionally nomadic peoples, Australian aborigines drew maps associated with important landmarks such as outcrops of rock, waterholes and creeks. These maps – created in sand or on bark – were also linked to the Dreamtime, a mythological period when ancestral beings and giant animals created the landscape, and thus had a deep spiritual meaning. The artist came from the Spinifex culture, who were displaced from their lands in the 1950s and 1960s to make way for British nuclear tests. The painting was made as part of the Spinifex Arts Project, a symbolic exchange with the Australian government by which the Spinifex reclaimed their historical homelands.

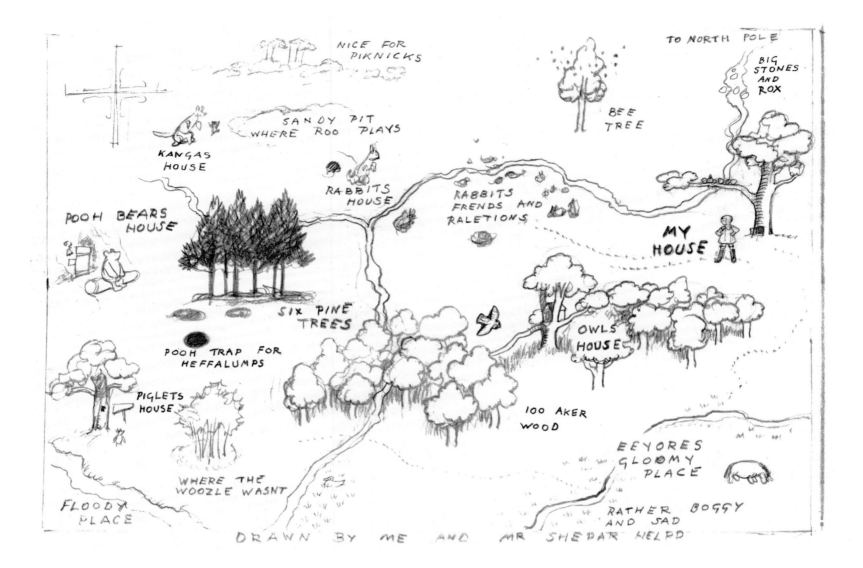

The Hundred Acre Wood | 1926 | Ernest H. Shepard

Pencil on paper. 9 × 25 cm / 3½ × 9⅞ in. Private collection

Fictional places have often provided inspiration for cartographic depiction. One of the simplest, earliest and most memorable is the depiction by the illustrator Ernest H. Shepard of the Hundred Aker Wood, the setting of A. A. Milne's children's stories about Winnie-the-Pooh. The small map for which this was the first sketch appears on the inside front cover of the books, where it immediately draws the reader into the

imaginary landscape that provides settings for the adventures to come. The map is whimsical and playful, with simplified geography, vignettes of key places, labels that refer directly to episodes in the stories and central characters positioned throughout. The imaginary wood is based on Five Hundred Acre Wood in Ashdown Forest in Sussex, England, and many locations in the stories can be linked to real places. Both the map and Shepard's

other illustrations can be matched to actual views, and were directly inspired by the distinctive high, open heathlands of heather, gorse, bracken and silver birch punctuated by hilltop clumps of pine trees. The map has become synonymous with the Winnie-the-Pooh stories, and reminds us of the power of maps to bring our imaginations to life.

Australia | 2012 | Aleksandra Mizielinska and Daniel Mizielinski

Hand-drawn map with digitially applied colour, printed in *Maps* (2012). 37 × 54 cm / 14½ × 21¼ in. Private collection

The maps we encounter in childhood shape not only our idea of the world but also our idea of what maps are. These illustrated guided tours for junior armchair travellers take inspiration from illustrated adult maps such as those of *National Geographic* (see p.53). The Mizielinskis, married Polish graphic designers, drew on their own childhood memories to produce the international bestseller *Maps*, a collection of fifty-two sump-tuously drawn images. Rather than the comprehensive-ness expected in an adult atlas, *Maps* leaves out much information in order to concentrate on aspects of life about which young people are more likely to care: plants and animals, sports, languages and flags, food, musical instruments and so on. A certain amount of cultural ste-reotyping is inevitable with such a snapshot approach – the Australia map includes such classics as a surfer, a didgeridoo and a meat pie – but taken as a whole *Maps* invites young explorers to think about their relation to the physical world on a scale of their own experience (although this large book will test the arm span of its youngest readers). In an era of extremely precise dig-ital maps, this playful hard-copy armful of information inspires children to return again and again to its beauti-fully rendered geography.

Map of the Northern Sky | 1515 | Albrecht Dürer

Hand-coloured woodcut. 44.5 × 61 cm / 17½ × 24 in. Collection Daniel Crouch Rare Books, London

The renowned German artist Albrecht Dürer created the first printed star charts: this woodcut of the northern hemisphere and its pair showing the southern hemisphere. In the northern hemisphere, the twelve signs of the zodiac are intended to be read anti-clockwise, as if the viewer were looking down from space. The figures representing the constellations are shown from behind, as they would appear on a celestial globe from 'outside' the sky. The charts use a coordinate system in an attempt to position accurately forty-eight constellations listed in the star catalogue contained in Claudius Ptolemy's second-century work *Almagest*. The portraits in the corners of the chart depict four ancient scientific authorities – each in national dress and holding a celestial globe – whose advances in knowledge informed Dürer's work. They are Aratus, representing Greek geometry; Ptolemy, Greek–Egyptian iconography; al-Sufi, Islamic scientific accuracy; and Marcus Manilius, the Roman tradition of astronomy. The charts may, therefore, be seen as a culmination of more than 2,000 years of science. They were produced by Dürer under the patronage of the Holy Roman Emperor Maximilian I, in cooperation with the mapmaker Johannes Stabius and the astronomer Conrad Heinfogel.

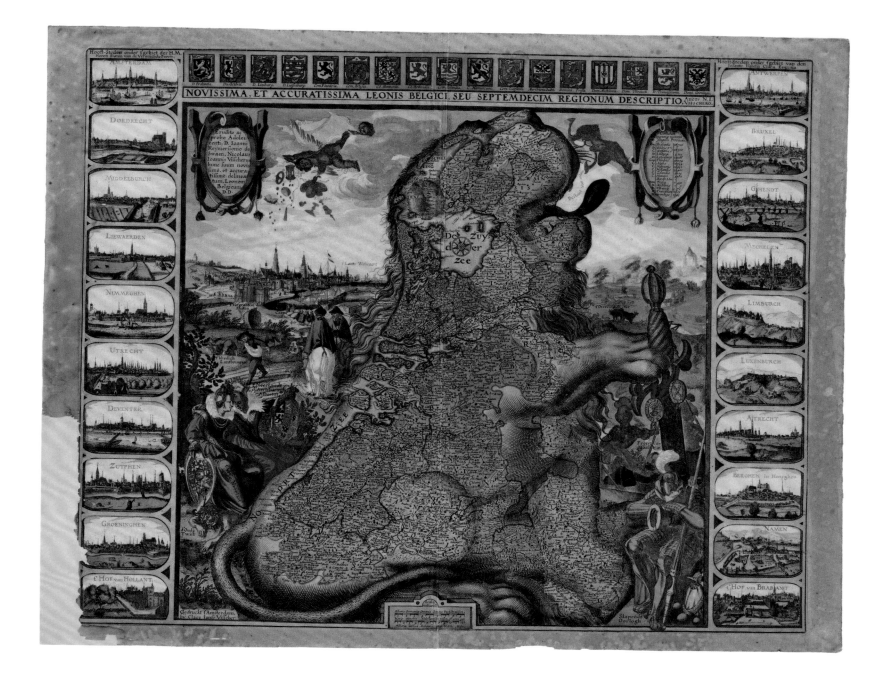

Leo Belgicus | 1609 | Claes Janszoon Visscher the Younger

Hand-coloured engraving and etching. 46.4 × 56.5 cm / 18 ¼ × 22 ¼ in. Atlas van Stolk, Rotterdam

Leo Belgicus (Lion of Belgium) is one of the most famous novelty maps, but it also carries a strong political message. It represents the Seventeen Provinces of the Low Countries (present-day Holland, Belgium and Luxembourg) in the form of a lion. The first design was conceived by the Austrian cartographer Michael Aitzinger in 1583, while the Netherlands waged the Eighty Years' War (1568–1648) for its independence from

Spain. The map soon achieved the status of a patriotic national emblem, and several versions appeared. After Aitzinger's, known as 'lion rampant', this second and most famous version was published by Claes Janszoon Visscher the Younger to mark the Twelve Years' Truce (1609–21). The lion now sits with its sword sheathed, surrounded by images symbolizing peace and prosperity: the growth of towns, agriculture, safe travel and an

allegorical figure of a sleeping Mars. Above the title is a frieze formed by the seventeen coats of arms of the provinces. The two side borders contain town views of the northern (left) and southern Netherlands (right). The third version of the map – known as *Leo Hollandicus* – shows only Holland and was published after the independence of the Dutch Republic was confirmed by the Peace of Westphalia (1648).

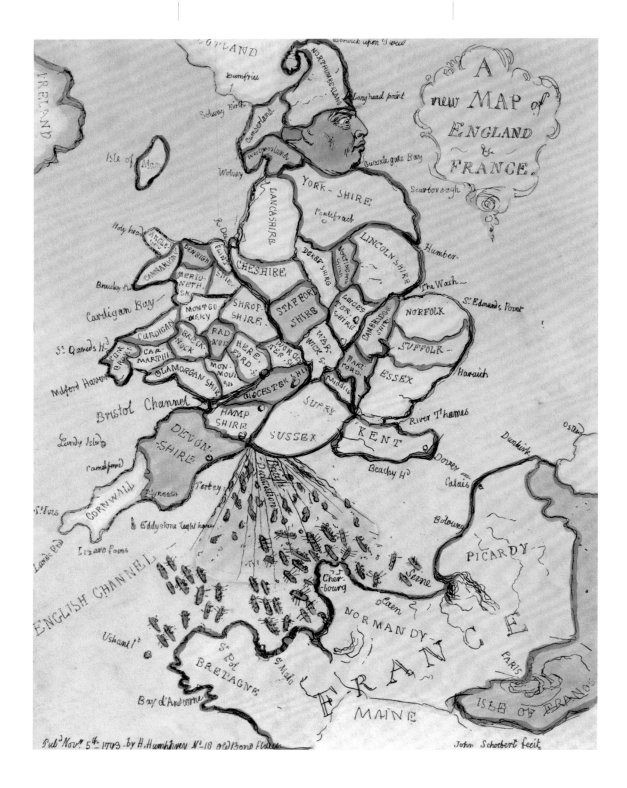

The French Invasion, or John Bull Bombarding the Bum-boats | 1793 | James Gillray

Hand-coloured etching. 35.3 × 25 cm / 14 × 10 in. New College, Oxford University

In this map by the leading British cartoonist James Gillray, King George III in the shape of England and Wales defecates directly into a French coastline configured to resemble a face, repelling a French invasion of 'bum-boats' – a type of small supply vessel. Maps are powerful objects with which to convey political messages or propaganda, and Gillray combines his with the late eighteenth-century British taste for scatalogical humour and caricature to express Britain's relationship with the rest of Europe, in particular its closest neighbour, France. The map was created amid rumours of an impending invasion as part of the revolutionary tendencies then running high in France, and Gillray creates a fervently patriotic show to increase sympathy with the ruling monarch and raise anti-French sentiment. Gillray was a master of satirical caricature and a cutting commentator on political and social topics, and skilfully summed up Britain's contempt of the potential threat. Cartography is a powerful vehicle for satire in the hands of a skilled craftsman, and although the sketch is merely that – a sketch rather than an accurate portrayal of topography, and dependent on crude stereotypes, such as the figure of John Bull himself – it needs no more than a general shape on which to hang the message.

СМЕРТЬ ФАШИЗМУ

Death to Fascism | 1941 | Vasilii Vlasov, Teodor Pevzner and Tatiana Vladimirovna Shishmareva

Lithograph. 60.4 × 90.5 cm / 23¾ × 35½ in. Ne boltai! Collection, Prague

On 22 June 1941 Nazi Germany abruptly ended the Nonaggression Pact it had formed in 1939 with the Soviet Union when it launched Operation Barbarossa, the largest invasion in history. Some three million troops crossed into Soviet territory. Soviet artists were immediately charged with generating propaganda to re-educate the people about their new enemy to the west. This is just one example of that campaign, designed in Leningrad (now St Petersburg) just days after the invasion. Aided by two other artists, Vasilii Vlasov – a film artist and book illustrator – created this simple vilification of the new monstrous German enemy, wielding an axe and a gun and with his paws all over the map of Europe, a reference to Adolf Hitler's territorial ambitions. With a caricature of Hitler's moustache and cropped hair, the subhuman enemy lumbers towards the Soviet Union, but is effectively repelled – at least visually – by the unified bayonets of the Red Army. This characterization of the German enemy as an apelike creature stretches back to World War I (1914–18), when American and British propaganda depicted the German Kaiser as the brutish enemy of civilization. The challenge facing Soviet propagandists in 1941 was to generate support for this unexpected new war, virtually overnight.

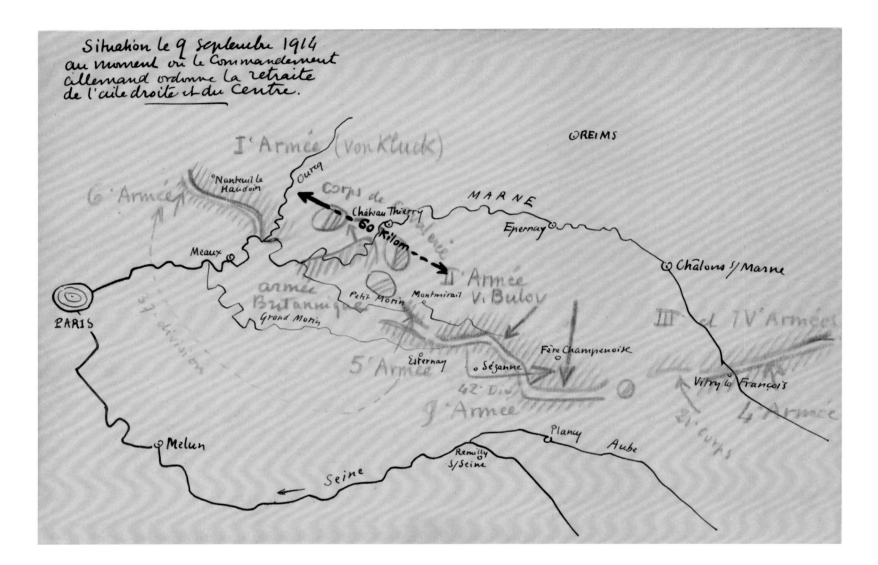

First Battle of the Marne | 1914 | Unknown

Ink and coloured pencil on paper. 22 × 34 cm / 8⅝ × 13⅜ in. Library of Congress, Washington, DC

The simple colour and broad detail of this French sketch of the First Battle of the Marne, fought in the opening weeks of World War I (1914–8) on 5–12 September 1914, disguise the perilous situation the map depicts. German armies had looped through Belgium to threaten Paris, in order to defeat the French before turning to fight the Russians on the Eastern Front. The French and their allies, the small British Expeditionary Force, fell back towards the French capital before making a desperate last stand on the Marne River. Probably drawn by a French officer, this map is one of a series showing the week-long battle, and reveals just how close to Paris the Germans had come. The cannon from the front could be heard in the capital, and fleets of Paris taxis were hired to rush French reserves to the front line. Black lines mark the rivers that were so important to the Allied lines of defence, and pencil notes the positions of the main forces. This map shows the situation on 9 September, when a German miscalculation opened a gap between the First Army of Alexander von Kluck and the Second Army of Karl von Bülow. The British pushed into the gap, forcing the German forces right and centre to retreat. The moment of crisis had passed, and within months the war settled into the stalemate of the Western Front.

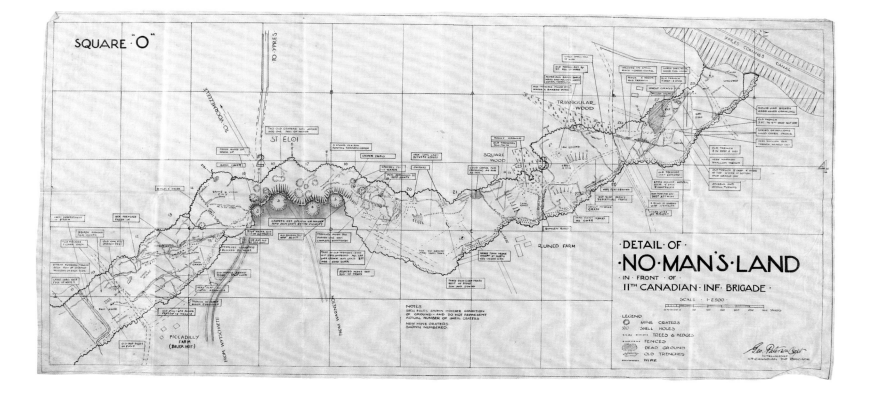

No-Man's-Land | 1916 | George Patterson

Ink on tracing linen. 49 × 103 cm / 19 ¼ × 40 ½ in. Library and Archives Canada, Ottawa, Ontario

Throughout the history of warfare, reliable maps have made the difference between life and death, or victory and defeat (see p.88). This is certainly true of this Canadian manuscript map of the trenches of the Western Front in 1916, which shows areas of cover and possible obstacles to soldiers in no-man's-land. George Patterson, an Intelligence Officer with the Canadian 11th Infantry Brigade, drew the map on tracing linen, so it

is a unique copy, probably produced to brief officers commanding the sector. The Canadian 4th Division had arrived in France only in mid-August 1916 before moving up to the line just south of Ypres later that month, so were not yet experienced in trench warfare. Ypres had experienced heavy fighting during two previous battles in 1914 and 1915, when mining had been used to destroy enemy trenches, producing the craters shown on the

map. When the war began, in 1914, the combatant nations expected lots of movement and issued their forces with medium-scale maps (at scales between 1:80,000 and 1:100,000). However, by the end of 1914 the Western Front was bogged down in static trench warfare and the existing maps no longer met the needs of the armies, so increasingly larger-scale maps like Patterson's were produced during the rest of the conflict.

5KM RIVER RUN

DISTANCE	**BEGINS IN:**	Florence, Italy	AVAIL. POINTS
5.06 kilometers	**CREATED BY:**	Elsie Cheshire Best Time: 30:00	**0** ?

DESCRIPTION: This is a 5.06 km Run in Florence, Italy. The Run has a total ascent of 35.88 m and has a maximum elevation of 119.09 m. This route was created by fb.ElsieCh.187 on 09/24/2009. View other Runs that fb.ElsieCh.187 has done or find similar maps in Djibouti.

RUN

CLIMB
35 ft

TYPE: Run / Jog

SHARE:

ACTIONS   PRINT   SEND TO PHONE   ★ BOOKMARK

ELEVATION (m)

START ELEVATION	MAX ELEVATION	GAIN	CLIMBS ON ROUTE
49 M	**119 M**	**35 M**	1

CLIMB DETAILS

Learn About Climb Ratings   Download Data

Rating	Start/End Points	Length	Start/End Elevation	Avg Grade
	0.10 km/1.35 km	1.24 km	55 m/89 m	2.8%

5km River Run (Florence) | 2009 | MapMyRun

Digital. Dimensions variable

The red line of MapMyRun is familiar to runners around the world. Robin Thurston, an avid cyclist, and Kevin Callahan, a dedicated runner, started MapMyRun in 2005 as the first fitness application for individuals. It uses GPS technology to enable users to track the route, distance and elevation of their runs, and calculates pace and calories burned. Each run can be compared to previous runs, to friends' runs or even to strangers' runs – all of which is meant to motivate people to keep it up. Over half of MapMyRun users admit to being overweight and using the app as part of a strategy to embrace a healthier lifestyle, receiving an immediate visualization of their latest achievement in the form of a red line of ground covered. The progress of a particular run can be studied and shared, and adjusted for unexpected detours, while runners seeking a new route or a route in an unfamiliar location can search for runs by location. Runners track everything, from the daily commute to marathons and further; some users have run around the world with the app. The parent company, MapMyFitness, has launched MapMyRide (for cyclists) and even MapMyDogWalk, and was purchased in 2013 by the clothing maker Under Armour, which plans to incorporate mapping technology into wearable objects.

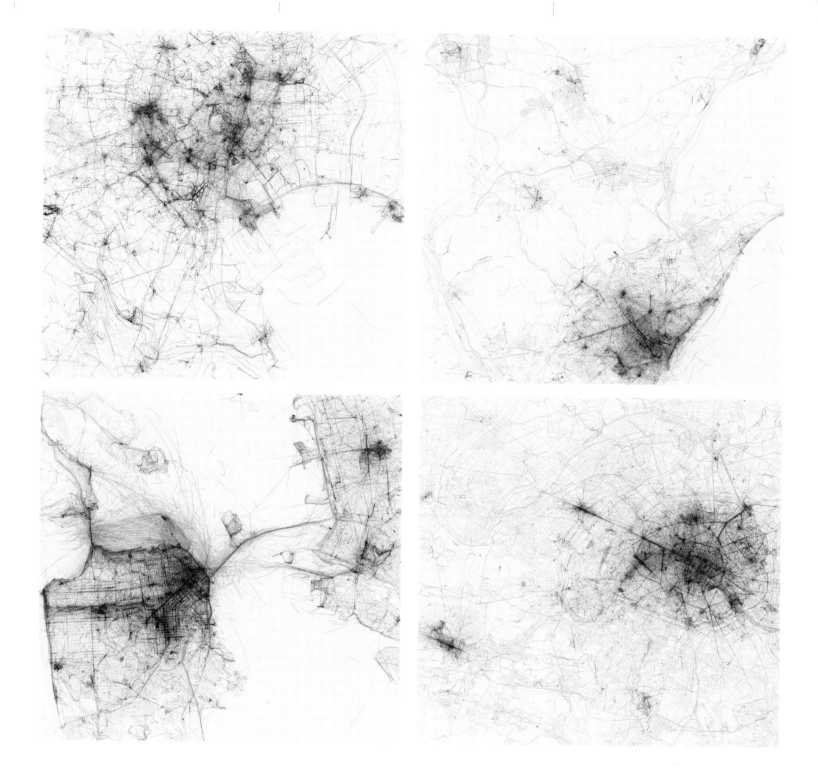

Locals and Tourists | 2015 | Eric Fischer

Digital. Dimensions variable

These four city maps – Tokyo (top left), Barcelona (top right), San Francisco (bottom left) and Paris (bottom right) – were generated by data artist and software developer Erich Fischer from data gathered from unknown users on the Internet. Fischer mapped the locations of which people posted images online and colour coded them blue (for people whose photographs of a location spanned at least a month) or red (for those whose photographs were concentrated into a period of shorter than a month). Fischer deduced that the former were probably locals and the latter tourists (where it was not possible to tell, he used yellow). The results seem to reveal the tourist hot-spots in each city (Fischer produced a similar set of maps based on where people sent tweets). This kind of crowd-sourced mapping – in which individuals provide their own experiences through mechanisms of collecting data designed for a project – creates maps that go beyond static issues to become useful in the moment. Whether needing to know where a parking spot becomes available, how a snow-storm is moving or if a friend has arrived at a restaurant, crowd-sourcing allows for live visualization of personal information. The cartographer defines the data, while the crowd collectively draws the lines and fills the spaces.

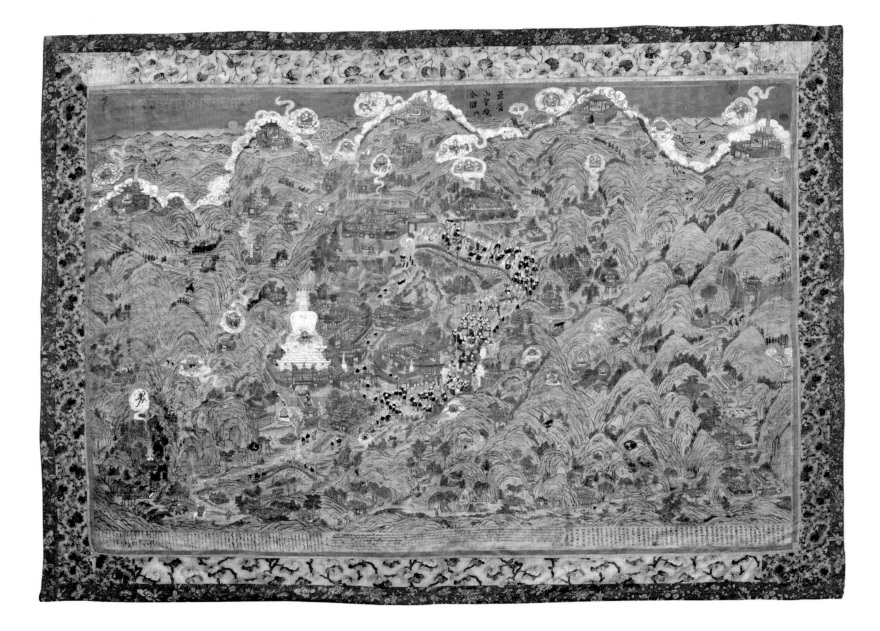

Panoramic View of Wutaishan | 1846 | Gelong Lhündrup

Hand-coloured woodcut. 144 × 194.6 cm / 4 ft 10¾ in × 6 ft 4¾ in. Rubin Museum of Art, New York

Wutaishan – the Mountain of Five Terraces – in China's Shanxi Province had a long history as a sacred mountain for Chinese pilgrims before innovations by the Qing emperors encouraged its popularity among Buddhists from Tibet and Mongolia. Drawn by a Tibetan monk at Wutaishan's Cifusi Temple, this woodcut print shows the mountain as an enternal landscape based closely on Buddhist scripture. Its five terraces spread across the top of the image, each with a temple dedicated to Manjusri, an important bodhisattva (a spiritual guide in Buddhism). In the heart of the map a large procession of pilgrims wearing straw hats winds its way past the prominent white stupa in Taihuai village towards the distant peaks, walking or riding animals along steep curving paths and roads. The peripheral parts of the map are dotted with sacred sites such Buddhist stupas, Taoist temples, sacred objects and vignettes of historical and miraculous events. Each major location and temple on the sacred mountain is marked with an inscription in both Tibetan and Chinese; some temples are further highlighted by hovering clouds containing deities or eminent monks. The walls and pillars of the temples are also picked out in red against a lush green typical of Tibetan painting and the azure blue sky.

Come All the Way! (Caminos Santiago) | 2011 | Cinta Arribas

Printed paper. 70 × 87 cm / 27½ × 34¼ in. Private collection

Although this is a recent map, drawn by the Spanish illustrator Cinta Arribas, its content is much older. It reflects the medieval belief that relics of the disciple St James were housed in north-west Spain on Europe's western edge. Thus Santiago de Compostela – named after the saint's Spanish name – became a pilgrimage centre that lay at the end of routes from all over Europe. Each path was a 'Camino de Santiago', a 'Way of St James', and for

centuries one might have met a German, an Italian and a Spaniard trudging side by side along muddy roads with the common aim of praying at the shrine. Arribas draws on a tradition of maps of pilgrim routes that dates back to the Middle Ages, but also reflects the modern revival of the pilgrimage to Santiago. Now backpackers march hundreds of kilometres as a challenge and a marker in their lives quite distinct from any interest in the saint's

relics. The scallop – the ancient pilgrims' symbol – can again be seen on backpacks and along the routes walkers follow. Arribas shows these routes, incorporates the symbols and downplays the obstacles presented by the mountains, the pilgrims' greatest enemy. Although it appears as a skeleton road map, her map functions to lead the viewer, like the pilgrim, to a single destination (see pp.24–25).

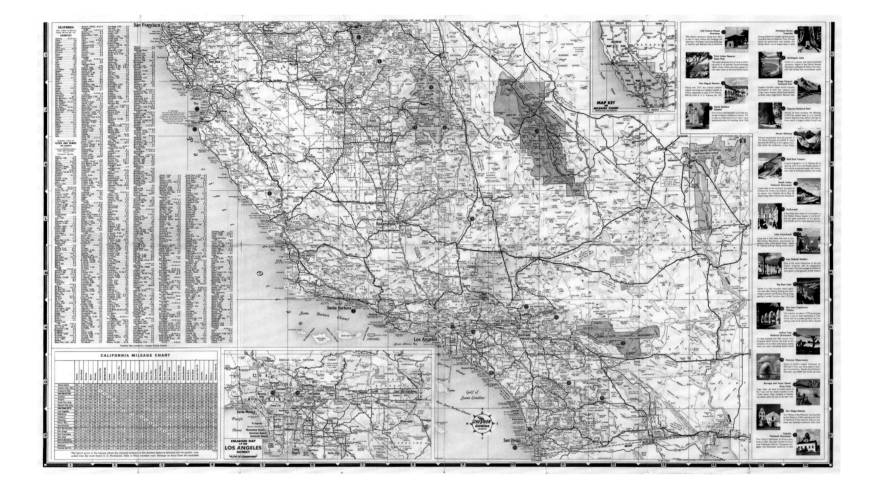

California Points of Interest and Touring Map (South) | 1956 | H. M. Goushá Company

Printed paper. 46 × 87 cm / 18 × 34¼ in. Private collection

The road maps given away by gasoline and oil companies at petrol stations all over the United States in the golden age of motoring – this one was produced for the Standard Oil Company – are classics of American cartography. Some 5 billion were printed from the 1920s through the late 1990s, when mobile GPS made them obsolete, in order to encourage the country's emerging middle classes to take road trips along the newly developed highway system. The most obvious features on such maps are roads, spreading in thick red lines across the landscape with virtually no attempt to give any hint of topography or vegetation. The prominent advertising featured not only the service stations of the oil companies but also roadside attractions meant to attract travellers to towns and local businesses. This example shows the high-speed interstate highway system in southern California and includes all the information a driver might need: a chart of mileage between cities, driving times between destinations, speed limits, state traffic laws and a list of national parks and monuments. A panel of vignettes illustrates attractions, including a number of California missions, the Mariposa Grove at Yosemite and Death Valley.

On the Road | 1949 | Jack Kerouac

Pencil on paper, from Jack Kerouac's unpublished journal. New York Public Library

Many readers of Jack Kerouac's seminal novel *On the Road* may have drawn their own maps in order to keep track of the back-and-forth exploits of Sal Paradise and Dean Moriarty as they criss-cross America. This sketch map is one of several by Kerouac himself that survive in his unpublished journals. It is thus simultaneously an itinerary for a real journey, a plan for the novel and an imagining of the fictionalized 'Beat' world in which the story takes place. From 1947 to 1950 Kerouac made a series of road trips around the United States, episodes of which he recorded in a series of notebooks and journals that became the raw material for the novel. He began drafting the novel as early as 1948, but became dissatisfied with the result. This sketch map, dating from November 1949, announces that Kerouac is reverting to a 'simpler style', perhaps reflecting his frustration with his earlier drafts. Besides showing some of the iconic places that appear in the final book, the map also lists some of the pseudonyms Kerouac made up for real-life characters, such as 'Old Bull', who was inspired by the writer William S. Burroughs. Kerouac finally typed out the final draft of *On the Road* on a continuous roll of paper in just three weeks in April 1951. It was published to critical acclaim in 1957.

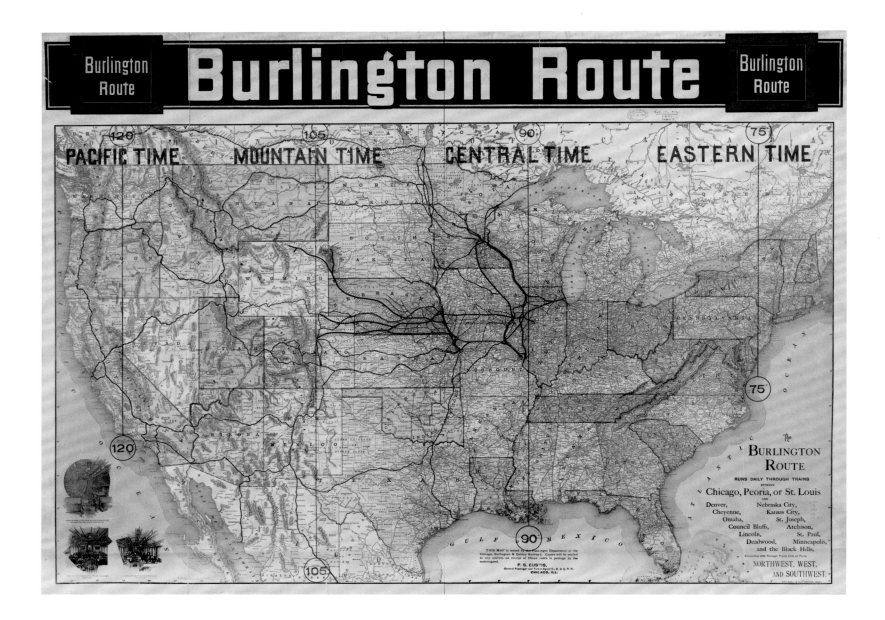

Burlington Route | 1892 | Rand McNally and Company

Printed paper. 81 × 111 cm / 31⅞ × 43¾ in. Library of Congress, Washington, DC

This map of the Chicago, Burlington and Quincy Railroad – the 'Burlington Route' – brings together geography and time. Before industrialization, towns and cities set their clocks by the sun, so each had its own time – but railways required uniform times to coordinate operations. In 1847 British railways had adopted a 'mean time' from the time at Greenwich, often called 'railway time' before it became law in 1880. North America was dominated by important lines like the Burlington (a major carrier between the industrialized Great Lakes and the resource-rich Rocky Mountains), and each adopted the local time of its primary cities, a practice that made it possible to be in different places at the same time or in the same place at different times. In 1883 a meeting of railway officials resulted in the adoption of four standard time zones an hour apart, so telling the time involved gauging one's relative proximity to one of the four meridians on which the divisions were based. This map appeared after the railways had adopted standard time but before that became law in the United States, in 1918, after which more precise time-zone boundaries were established. The lines of the Burlington Route appear on this map in black; railways connecting to points west appear in red.

Albert Richard Football Map | 1938 | E.E. Cheeseman

Lithograph. 49 × 66 cm / 19¼ × 26 in. Private collection

It became a standard technique of advertising in the twentieth century to associate whatever was being sold with something people already liked. Sometimes the connection was more or less clear, such as selling gasoline by giving away road maps to encourage automobile vacations (see p.272) or selling tires by judging restaurants to be 'worth a trip'. Why not sell overcoats by linking them with the popular fall and winter sport of American football? That's what outerwear manufacturer Albert Richard did from 1938 to 1941, when the popularity of college football was reaching new heights, placing advertisements in magazines that offered this free college football poster to anyone who wrote in. The map is packed with information for fans, including a legend identifying the conferences (only nine at the time), the states colour-coded into regions, a key of official nicknames, pennants marking the home of each team – with stars to indicate their conference – and college banners around the perimeter and a wheel of pennants around a central 'Albert Richard' flag. The back of the map shows Richard's coats and information on where to find them – keeping his coats on people's minds throughout the season, until the Horned Frogs of Texas Christian University became the number one team of 1938.

Utopia | 1518 | Ambrosius Holbein

Woodcut, printed in *Utopia* by Thomas More (1518). 20 × 13.7 cm / 7⅞ × 5½ in. Private collection

For the third edition of Thomas More's *Utopia*, the German-Swiss artist Ambrosius Holbein – older brother of the more famous Hans – drew a map of the allegorical ideal island in the hidden shape of a distorted human skull. The large 'ship of teeth' reveals the hidden image: its main mast and rigging indicate the skull's nasal cavity, while the other two masts define the sides of the upper jaw; the large church defines the right eye socket. The skull often symbolized *memento mori* – Latin for 'remember that you must die' – a common motif in medieval and Renaissance art. Such images were meant as a reminder of one's mortality, the vanity of earthly life and the transitory nature of worldly goods and human endeavour. The publisher and scholar Erasmus seems to have asked Holbein to provide a graphic pun on *mori*, which in Latin means both 'of More' and 'of death'. Fifteen years later, after Ambrosius's death, his brother Hans Holbein the Younger included an enigmatic anamorphic skull, similarly representing *memento mori*, in his famous painting *The Ambassadors*. Utopia itself appeared in English in More's homeland only in 1551, long after More's execution in 1535 for denying Henry VIII's right to become spiritual head of the English Church.

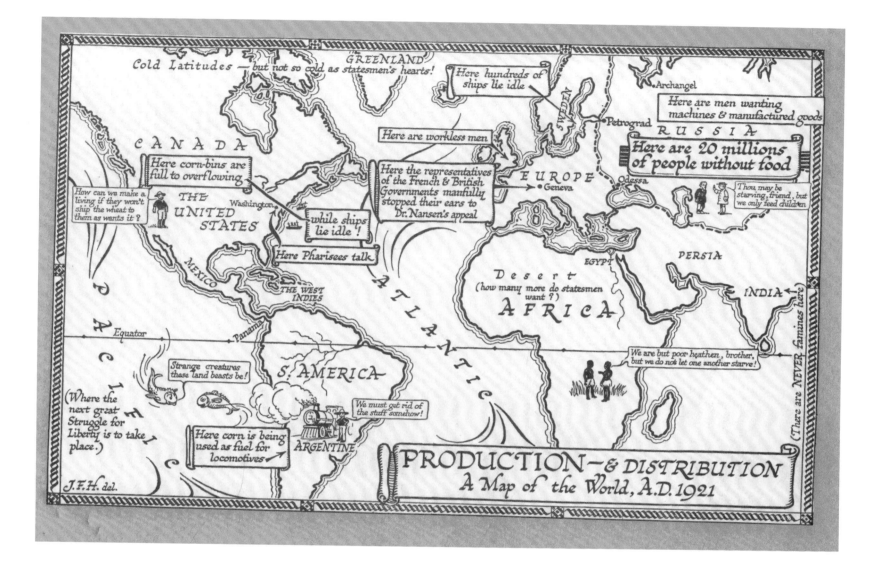

Production & Distribution: A Map of the World, AD 1921 | 1921 | James Francis Horrabin

Printed paper. 25 × 38 cm / 9¾ × 15 in. Private collection

Published in *The Communist* in December 1921, this map is a commentary by James Francis Horrabin ('JFH') on the chaos following World War I (1914–18), when political stupidity continued to cause suffering, particularly world hunger. A label attached to Geneva damns the international response to the polar explorer Fridtjof Nansen's unsuccessful appeal on behalf of the League of Nations for food to alleviate famine in post-revolutionary Russia.

Washington, DC is labelled as a venue for 'Pharisees': smug hypocrites. 'JFH' was a British polymath – an economist, geographer and historian who was also a gifted cartographer and cartoonist – whose passion for politics saw him by turns a communist and, briefly, a Labour MP. He drew his first maps during the Balkan Wars of 1912–13 and became captivated by maps' communicative power, producing dozens of atlases and thousands of maps that

combine elegantly simple drawing, masses of facts and striking ways to re-envisage the world. This map owes much to wartime developments in the use of maps to communicate with the home front, and it anticipates much later cartography conveying complex social, economic and political problems, such as the work of modern map-makers like Michael Kidron and Dan Smith.

Systema Ideale
PYROPHYLACIORUM
Subterraneorum, quorum montes
Vulcanii, veluti spiracula
quædam existunt.

Hoc Schema exprimit Caloris sive Ignis nidos, vel quod idem est, pyrophylacia per universa Geocosmi viscera, admirando DEI opificio, varie distributa ne alicubi deesset; quod conservationi Geocosmi tantopere foret necessarium; Nemo autem sibi persuadeat Ignem revera hoc pacto quo schema refert constitutum esse; eoq; prorsus ordine disposita æstuaria, nequaquam. Quis enim hæc observavit? quisnam illuc penetravit unquam ex hominibus? Hoc itaq; Schemate solummodo ostendere voluimus, Telluris viscera plena esse æstuariis et pyrophylaciis, sive ea jam hoc modo, sive alio, disposita sint. Ex centro igitur Ignem per omnes Subterrestris mundi semitus usq; ad ipsos exterioris superficiei montes Vulcanos deduximus; Ignis Centralis signetur A litera. Reliqua sunt æstuaria Naturæ, signata B. Canales pyragogi C. minimi vero rivi sunt fissuræ Terræ, per quas Ignei spiritus pervadunt.

Mundus Subterraneus | 1664 | Athanasius Kircher

Engraving, printed in *XII Libros Digestus*. 39.5 × 43.5 cm / 15½ × 17⅛ in. Bibliothèque Universitaire de Poitiers

This remarkable map was created by 'the last Renaissance man', a common description of the seventeenth-century Jesuit priest, historian, theologian and geographer Athanasius Kircher. It is probably the last world map to present the medieval world view as fact, although it also marks Kircher's attempts to take into account new discoveries. Kircher saw the geocentric cosmos as being made up of the four Aristotelian elements – earth, water, air and fire – which caused geological change as each sought its 'proper position' relative to its weight. Earth was the heaviest element and fire the lightest, which is why Kircher shows fire from a central underground source erupting on the surface as volcanoes. But Kircher had also to explain such facts as geysers and springs and accommodate such geological phenomena within his world view. His scientific account had also to accommodate what for him were the equally certain facts of religion: a fiery hell must lie at matter's dark core, while 'purgatory' – a place of transient punishment – must also be located deep within the Earth. This cross-section of the planet made room for all these 'facts' and related them to one another. As such, it combines a new observational approach within the older vision such empiricism was undermining.

Panorama of the Washoe from the Summit of Mount Davidson | 1861 | Edward Vischer

Lithograph. 45 × 51 cm / 17¾ × 20 in. Private collection

The German-born painter and photographer Edward Vischer's inventive approach to visual geography sits somewhere between a map and a picture, and captures the drama of California's Eastern Sierra range in a wholly unfamiliar but inviting way. Vischer came to California in 1842, after having emigrated from Germany to Mexico at the age of nineteen. The discoveries of silver in the Comstock Lode of the Eastern Sierras in 1859 drew hordes of young men to the newly established mines, and in the spring of 1861 Vischer made his own visit. A guide took him from the 'bowels of Mount Davidson' – its mines and tunnels – to its 2,745-metre (9,000-foot) summit, where he tried to make sense of the stunning scenery that surrounded him. To do this he departed from a traditional approach to scale through an unconventional yet arresting image that shows the enormous, complex mountain chain from the air, 360 degrees around. The surrounding vignettes illustrate the mining locations of Washoe: Virginia, Gold Hill, Silver City, Ophir Works in Washoe Valley and some of the nearby crushing mills. As was his practice, Vischer made a quick sketch on site, and later developed a more sophisticated drawing, which he reproduced through lithography.

Septentrionalium Terrarum Descriptio | 1613 | Gerard Mercator and Jodocus Hondius

Hand-coloured engraving. 36.7 cm × 39.2 cm / 14½ × 15⅜ in. Elmer E. Rasmuson Library, University of Alaska, Fairbanks

In 1604, a decade after the death of the celebrated Flemish cartographer Gerard Mercator, his countryman Jodocus Hondius bought the copper plates used to produce Mercator's *Atlas* (see p.155). Over the next decades, Hondius published twenty-nine more editions of the *Atlas* – including new and revised maps by himself – making Mercator a household name across Europe. This edition of 1613 is a fascinating example of the relationship between conjecture and certainty. Many of Mercator's maps needed updating, including his famous map of the North Pole (1595). In common with his contemporaries, Mercator believed that Earth's magnetic forces derived from a large black rock or *rupes nigra* at its northernmost point, surrounded by four rivers and four mythical islands. Hondius revised the map to incorporate information from explorers such as Willem Barentsz, who had sailed to Spitsbergen and Novaya Zemlya. Hondius opened up the outlines of two mythical islands, altering the profiles of Novaya Zemlya. Two of the corner inserts show the Faroe and Shetland islands, but the third shows another land of conjecture, Frisland, the result of a long-standing error. Hondius's editions of this polar map are usually hand-coloured, making this an attractive monument to cartography's shifting conceptions of the unknown.

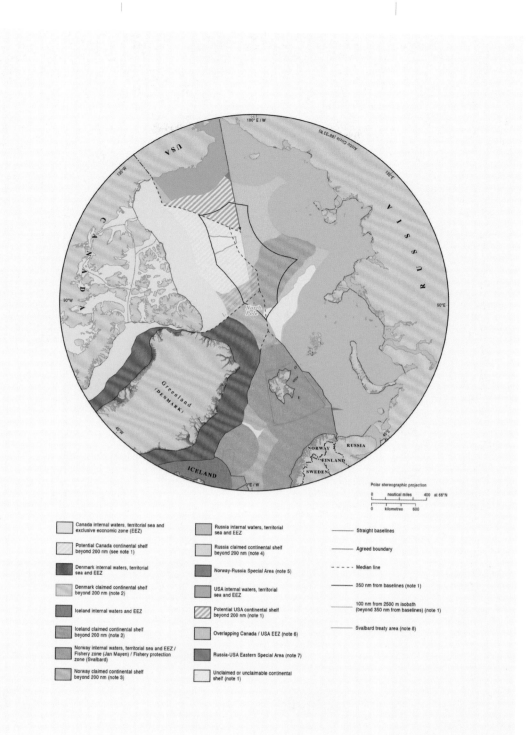

Canada internal waters, territorial sea and exclusive economic zone (EEZ)

Potential Canada continental shelf beyond 200 nm (see note 1)

Denmark internal waters, territorial sea and EEZ

Denmark claimed continental shelf beyond 200 nm (note 2)

Iceland internal waters and EEZ

Iceland claimed continental shelf beyond 200 nm (note 2)

Norway internal waters, territorial sea and EEZ / Fishery zone (Jan Mayen) / Fishery protection zone (Svalbard)

Norway claimed continental shelf beyond 200 nm (note 3)

Russia internal waters, territorial sea and EEZ

Russia claimed continental shelf beyond 200 nm (note 4)

Norway-Russia Special Area (note 5)

USA internal waters, territorial sea and EEZ

Potential USA continental shelf beyond 200 nm (note 1)

Overlapping Canada / USA EEZ (note 6)

Russia-USA Eastern Special Area (note 7)

Unclaimed or unclaimable continental shelf (note 1)

Straight baselines

Agreed boundary

Median line

350 nm from baselines (note 1)

100 nm from 2500 m isobath (beyond 350 nm from baselines) (note 1)

Svalbard treaty area (note 8)

Maritime Jurisdiction and Boundaries in the Arctic Region | 2008 | IBRU, Durham University

Digital. Dimensions variable.

The colours on this map of the Arctic relate more to claims of sovereignty reflecting the conflicting claims of bordering nations to the Arctic Ocean's resource-rich continental shelf. The map was drawn by the International Boundaries Research Unit (IBRU) in response to a Russian decision to use a mini-submarine to plant a titanium Russian flag on the seabed beneath the North Pole in August 2007, Russia caused international uproar and triggered a race for potential resources, including oil and natural gas, beneath the ice. The IBRU compiled this map to show all national claims to the Arctic. Russia (shown in green), Canada (yellow), Denmark/Greenland (pink), Norway (orange) and the United States (blue) all claim sovereignty based on the United Nations Convention on the Law of the Sea (UNCLOS, 1982). The IBRU, part of Durham University, leads the world in researching boundary laws. It uses maps to help resolve complex boundary issues. On this map, darker colours indicate the extent of the exclusive economic zones (EEZs), stretching 370 kilometres (198 nautical miles) from the coasts of Arctic-bordering nations. The lighter colours and diagonal stripes highlight conflicting claims to the seabed to be resolved by the Commission on the Limits of the Continental Shelf, which is part of UNCLOS.

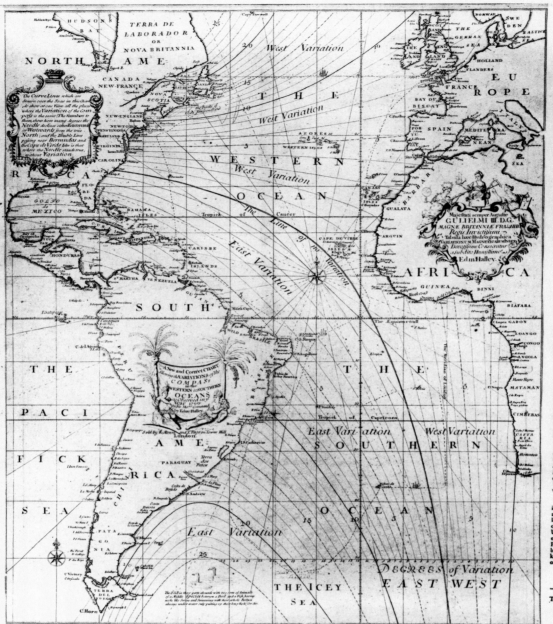

Magnetic Chart of the North and South Atlantic Oceans | 1701 | Edmond Halley

Printed paper. 42 × 36 cm / 16½ × 14⅛ in. Royal Astronomical Society, London

Today the English astronomer Edmond Halley is best remembered for predicting the return of the comet that bears his name, but for sailors he had a far more practical legacy. In the late seventeenth century, one of the great problems facing navigators was a deviation – first noticed a couple of decades earlier – between magnetic north as indicated by a compass needle and true north as indicated by meridians of longitude. This variation – magnetic declination – was originally attributed to the effect of landmasses on compass needles. From 1698 to 1700 Halley made the first purely scientific voyages undertaken by an English naval vessel into the Atlantic Ocean to observe variations in magnetic declination. The results, published in 1701, included this chart. Halley had concluded that variations in the compass needle were not influenced by the proximity of land. Instead, he suggested that Earth had its own magnetic field, as we now know to be true. His map was the first to show variations in magnetic declination and to use isogonic or Halleyan lines to join points of equal declination, allowing navigators to adjust compass readings accordingly. It was the first time lines of equal value were used to show a variable surface, a practice later extended to topographic mapping and hydrographic charting.

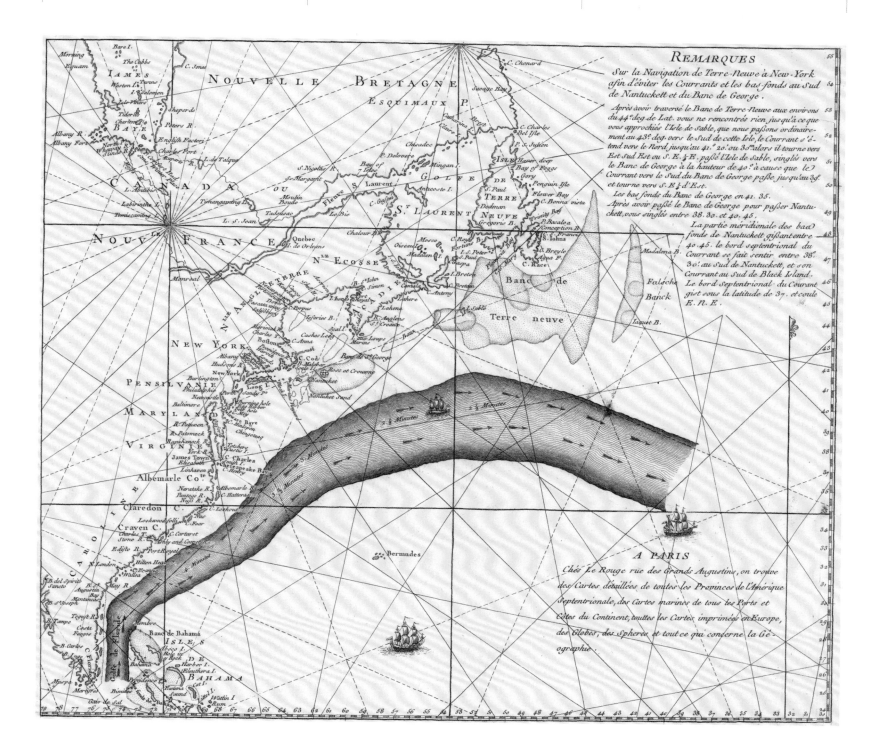

The following text appears within the map image:

REMARQUES

Sur la Navigation de Terre-Neuve à New-York afin d'éviter les Courrants et les bas-fonds au Sud de Nantuckett et du Banc de George.

Après avoir traversé le Banc de Terre-Neuve aux environs du 44.º deg de Lat. vous ne rencontrés rien, jusqu'à ce que vous approchiés l'Isle de Sable, que nous passons ordinairement au 43.º deg. vers le Sud de cette Isle, qui s'étend vers le Nord jusqu'au 41.º 20.' ou 30' alors il tourne vers Est Sud Est ou S. E. ¼ E. passé l'Isle de Sable, singlés vers le Banc de George à la hauteur de 40.º à cause que le Courrant vers le Sud du Banc de George passe jusqu'au 39.º et tourne vers S. E ¼ d'Est.

Les bas fonds du Banc de George en 41. 35.

Après avoir passé le Banc de George pour passer Nantuckett, vous singlés entre 38. 30. et 40. 45.

La partie méridionale des bas fonds de Nantuckett, gisant entre 40. 45. le bord septentrional du Courrant se fait sentir entre 38.º 30.' au Sud de Nantuckett, et son Courrant au Sud de Black Island. Le bord Septentrional du Courant gist sous la latitude de 37. et coule E. N. E.

A PARIS

Chés Le Rouge rüe des Grands Augustins, on trouve des Cartes détaillées de toutes les Provinces de l'Amérique Septentrionale, des Cartes marines de tous les Ports et Côtes du Continent, toutes les Cartes imprimées en Europe, des Globes, des Spheres et tout ce qui concerne la Géographie.

Franklin-Folger Chart of the Gulf Stream | 1785 | Benjamin Franklin and Timothy Folger

Engraving. 32 × 36 cm / 12⅝ × 14⅛ in. Princeton University, New Jersey

This chart of the Gulf Stream belongs to the founding stories of both the United States and modern oceanography. Its co-creator, Benjamin Franklin, was one of the Founders who led the fight for independence from the British during the American Revolution (1775–83). Franklin had lived in Britain on and off for twenty years, representing the American colonies in various capacities. As postmaster general, he noticed that British mail packets took much longer to cross the Atlantic to America than did American merchant ships. Franklin's first cousin Timothy Folger, a master mariner from Nantucket Island, explained that British captains did not avoid the Northeast Current when crossing from east to west. Atlantic mariners in North America had for centuries been aware of the warm current – which Franklin renamed the Gulf Stream – that flowed out of the Gulf of Mexico around the end of Florida and north-east across the Atlantic. Folger sketched out the current on a Mercator sailing chart of the Atlantic, and Franklin printed copies for the benefit of British mail boats. He withdrew the map during the American Revolution to remove the British advantage, but secretly gave copies to his French allies. After American independence, Folger and Franklin published the map widely, as did others.

The Earth Seen Through the Sphere of the Stars | 1661 | Andreas Cellarius

Engraving. 42.5 × 49.4 cm / 16¾ × 19½ in. Private collection

This novel view of the Pacific and Arctic regions of the Earth, as if seen from a point far out in space through a layer of starry constellations, was the creation of the Dutch-German Andreas Cellarius, a Protestant astronomer who became famous for his star and celestial atlas titled *Harmonia Macrocosmica*, which first appeared in 1660 and was reprinted numerous times (this plate comes from the second issue) The thirty colour plates avoid the controversy raging at the time by including different versions of the cosmographical order. Cellarius drew verions of the skies following classical authorities, including the second-century Greek-Egyptian Ptolemy – who put Earth at the centre of the planets – and according to Copernicus, who in the sixteenth century developed a revolutionary heliocentric solar system. This engraving shows the Earth inside the sphere of the stars, with illustrations of the constellations of the northern hemisphere and, in a surrounding belt, the astrological signs of the zodiac. The upper background shows clouds over a light blue background representing the heavens, with angels in each corner holding banners giving the map's title. In the lower corners astronomers use astrolabes, compasses, a Jacob's staff and books to study the heavens.

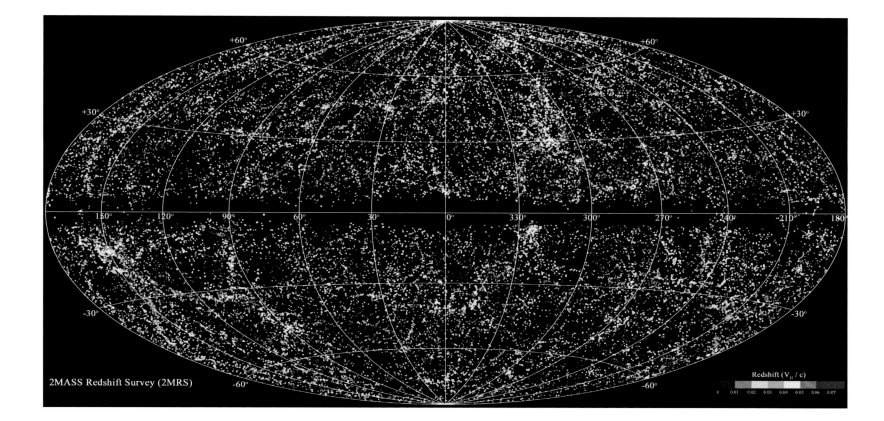

2MASS Redshift Survey (2MRS)

+60°   +60°

+30°   +30°

150° 120° 90° 60° 30° 0° 330° 300° 270° 240° 210° 180°

-30°   -30°

-60°   -60°

Redshift (V$_H$ / c)

0   0.01 0.02 0.03 0.04 0.05 0.06 0.07

2MASS Redshift Survey | 2012 | John Huchra, Thomas Jarrett and others

Digital image. Dimensions variable

This map represents a decade's work by the 2MASS Redshift Survey, which uses 'redshift' – an increase in the wavelength of light as it moves away from the viewer – to map an area of space extending 380 million light years from Earth. The survey is a legacy of a development that began in the 1990s, when universities and astronomical observatories began piecing together data from millions of galaxies to map their type and relative position. Several surveys using different methods competed to present the first complete picture of the universe, including the Sloan Digital Sky Survey, the Two-degree-Field Galaxy Redshift Survey and the 2-Micron All-Sky Survey. In the decades since, such surveys have changed our fundamental ideas about the structure of the universe, the acceleration of its expansion and the nature of dark matter. A consensus has emerged that galaxies are not evenly distributed but rather cluster together in arrangements often described as being like soapsuds. Although the dark horizontal gap on this image is the plane of our own galaxy, which is hard to 'look' through to gain data, the 2MASS survey has garnered more information near that zone than ever before, making that part of the sky more visible and increasing our understanding of the motion of our own galaxy.

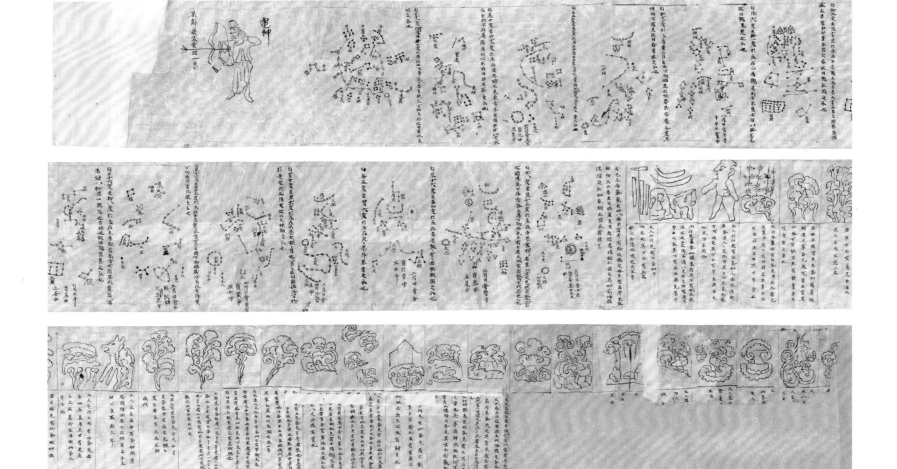

Dunhuang Star Atlas | c.700 | Unknown

Ink on paper. 24.4 × 330 cm / 9⅝ × 130 in. British Library, London

The world's oldest star atlas, the Dunhuang star atlas was sealed in a Buddhist cave at Dunhuang, on the Silk Road in the Gobi Desert, in about 700 AD. The dry desert air proved ideal for preserving documents, and the star atlas – together with thousands of other, largely Buddhist documents – was rediscovered in the early twentieth century in nearly original condition. It is read from right to left. A section on clouds and their religious meanings is followed by a twelve-panel sequence of diagrams of the night sky; the scroll ends with the image of an archer. Early astronomers had different opinions on the constellations, a fact that explains the different-coloured stars associated with each. Overall, the chart portrays more than 1,300 stars and 257 constellations, all of which have been confirmed as accurate representations of the sky at that time and in that place. Stars were vital for tracking time and navigating distance and direction, and Chinese astronomers of the time were accomplished mathematicians who successfully worked out the number and time of eclipses, the length of a degree of a meridian and the exact length of a year to within a minute. It is likely that this version of the star atlas is a traced copy from observations made by the revered contemporary astronomer Li Chunfeng.

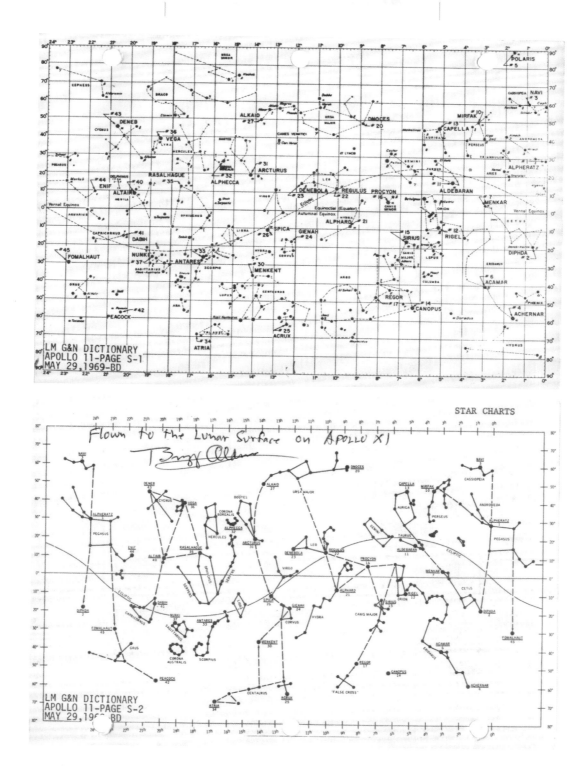

Apollo 11 Flown Star Chart | 1969 | NASA

Printed card. Private collection

With minor variations, the star chart that guided Edwin 'Buzz' Aldrin as he piloted the Apollo 11 lunar module to the surface of the moon on 20 July 1969 would have been entirely intelligible to navigators sailing the oceans a millennium earlier. The lunar mission was completed with limited computing power, so NASA fell back on traditional technology when it could. The astronauts' Guidance and Navigation file contained star charts – still with punched holes for the folder – to help them navigate. They used the chart with a scanning telescope to work out the position of three stars, as determined by the chart's grid, then used a numeric keypad to enter the coordinates into the Apollo Guidance Computer, which would triangulate the desired trajectory. This particular version of the chart has been authenticated by Aldrin as being used on the historic landing of the lunar module, *Eagle*. The chart also contains a reminder of the dangers and difficulties of the Space Race. The star names contain a poignant tribute to the astronauts of Apollo 1, who died during a training fire in 1967. Stars 3, 17 and 20 are anagrams on the names of the three astronauts, first included on the charts by one of them – Gus Grissom – and retained as a tribute.

Selden Map of China | 1620s | Unknown

Watercolour on paper. 158 × 96 cm / 5 ft 2 in × 3 ft 1¾ in. Bodleian Library, University of Oxford

This early seventeenth-century chart of China and its adjacent seas is one of the most important Chinese maps of the last seven centuries – although the details of its story before it was presented to the Bodleian Library in 1659 remain a mystery. As recently as 2008, a visiting scholar noticed very faint lines covering trade routes and compass bearings radiating from the Chinese port of Quanzhou, where it is assumed the chart was made.

Unusually for a Chinese map, the hand-painted watercolour shows China as part of a larger region that stretches from the Indian Ocean in the west to the Spice Islands in the east, from Java in the south to Japan in the north, including the Philippines, Borneo, the coast of Vietnam and the Malay Peninsula. It includes much information for sea pilots, such as how best to avoid shoals, pirates or sailors claiming rights of 'salvage'. The map was created

by an unknown Chinese cartographer in the late Ming dynasty, and is named the Selden Map after its donor to the Bodleian, the English lawyer and scholar John Selden. One suggestion from Chinese researchers is that the chart's uniqueness among Chinese maps might reflect the fact that it was produced by the community of sinicized Arabs who lived in Quanzhou at the time.

中和橋 山方 水西橋 五屑橋
天地壇 石城橋 自寶船廠開船從
皇城 龍江開出水直抵
天妃宮 外國諸番圖
菜園
太子洲
腰段

Route of Admiral Zheng He | 1628 | Zheng He

Woodcut. 30 × 38 cm / 11¾ × 15 in. Library of Congress, Washington, DC

This sailing chart (a 1644 copy of a 1628 original by Yuanyi Mao) shows a small part of the route taken by the Chinese admiral Zheng He in the early fifteenth century, when he made seven voyages into the Indian Ocean, sailing as far as East Africa. The illustration – from a series of maps in the form of a scroll more than 5.5 metres (18 feet) long that was later divided into forty pages – shows part of the route Zheng took from

Nanjing through South-east Asia, the Indian Ocean and the Red Sea to the Persian Gulf. The maps vary in scale from 7 miles to the inch around Nanjing to 215 miles to the inch in parts of the African coast. The chart comes from the last part of the *Wubei Zhi*, the most comprehensive military book in Chinese history, written in 1621 and published in 1628. Zheng made his first voyage for the Ming emperors – with 317 junks crewed by over

28,000 men – in 1405 and his last in 1431. Dotted lines show more than fifty sea routes, with either sailing times or distances, making allowances for local currents and winds. Some depth soundings are shown, as are coastal features such as bays, estuaries, capes and islands, ports, mountains, landmarks and rocks. About 300 place names are marked along the route; 260 or so can be identified today.

World Map | *c.*1154 | al-Idrisi

Manuscript. 1553. 30 × 21.8 cm / 11¾ × 8⅝ in. Bodleian Library, University Oxford

'England is set in the Sea of Darkness. It is a considerable island ... most fertile, its inhabitants are brave, active and enterprising, but all is in the grip of perpetual winter.' So wrote the Arab geographer Mohammed al-Idrisi in 1154 in the *Book of Pleasant Journeys into Far Away Lands*, also known as the *Book of Roger*, an Arabic description of the world with seventy regional maps and this circular world map, orientated with south at the top. The map

shows the world surrounded by ocean, with the Indian Ocean (left) and Mediterranean (right) protruding into the landmasses. In Africa (top right), al-Idrisi shows the Nile flowing northwards to its delta from a source in the mountains. Next to a curiously flattened India, he shows the island of Sri Lanka. Al-Idrisi worked on the commentaries and maps for fifteen years at the court of the Norman king Roger II of Sicily, drawing on his own travels

in Europe, North Africa and Central Asia. The texts are based on Arabic geographical treatises and interviews with travellers and informants, and give extensive descriptions of the physical, political, cultural and economic conditions of each region. Although little used by European geographers, the book and maps served as a model for Muslim scholars for centuries. The original maps are lost but survive in several copies.

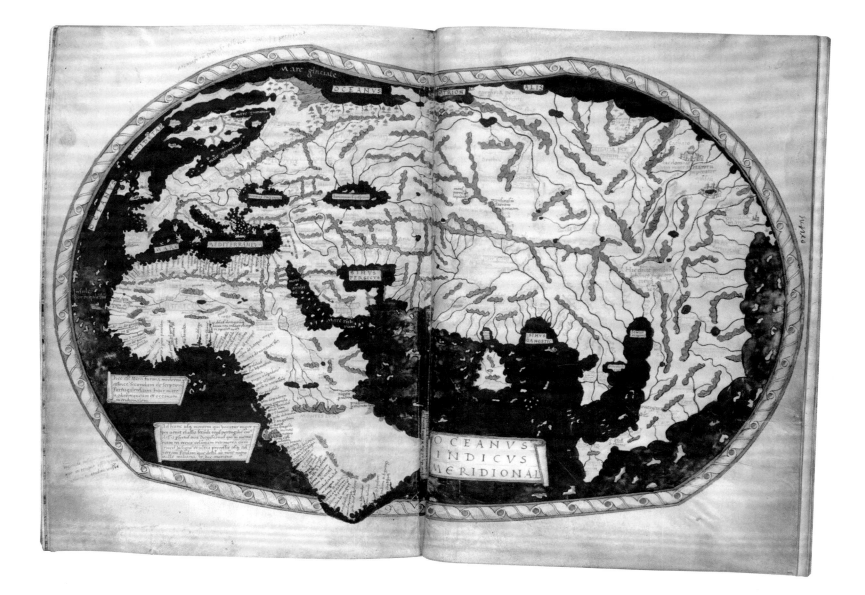

World Map | 1489 | Henricus Martellus

Manuscript on vellum. 47 × 30 cm / 18½ × 11¾ in. British Library, London

In this world map, the German cartographer Henricus (or Heinrich) Martellus set out to reconcile maps derived from the second-century Greek-Egyptian geographer Ptolemy, whose *Geography* was still highly influential (see p.139), with new discoveries being made by fifteenth-century European sailors. In particular, it resolved a conflict between two opposing models of the Indian Ocean. The generally accepted Ptolemaic model portrayed the Indian Ocean as an enclosed sea, rather like the Mediterranean. The Macrobian model – named after the fifth-century Roman geographer Macrobius (see p.166) – held that a seaway linked the Atlantic and Indian oceans. Portuguese mariners had been exploring the west coast of Africa since about 1418, trying to locate the sources of the gold and slaves transported north across the Sahara Desert to the Mediterranean coast. Gradually, they extended their explorations further south until, in 1488, Bartolomeu Dias rounded the Cape of Good Hope and sailed north to the Fish River (now in Namibia), proving that there was a seaway to the Indies (the border of Martellus's map actually shows an endless African coast-line). Martellus, who worked in Florence, Italy, was the first cartographer to be able to show Dias's discovery while it was still fresh news.

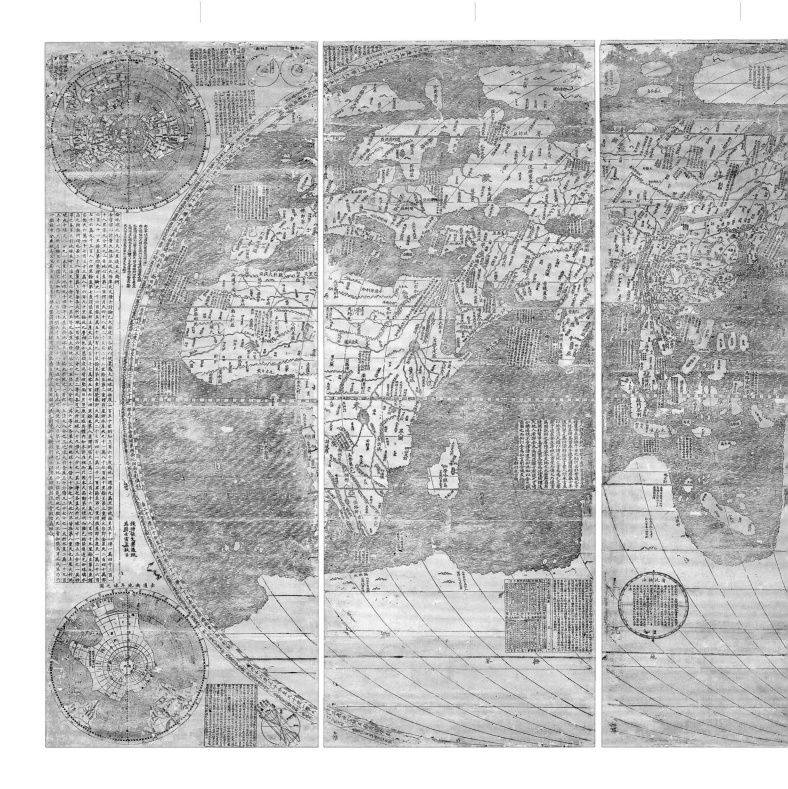

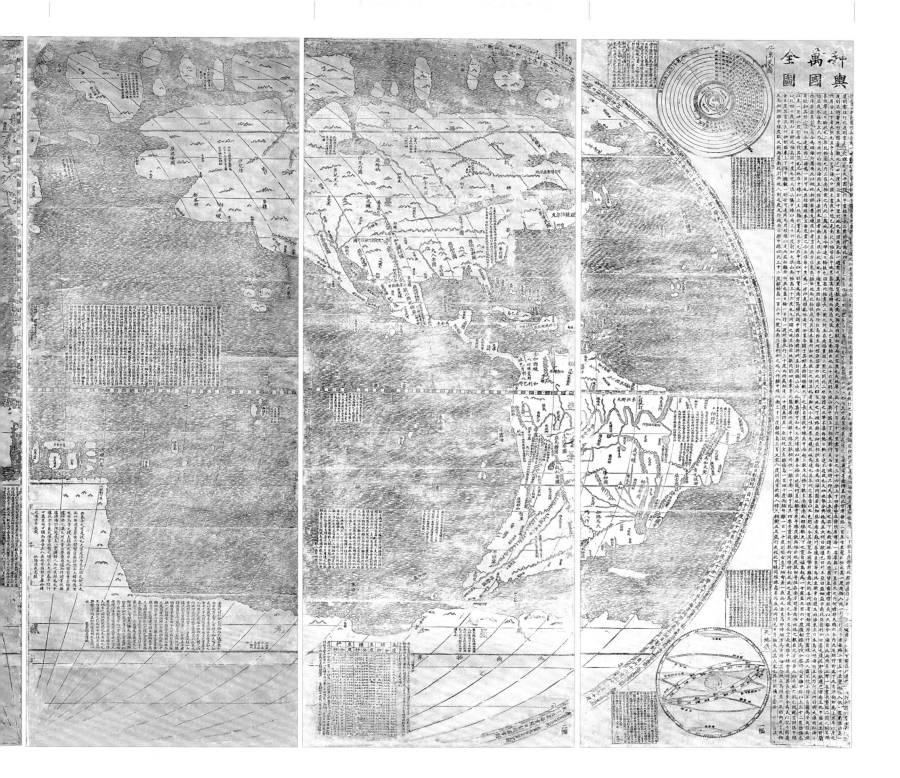

Map of the Ten Thousand Countries of the Earth | 1602 | Matteo Ricci and Li Zhizao

Woodcut on rice paper. 167 × 380 cm / 5 ft 6 in × 12 ft 6 in. James Ford Bell Library, Minneapolis, Minnesota

The Italian Jesuit priest Matteo Ricci is credited with introducing Western science to China in the sixteenth century, and this remarkable world map was part of the process, being the first map known to combine Eastern and Western cartography and the first Chinese map to show the western hemisphere. Ricci, 'the Apostle of China', trained at a Jesuit seminary in Rome before travelling to Macao in 1582. His mission at Shiuhing was decorated with a Western world map of which the provincial governor asked Ricci to provide a Chinese translation. Ricci – one of the first Western scholars to make a study of Chinese – duly obliged, but was prudent enough to change the projection so that the map was centred on the meridian of 170°E, thus placing China at its heart, in accordance with the Chinese view of their homeland as the 'Middle Kingdom'. In 1601 Ricci entered Peking (present-day Beijing) – he was the first Westerner to enter the Forbidden City – and received the favour of the Yanli emperor, who commissioned this woodcut version of the map (a copy of a version from 1584, now lost). Ricci and the engraver, Li Zhizao, drew the map to incorporate as much Jesuit and Chinese knowledge as possible, demonstrated both graphically and in Chinese characters surrounding the map.

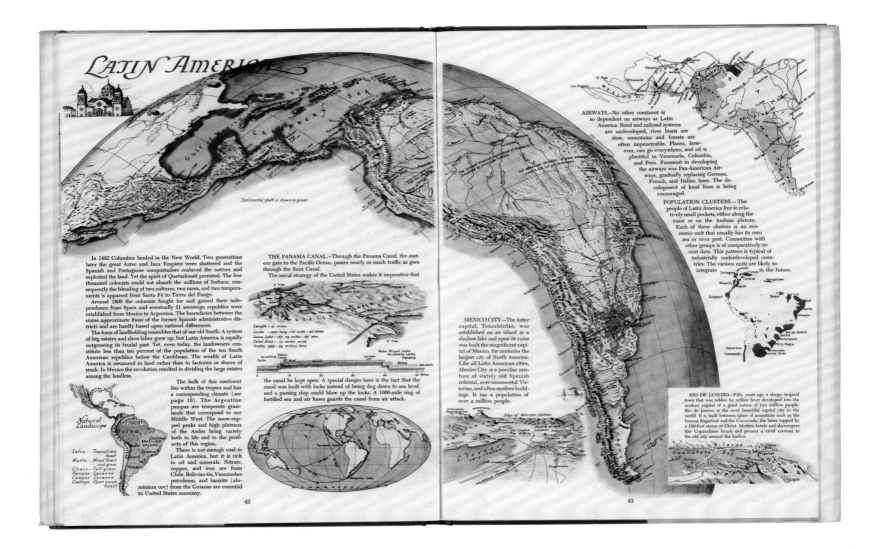

Latin America | 1944 | Erwin Raisz

Printed in *Atlas of Global Geography* (1944). 34 × 50 cm / 13⅜ × 19¾ in. Private collection

The surface of the Earth is highly complicated. A satellite photograph can show an assortment of vegetation, hills, mountains and streams that may appear almost random. For us to understand it, this complexity must be simplified and generalized by a cartographer who can show us the big picture. A map-maker can reveal a forest where we saw only a scattering of trees, or a watershed where we saw only rivers. Few have been as good at capturing the essence of the planet – extracting the signal from the noise – as the Hungarian-born American cartographer Erwin Raisz. While Raisz excelled in many areas of cartography – he taught for years at the Harvard University Institute of Geographical Exploration – he is perhaps best remembered for his depictions of landforms, as seen in the *Atlas of Global Geography*, in which this map appears. He was a skilled illustrator who continued to draw his maps by hand despite the growing use of photo-mechanical mapping, and who used his abilities to capture a caricature of the planet. His pen-and-ink style promised not a perfect mimicry, but a fair and authentic simplification of the larger patterns at work. Raisz's terrain drawings possess a delicate balance of verisimilitude: less exact than a photograph, but more believable than a cartoon.

Amazon Deforestation | 2000 | NASA

Digital. Dimensions variable

This picture of the remote Brazilian state of Rondônia was taken on 30 July 2000 by the Moderate Resolution Imaging Spectroradiometer (MODIS) on Terra, a satellite of NASA's Earth Observing System. It shows the effects of largely unrestricted development on a large area of what was only thirty-five years earlier largely virgin rain forest. At the edge of the wooded areas (dark green), the deforestation takes on a characteristic herringbone pattern: loggers cut a road into the forest and clear the trees along it, after which settlers arrive to plant the cleared land or use it as cattle pasture. The loss of tree cover causes soil erosion, which leaves more barren land (pale brown). Terra was launched in 1999 as part of NASA's programme to monitor changes – largely but not entirely caused by humans – on land, at sea and in the atmosphere. The MODIS sensor on board creates an electromagnetic image of the whole planet every two days, so it can monitor even small changes. It can map surface reflectance and land-surface temperature, and can distinguish eleven types of vegetation and also non-vegetated areas – a total of seventeen different types of land cover.

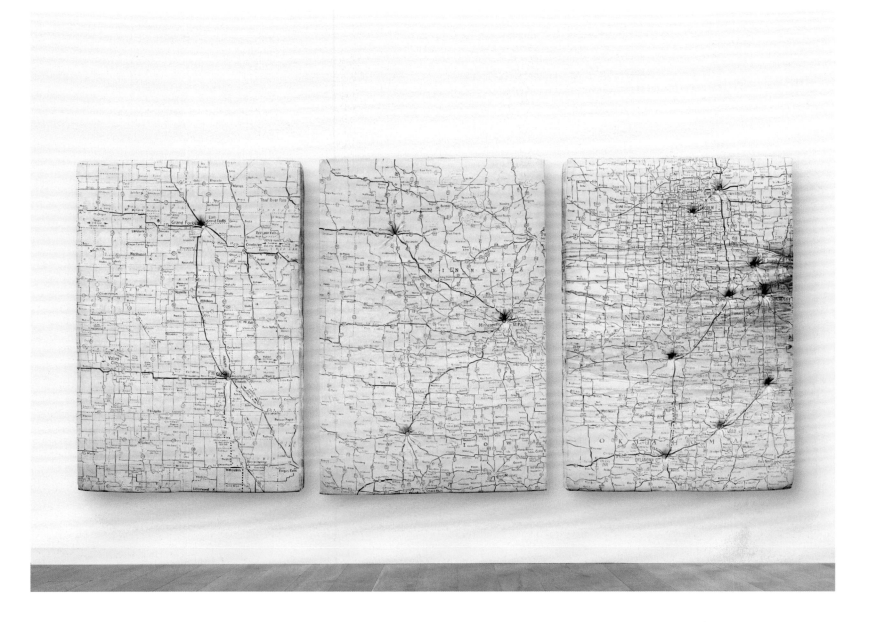

Untitled | 1990 | Guillermo Kuitca

Mixed media on mattress. Three parts, each: 198 × 140 cm / 78 × 55⅛; overall: 198 × 437 cm / 78 × 172 in. Private collection

The Argentine artist Guillermo Kuitca frequently uses maps and plans of geographical locations and interior spaces as starting points for paintings. Here three ready-made mattresses become the surface for carefully transcribed road maps, rendered in paint and ink. Hanging on a wall, these maps are surely impractical for a road trip. They feature areas of the American Midwest, – town names and road numbers are real and legible – yet Kuitca claims not to be interested in specific places. Rather, the locations are chosen precisely because they have no particular personal significance, and closer inspection reveals that Kuitca sometimes repeats or dislocates cities. Although the maps are not overtly political, themes of absence, alienation and institutional anonymity may be a reflection on the turbulent, sometimes repressive, recent history of Argentina. Irregularly placed buttons – of the type typical of mattresses – create indentations that draw attention to certain towns and junctions, plotting a set of coordinates that invite speculation on narrative connections. Mattresses also reference the most intimate of places – the bed. Kuitca thus conflates private and public spaces, with the possibility of dreams offering a disorder and chaos that defies the systemized world of maps.

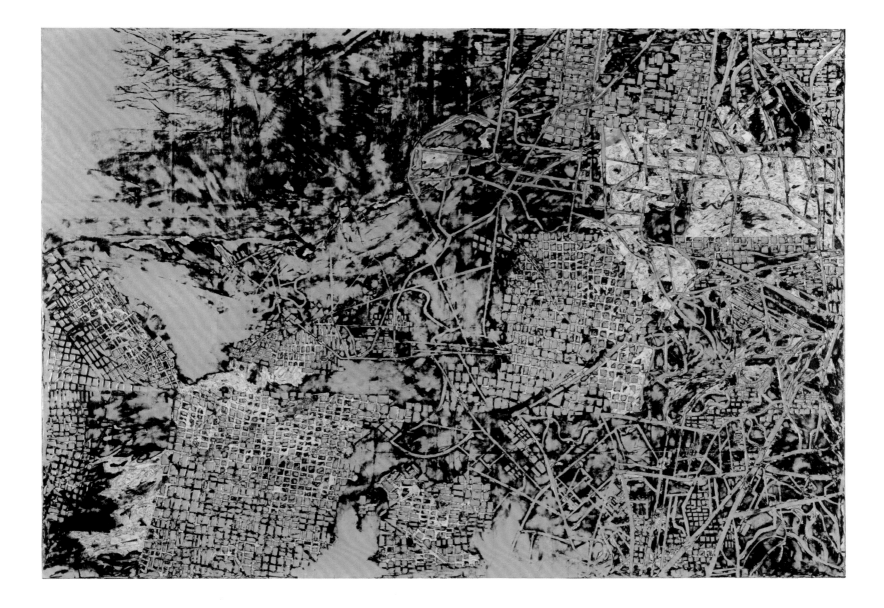

My Whole Family is from Philly | 2014 | Mark Bradford

Mixed media on canvas. 259.1 × 365.8 cm / 102 × 144 in. Private collection

Without any text or symbols, this map by the Los Angeles artist Mark Bradford is not usable as such – and even a resident of Philadelphia might struggle to recognize the location without reading the title. In this way, Bradford reminds us that all maps are abstractions of reality, which rely on cartographic conventions and a known context in order to function. Bradford is known for semi-abstract paintings that incorporate everyday materials found in his urban environment, such as billboard posters and newsprint. This work presents an intricate network of pathways that echoes a map of the city of Philadelphia. It was made by collaging different types of paper and paint, and then cutting and sanding through the strata to reveal varying colours and textures and to form grid patterns. As the location where both the Declaration of Independence (1776) and the US Constitution (1788) were originally signed, 'Philly' is the symbolic cradle of American democracy and nationhood. Bradford's painting was first presented alongside other works – *Amendments #5–10* – in which quotations from the Bill of Rights go from being clearly readable to almost illegible, emphasizing the way their original meaning has been manipulated and abstracted far beyond the intention of its creators.

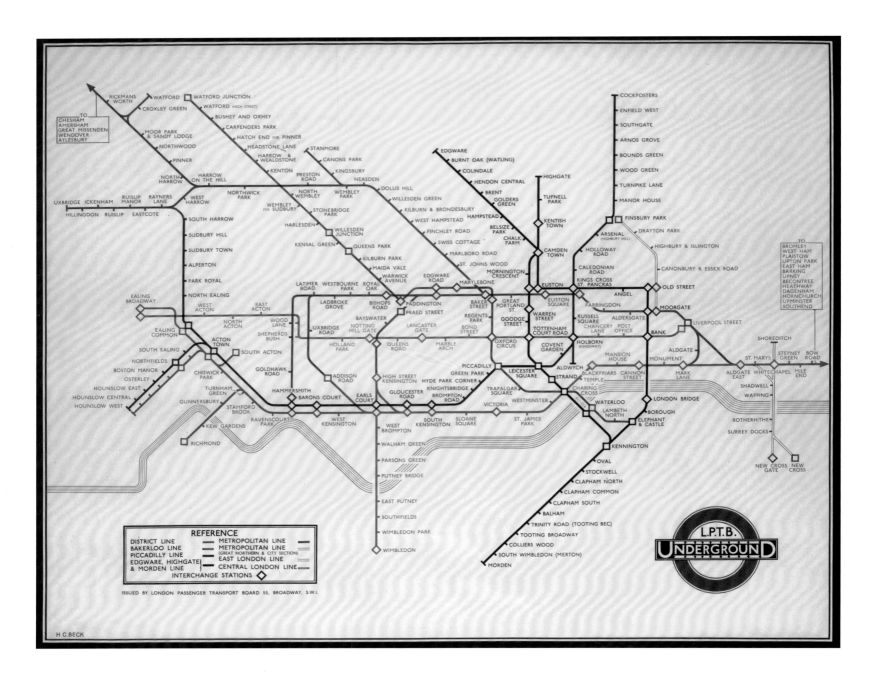

London Underground | 1933 | Harry Beck

Printed paper. 15.4 × 22.7 cm / 6 × 9 in. London Transport Museum, London

This renowned schematic diagram was the engineering draughtsman Harry Beck's solution to mapping the London Underground for travellers. Simplified and heavily generalized, the map shows stations linked by colour-coded straight lines that run vertically, horizontally or at 45-degree angles. Ordinary stations are differentiated from interchanges, and the map's central area is exaggerated, while the outer scale is contracted. The map shows nothing of the geography above ground, other than the River Thames, and this is its key design feature: Beck argued that it was unnecessary for passengers to know what was going on above. Although the London Underground company was uncertain, the map's initial print run was hugely successful. While not entirely original – design cues can be traced to many earlier works – Beck's idea was innovative and *avant-garde*. It matched both the contemporary vision of the city as a machine and the way Frank Pick, vice chairman of the London Passenger Transport Board, wanted to rebrand the Underground as modern and streamlined. Although the map has gone through many revisions and design changes, its essential graphic approach is still used today, and the beauty Beck found in simplicity is a model for transport-related maps around the world.

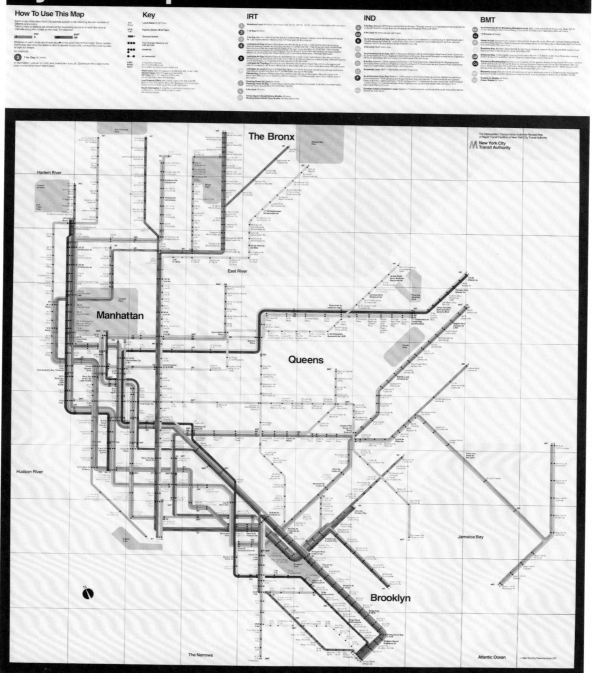

New York Subway Map | 1972 | Massimo Vignelli

Lithograph. 149.9 × 118.7 cm / 59 × 46¾ in. Museum of Modern Art, New York

This map of New York City's subway system by Massimo Vignelli polarizes opinion. It is a striking piece of design and has a strong aesthetic appeal, but at the time of its release the MTA received complaints about its perceived inaccuracies. Central Park, for example, is square rather than rectangular and geographically speaking, some of the stations appear to be in the 'wrong' places. While previous maps of New York's subway provided a geographically accurate representation of the city above ground in addition to the transit system, Vignelli's map is far more abstract and was intended only for use on the subway. Taking inspiration from Harry Beck's famous 1933 map of London Underground (see opposite), Vignelli reimagined the complex transit subway system as a neat grid of coloured lines, instead of a more realistic tangle of curved paths, with only a few above-ground landmarks.

Design fans celebrated Vignelli's map and it became a coveted souvenir of trips to New York but it was replaced after only seven years with a more topographical version in 1979. However, Vignelli's map remains a classic of cartographic design and later became part of the postwar design collection at the Museum of Modern Art.

AERIAL SURVEY
MANHATTAN ISLAND, New York City
Made by
FAIRCHILD AERIAL CAMERA CORPORATION
New York City   August 4, 1922
This Mosaic was made by assembling 100 Aerial Photographs taken
while flying over the area at an altitude of 10,000 feet

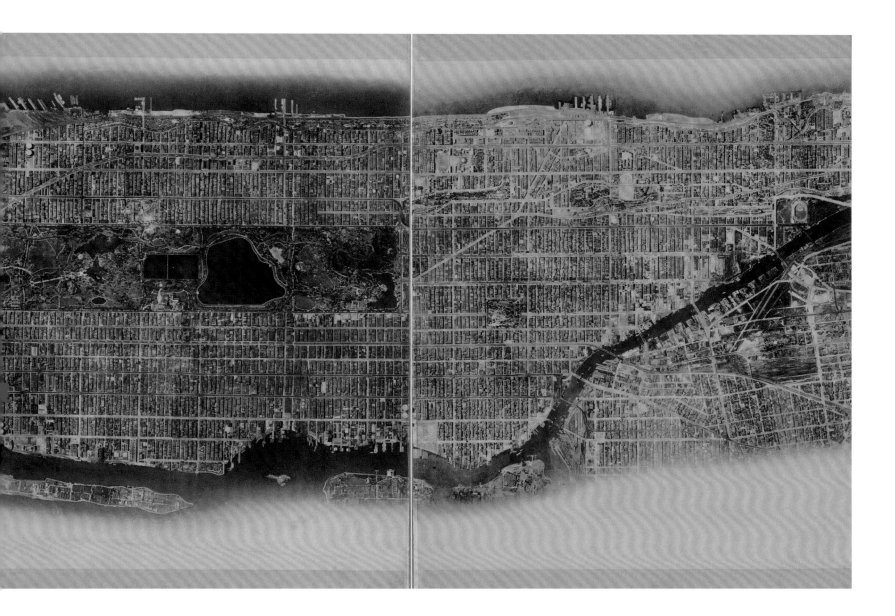

Aerial Survey of Manhattan Island, New York City | 1921 | Fairchild Aerial Camera Corporation

Composite aerial photograph on six sheets (detail shown here). 56 × 253 cm / 1 ft 10 in × 8 ft 3⅝ in. Library of Congress, Washington, DC

This aerial survey captures Manhattan Island at the start of the building boom of the 1920s. The project was intended, in part, to demonstrate how aerial photography could help to map a city changing so rapidly that conventional line maps soon became out of date without time-consuming revision. Aerial photography had been in its infancy at the outbreak of World War I (1914–18), but trench warfare, particularly on the Western Front, led to a rapid development

of technology for reconnaissance. At the end of the war, the aircraft and aerial cameras were no longer required by the armies, while large numbers of men had been trained to take aerial photographs for use in map-making. In addition, companies such as the Fairchild Aerial Camera Corporation needed to find new outlets for cameras previously bought by the military. A relatively poorly mapped country at the end of the war, the United States saw the

greatest expansion in civilian aerial surveying. The six-sheet photographic mosaic produced by Fairchild from 100 images taken from an altitude of 305 metres (1,000 feet) on 4 August 1921 was quick to produce and showed all the new buildings in the city. Despite the obvious advantages, photographic mosaics were not widely adopted until after World War II (1939–45).

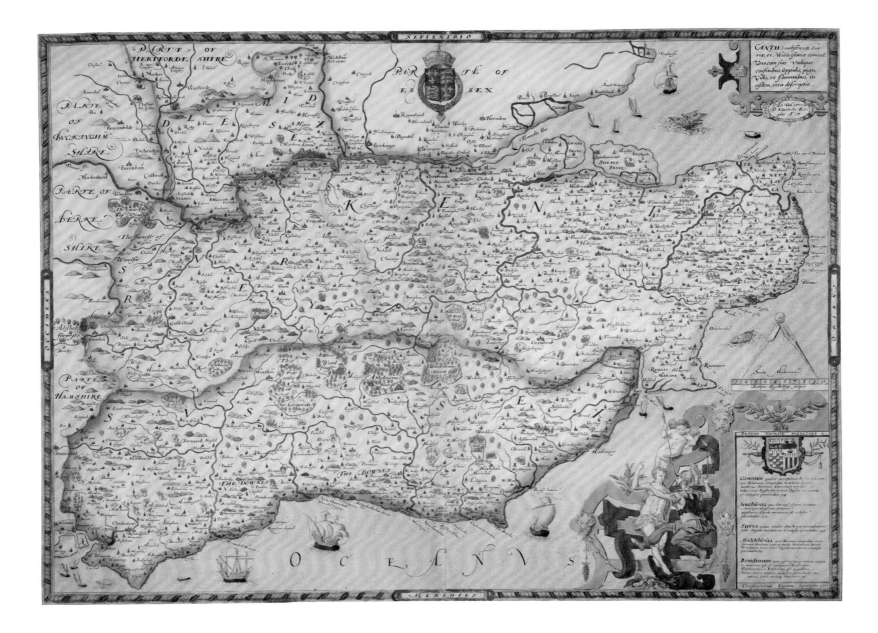

Map of Kent, Sussex, Surrey and Middlesex | c.1579 | Christopher Saxton

Hand-coloured engraving. 40.5 × 54.5 cm / 16 × 21½ in. British Library, London

The maps of Christopher Saxton – often dubbed the father of British cartography – formed the basis of county mapping in England and Wales for more than 150 years. This map of the south-eastern counties comes from his major work, *An Atlas of England and Wales*, the first comprehensive survey of the counties of England and Wales and the first atlas anywhere to be devoted to the complete depiction of a country. Behind Saxton's work was a concern with national defence. During the reign of Queen Elizabeth I (1558–1603), maps were increasingly used in the business of government, requiring both a more consistent use of scales and symbols and improved surveying techniques. With an obvious concern for the country's territorial integrity – the coastal counties were surveyed first – Thomas Seckford, Master of Requests at Elizabeth's court, financed the project, which was commissioned from Saxton in 1574. The resulting thirty-four county maps and one general map were first issued as an atlas in 1579. Seckford's arms appear at the lower right of the map, while the royal arms are displayed at upper centre. London is shown in some detail: London Bridge is clearly visible, and St Paul's Cathedral is depicted without its steeple, which was destroyed by lightning in 1561 and not replaced.

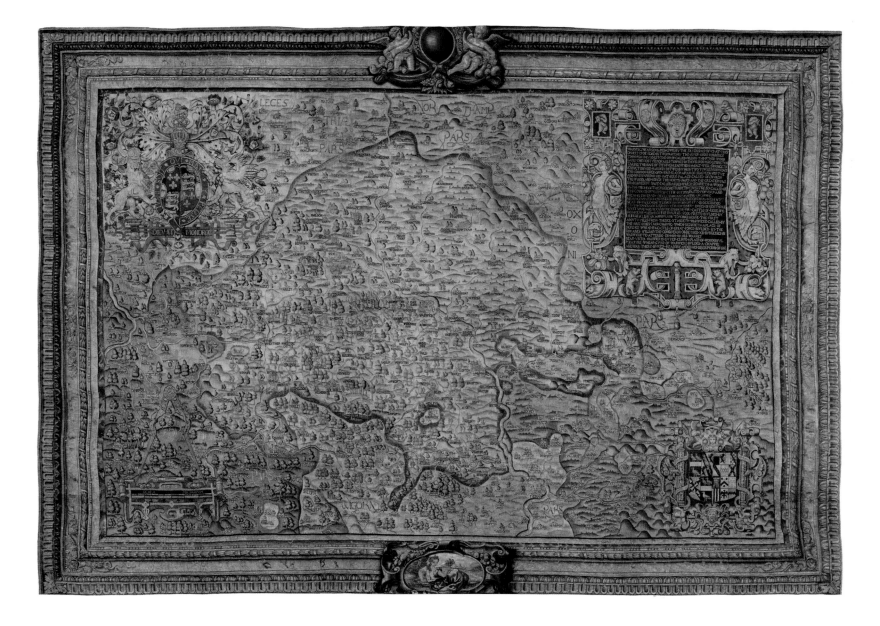

The Tapestry Map of Warwickshire | c.1590 | Unknown

Tapestry. 390 × 510 cm / 12 ft 9½ in × 16 ft 7 in. Market Hall Museum, Warwick

This magnificent tapestry map is the only complete survivor of a set of four centred on Gloucestershire, Oxfordshire, Worcestershire and Warwickshire, commissioned by Ralph Sheldon in the late 1580s for his house at Weston in Warwickshire. Tapestries were widely used as wall hangings to decorate – and insulate – large houses. The complete set stretched for over 24 metres (78 ¾ feet) and showed a panorama from London to the Bristol Channel. The maps are based on Christopher Saxton's atlas of 1579 (see opposite), but the vignettes representing settlements are more detailed, with additional roads and bridges and many more trees, to give a lively impression of the English countryside (the colours on the Warwickshire map are somewhat faded). In the top left corner is an elaborate Royal Arms; in the bottom right the arms of Edward Sheldon and Elizabeth Markham, who married in 1588; in the bottom left a decorated scale bar surmounted by dividers; and in the top right a panel within a cartouche containing a text based on Camden's county-by-county description *Britannia* (1586). The Warwickshire map had its original decorative border replaced by a simpler one to match new versions of the Oxfordshire and Worcestershire maps woven for Sheldon's great-grandson, William, after 1660.

Srinagar | c.1860s | Unknown

Wool embroidery on cloth. 229 × 198 cm / 90 × 78 in. Victoria & Albert Museum, London

This woven shawl, embroidered with a bird's-eye view of Srinagar, the capital of Kashmir, may have been made for a prince: the future British king (and emperor of India) Edward VII, who made an eight-month trip to the Subcontinent in 1875–6. The ruler of Kashmir from 1857 to 1878, Maharaja Ranbir Singh – shown on the woven map as a passenger on one of the tiny boats on Dal Lake – is said to have had the shawl created especially to present to the then Prince of Wales, who did not in fact visit Kashmir on his tour, leaving the gift ungiven and unworn. The highly detailed map of the city's buildings, gardens and people is both decorative and informative. It is inclusive but not entirely accurate, and ornamented with distinctive birds, recognizable landmarks and people engaged in conversation, gardening, trade and prayer. The renowned weavers of Kashmir used two kinds of wool to make their shawls: one from a wild goat, the other – softer and harder to find – from a wild antelope of the Himalayan foothills. Srinagar was a centre of tourism at the time, known by Westerners as the 'Venice of the East'. This shawl is a reminder that the wearable maps common on scarves and ties today are part of a long and rich tradition.

Imperial Cities | 1994 | Joyce Kozloff

Watercolour, lithograph and collage on paper. 140 × 140 cm / 55 × 55 in. Private collection

Some maps can say something about the world without depicting a particular territory. To make this collage, the American artist Joyce Kozloff pasted together strips from maps of Rome, Vienna, Istanbul and Amsterdam to re-create and combine all four cities in a deceptively homogenous whole. Kozloff discovered that both Vienna and Amsterdam radiate from a centre – in Vienna the rings are roads, in Amsterdam they are canals – and

she blended Rome and Istanbul with little difficulty. The cartographical quarters of the work are separated by old etchings of these cities in their heyday, when they held sway over huge territories: Rome as the head of the Catholic Church, Istanbul as the heart of the Ottoman Empire, Vienna as the capital of Austria-Hungary and Amsterdam as the centre of a commercial empire that stretched to the East Indies. Pasted on to the collage

are images of conquered peoples within those empires. Kozloff finishes the piece with mosaic streets of tiny paper tiles that echo the decorative flourishes of the early Christian Church, suggesting that these imperial cities – once rivals – were not so very different from one another. An artist who combines the temperament of an activist with the patience of an artisan, Kozloff has used maps as the basis of her work since 1993.

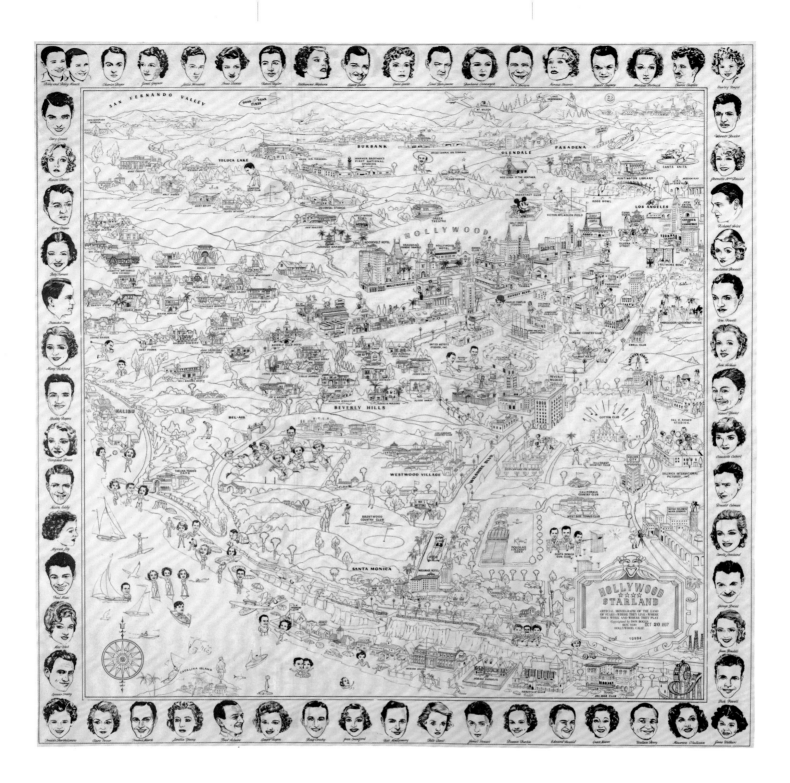

Hollywood Starland | 1937 | Don Boggs

Lithograph. 67 × 66 cm / 26½ × 26 in. Library of Congress, Washington, DC

Hollywood, the home of the US entertainment business, has become synonymous with the motion-picture industry and is a huge tourist attraction. Maps purporting to show the homes of film stars have been a Hollywood staple since tourists first started visiting Los Angeles in their cars. The maps, which were sold on street corners, allowed visitors to drive past and marvel at the stars' glamorous homes and imagine living in them. The 1930s,

when this celebratory paean to the cinema greats was produced, was the golden age of Hollywood, when dozens of studios produced films on their own lots with creative personnel under long-term contract. The map has a border containing the names and faces of sixty-one of the top stars of the cinema at the time. Although the map claims to show 'Where They Live', there is not a single address to help the adoring fans find their way; like the

dreams of Hollywood itself, the map was an exercise in smoke and mirrors. Most of the studios 'Where the Stars Work' and the places in the city 'Where They Play' went out of business long ago, so for us the map – like the stars it pictures – is a record of a vanished world.

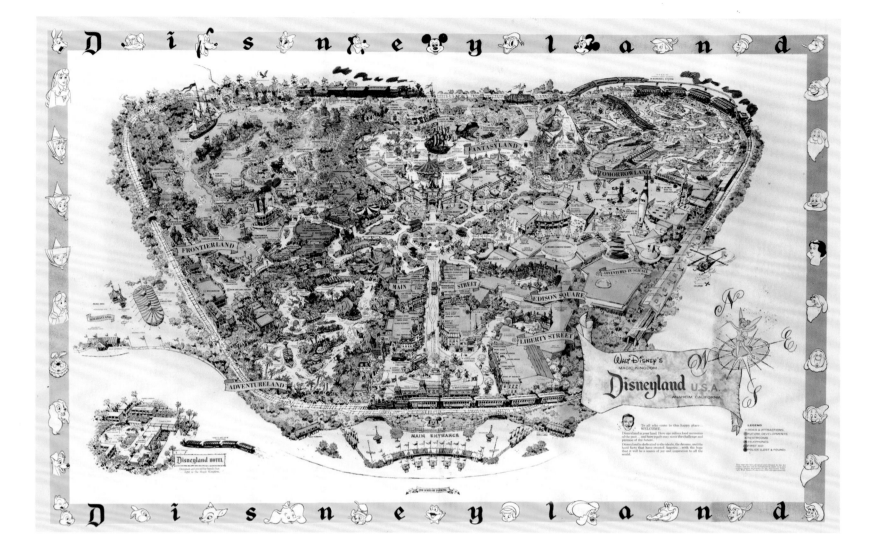

Disneyland | 1958 | Sam McKim

Printed paper. 61 × 91 cm / 24 × 36 in. Private collection

How do you map a world of fun? In 1958 the Disney artist Sam McKim designed the first large-format souvenir map of Disneyland, California, which opened on 17 July 1955. A decades-long dream of Walt Disney, Disneyland brought alive characters and landscapes from Disney's celebrated animated and live-action films in a transformed 64-hectare (158-acre) orange grove near Los Angeles. During planning and construction, McKim – himself a former child actor – had drawn inspirational sketches of Disneyland attractions as an 'imagineer', a combination of 'imagination' and 'engineer'. Once the project was complete, he made Disneyland maps from 1958 to 1964 as the park developed. McKim gives loving detail to Disneyland's themed areas: Main Street, Adventureland, Fantasyland, Frontierland and Tomorrowland. The maps were a wildly successful tool in marketing the theme park and increasing attendance. Today the McKim maps are collectors' items thanks to their intricate detail and almost magical quality. Back in the 1960s, countless children and adults spent hours poring over these maps, dreaming of their next visit to Disneyland.

Minecraft Map of Snowdonia | 2014 | Joseph Braybrook for Ordnance Survey

Digital. Dimensions variable

This map of Snowdonia in northern Wales is clearly not 'real': it was constructed from thousands of square blocks in the popular online building game Minecraft. Nevertheless, it is an accurate – albeit stylized – representation of the topography of the mountainous region, and it may also represent a possible way forward for cartography. Minecraft was officially released in late 2011 and soon became a huge success among players attracted by the chance to create their own Lego-like worlds by digging into the terrain or building with various types of block: within four years the game had sold more than fifty million copies. This detail is taken from a map of the whole of Britain created in 2013 by an intern at Ordnance Survey, Joseph Braybook, and refined a year later. The map was intended only for Minecraft players to use and explore within the game, yet the technology clearly had potential for generating online maps with practical uses in the real world. In 2014 the Danish Ministry of the Environment fed topographic data into a computer program to generate a map of the whole country using four trillion individual blocks. Minecraft users have also cooperated with the United Nations to map parts of Kibera – Africa's biggest slum – in Nairobi, to aid a regeneration project.

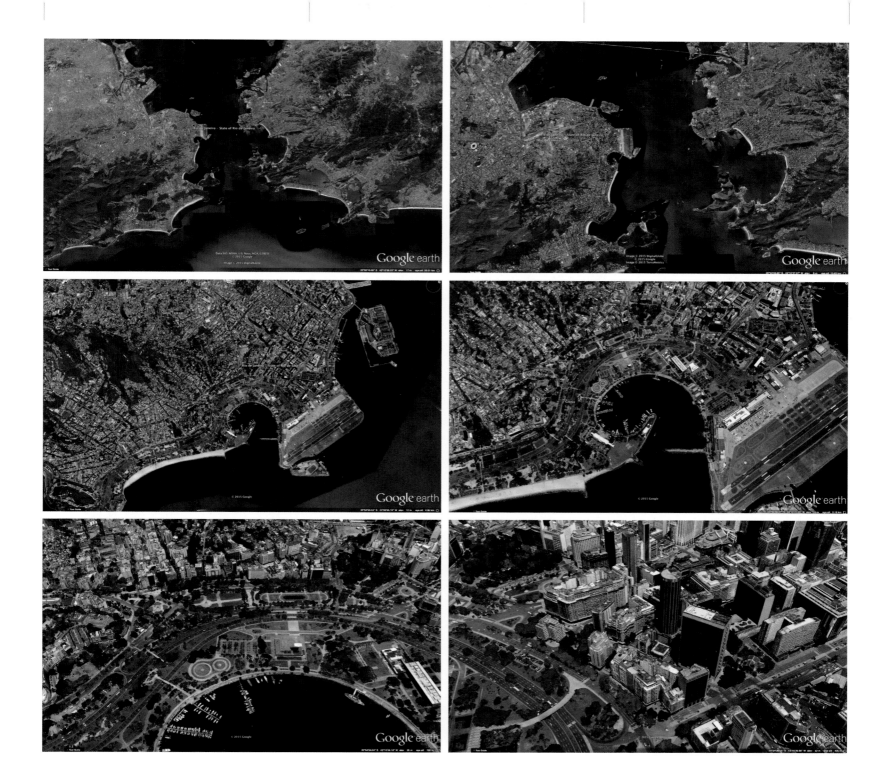

Rio de Janiero | 2015 | Google Earth

Digital. Dimensions variable

Google Earth created a revolution in cartographic visualization when it was launched in 2005. It put in the hands of anyone with a computer, tablet or cell-phone striking images of Earth and accurate high-scale mapping in a format that was easy to use and free. Users can zoom seamlessly from a wide view – as if from space – to a street or addres, 'flying' through layers of information, from roads to demographics. The views can be tilted or rotated as required by the user. The visualization platform for Google Earth was created by Keyhole Corp., which produced mapping and remote sensing imagery for the Central Intelligence Agency. Keyhole – bought by Google in 2004 – based its visualizations on a superimposition of images from satellites, aerial photography, ground-based observations and other mapping tools that could interface with Geographic Information Systems. This was a significant technical achievement, as maps and images change resolution as the viewer zooms in, an effect achieved by the precise layering and geo-rectification of geospatial databases and remote-sensing images from a range of sources. Google Earth also uses high-resolution radar topography data to generate digital-elevation models that allow the user to view large parts of Earth's surface in three dimensions.

Copenhagen | 2015 | Google

Digital. Dimensions variable

Few specific dates can be said to have changed cartography completely, but 8 February 2005 was one. On that date Google released Google Maps, following its acquisition the previous year of Lars and Jens Rasmussen's mapping company. Google Maps has revolutionized the way the people view, use and make maps to an unimaginable extent, thanks partly to the spread of other technology, particularly the Internet and mobile devices.

Google's early problems – disjointed data and poor cartographic design – have been addressed to create a design that is instantly recognizable and consistent at a local scale, all over the world. The integration of complementary functionality – routing, traffic information, overlay of social media and pho tographs, zooming, panning, querying and measuring – serves a multitude of purposes far beyond that of a general reference map.

Different views are available – a satellite image, a map, or a hybrid of the two, incorporating map symbols and labels on a photograph – and the design is automatically modified depending on use. For instance, secondary roads widen at some scales when traffic information is overlaid. The appearance of three-dimensional buildings and moving shadows at large scales (in some cities) represents the built environment as never before.

Bahrain | 2014 | Micro CADD Services

Paper and adhesive. 5.4 × 2.2 m / 17 ft 8 in. × 7 ft 3 in. Private collection

Map-makers have found various solutions to the problem of representing relief on maps, from hachure and contour lines to delicate relief shading (see p.196). This giant map of the Gulf state of Bahrain reveals the latest solution to the problem: create a three-dimensional map. The map produced by the Bahrain-based modelling company Micro CADD Services uses inexpensive three-dimensional printing technology, which creates shapes from paper, printed and cut into shape by a roller cutter that then presses it and applies a layer of glue before repeating the process. The roads were printed separately on grey paper and stuck on to the map, raising them just off the surface – as they are raised above the desert in real life. The images were created using only Google Earth and the appropriate software, promising to bring three-dimensional mapping within the reach of anyone, from small firms to individuals. It might be argued that what is produced is not so much a map as a model, without either labels and gridlines. There is a precedent for shaped maps, however. Many children's first familiarity with maps comes at school in the form of moulded plastic sheets, their surface shaped to reflect the topography of the land, with mountains, valleys and continental shelves around the coasts.

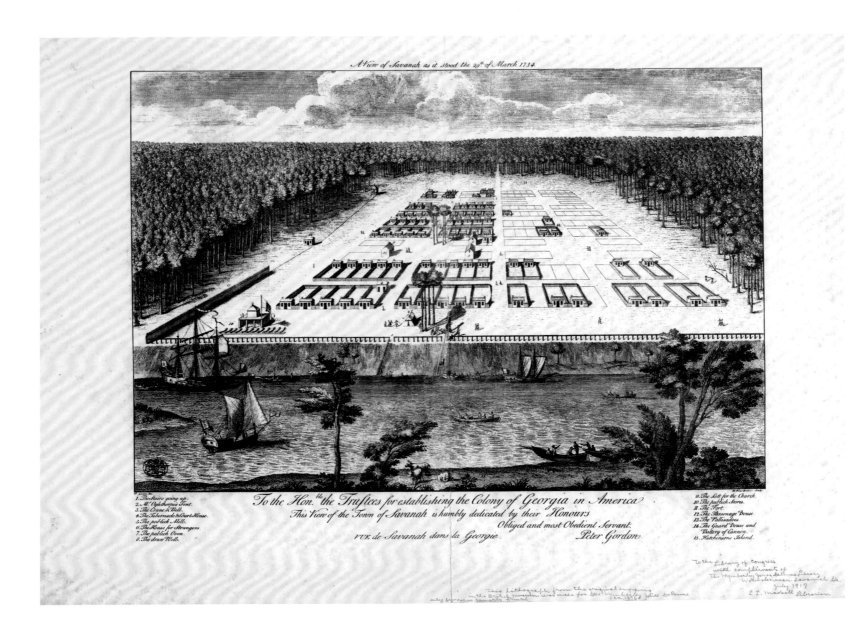

A View of Savannah as it Stood the 29th of March 1734 | 1734 | Peter Gordon

Engraving. 39 × 56 cm / 15¾ × 22 in. Library of Congress, Washington, DC

Founded in 1733, Savannah is the United States' oldest planned city, and the historic section of the modern city still reflects its original design. In this copperplate map – drawn from a rather unusual oblique perspective – the streets of Savannah are still little more than outlines in an area of newly cleared forest on a bluff overlooking the Savannah River, which is already busy with ships. The city is laid out following a typical rational planning scheme of the early Enlightenment, with blocks separated by the larger open squares for which it is so famous today. These squares were originally intended in part to act as natural air conditioners to provide the city's northern European residents with some relief from the humid semi-tropical climate. Savannah was the capital of Georgia, the last of the original Thirteen Colonies that would become the United States, founded by General James Oglethorpe partly as a haven for debtors and Catholics who were unwelcome in other British colonies. While this first published plan of the city is usually associated with Peter Gordon, who was made Savannah's first bailiff in 1733, it is actually the work of several individuals, including Oglethorpe, who formally laid out the future city in 1733, and Noble Jones, the colony's first surveyor.

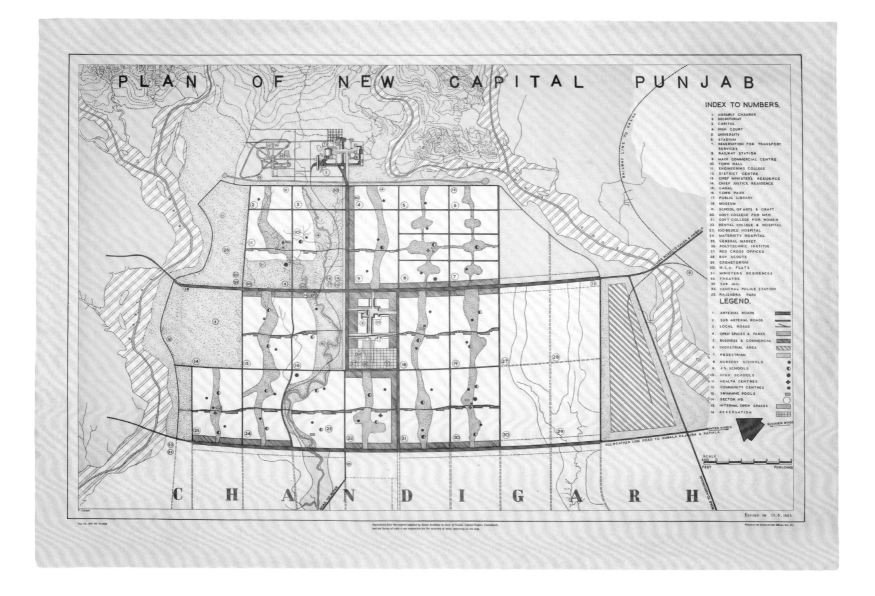

Plan of New Capital, Punjab, Chandigarh | 1951 | Le Corbusier

Printed paper. 58 × 82 cm / 23 × 32¼ in. Fondation Le Corbusier, Paris

The Swiss-French architect Le Corbusier designed Chandigarh – 'the City Beautiful' – in four days in February 1951. Such speed is not entirely surprising. Le Corbusier had been thinking about the ideal city for the machine age for decades before he received the commission for India's first new city after its independence in 1947, after the death of one of its original architects, the Pole Matthew Nowicki. Nowicki and his partner, the American planner Albert Mayer – who withdrew from the project after Nowicki's death in a plane crash – had planned a delta-shaped city, making plenty of allowance for the rolling northern Indian landscape. In contrast, Le Corbusier's plan is a simple grid, but its apparent rigidity is softened by chains of parkland – marked by undulating green lines – and irregular cross streets for commercial or retail use. The grid divides the city into leisure, civic and industrial zones, as well as smaller, discrete neighbourhoods. There are cycle routes and some striking mid-century buildings. Detractors say Le Corbusier's Chandigarh lacks an understanding of the climate or culture of the region: that it is as artificially imposed from without as the plan might suggest. Yet today Chandigarh is both a prosperous city and the only urban plan ever fully realized by this arch-Modernist.

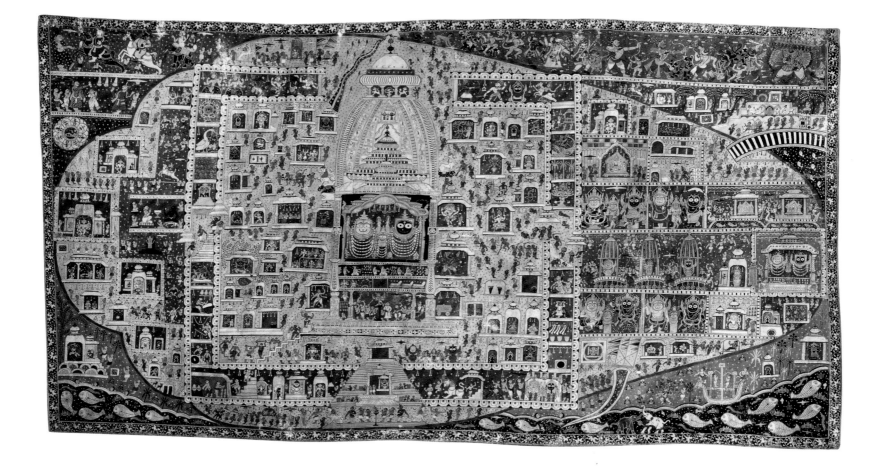

Jagannatha Temple and the City of Puri | c.1820 | Unknown

Paint on canvas, lacquered. 150 × 270 cm / 59 × 106¼ in. Bibliothèque nationale de France, Paris

This early nineteenth-century Indian painted canvas map of the Jagannatha temple in the eastern coastal city of Puri in Orissa brings together the divine and earthly worlds. The temple itself – marked by its tall dome – houses venerated wooden statues of three gods whose worship brings together Hinduism with elements of Buddhism and Jainism: the siblings Jagannatha (Lord of the World and an avatar of Vishnu), Balabhadra and Subhadra. The threesome also appear elsewhere on the map – represented by a large dark figure (Jagannatha), a large pale figure (Balabhadra) and a smaller pale figure usually between her brothers (Subhadra) – along with incarnations of other deities, such as Shiva and other avatars of Vishnu. The temple was established in the twelfth century and became an important pilgrimage destination: millions of people attended Rath Yatra, the annual chariot festival, when the gods' statues were paraded on elaborate carts (centre, right). Judging by its size, this map of the temple was probably created for a wealthy pilgrim as a souvenir of the festival. Details of the physical surroundings show bridges and stairs, and the sea is full of crabs, smiling fish and turtles.

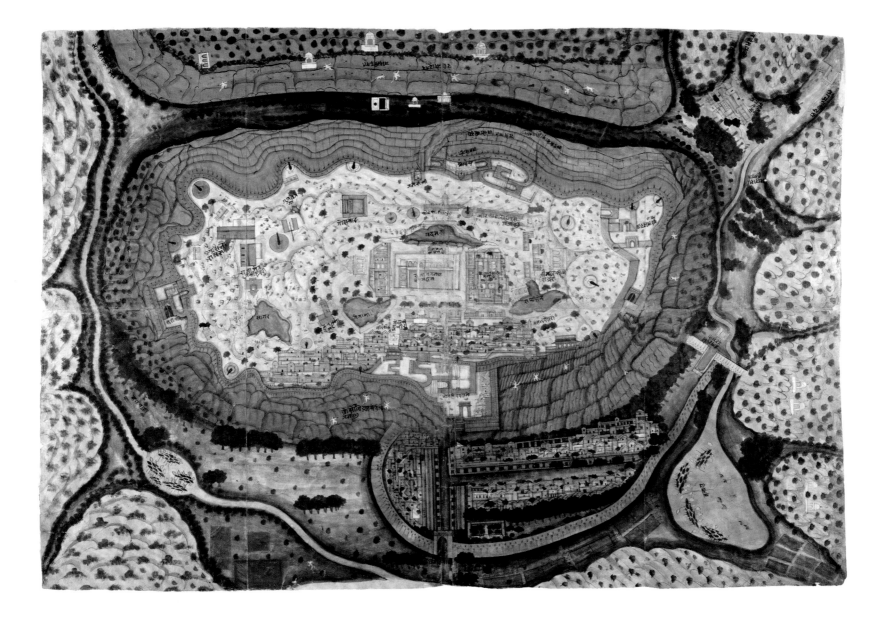

The City and Hill Fortress of Ranthambhor | c.1810–18 | Unknown

Ink and opaque watercolour on paper. 73.7 × 102.2 cm / 29 × 40¼ in. Metropolitan Museum of Art, New York

This early nineteenth-century painted map of the hill fortress of Ranthambhor, high on a rocky bluff above a moat, represents a novel solution to a long-standing cartographic puzzle: how to depict height from an overhead perspective. One of the famed hill forts of Rajasthan, Ranthambhor was built in the tenth century some 215 metres (700 feet) above the plain, protected by a steep stone wall that rises from dense forest. The artist's approach to the buildings is conventional enough for the time: they are shown in the usual way, in rows with their fronts facing skyward as if flat. This allows the various structures, including both Hindu and Jain temples, to be identified easily. But the cliffs above the river moat are shown as if from above, and tiered rather than contoured, in a break from previous renderings of the subject. This attempt at topography goes beyond what was common in Indian maps of the time, possibly reflecting European influence on topographical maps. The shading is not entirely successful, but the artist used white climbing figures against the dark angles to add another indication of gradient. Today the famous fortress is in ruins and sits at the heart of a national park that is itself part of a large tiger reserve that draws many tourists to the area.

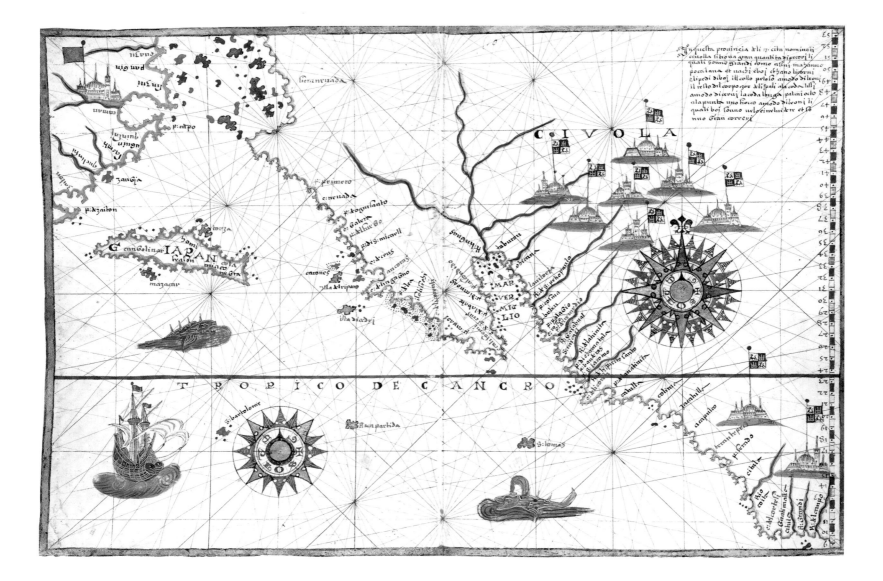

California and the Seven Cities of Cibola | 1578 | Joan Martines

Manuscript on vellum. 24 × 35.5 cm / 9½ × 14 in. British Library, London

The key features of Joan Martines' map of what is now the southwestern United States are the seven cities of Cibola, which were thought to be so fabulously rich that Spaniards in Latin America knew them as the 'cities of gold'. The quest to find Cibola drew Spanish conquistadors deep into the interior of North America, most notably Francisco Vásquez de Coronado and Hernando de Soto in the early 1540s, but long before Martines drew his map

Spanish explorers had come to the reluctant conclusion that the rumours of wealthy cities were just that. They found not the storied walled cities, with battlements and towers, but the mud-brick pueblos of the Native Americans. That did not prevent the story persisting, however, nor the efforts of the Spaniards to ensure that – if they did prove to exist – they were claimed by Spain. Martines showed them as walled cities with towers and

battlements, flying Spanish heraldic banners. In his 1578 atlas, from which this map comes, Martines brought together two cartographic traditions: the decorative portolans of the Majorcan school and the increasingly geographically accurate maps being produced by mapmakers in the Netherlands and Belgium.

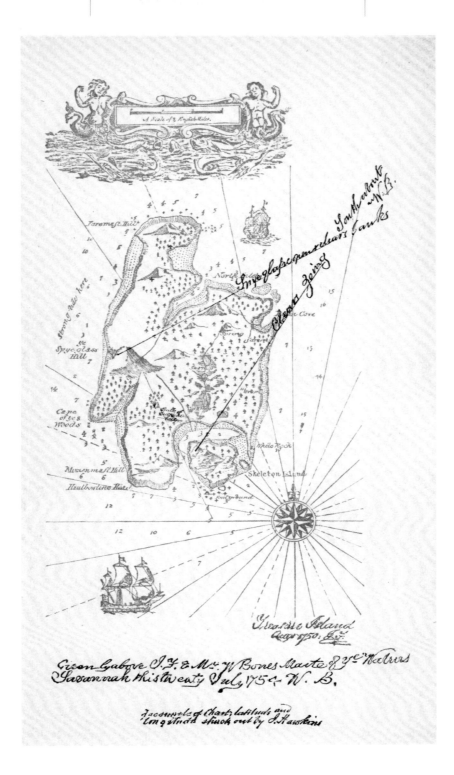

Treasure Island | 1883 | Robert Louis Stevenson

Printed paper. 19 × 11 cm / 7½ × 4¼ in. Yale University Library, New Haven, Connecticut

X marks the spot: although no real pirate maps have ever been discovered, they remain an enduring legend and are familiar to children the world over. The idea may have originated in an unsuccessful attempt by Captain William Kidd to avoid death by hanging in 1701. Kidd hinted that he had buried some of his pirated booty in the Caribbean or North America. No treasure has been found – but the promise of easy riches for the digging persisted. Fast-forward to a rainy day in late nineteenth-century Scotland, where a bored boy, stuck inside during his school holiday, let his mind wander to pirates, islands and buried treasure and drew a map of the adventure. The boy's stepfather, Robert Louis Stevenson, was so excited by the map that he wrote the first several chapters of *Treasure Island* by the end of the holiday. Since then, the idea of buried treasure marked on a map has gripped the imaginations of children and adults alike. Treasure maps can take many forms, but they usually have geographic hints or landmarks, directions in the form of a puzzle – and an 'X' to mark the loot. From books and cinema to computer games and geo-caching, the notion of receiving a reward in return for correctly interpreting coded directions and following a visual key remains as alluring as ever.

Europe Divided into its Kingdoms | 1766 | John Spilsbury

Painted wood. 30 × 28 cm / 11¾ × 11 in. British Library, London

Many children's earliest introduction to maps comes from jigsaws or board games based on the shapes of countries or regions. The practice is not new: this example is not just the earliest jigsaw map but arguably one of the very first jigsaws. Its creator, John Spilsbury, was an apprentice to Thomas Jefferys, royal geographer to King George III, and believed to be the first commercial manufacturer of jigsaw puzzles. Spilsbury's earliest jigsaws were

referred to as 'dissected maps' and set a trend for puzzles for many years to come. These puzzles were initially produced as aids in geography teaching. Countries were dissected along national boundaries so that piecing the puzzle together allowed children to learn how the different countries connected to one another. Beyond the land, Spilsbury continued the dissection along lines of latitude and longitude to produce what was both an ingenious

educational aid and an early indicator of the commercial value of using maps for a non-cartographic product. The dissected puzzles were a commercial success, and Spilsbury went on to create them on eight themes: the World, Europe, Asia, Africa, America, England and Wales, Ireland and Scotland. His legacy is the continued use of maps in jigsaw puzzles in many different forms.

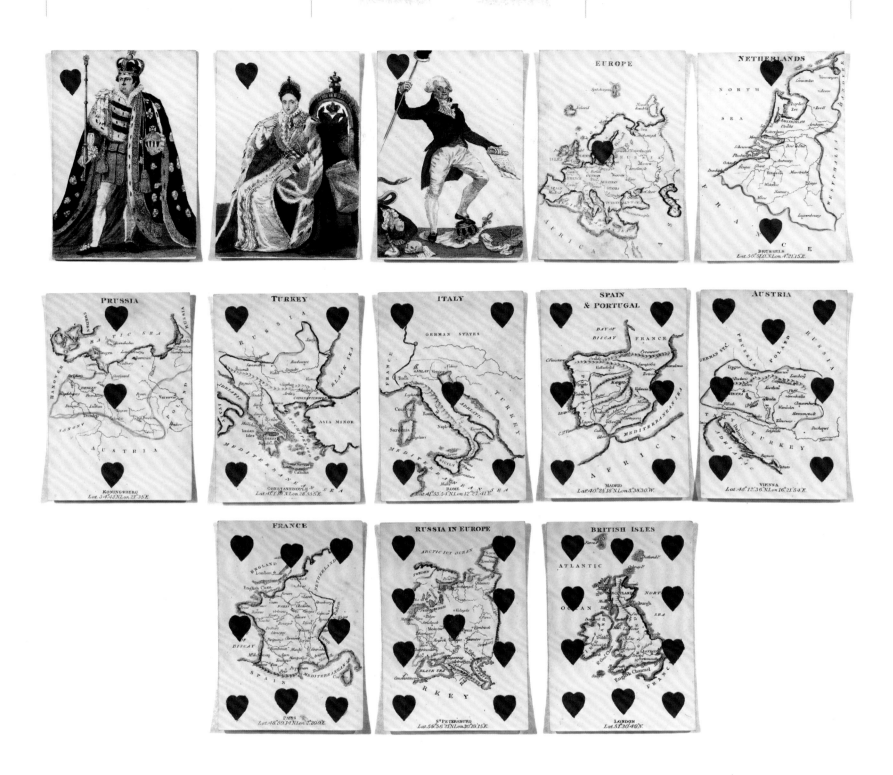

The Court Game of Geography | c.1840–3 | W. & H. Rock

Engraved, hand-coloured cards. Each card 9.6 × 6.4 cm / 3¾ × 2½ in. Royal Geographical Society, London

Images from geography and science had been used in educational games since the late sixteenth century, but this deck with maps is striking for its clarity and accuracy, however, and for its portrayal of British attitudes towards the rest of the world. The cards – finely engraved maps over which the suit symbols are simply stencilled – could be used either as normal playing cards or to play the 'Court Game of Geography', the rules of which were contained in a booklet that also gave a brief description of each country and the characteristics of its population (the British were 'enterprizing [sic]', the Chinese 'deceitful', for example). Each suit represents a continent: hearts is Europe, diamonds Asia (including Australia), spades America and clubs Africa. The ace shows the whole continent, the royal cards are portraits of selected rulers from that continent (including George Washington as the King of the United States) and the numbered cards are maps of countries, with the higher numerical values being assigned to the more important nations. The game itself involved trying to achieve international domination – with the rules clearly suggesting that a European triumph was the most desirable outcome.

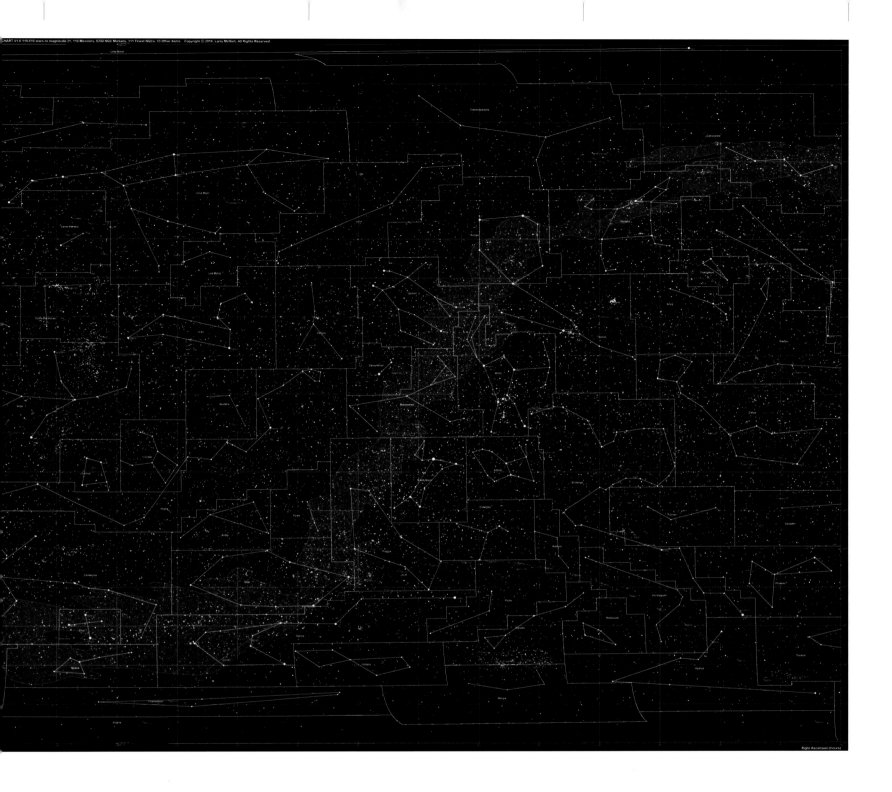

Rectangular Declination vs. Right Ascension Mega Star Chart | 2014 | Larry McNish

Digital image. Dimensions variable

Any view of deep space is a view into the past, as the light reaching Earth may be millions of years old. The sheer size of Larry McNish's star chart gives some indication of the challenge facing mapmakers who turn their attention to the heavens: the vastness of space. McNish's chart includes 119,616 of the brightest stars in the sky, plus other astronomical phenomena such as Messier objects – nebulae, star clusters and galaxies – and other highlights from the New General Catalogue (NGC), a list of features in the night sky. As in older celestial charts (see p.262), McNish also added boundary lines to define constellations and drew stick figures to join asterisms (patterns within the constellations). The stars are scaled according to their apparent brightness. The irregular 'U'-shaped shaded belt that crosses the chart indicates the Milky Way – that galaxy that contains our solar system. The chart is a remarkable testimony to what an amateur astronomer – McNish is a retired computer expert – can do with patience, tables of astronomical coordinates and other data, computers and a decent telescope camera, but it is still only fractional. The observable universe has some 170 billion galaxies – some of which contain 100 trillion stars each.

Prehistory

c.16,500 BC

Neolithic artists include a map showing the Pleiades star cluster among their paintings of animals and other subjects in the Lascaux Caves in southern France

c.2300 BC

The first Babylonian map is created on a clay tablet; it may show a noble's estate

c.1200 BC

In the foothills of the Alps in northern Italy, people begin carving a plan of fields and paths into a large, smooth rock at Bedolina; the map is completed three to five centuries later with the addition of houses

c.1160 BC

An Egyptian scribe creates a papyrus map to show the way to mines in the Eastern Desert – the earliest known navigational map in the world

1000 BC

c.750 BC

Chinese literature contains the first references to maps

c.725 BC

Assyrian astronomers begin to chart the heavens in a methodical way

c.700–500 BC

A Babylonian scribe draws a world map on a clay tablet, showing Babylon at the centre and noting that the map is based on an older original (1; see p.74)

c.570 BC

The Greek philosopher Anaximander of Miletus creates an early world map

500 BC

c.500 BC

Pythagorean philosophers in Greece deduce that the Earth is a sphere

c.500 BC

The Greek traveller Hecataeus of Miletus describes the geography of Europe, northern Africa and Asia in the first known travel narrative, *Tour Around the World*

c.330 BC

A Greek known as Pseudo-Scylax writes a periplus, a list of landmarks and ports used to navigate around the Mediterranean and the Black Sea

c.300 BC

The earliest surviving Chinese maps are created

250 BC

235 BC

The Greek mathematician Eratosthenes calculates the circumference of the Earth

c.200 BC

The development of the astrolabe in Alexandria, Egypt increases the accuracy with which the positions of the stars can be measured

c.140 BC

Crates of Mallus creates the first known globe in Asia Minor (now Turkey)

12 BC

In Rome, the politician Marcus Agrippa creates a map of the world that is carved into marble and set up at the beginning of the Via Flamina to remind travellers of the extent of the Roman Empire

1

2

3

c.3000 BC

Egyptians invent papyrus, a form of paper made from plant fibres

c.2000 BC

Austronesian peoples begin spreading throughout Maritime Southeast Asia, the South Pacific, Australia and Madagascar

c.1400 BC

Settled communities are established all over Europe

c.800 BC

The Greeks establish city states

753 BC

Traditional date for the founding of Rome

c.660 BC

Jimmu becomes the legendary first emperor of Japan

c.563 BC

Birth of Siddhartha Gautama, the founder of Buddhism, in India

c.475 BC

A period of upheaval known as the Warring States begins in China

c.432 BC

The Parthenon is built in Athens

c.331 BC

Alexander the Great completes his conquest of Persia

221 BC

Qin Shihuangdi becomes first emperor of a unified China

c.146 BC

Rome's victory in the Third Punic War finally destroys the power of its rival city, Carthage

27 BC

The Roman Republic becomes the Roman Empire

c.50

The *Periplus of the Erythraean Sea* is a Greek navigational document for trading in the Red Sea and along the East African coast to India

c.78–139

The Chinese geographer Zhang Heng produces the first map with parallels running north-south and east-west, introducing mathematical precision to cartography

c.90–168

The Greek-Egyptian geographer Claudius Ptolemy's *Geography* sets out the Roman world. (3; see p.138)

203–11

The *Forma Urbis Romae* is created under the Emperor Severus Septimius; it is a huge carved marble map of the city (2; see p.188)

c.300–50

Roman cartographers create a large map of the empire showing roads and distances between major cities; in about 1200 the original was copied to create what is now known as the *Peutinger Table* (see p.24)

333

The first known pilgrim itinerary describes the journey from Bordeaux to Jerusalem

c.410

Using the theories of the second-century BC Greek scientist Crates of Mallos, the Roman writer Macrobius produces a map of the Earth divided into climatic zones (see p.166)

c.560

Byzantine Christians create a mosaic map of the Bible lands on the floor of an Orthodox church in Madaba, in Jordan; the map shows many biblical locations, with Jerusalem at its centre (4; see p.144)

c.620s–630s

Isidore of Seville creates a T-O map dividing the world into three continents (see p.136)

c.650

A Chinese astronomer, probably Li Chunfang, draws the extensive Dunhuang Star Chart of constellations (see p.286)

c.685

A monk in Ravenna, Italy, compiles the Ravenna Cosmography, a list of towns, rivers, countries and other place names in the Roman Empire

c.750

The Albi World Map is an early attempt to depict the world in a more realistic way than contemporary T-O maps

776

Beatus of Liébana, a Spanish monk, writes a commentary on the Book of Revelation with a world map that was later widely copied (5; see p.12)

c.900

The Cottonian World Map, created by Anglo-Saxon monks in England, attempts to combine biblical and geographical knowledge

964

The Persian astronomer al-Sufi creates charts of the major constellations based on the work of Ptolemy; al-Sufi's illustrations were widely reproduced over the following centuries (6; see p.42)

c.1050

An Egyptian mapmaker draws maps of the Islamic Mediterranean for an Arabic cosmology now known as the *Book of Curiosities* (see p.220)

1120

Prior Walcher of Malvern Priory, England, uses degrees to express longitude and latitude on maps

c.1137

A Chinese cartographer carves the *Map of the Tracks of Yu*, a stone map of China that illustrates the travels of a legendary Chinese hero (see p.104)

1154

Mohammed al-Idrisi writes the *Tabula Rogeriana* (Book of Roger), an Arabic map and description of the world produced for King Roger II of Sicily

1175

Gerard of Cremona translates the *Almagest* by Ptolemy into Latin, helping to introduce Ptolemaic astronomical knowledge to Europe

4

5

6

79

Vesuvius erupts in southern Italy, burying the Roman cities of Pompeii and Herculaneum

105

Chinese official Cai Lun describes how to make paper, which may have been invented about 150 BC

117

The Roman Empire reaches its greatest extent, under Trajan

259

Barbarian peoples sweep into Roman Gaul (France)

c.400

Polynesians settle the Hawaiian Islands

476

The Roman Empire in the West comes to an end when the final emperor is overthrown by the soldier Odoacer, who becomes king of Italy

c.570

Birth of Mohammad in Medina; he becomes the founder of Islam

593

Printing blocks invented in China

609

The Grand Canal is built in China

638

Jerusalem is captured by Arab invaders

786

Harun al-Rashid becomes caliph, ruler of the Islamic world

800

Charlemagne is crowned emperor of much of western Europe

866

The Fujiwara Period begins in Japan

c.950

Arabic becomes the main language of scientific development

1054

Christianity splits between the Catholic and Orthodox churches

1096

The First Crusade begins; it recaptures Jerusalem in 1099, opening the city to Christian pilgrims

1106

The Aztec leave their legendary homeland in Aztlán and begin their long journey to Mexico

1200

c.1200

Abdallah al-Rumi writes an Arabic geographical encyclopedia

c.1200

A French artist illustrates the Crusades with a map showing Jerusalem as the centre of the world (see p.26)

1230

1240

The English mathematician Johannes de Sacrobosco publishes *On the Sphere of the World*, which becomes a standard astronomical text for 400 years

1247

A star map is carved on to a stela in the Confucian temple at Suzhou in Jiangsu province, China (7; see p.44)

c.1250–9

The English monk Matthew Paris draws a strip map of the pilgrim route from England to Rome and Jerusalem (8; see p.25)

1260

1270

The first reference to a sea chart is noted in an account about Louis IX of France

c.1280

The Persian or Arabic geographer al-Qazwini creates an influential *Cosmography* (see p.68)

1290

c.1290

The *Carte Pisane* is drawn to help navigators in the Mediterranean (9; see p.152)

c.1300

The largest medieval map, the Ebstorf World Map, is drawn on thirty goatskins; it is destroyed in the twentieth century (10; see p.148)

c.1300

The Hereford *Mappa Mundi* is created; it incorporates geographical and Christian views of the world (see p.13)

c.1300

A school of cartographers in Majorca produces charts for Portuguese sailors to use for coastal navigation

1320

1325

Pietro Vesconte produces a portolan of the Atlantic coast, one of the earliest surviving chart for practical sea navigation

1330s

Opicinus de Canistris, a cleric at the papal court in Avignon, produces an anthropomorphic novelty mappa mundi showing human features

1331

Traveller Ibn-Battuta begins his journey through Islamic lands and on to India and China

1337

William Merlee of Oxford attempts the first weather forecasts

1339

The Majorcan cartographer Angelino Dulcert draws a chart that helps to spread the popularity of portolans

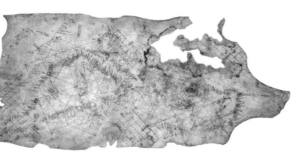

9

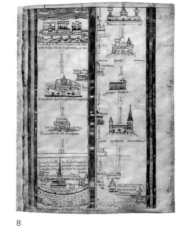

8

10

1204

The sack of Constantinople during the Fourth Crusade begins the decline of the Byzantine Empire

1206

Genghis Khan becomes chief of the Mongols

1215

King John I of England signs Magna Carta, giving rights to his nobles; the document is now seen as an early step towards democracy

1240

The Mongols defeat Rus, establishing a state that becomes known as the Golden Horde

c.1250

The Mexica arrive in central Mexico from a homeland to the north; they are now better known as the Aztec

1258

The Mongol siege of Baghdad marks the declining power of the Islamic

1269

The French soldier Petrus Peregrinus suggests that a magnet has poles that influence a compass needle

1271

The young Marco Polo leaves Venice with his father and uncle to travel to East Asia

1274

Japan repels an invasion by the Mongols; it repels another in 1281

1291

The Crusades come to an end

1295

Marco Polo returns to Venice from his travels to China and dictates his memoirs, published in 1298

1299

The Ottoman Empire is founded in Anatolia

1310

The Italian poet Dante writes *The Divine Comedy*

1324

Mansa Musa travels to Mecca, a visit recorded in the *Catalan Atlas*

1325

The Aztec found their capital at Tenochtitlán

1337

The Hundred Years' War begins between England and France

1347

The Black Death arrives in Europe

1350

c.1360

The Gough Map, produced during the reign of Edward I, is the first detailed map of England and Wales

1361

Astronomers in Catalonia, Spain, draw maps of the constellations

c.1375

The *Catalan Atlas*, drawn by Cresques Abraham or Abraham Cresques, shows the Malian ruler Mansa Musa; it also shows Marco Polo, whose knowledge about China is reflected in the map, and his family (11; see pp.14–15)

1380

1389

The Great Ming Amalgamated Map is a new, comprehensive map of the world with China at its centre

1402

Korean cartographers produce the first examples of the Kangnido world map

1406

Ptolemy's influential *Geography* becomes more accessible when Jacobus Angelus translates it into from Greek into Latin

1410

1422

The Florentine monk Christoforo Buondelmonti creates the earliest surviving map of Constantinople shortly before it is taken over by the Ottomans (see p.208)

1431–3

The Chinese admiral Zheng He maps his final voyage to the Indian Ocean; the maps are printed two centuries later (see p.289)

1440

c.1450

Fra Mauro, a Venetian mapmaker, completes a mappa mundi for Alfonso V of Portugal. It reflects the most up-to-date European knowledge of East Asia

c.1450s

The Portuguese begin using the astrolabe to fix latitude at sea

c.1459–63

The European artist Simon Marmion paints a miniature T-O world map showing Noah's three sons ruling the three continents (12; see p.137)

1470

1472

The first printed map is a T-O diagram in an edition of Isidore of Seville's *Etymologia*

1477

The first edition of Ptolemy's *Geography* to include maps is printed in Bologna, Italy

1484

The first European nautical almanac and manual of navigation are published

1492

Columbus crosses the Atlantic; his crew includes Juan de la Cosa, who later maps the discoveries (see p.153)

1492

Martin Behaim constructs the earliest surviving terrestrial globe in Nuremberg, Germany

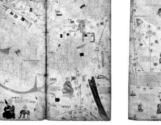

11

12

1356

Widespread rioting against Mongol rule breaks out in China

1370

Tamerlane establishes the Timurid Dynasty of Persia

1378

During the Great Schism, three different men claim to be pope at the same time

1381

John Wycliffe translates the first English edition of the Bible

1392

The Joseon Dynasty is founded in Korea

c.1405

The Chinese admiral Zheng He leads the first of seven voyages through the Indian Ocean

1428

Joan of Arc leads French resistance against English forces

1430s

Encouraged by Prince Henry the Navigator, Portuguese navigators begin exploring the West African coast

c.1439

The German Johannes Gutenberg invents a printing press

1450

Florence under the Medicis becomes the centre of the Renaissance

1453

The end of the Hundred Years' War leaves English territory in France greatly reduced

1453

The Ottoman Turks capture Constantinople, ending the Byzantine Empire

1485

The Tudor dynasty comes to the throne in England at the end of the Wars of the Roses

1494

The Treaty of Tordesillas divides the 'New World' between Spain and Portugal along a meridian 370 Castilian leagues (1,185 miles/1,907 km) west of the Cape Verde Islands

1500

c.1500

The Italian artist Jacopo de Barbari's map of Venice is the first bird's-eye-view city map (13; see p.36)

1502

The Italian artist Leonardo da Vinci maps the town of Imola as part of his duties as an engineer for Cesare Borgia (14; see p.76)

1502

The Italian diplomat Alberto Cantino smuggles a map of Spanish and Portuguese discoveries out of Lisbon for his employer, Duke Ercole d'Este of Ferrara; it is now known as the *Cantino Planisphere* (see p.223)

1507

The German cartographer Martin Waldseemüller produces a woodcut world map and uses the name America for the first time (see p.228)

1510

1511

Bernard Sylvanus publishes a cordiform map of the world, based on a heart-shaped projection

1513

Piri Reis, an Ottoman geographer, draws a world map; the fragment that survives today includes the Americas (15; see p.154)

1515

The renowned German artist Albrecht Dürer publishes the first printed star chart (see p.262)

1516

Martin Waldseemüller publishes the *Carta Marina*, a nautical chart (see pp.120–121)

1520

1522

The Portuguese explorer Ferdinand Magellan's expedition completes the first circumnavigation of the globe (although Magellan himself has been killed on the voyage)

1524

The Spanish conquistador Hernán Cortés sends the Spanish king a map of the Aztec capital city, Tenochtitlán, captured by Cortés three years earlier (see p.77)

1529

A Portuguese in Spanish service, Diogo Ribeiro, produces the Universal Chart to support Spanish claims to the Spice Islands (see p.178)

1530

1533

The Dutch cosmographer Regnier Gemma Frisius publishes an explanation of the use of triangulation for use in surveying and map-making

c.1536

The French mathematician Oronce Fine creates a cordiform (heart-shaped) world map (16; see p.158)

1537

Johann Putsch (Bucius), from the Tirol in the Habsburg Empire, produces one of the first novelty maps, showing Europe in the shape of a woman

1539

The Catholic priest Olaus Magnus produces the first realistic map of Scandinavia during the Counter-Reformation (see p.184)

1540

c.1540

Native Aztec artists in Mexico draw maps of disputed land for use in Spanish courts (see p.186)

1546

The Flemish geographer Gerard Mercator describes Earth's magnetic poles

1547

The Vallard Atlas is published with fifteen maps, including three that show Terra Incognita Australis, the hypothetical undiscovered Southern Continent and one showing Jacques Cartier's explorations of Canada (see p.258)

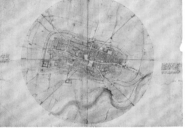

14

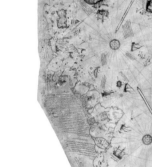

16

13

15

1502

The first African slaves are brought to the New World

1505

The Ming Dynasty begins in China

1506

The Safavid Dynasty comes to power in Iran

1509

Portuguese seafarers reach the Moluccas, or Spice Islands

1511

The Portuguese conquer the Spice Islands and establish a monopoly on the spice trade

1517

The German monk Martin Luther begins the Reformation when he makes a list of objections to the Catholic Church

1520

Suleyman the Magnificent becomes Sultan of the Ottoman-Turkish Empire

1521

The Spanish conquistador Hernán Cortés overthrows the Aztec empire in Mexico

1526

Babur founds the Islamic Mughal Empire in northern India

1532

The conquistador Francisco Pizarro and a handful of men overthrow the Inca Empire of Peru

1534

The Frenchman Jacques Cartier explores the St Lawrence River in Canada

1539

Hernando de Soto explores inland North America on behalf of Spain

1540

The Spanish conquistador Francisco Vásquez de Coronado explores New Mexico seeking the Seven Cities of Gold (see p.316)

1543

The Polish astronomer Nicolaus Copernicus publishes his theory that the Earth orbits the Sun

1547

Ivan IV ('the Terrible') becomes the first czar of Russia

1550

1550s |

Copperplate engraving takes over from woodcuts as cartographers' preferred means of working; Antwerp becomes the first commercial centre of Europe's map trade

c.1550s |

The cartographer Diogo Homen flees his native Portugal after killing a man in a fight, visits England and settles in Venice

1558 |

The Portuguese cartographer Luis Teixeira maps the captaincies of Brazil during Portugal's early exploitation of its new territory (see p.124)

1560

1561 |

The Italian cartographer and humanist Girolamo Ruscelli publishes the first double-hemisphere world map

1564 |

The Italian engineer and cartographer Jacopo Gastaldi prints the first large-scale map of Africa, combining accurate and fictitious details

1564 |

Abraham Ortelius of Antwerp publishes his first world map (17; see p.229)

1569 |

Gerard Mercator creates the Mercator projection; it becomes standard for world maps (see p.155)

1570

1570 |

Abraham Ortelius publishes the *Theatrum Orbis Terrarum*, the world's first atlas; by his death in 1598 the atlas contains 119 contemporary and 36 historical maps

1572 |

The German cleric Georg Braun and the Flemish artist Frans Hogenberg publish their first maps of Europe's cities; the sixth volume is published in 1618 (18; see p.28)

1574 |

The English surveyor Christopher Saxton begins a five-year project to map the counties of England and Wales (see p.302)

1580

1581 |

The German theologian Heinrich Bünting publishes a cloverleaf map of the world based on Protestant theology (19; see p.18)

1583 |

The Austrian historian Michael Aitzinger publishes a novelty map showing Belgium in the shape of a lion (see p.263)

1585 |

The Dutch cartographer Lucas Waghenaer prints the first book of sea charts

1585 |

Gerard Mercator uses the word 'atlas' to describe a book of maps

1590

1590 |

The Flemish engraver Jodocus Hondius publishes a double-hemisphere world map showing the circumnavigation 1577–89 by Francis Drake

c.1590 |

The English nobleman Ralph Sheldon commissions a series of tapestry maps of England (see p.302)

1594 |

The Flemish astronomer and cartographer Petrus Plancius produces the first charts using the Mercator projection for Dutch seafarers sailing to the Spice Islands (see p.62)

1599 |

The English mathematician Thomas Wright publishes the mathematical explanation of Mercator's projection that helps to popularize its use

17

18

19

1553 |

The navigator Richard Chancellor leads the first English expedition to Russia

1556 |

Akbar becomes emperor of India; he will encourage religious tolerance and promote art and trade

1558 |

Queen Elizabeth I comes to the English throne, beginning a period of prosperity and cultural achievement

1562 |

In India, Emperor Akbar tries to unify his Muslim and Hindu subjects

1562 |

The Wars of Religion break out between Catholics and Protestants in France

1566 |

The Eighty Years' War breaks out between the Spanish and their subjects in the Netherlands

1571 |

The Catholic Holy League defeat's the Ottomans at the Battle of Lepanto in the eastern Mediterranean

1578 |

The English navigator Sir Francis Drake claims the west coast of North America for England

1580 |

Francis Drake completes the second circumnavigation of the globe

1584 |

The English politician and explorer Walter Raleigh claims Virginia for England

1588 |

The English navy defeats an invading Spanish force, the Armada

1597 |

The Dutch establish a colony at Batavia, on Java in the East Indies

1598 |

The Edict of Nantes ends the French Wars of Religion

1599 |

The first Dutch fleet returns from the East Indies with a cargo of valuable spices, signalling the beginning of the Dutch golden age

1600

1602

The Italian Jesuit missionary Matteo Ricci publishes a Chinese atlas of the world, reviving Chinese cartographic traditions and introducing European discoveries to Asia (20; see pp.292–293)

1607

The French explorer Samuel de Champlain maps New France (Canada) (see p.218)

1610

1611

English cartographer John Speed's *Theatrum* contains a popular map of the Heptarchy – Anglo-Saxon Britain from about 600 to 800 – that is later copied by Johannes Blaeu and Jan Jansson; Speed also publishes a series of maps showing the changing counties and towns of England

1616

Captain John Smith, the English governor of Virginia Colony, publishes a map of New England in the hope of attracting more settlers

1617

Jesuits publish the first accurate map of Japan available in Europe

1620

c.1620

Late Ming mapmakers produce a beautiful watercolour map of East and Southeast Asia, the first Chinese map to show shipping routes (see p.288)

1622

As cartographer of the Dutch East India Company, Hessel Gerritsz maps the latest Dutch discoveries in the Pacific Ocean (21; see p.255)

1630

1630

The Dutch cartographer Willem Janszoon Blaeu produces his first atlas, the *Atlas Appendix*, with sixty maps including some plates bought from the earlier Hondius/Mercator atlases

1633

The Italian scientist Galileo Galilei is condemned by the Inquisition for supporting the Copernican view that the sun is at the centre of the solar system

1635

In Amsterdam, Willem Blaeu and his son Johannes publish the *Novus Atlas* (see p.209)

1638

Johannes Blaeu replaces his father, Willem, as mapmaker to the Dutch East India Company

1640

1644

Having explored New Zealand, New Guinea, Fiji and Tasmania, the Dutch navigator Abel Tasman explores the northern coast of Australia, which is by now known to be a huge island (see 22; p.256)

1645

The Flemish cartographer Michael Langrenus publishes the first map of the moon

1648

A former apprentice of Willem Blaeu, Frederik de Wit, sets up an influential map-printing house in Amsterdam

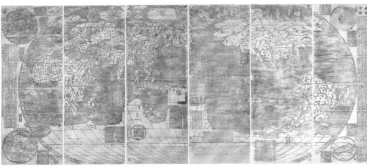

20

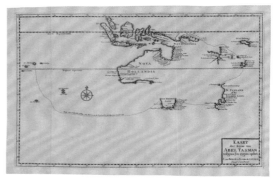

22

21

1600

The English found the East India Company to trade with Asia; the Dutch form their own company two years later

1608

The Italian scientist Galileo Galilei builds a telescope

1609

The provinces of the Netherlands gain independence from Spain

1610

The English navigator Henry Hudson explores Hudson Bay

1618

The Thirty Years' War breaks out in Europe

1619

The Dutch seize Batavia and make it the capital of their colony in the Spice Islands

1620

The Pilgrims arrive in Massachusetts on the *Mayflower*

1625

Dutch settlers in North America found New Amsterdam, later New York

1626

The basilica of St Peter's is completed in the Vatican in Rome

1635

The Japanese shogun Tokugawa Iemitsu forbids the Japanese from travelling overseas and bans all books from abroad

1639

The first printing press is set up in North America

1644

The Manchus conquer China and found the Qing Dynasty

1648

Peace of Westphalia ends the Thirty Years' War, signalling the end of the political influence of Spain and the Holy Roman Empire

1650

1651

The English cartographer John Farrer maps the English colony in Virginia (23; see p.219)

1651

The Italian Giovanni Battista Riccioli publishes a map of the moon

1655

Johannes Blaeu completes the *Novus Atlas*, which now covers six volumes

1656

Nicolas Sanson, France's first royal cartographer, publishes a map of New France (Canada), which is the first to show all the Great Lakes

23

1660

1660

The Dutch–German cartographer Andreas Cellarius creates his *Atlas of the Heavens* (24; see p.284)

1662

Johannes Blaeu publishes the *Grand Atlas*, in eleven volumes; it may be the most expensive publication of the century

1664

The English seize New Amsterdam and rename it New York; the Duke's Plan is the first English-language map of Manhattan (25; see p.98)

1669

The Italian Giovanni Domenico Cassini becomes director of the new Paris Observatory; he takes the French name Jean-Dominique

1670

1670

The French astronomer Jean Picard measures part of the meridian, allowing the accurate calculation of the circumference of the Earth

1670s

Frederik de Wit buys the plates of the Blaeu and Johansson firms when the latter goes out of business

1672

King Charles II of England bans the import of Dutch maps to try to lessen English dependence on Dutch maps and charts

1674

The French explorer Louis Joliet draws a map of his exploration of the Mississippi River (see p.114)

1675

Greenwich Observatory is built and gives its name to the Greenwich Meridian, 0 degrees longitude

1675

John Ogilby publishes the first strip maps of England's roads in the atlas *Britannia* (see p.60)

24

1680

1681

The British Admiralty commissions Captain Grenville Collins to carry out the first complete survey of the British coasts, published in 1693 as *Britain's Coasting Pilot*

1681

Jean Picard completes his triangulation of the French coast

1683

A map by the German scholar Hiob Ludolf correctly identifies Lake Tana in Ethiopia as the source of the Blue Nile

1685

The English surveyor William Petty publishes the first atlas of Ireland, with thirty-six maps originally drawn to survey land seized by Anglo-Irish Protestants from the native Catholics after the campaigns of Oliver Cromwell

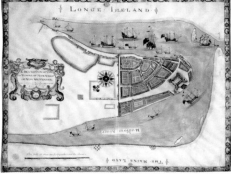

25

1690

1690

The English cartographer William Hacke charts the coast around Bombay in India, the new port of the East Indian Company (see p.226)

1696

The Italian-born French astronomer and cartographer Jean-Dominique Cassini publishes a highly accurate world map based on his own tables for determining longitude on land

---

1651

The English Civil War ends in a victory for Parliamentarian forces

1652

The Dutch East India Company sets up fortifications at the Cape of Good Hope and plants gardens to grow fresh food

1653

Britain's lord protector, Oliver Cromwell, completes the English conquest of Ireland

1660

Royal Society chartered in London to advance the sciences

1660s

The Mughal Empire reaches its greatest extent in India

1666

The Great Fire of London devastates much of the English capital

1670

The English establish the Hudson's Bay Company to coordinate the fur trade in Canada; the company encourages the exploration of northern North America

1674

The French establish a trading post in India

1683

Ottoman forces besiege the Habsburg capital in the Second Siege of Vienna

1687

The English scientist Isaac Newton proposes his universal law of gravitation

1688

The Glorious Revolution in England; the crown passes to the Protestant Dutch prince William of Orange

1690

The English East India Company founds Calcutta (Kolkata) in the Ganges Delta in India

1692

Colonial Americans in New England begin the Salem Witch Trials

1696

Peter the Great becomes czar of Russia

1700

The French cartographer Guillaume Delisle publishes a map of Africa that leaves blank spaces for unknown regions rather than the fanciful details included by his predecessors

1701

Semyon Remezov is the first Russian to map the newly conquered territory of Siberia (26; see p.94)

1701

The English astronomer Edmond Halley publishes a map showing the Earth's magnetic field, using contour lines (27; see p.282)

1702

Johann Baptist Homann sets up as a map publisher in Nuremberg; he and his family – 'Homann's Heirs' – become the leading German mapmakers of the century

1712

The English astronomer John Flamsteed publishes the first volume of *Historia Coelestis Britannica*, cataloguing the position of 3,000 stars

1714

The English government offers £20,000 for a method to determine longitude at sea; the reward is claimed in 1759 by the clockmaker John Harrison, who has to wait fourteen years to be paid

1715

Herman Moll's 'Beaver Map' of north-eastern North America shows the colonies following the Peace of Utrecht (28; see p.252)

1720S

English landowners commission local surveyors to map their estates; some of these estate maps are largely practical, but some are highly decorative and are put on display in the owner's home as a status symbol (see p.175)

1729

The French cartographer Jean D'Anville maps European slave forts along the so-called Gold Coast in West Africa (see p.250)

1730S

Jacques and César-François Cassini – son and grandson of Jean Dominique – undertake the national triangulation of France, financed by the French Crown

1736

The French mathematician and astronomer Alexis Clairaut measures the length of 1 degree of the meridian arc

1745

The Cassinis publish an accurate map of France

1746

The Frenchman Philippe Buache makes the first maps of European rock formations and minerals

1747

The Russian Academy of Sciences publishes the first official atlas of the Russian Empire

1747

The British begin a military survey of Scotland, in part to help the army effectively fight Highland supporters of Bonnie Prince Charlie

27

28

26

1703

The Russian czar Peter the Great founds a new capital at St Petersburg

1707

England and Scotland unite to create Great Britain

1707

Mount Fuji erupts in Japan, causing a massive cloud of smoke over much of the country

1713

The Peace of Utrecht ends Queen Anne's War, passing French territory in North America to Britain

1718

French colonists in North America found New Orleans near the mouth of the Mississippi River

1719

Daniel Defoe writes *Robinson Crusoe*, a novel based on the real experiences of a shipwrecked sailor

1720

English investors are ruined by the collapse of the South Sea Company, whose shares have become vastly overvalued on the basis of its theoretical monopoly over trade with South America – which remains dominated by Spain

1720S

The city of Jaipur, India, is laid out on a grid system

1730

The English mathematician John Hadley develops the quadrant for use in navigation

1735

The self-taught English clockmaker John Harrison makes his first chronometer, used for measuring longitude at sea

1740

Frederick the Great becomes king of Prussia and sets out to modernize the state and its army

1742

The first cotton mills open in Britain, heralding the start of the Industrial Revolution

1747

Nader Shah of Iran is assassinated after trying to unify Sunni and Shiite factions

1750

1750

A final edition of the city atlas by Braun and Hogenberg is published

1753

Mikhail Makhaev publishes a map of St Petersburg to celebrate the fiftieth anniversary of the city's founding (29; see p.96)

1755

The American physician John Mitchell draws the 'most important map in American history' showing the French and British colonies in North America; the map was used as the basis for negotiations in 1783 to set the boundaries of the United States after the Revolution (30; see p.253)

1756

César-François Cassini de Thury completes the first sheet of the French national survey (see p.90)

1760

1766–77

English artist John Spilsbury begins mass-producing jigsaw maps (see p.318)

1767

The English astronomer Nevil Maskelyne publishes the *Nautical Almanac*

1768

The American politician and inventor Benjamin Franklin maps the Gulf Stream (see p.283)

1769

The Polynesian chief Tupaia draws a map of Tahiti for the British navigator Captain James Cook (31; see p.221)

1770

1770

James Cook charts New Zealand as he sails around the islands (see p.257); he later claims south-east Australia for Britain

1776

The British lieutenant Bernard Ratzer's survey of the city of New York is published in London a decade after he completed it (see p.99)

1780

1783

Negotiators in Paris use the Mitchell map to begin defining the new United States

1784

The American physician Abel Buell publishes the first map of the United States printed in America

1784

Major General William Roy measures a baseline on Hounslow Heath near London as a basis for a triangulation survey of Britain

1788

The *Cassini Carte de France*, a complete topographical survey, is published by the four generations of the family of cartographers

1790

c.1790

A Gujurati cartographer draws a chart of the Red Sea and the Gulf of Aden to help ships' captains taking Muslim pilgrims to Arabia on the Hajj (32; see p.61)

1791

The Trigonometric Survey of the Board of Ordnance, later the Ordnance Survey in Britain, buys its first theodolite

1797

The British naval surgeon George Bass explores the coast of eastern Australia

29

30

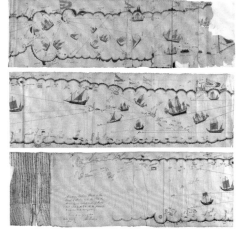

32

31

1750

The Chinese take power in Tibet

1754

The French and Indian Wars begin as France and Britain dispute territory in North America

1757

At the Battle of Plassey, East India Company troops defeat a French and Indian army, leaving the British in charge of much of India

1763

End of the French and Indian Wars; France cedes all of Canada and Louisiana west of the Mississippi to Britain

1765

James Watt invents a steam engine

1769

The English navigator James Cook visits Tahiti to observe a transit of Venus and begins his exploration of the Pacific Ocean

1771

In England, Richard Arkwright builds the first water-powered cotton mill, further speeding the progress of the Industrial Revolution

1775

Colonial Americans known as Patriots begin the Revolutionary War against their British governors; in 1776 the Patriots issue the Declaration of Independence

1783

The Treaty of Paris confirms the creation of the United States

1788

The African Association is founded in London to sponsor exploration of Africa, including Mungo Park's expedition to the Niger

1789

The French Revolution begins the overthrow of the *Ancien Régime*

1791

The English seaman George Vancouver begins a four-year exploration of the north-west coast of North America

1795

The metric system is adopted in France

1796

The German printer Aloys Senefelder invents lithography

c.1800

Korean cartographers produce a *Ch'onhado* (All Under Heaven), a traditional cosmographic map (33; see p.72)

1801

The British Board of Ordnance publishes its first survey map, of Kent (see p.29)

1802

The British soldier William Lambton measures the baseline for what becomes the Great Indian Trigonometrical Survey (see p.48)

1807

The German explorer and naturalist Alexander von Humboldt publishes a cross-section map of vegetation zones on Mt. Chimborazo in the Andes (see p.50)

1814

American explorers Meriwether Lewis and William Clark produce a map of North America detailing their expedition to and from the Pacific coast in 1804–6 (34; see p.201)

1815

The British engineer William Smith publishes a geological map of England and Wales; he publishes more detailed maps in an atlas in 1822 (see p.46)

1819

The American Geological Society is founded; it will spearhead geological surveys of the country until 1879, including John Wesley Powell's journey through the Grand Canyon in 1869

1820s

Steel engraving becomes an increasingly popular medium for cartography

1823

The American educator William C. Woodbridge publishes an early isothermic map of the world, based on Alexander von Humboldt's observations (see p.167)

1826

The French mathematician Charles Dupin publishes the world's first chloroplethic map, of France, using shading to represent variables in different areas (see p.91)

1832

Baron Walckenaer, the Dutch ambassador to France, discovers Juan de la Cosa's world map in an antique shop in Paris (see p.153)

1834

Wilhelm Beer and Johann Heinrich van Mädler publish the first quadrant of a lunar map made by using a telescope to map the surface of the moon (see p.235)

1835

Britain establishes the first official national survey

1837

The American educators Samuel Gridley Howe and Samuel P. Ruggles produce the first known atlas for the blind (see p.131)

1839

The Ordnance Survey begins to use contour lines rather than hachures to indicate high ground

1845

The German geographer Heinrich Berghaus produces a map of the world's vegetation zones (see p.51)

1847

British surveyors of the Great Trigonometrical Survey in India identify a mountain in the Himalayas they name Peak B, later known as Mount Everest

1848

The American explorer John C. Frémont maps the western United States at the start of a period of increased migration to the West (see p.241)

1849

Augustus Petermann produces the first hydrographical map of the British Isles, showing its canals and rivers (see p.204)

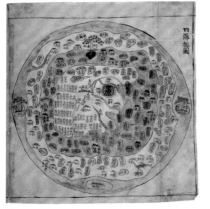

33

34

1803

Louisiana Purchase: the United States buys a huge area of land west of the Mississippi from France

1803

Richard Trevethick builds the first steam locomotive

1805

The Battle of Austerlitz leaves the French emperor Napoleon Bonaparte as supreme ruler of Europe

1812

Britain and the United States begin an inconclusive three-year war

1815

Napoleon is defeated at the Battle of Waterloo

1819

Large-scale whaling begins in the Pacific Ocean

1821

Mexico and Peru gain independence from Spain

1822

Brazil becomes independent from Portugal

1823

The Monroe Doctrine: American president James Monroe excludes European nations from political or military interference in the Americas

1833

Slavery is abolished in the British Empire

1835

Texas declares independence

1836

The English scientist Charles Darwin completes his voyage on HMS *Beagle*

1839

China goes to war with Britain in the First Opium War

1844

The US inventor Samuel Morse invents the telegraph

1846

Oregon Territory is divided between the United States and Canada along the 49th Parallel

1848

After victory in the Mexican–American War, the United States acquires much of what is now California and the South-west

1850

1850s

By now lithography (invented in 1796) is an increasingly popular method of producing maps and posters, allowing the production of finer detail and more controlled colour

1851

The Oceanographer Matthew Fontaine Maury of the US Naval Observatory produces a map of whale occurrence based on sightings (see p.40); among his other innovations are a unique chart of trade winds (37; see p.162)

1855

1855

Astronomer Friedrich Georg Wilhelm Struve completes the Struve Arc, the first accurate mapping of a long segment of a meridian

1855

The English physician John Snow maps incidences of cholera in Soho in London, revolutionizing medical understanding of the disease

1856

William C. Reynolds publishes an influential map of the United States, showing slave and free areas; the map is copied many times (see p.251)

1860

1861

The start of the American Civil War leads to increased surveying of the eastern states as engineers create maps for military commanders

1861–5

During the American Civil War, newspapers frequently print battle maps to inform readers about the progress of the conflict (35; see p.239)

1862

Christian missionaries in the Pacific record the use of stick charts for navigation in the Marshall Islands (38; see p.63)

1865

1867

France establishes a national survey organization

1867

In the United States the Sanborn Map Company begins mapping North American cities for insurance purposes (see p.190)

1869

The French statistician Charles Joseph Minard produces a celebrated 'infographic' mapping Napoleon's advance to and retreat from Moscow in 1812 (36; see p.89)

1870

1870

The Ordnance Survey completes the first national survey of Britain

1870

The Great Trigonometrical Survey is finished in India, marking the complete mapping of the Subcontinent

1873

The Scottish missionary David Livingstone maps the interior of Africa based on his own travels (see p.202)

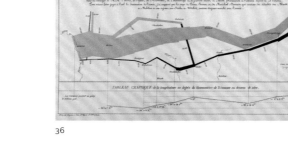

36

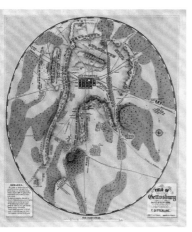

35

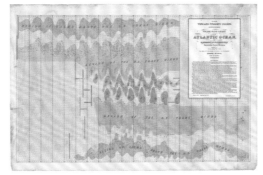

37

38

1851

The Great Exhibition is held in London to celebrate the manufacturing power of the British Empire

1852

The British let the Boers of southern Africa govern themselves

1853

US Commodore Matthew Perry sails gunboats into Edo harbor to force Japan to permit international trade

1858

After the extensive and bloody Indian Mutiny, the British government takes over control of India from the East India Company, marking the start of the period known as the Raj

1859

Charles Darwin publishes *On the Origin of Species*, a theory of biological evolution

1860

The Australian explorers Robert O'Hara Burke and William John Wills become the first men to cross Australia, but die on the return journey

1861

Italy becomes a unified country

1861

The American Civil War begins when Southern states leave the Union

1869

Thomas Cook escorts his first party of tourists to Egypt and Palestine

1869

The Suez Canal is completed between the Mediterranean and the Red Sea, dramatically cutting the sea voyage from Europe to Asia

1869

The Union Pacific transcontinental railway is completed in the United States

1871

A German victory in the Franco–Prussian War helps to complete the process of German unification

1873

As part of a modernization process, the Meiji rulers of Japan abandon Confucianism as the state religion

1873

The English astronomer Richard Proctor proposes that the moon's craters were formed by meteorite impact

1875

1876

The Scottish marine biologist Wyville Thomson uses findings from the British Challenger Expedition to map the floor of the North Atlantic Ocean, showing for the first time the location of the mid-Atlantic Ridge

1878

The German astronomer Johann Schmidt publishes the last detailed map of the moon based on visual observation

1879

The United States sets up a national geological survey to map the continent

1880

1883

Maps in the United States begin to reflect the adoption of standard time zones by railway companies

1883

The Scottish writer Robert Louis Stevenson is inspired by a treasure map to write his story *Treasure Island* (39; see p.317)

1883

The Argentine adventurer Julio Frey Popper publishes maps and business directories of cities, including Mexico City and New Orleans (see p.187)

1885

1885

The US public official Willard B. Farwell publishes a map of vice in Chinatown as part of an official survey of housing in San Francisco (40; see p.30)

1886

The British naval strategist John Colomb publishes an influential map of the British Empire that is one of the first to colour the colonies pink (41; see p.150)

1890

1891

Charles Booth publishes his famed poverty map of London, showing income levels by street (see p.92)

1893

The Durand Line is drawn to separate British India and Afghanistan

1893

A detailed *International Map of the World* representing the entire globe on the scale of one-to one-million is proposed at the Sixth International Geographical Congress in Chicago

1895

1895

The social reform organization Hull House publishes maps of Chicago showing the distribution of nationaliities and average incomes

1897

In Britain, the Ordnance Survey publishes its first full-colour maps

1899

Alexander Supan publishes the first modern map of the world's ocean floors (see p.160)

41

39

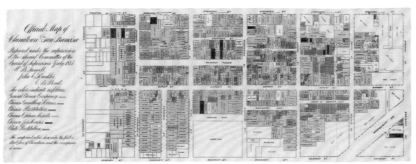

40

1876

The British queen Victoria becomes empress of India

1879

In southern Africa, native peoples clash with European settlers in the Zulu War

1879

The US inventor Thomas A. Edison demonstrates the electric light bulb

1883

The eruption of the volcanic island of Krakatoa in Indonesia is one of the biggest eruptions ever recorded

1884

The Berlin Conference divides Africa into European spheres of influence, triggering the 'Scramble for Africa'

1889

The British businessman Cecil Rhodes is given a charter to seize territories north of South Africa

1886

The German inventor Gottlieb Daimler builds a four-wheeled petrol-driven car

1886

The discovery of gold in Transvaal in South Africa sparks a gold rush

1889

The Eiffel Tower is completed in Paris

1893

New Zealand becomes the first country to introduce female suffrage

1893

The American economy enters a depression that lasts for two years

1894

In France, the Jewish soldier Alfred Dreyfus is accused of passing secrets to Germany; the case becomes a scandal that reveals anti-Semitism in the French establishment

1896

Abyssinia defeats Italy at Adwa (now in Ethiopia) in the first victory by a traditional African force over a modern European army

1898

The United States acquires an overseas empire after its victory in the Spanish–American War, obtaining Puerto Rico, Guam and the Philippines

1900

The tyre manufacturer Michelin begins publishing road maps to encourage car travel in France

1900

The German geographer and biologist Wladimir Köppen proposes a system of global climate classification (see p.165)

1907

The British publisher Bartholomew's *Atlas of the World's Commerce* contains a map of the trade in opium

1908

In Britain, the Philips company prints a series of relief maps without labels for schoolchildren to copy when making their own clay models of the continents

1913

The English artist and illustrator MacDonald Gill draws a celebrated map of London as 'Wonderground' (42; see p.79)

1914

The British explorer Ernest Shackleton sketches out his trans-Antarctic expedition at a fund-raising dinner (see p.117)

1915–18

After fighting in World War I becomes largely static, military engineers produce large-scale maps of the fixed trenches of the Western Front (43; see p.266)

1916

In the Sykes-Picto Agreement, Britain and France map a division of the Middle East in preparation for the defeat of the Ottoman Empire

1920S

As car ownership spreads, firms increasingly sponsor the production of road atlases with advertisements; the movement is led by the United States and France (44; see p.272)

1920S

Mapping companies take advantage of the availability of aircraft, aerial pilots and cameras after the end of the war to create photographic maps (see p.301)

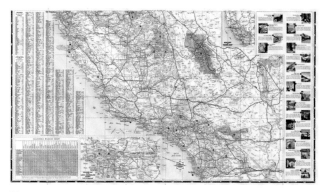

44

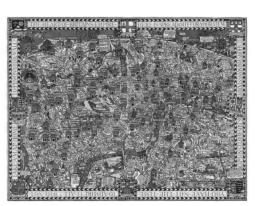

42

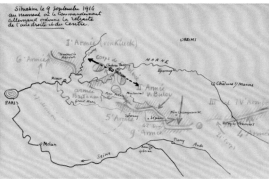

43

1901

Australia becomes a unified nation

1903

The Wright brothers achieve the world's first powered flight

1904

First lines of the New York City subway open

1904

Work begins on the Panama Canal

1908

The Young Turk movement is formed to try to introduce reform to the Ottoman Empire

1908

Henry Ford's motor company introduces the Model T Ford

1909

The US explorer Robert B. Peary claims to be the first man to reach the North Pole; his claim is widely disputed

1910

At its peak, the British Empire covers about a quarter of the globe

1911

Roald Amundsen is the first person to reach the South Pole

1914

World War I breaks out in Europe when the assassination of the Habsburg Archduke Franz Ferdinand triggers a series of alliances and declarations of war

1917

In Russia, the provisional government established with the overthrow of the czar is itself overthrown by the Bolsheviks led by Vladimir Lenin; the czar is later murdered with his family

1919

At the end of World War I, peace settlements redraw the map of Europe and partition countries of the Middle East under European protectorates

1922

The Soviet Union is established

1923

Kemal Atatürk becomes the first president of the modern nation of Turkey

1924

Lenin dies; after a power struggle, he is succeeded by Joseph Stalin as Soviet premier

1925

1926

The Inuit fisherman Silas Sandgreen uses carved driftwood to produce a three-dimensional map of the Crown Prince Islands in Disko Bay, Greenland, for an American visitor (see p.119)

1926

The British illustrator Ernest H. Shepard draws a map of the Hundred Acre Wood to accompany A.A. Milne's Winnie the Pooh books (see p.260)

1930

1932

The African American artist E. Simms Campbell maps the nightlife of Harlem, New York (see p.32)

1932

The artist K.M. Leuschner creates a map of Los Angeles for the city's Olympic Games (45; see p.80)

1933

The British draughtsman Harry C. Beck produces his famed map of the London Underground (see p.298)

1935

1936

Phyllis Pearson produces the first edition of the A–Z street plan of London (see p.189)

1938

The coat manufacturer Albert Richard commissions a series of American football maps (see p.275)

1939

Daniel K. Wallingford's map satirizes the view New Yorkers have of the rest of the United States (see p.10)

1940

1941

The British games company Waddington produces silk escape maps for British prisoners of war.

1943

Richard Buckminster Fuller produces a map of the world on a dymaxion projection (46; see p.231)

1944

Harold Fisk maps the historical courses of the Lower Mississippi River (47; see p.199)

1945

1945

The Palestinian cartographer Sami Hadawi maps the growing share of Palestinian territory under Jewish ownership (48; see p.142)

1947

The first Oblique Mercator projection map is produced to help pilots

1947

India and Pakistan are partitioned along a line decided by a British commission, but the process does not involve geographers and cartographers and in some places the new border seems arbitrary

46

47

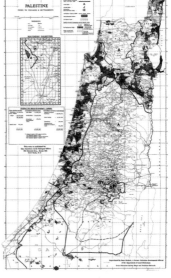

48

45

1927

The US aviator Charles Lindbergh makes the first solo flight across the Atlantic Ocean

1928

The Scottish biologist Alexander Fleming develops penicillin

1929

The Wall Street Crash: a collapse of the share market in the United States marks the end of a decade of comparative prosperity

1933

The first modern airliner, the Boeing 247, enters service

1933

Adolf Hitler becomes chancellor of Germany

1933

In the United States, Franklin D. Roosevelt is elected president and launches the 'New Deal' to tackle the effects of the Great Depression

1936

Civil war breaks out between Nationalists and Republicans in Spain

1939

World War II begins after Germany's invasion of Poland

1939

The US zoologist Victor Shelford conceives of biomes, major geographical areas that support their own organisms

1941

Japan's surprise attack on the US Pacific Fleet at Pearl Harbor, Hawaii, triggers US entry into World War II

1943

The surrender of a German army at Stalingrad marks a turning point on the Eastern Front

1944

After years of planning, the Allies invade mainland Europe in Normandy, France, on D-Day

1945

World War II ends in the defeat of Germany and Japan

1948

Israel declares its independence

1949

Mao Zedong announces the creation of the People's Republic of China

1949

Germany is divided into two states, East and West

1950

1952

The British walker Alfred Wainwright begins a thirteen-year project to map and describe walks in the Lake District of north-east England (see p.194)

1954

The British fantasy writer J.R.R.Tolkien draws a map of Middle-earth that is folded into the first volume of his epic novel *The Lord of the Rings*

1955

1958

The *Times Atlas of the World Mid-Century Edition* includes innovative projections devised by the Edinburgh cartographer John Bartholomew (49; see p.151)

1958

Britain's Ordnance Survey maps the effects of a hypothetical nuclear explosion on the city of Southampton, using contour lines to shows levels of radioactive fallout

1960

1960

The first Geographic Information System (GIS) is introduced by Canada's Department of Forestry and Rural Development

1961

Jasper Johns paints *Map*, a celebrated depiction of the US states (see p.243)

1963

The German-born graphic artist Hermann Bollmann produces a celebrated map of Manhattan (50; see p.33)

1964

Howard T. Fisher forms the Laboratory for Computer Graphics and Spatial Analysis at the Harvard Graduate School of Design; it will lead the development of early Geographic Information Systems

1965

1966

The American geographer William 'Bill' Bunge publishes *Theoretical Geography*, a key work in the development of his theories of radical cartography (see p.210)

1968

The popular strategy board game Risk is launched; it is based on a stylized map of the world

1969

The astronauts of Apollo 11 use star charts to land on the moon (see p.287)

1970

1971

The Italian artist Alighiero Boetti begins creating *Mappa*, a series of woven and embroidered maps (see p.122)

1972

Massimo Vignelli creates a map of the New York subway system based on Harry Beck's celebrated London Underground map (see p.299)

1972

NASA launches Landsat 1 (ERTS-1), the first Earth resources satellite, to take images of the planet

1973

Arno Peters creates the Peters projection, which he intends to reflect the size of the world's southern continents more accurately than the standard Mercator projection (see p.156)

1974

The Hungarian-born artist Agnes Denes begins a series of experimental global projections, *Isometric Systems* (51; see p.159)

49

50

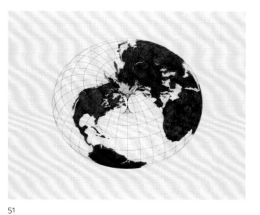

51

1950

The Korean War pits UN forces led by the United States against communist North Korean and Chinese forces backed by the Soviet Union

1952

Scheduled flights by a jetliner begin

1953

The Soviet dictator Joseph Stalin dies

1956

Suez Crisis: France, Britain and Israel defeat Egyptian forces on the Suez Canal but are forced to withdraw under US pressure

1957

The Russians put the first artificial satellite, Sputnik 1, into Earth orbit

1958

Formation in the United States of the National Aeronautics and Space Administration (NASA)

1961

The Berlin Wall is built

1961

The Soviet cosmonaut Yuri Gagarin becomes the first man in space

1963

US president John F. Kennedy is assassinated in Dallas, Texas

1964

Civil Rights Act comes into effect in the United States

1966

Mao Zedong begins the Cultural Revolution in China: its economic and social effects are disastrous

1968

In Vietnam, communist forces launch the Tet Offensive against cities in South Vietnam

1969

Apollo 11 lands on the moon and Neil Armstrong becomes the first man to walk on the lunar surface

1970

King Sihanouk is driven from power in Cambodia, hastening the rise of the Khmer Rouge

1971

The microchip is developed for use in computers

1973

The Watergate scandal begins in the United States, in which the Republican Party is accused of illegal activities

1975

1975

The British artist Richard Long maps his walks in the English countryside (see p.195)

1976

The American writer Saul Steinberg produces *View of the World from 9th Avenue*, a drawing that illustrates New Yorkers' attitudes towards the rest of the world (see p.11)

1977

Britain's Ordnance Survey has its first non-military director

1977

The American oceanographers Bruce Heezen and Marie Tharp map the ocean floors (52; see p.161)

1980

1982

The ESRI (Environmental Systems Research Institute) releases Arc/Info for microcomputers; it is the first modern Geographic Information System (53; see p.171)

1983

The first English version of a Peters projection map is published

1983

The Brisbane-based mapping and publishing company Hema is founded

1985

1986

Mapping Display and Analysis System (MIDAS) is the first desktop GIS program; it is later renamed MapInfo for Windows

1988

The radical American cartographer Bill Bunge publishes the *Nuclear War Atlas*

1989

The American entrepreneur Jill Amen publishes the first in a series of maps charting the rise and fall of IT companies in Silicon Valley, California (see p.81)

1990

1990

The US artist Tom Van Sant publishes the first satellite map of the world (see p.123)

1991

The European Radar Satellites (ERS1 and ERS2) begin mapping ground movement on Earth from space

1992

The US artist Dennis Wood publishes *The Power of Maps*, a key publication in the development of 'new cartographies' (see p.193)

1993

The US artist Joyce Kozloff begins working with cartography, which comes to dominate her work (54; see p.305)

1995

1996

Digitization begins of the David Rumsey Map Collection, one of the largest private collections in the world

1997

Mars Global Surveyor goes into orbit around Mars and begins mapping its topography, gravity and magnetism

1997

The ocean floors are mapped by sonar and satellite altimetry, creating ever more detailed maps

1999

NASA launches the Terra satellite to orbit the Earth as part of the Earth Observing System (EOS)

1999

ESRI and the National Geographic Society host the first GIS Day to encourage public involvement in mapping projects

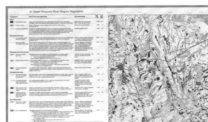

53

52

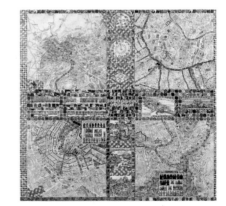

54

1975

The first commercial PC, the Altair 8800, is marketed

1975

Saigon falls to the North Vietnamese, marking the end of the Vietnam War

1979

Soviet forces invade Afghanistan, beginning a ten-year war

1980

The Iran–Iraq War begins

1981

The Space Shuttle makes its maiden flight; over the next thirty years, six shuttles fly 135 missions

1983

Global Positioning System (GPS) software becomes available to the public for the first time

1987

Palestinians launch an intifada – uprising – against Israel

1988

The Soviet premier Mikhail Gorbachev introduces reforming policies known as perestroika ('listen') and glasnost ('openness')

1989

Communist regimes collapse throughout eastern Europe

1990

East and West Germany are reunified

1990

The Hubble Space Telescope goes into orbit

1994

Nelson Mandela is elected president of South Africa

1994

The Channel Tunnel opens between England and France

1995

The Dayton Agreement ends wars that began in the former Yugoslavia in 1991

1995

The Oslo Accords create a peace plan for the Middle East

1999

The euro is introduced as a common currency for many countries in Europe

2000

2000

The aeronautical charting division of the US Coast and Geodetic Survey is transferred to the Federal Aviation Administration

2001

After the terrorist attacks on 9/11 in the United States, the software firm ESRI provides emergency GIS mapping services

2003

The US Library of Congress announces its purchase of the 1507 world map by Martin Waldseemüller for $10 million

2003

2004

Michael T. Gastner and M.E.J. Newman devise a new method to produce density-equalizing maps, allowing the creation of cartograms

2005

Academics from the University of Sheffield in the UK found the Worldmapper project to produce a range of cartograms (see p.93)

2005

Web giant Google releases Google Maps and Google Earth, a satellite survey of the planet (55; see p.309)

2006

2007

The interactive website MapMyRun is launched, allowing users to map their own activity (see p.268)

2007

Google Street View is launched in the United Kingdom and the Netherlands

2009

2010

Paul Butler maps relationships between Facebook users around the world (see p.110)

2010

MapBox is founded in Washington DC to improve the creation of data-drive maps for use by non-governmental organizations; it becomes a major provider of open-source mapping software (see p.269)

2012

The Internet is mapped by hacking into users' machines

2012

2014

The Danish government maps the whole country using the popular video game Minecraft (56; see p.308)

2014

The United States Geological Survey and ESRI produce the first Ecological Land Units map of the whole world (see p.225)

2014

In the search for missing flight MH-370, probes survey the seabed of the southern Indian Ocean

2014

Using data from a handful of probes, a team at the US Geological Survey creates the most detailed geological map yet of the surface of Mars (57; see p.45)

56

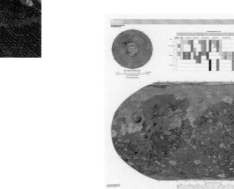

55

57

2000

Israel ends its occupation of Lebanon

2001

After the 9/11 terrorist attacks in the United States, a US-led coalition invades Afghanistan

2003

US-led forces invade Iraq, which is claimed to possess weapons of mass destruction

2004

A tsunami in the Indian Ocean on Boxing Day kills at least 228,000 people

2005

Hurricane Katrina hits New Orleans

2005

Brazilian government figures reveal that the Amazon rainforest is being destroyed more quickly than ever

2006

The former Iraqi dictator Saddam Hussein is executed

2007

Benazir Bhutto, the former president of Pakistan, is assassinated while campaigning in a national election

2008

Barack Obama becomes the first black president of the United States

2009

A civil war in Sri Lanka ends in victory for government forces

2010

The Arab Spring sees a wave of popular movements in support of democracy in the Middle East

2011

Osama bin Laden is killed by US special forces in an operation in Pakistan

2014

The world's worst outbreak of the deadly Ebola virus sweeps through countries in West Africa

2014

Fundamentalist Muslim extremists who describe themselves as 'Islamic State' seize control of territory in Iraq and Syria

SELECTED BIOGRAPHIES

Ai Weiwei

(China, 1957–) The Chinese artist Ai Weiwei has forged an international reputation both for his artworks and as a prominent political activist and critic of the Chinese government, which detained him in 2011. His artworks take the form of sculpture, woodwork, photography and video, and often include comment on human rights and democracy in his home country.

John Auldjo

(Britain, 1805–86) Born into a wealthy Canadian family, John Auldjo moved to London at the age of sixteen. He enjoyed the life of a young English gentleman, making the Grand Tour to Europe, during which he became the first Englishman to climb Mont Blanc. While living in Naples, he mapped and wrote about the volcano Vesuvius, becoming a fellow of both the Royal Society and the Royal Geographical Society. In his old age he served as the unpaid British consul in Geneva, Switzerland.

Jacopo de' Barbari

(Venice, c.1450–c.1516) Details of Barbari's life are obscure, but he was probably born in Venice in the middle of the fifteenth century. By 1500 he was working in Nuremberg, Germany, as a painter to the emperor Maximilian I; he later worked for other German princes and for Mary of Austria. Barbari was an accomplished artist whose few surviving works include the first Renaissance example of *trompe l'oeil*. His work shows the influence of Northern Renaissance artists such as Albrecht Dürer, with whom he corresponded.

Harry Beck

(Britain, 1902–74) Henry 'Harry' Beck was an engineering draughtsman working for London Transport when, in his spare time, he began to draw a simplified map of the London Underground, which was published in 1933. Beck's simplified topological design became an icon and set the direction for public transportation maps. Beck later drew maps of the rail system of the London region and the Paris Métro.

Heinrich C. Berann

(Austria, 1915–99) In 1934, while struggling to make a living as an artist during the Depression, the self-taught Austrian designer Heinrich Berann won a competition to design a panoramic map of a new mountain pass. He subsequently developed a unique combination of mapping and landscape painting to create the modern tourist panorama.

Johannes Blaeu

(Netherlands, 1596–1673) The son of leading Dutch cartographer Willem Blaeu, Johannes (or Joan) Blaeu initially trained as a lawyer before joining his father's studio and collaborating with him on the *Atlas Novus* (1635). Johannes and his brother, Cornelius, took over the business on their father's death in 1638 and maintained the family's position at the forefront of European cartography with publications such as Johannes' 1648 world map – showing the world as part of a heliocentric universe circling the sun – and the *Grand Atlas* of 1664. Johannes produced various maps incorporating ongoing Dutch discoveries in Australasia, with which he was familiar thanks to his position as official cartographer to the Dutch East India Company. He died a year after the business had been destroyed by fire in 1672.

Hermann Bollmann

(Germany, 1911–71) The German map-maker Hermann Bollmann established his reputation as a woodcarver and engraver in his homeland in the years before World War II. After the conflict he made a name for himself with his artistic three-dimensional maps, which revived the nineteenth-century practice of *Vogelschaukarten* – three-dimensional axonometric projections. Bollmann and his team relied on aerial photography to produce thirty-nine projections of cities in the United States and Europe, including his masterpiece, the map of New York City (1963).

Charles Booth

(Britain, 1840–1916) Booth was the son of a wealthy family from Liverpool, who inherited the family business and made a fortune. While campaigning in Liverpool to become a liberal member of parliament, he became concerned about the plight of the poor and began surveying social class; in London, he continued his campaign documenting social poverty, including on his influential map of 1898–99. He was one of the major social reformers whose work led to political change in the early twentieth century.

Georg Braun

(Germany, 1541–1622) A Catholic churchman in Cologne, Braun spent forty-five years writing texts and commissioning artists to create the *Civitates orbis terrarum*, a six-volume collection of prospects and bird's-eye views of more than 500 cities, mainly in Europe but also as far afield as Mexico. Braun's main collaborator on the first four volumes was the Flemish engraver and artist Frans Hogenberg (1535–90), with whom his name is most often linked.

William Bunge

(United States, 1928–) After serving in the United States military during the Korean War (1950–53), William Bunge studied quantitative geography before a short-lived academic career was ended by his radical politics and dissatisfaction with the establishment; he was blacklisted as a Communist sympathizer. Bunge used cartography and applied geography to promote social change in the United States and Canada, particularly with his books *Theoretical Geography* (1962) and *Fitzgerald* (1971).

Heinrich Bünting

(Germany, 1545–1606) Heinrich Bünting was a Protestant pastor in Germany during the height of the Catholic Counter-Reformation. In his major work, *Itinerarium Sacrae Scripturae* (Itinerary of Holy Scripture) (1581), he used woodcut maps to trace the travels of Old and New Testament characters in the Holy Land, creating a popular overview of biblical geography supplemented by figurative maps.

Cristoforo Buondelmonti

(Italy, 1386–c.1430) The monk Cristoforo Buondelmonti – a junior member of a distinguished Florentine family – left Italy in his late twenties to travel in the Aegean under the influence of the humanist book collector Niccolò Niccoli. He used his experiences to write two works of travel and history illustrated by maps: *Description of the Island of Crete* (1417) and *Liber insularum archipelagi* (Book of Islands) (1420). Buondelmonti's work did much to promote the study of Greek civilization in the early Renaissance.

César-François Cassini de Thury

(France, 1714–84) A son of the celebrated astronomer Jean Cassini, César-François Cassini de Thury was an astronomer, a member of the French Academy of Sciences and a Fellow of the Royal Society. In 1744 embarked on a cartographical landmark, the first scientific national survey. The 180-plate topographical map of France was completed by his son Jean-Dominique nearly fifty years later.

Andreas Cellarius

(Netherlands/Germany, c.1596–1665) Little is known of the life of Andreas Cellarius, who drew the star atlas *Harmonia Macwerlands*, where he worked as a teacher and wrote about astronomy, among other subjects.

Samuel de Champlain

(France, c.1567–1635) Samuel de Champlain was an accomplished navigator whose attempts to discover a Northwest Passage to Asia led him to chart the east coast of North America from Nova Scotia south to Rhode Island. He established a French settlement at Quebec in 1608 and lived in the colony for most of the period until his death.

Christopher Columbus

(Italy, 1451–1506) Columbus has a reputation for being one of the most successful navigators in history for his four voyages to the 'New World' (1492, 1493, 1498, 1502), in which he visited first the island of Hispaniola and later Cuba and the coasts of Central and South America. Columbus opened the Americas to European exploration, although he himself was convinced that he had discovered a sea route to the Indies of Asia.

James Cook

(Britain, 1728–79) James Cook learned to chart coastal waters in the Royal Navy before being given command of the *Endeavour* and ordered to Tahiti to observe a transit of Venus in 1796. Cook subsequently charted New Zealand and the east coast of Australia, which he claimed for Britain. On a second voyage (1772–75) he visited the coast of Antarctica – the first European contact with the legendary 'Southern Continent'. On a third voyage to find the Northwest Passage (1776–80) Cook was killed in a skirmish with local warriors in Hawaii.

Juan de la Cosa

(Spain, c.1450–1510) Juan de la Cosa was a Spanish navigator and ship-owner – he owned Christopher Columbus's flagship, the *Santa María* – who sailed with Columbus on his first and second voyages to the Americas before charting the coasts of South America as a pilot on later expeditions led by Alonso de Ojedo (1499, 1509) and Rodrigo de Bastidas (1500). He drew a number of maps, the only one of which to survive is the world map of 1500, the first European map to show the Americas.

Abraham Cresques

(Spain, 1325–87) Abraham Cresques (also known as Cresques Abraham) was a Jewish cartographer and clockmaker from the island of Majorca. With his son Jehuda he was commissioned by Prince John of Aragon to make nautical charts of as much of the world as possible. The Cresques drew the so-called *Catalan Atlas*, but no other works have been definitively attributed to either man.

Agnes Denes

(Hungary, 1931–) Agnes Denes was a leading member of the concept-based artists of the 1960s and 1970s, and uses a range of media to investigate science, philosophy, psychology, history and other subjects. She has a reputation as a pioneer, creating important early environmental artworks and using non-traditional materials for delicate drawings and prints.

Charles Dupin

(France, 1784–1873) Born under the *ancien régime*, Charles Dupin was educated during the years of the French Revolution and Republic and spent much of his career working under the Restoration. An outstanding mathematician, and later a naval engineer, Dupin was inspired by a visit to Britain to improve the living conditions of French workers, whom he saw as less healthy, less efficient and less educated than their British equivalents. His promotion of workers' education – supported by the world's first chlorpleth map – was pioneering but ultimately fruitless in the competitive world of the Industrial Revolution.

Albrecht Dürer

(Germany, 1471–1528) Albrecht Dürer was one of the leading artists of the Northern Renaissance, noted in particular for his paintings and engravings, and for woodcuts that achieved a new level of precision in what had traditionally been a somewhat crude medium. Dürer, who lived and worked in Nuremberg, travelled to Italy to study the techniques of Renaissance artists such as Giovanni Bellini.

Olafur Eliasson

(Denmark, 1967–) The Icelandic-Danish artist Olafur Eliasson studied in Denmark before establishing a studio in Berlin in 1995. His exploration of perception, movement and experience covers a wide range of media, including sculpture, painting, photography and film. Eliasson is also an accomplished public artist whose installations have appeared in New York, London and Reykjavik, among other cities.

Harold Fisk

(United States, 1908–64) Harold Fisk, a professor in the Department of geology at Louisiana State University, was commissioned by the United States Army Corps of Engineers Mississippi River Commission in 1941–44. He and his team used aerial photography to trace the river's meandering course over time.

Fra Mauro

(Italy, died 1460) After spending his youth travelling widely as a soldier and a merchant, Fra Mauro became a monk in the Camaldolese (Benedictine) Monastery of St Michael in Venice, where he took up cartography, consulting regularly with Venetian navigators about new discoveries. Commissioned by King Afonso V of Portugal to encourage the explorations of his nephew Prince Henry the Navigator, Fra Mauro completed his renowned world map in 1459, including the latest information about the geography of Cathay (China). The original does not survive, but a copy was created by Mauro and a collaborator, Andrea Bianco.

John C. Frémont

(United States, 1813–90) The American press dubbed John C. Frémont 'the Pathfinder' for his role in mapping the American West in the 1840s and 1850s as the leader of five expeditions by the United States Corps of Topographical Engineers. Frémont used the legendary mountain man Kit Carson as a guide to routes to Oregon and California; his maps helped many settlers and goldminers make the journey west in the mid-nineteenth century. Frémont went on to become the first Republican Party candidate for President (he was unsuccessful) and had a moderately successful military career in the Civil War (1861–65), after which unwise business investments left him destitute.

Richard Buckminster Fuller

(United States, 1895–1983) The Futurist architect Richard Buckminster Fuller spent his life developing new structures, particularly the geodesic dome. He developed the Dymaxion map projection, a world map projected onto a twenty-faced icosahedron, which is then unfolded in different ways to emphasize different aspects of Earth, particularly Fuller's view of the landmasses as a single island.

Giacomo Gastaldi

(c.1500–66) The Venetian engineer and cartographer Giacomo Gastaldi is credited with producing the first pocket atlas in 1548, when he published a highly accurate edition of Ptolemy's *Geography*; it included regional maps of the Americas, and was one of the first to use copper engraving to increase the level of detail.

Hessel Gerritsz

(Netherlands, c.1581–1632) Hessel Gerritsz served as an apprentice to the leading Dutch cartographer Willem Janszoon Blaeu before setting up as a printer in Amsterdam in 1610, publishing pioneering maps of the Pacific and northern Russia. In 1617 he became the first exclusive cartographer of the Dutch East India Company (the post passed to Johannes Blaeu after his death), in which position he gained information that enabled him to draw some of the earliest maps to include the coastline of Australia (helping to popularize that name). In 1628 he pursued his interest in the New World by sailing to Brazil and the Caribbean, producing maps of the West Indies and Florida.

MacDonald Gill

(Britain, 1884–1947) MacDonald Gill, brother of the artist Eric Gill, drew his first maps at school and went on to study architecture and calligraphy. While running an architectural practice, he also established a reputation as the leading decorative cartographer of the time. He received his first cartographic commission in 1909 from the architect Edwin Lutyens and followed it in 1913 with *The Wonderground Map of London Town* for London Electric Railways, intended to entertain passengers as they waited for trains. Gill worked widely on maps for marketing in the 1920s and 1930s, and on propaganda maps during World War II.

Charles Francis Hall

(United States, 1821–71) Charles Francis Hall was a journalist when he became fascinated by the fate of the missing expedition of the British Arctic explorer Sir John Franklin (1847) and raised money for his own expedition to the Arctic. In 1860 he visited Frobisher Bay and concluded that some of Franklin's men might still be alive; on a second expedition (1864–69) he found artefacts of the Franklin expedition on King William Island. On a third expedition in 1871, Hall died after drinking coffee that may have been poisoned by a member of his team.

Edmond Halley

(England, 1656–1742) Edmond Halley became Britain's Royal Astronomer in 1720, after a long career during which he identified the comet that now bears his name and calculated its period (every 75 or 76 years); he correctly predicted its return in 1758. As a cartographer, Halley added details of 341 southern stars to published star charts (1679), charted the trade winds (1686) and sailed into the Atlantic in 1698 to map differences in magnetic declination.

Richard Edes Harrison

(United States, 1902–94) The product designer Richard Edes Harrison came to cartography by chance, when he covered for a sick colleague. He established a reputation at the media company Time Life, where he worked for *Fortune* magazine, producing some of the most novel but revealing and popular maps of the 1930s and 1940s, using new projections and techniques such as shading to introduce relief to terrain. Believing his lack of formal cartographic training to be an advantage, Harrison created projections to suit the specific purpose of his maps, most notably in *Look at the World: The Fortune Atlas for World Strategy* (1944), which made Harrison a minor cartographic celebrity. He continued to work until the mid-1980s.

Johann Baptiste Homann

(Germany, 1664–1724) Johann Baptiste Homann's early plans for a career in the Catholic Church were abandoned after he converted to Protestantism and became first a notary and then an engraver, cartographer and publisher. His status as the leading German cartographer of the age was confirmed by his appointment as Imperial Geographer to the Holy Roman Emperor Charles VI, giving Homann valuable privileges over the copyright of his works. His *Grand Atlas*, produced with the engraver Christoph Weigel the Elder, was published in 1715.

Jodocus Hondius

(Netherlands, 1563–1612) The Flemish cartographer and engraver Jodocus Hondius was a leading map-maker at the turn of the seventeenth century in Amsterdam, where he moved in 1593 after a brief stay in England. He bought the plates of Gerard Mercator's *Atlas* from the cartographer's grandson and reprinted it, with thirty-six new maps. The edition sold out within a year.

James Francis Horrabin

(Britain, 1884–1962) A lifelong socialist, writer and cartoonist, James Francis Horrabin drew his first maps as art editor of the *Daily News* during the Balkan War of 1912–13. Horrabin used cartography – as he also used his illustration and writing – to raise workers' understanding of economics and to promote a socialist approach to economic organization. He was a Labour member of parliament for two years (1929–31). In 1934 he published a collection of his own maps – *An Atlas of Current Affairs* – which ran to several editions.

Alexander von Humboldt

(Germany, 1769–1859) Hailed as the 'father of modern geography', the mining engineer Alexander von Humboldt used his inheritance to travel with the botanist Aimé Bonpland to South America to study the continent's flora, fauna and topography. Humboldt mapped the Orinoco River, and the two men climbed Mount Chimborazo in Ecuador, then thought to be the highest mountain in the world. Humboldt also discovered and mapped the Peruvian Current, which is now known as the Humboldt Current.

Eduard Imhof

(Switzerland, 1895–1986) A surveyor, Eduard Imhof spent much of his career at the Swiss Federal Institute of Technology in Zurich, where he became a professor of cartography in 1925. He made a reputation for his influential use of relief shading on a wide range of maps, particularly when illustrating the landscapes of Switzerland and Austria.

Isidore of Seville

(Spain, 560–636) Famously described in the nineteenth century as 'the last scholar of the ancient world', Saint Isidore was archbishop of Seville for thirty years. He compiled the first Christian encyclopedia, the *Etymologiae*, a summary of classical works that had great influence on learning in the Middle Ages. He was canonized in 1598.

Alfredo Jaar

(Chile, 1956–) The Chilean artist, architect and filmmaker Alfredo Jaar works mainly in New York, where he creates installations and other works incorporating photography and performance. His work, which often takes the form of public interventions, is frequently politically motivated and reflects a particular concern with war and its victims.

Jasper Johns

(United States, 1930–) The artist Jasper Johns was born in Augusta, Georgia, and studied at the University of South Carolina and Parsons School of Design before serving in the Korean War. His paintings and prints from the late 1950s and 1960s made him one of the most influential American painters of the late twentieth century as a pioneer of the Conceptual, Minimal and Pop art movements, often incorporating familiar images such as the Stars and Stripes, targets and, later, maps of the United States and images from renowned works of art.

Louis Jolliet

(Canada, 1645–1700) Louis Jolliet was a French-Canadian fur trapper who was born and grew up in Quebec, then the centre of the fur trade. With a Jesuit priest, Jacques Marquette, he became the first explorer to sail down virtually the whole length of the Mississippi River in 1673, returning to Canada via the Illinois River. He later established a settlement on the island of Anticosti in the St Lawrence River and mapped the coast of Labrador. He disappeared on a trip in 1700.

Jack Kerouac

(United States, 1922–69) The leading Beat writer of the 1950s, Jack Kerouac moved in the 1940s from small-town America to New York, where he was inspired by the jazz he heard in clubs. With his friend Neal Cassady, Kerouac made a number of cross-country road trips, which inspired his greatest work, *On the Road*, typed out on a single 36.5-metre (120-foot) scroll of paper in 1951. Published in 1957, the book became an instant classic and defined the 'Beat' generation. Kerouac continued to write, but he never again achieved a similar degree of success.

Aaron Koblin

(United States, 1982–) Aaron Koblin led the Data Arts Team at Google before establishing his own career as a digital media artist. He specializes in data visualization and using community-generated data to reflect cultural trends and humans' relationships with technological systems. His *Flight Patterns* of 2006 won a National Science Foundation prize for science visualization.

Joyce Kozloff

(United States, 1942–) A founder of the Pattern and Decoration movement of the 1970s, which aimed to use patterns to challenge the perceived primacy of 'high art', Joyce Kozloff is a feminist, politically motivated artist who has used maps as the basis for her work for more than twenty-five years. Kozloff uses cartography to explore historical themes such as colonialism, geographical knowledge and exploration in a variety of media.

Maya Lin

(United States, 1959–) The sculptor and landscape artist Maya Lin shot to fame when, as a student at Yale University, she won the competition to design the US Vietnam Veterans Memorial in Washington DC. Lin's design – a V-shaped wall of black granite dug into the earth bearing the names of 57,661 dead – has become one of the most enduring and poignant of all war memorials. Much of Lin's later work has also concerned landscape, and the importance of making a place for individuals within it.

Olaus Magnus

(Sweden/Poland, 1490–1557) The writer Olaus Magnus was a Swedish Catholic clergyman who moved to Poland after the Swedish Reformation. He wrote numerous works, including *Carta Marina*, which includes the most accurate map of northern Europe for the period.

Matthew Fontaine Maury

(United States, 1806–73) Having spent a decade serving in the United States Navy, Matthew Fontaine Maury began writing about navigation in the 1830s, and in 1842 became superintendent of the Depot of Charts and Instruments of the Navy Department in Washington DC. Over the next decade he established an international reputation for his studies of oceanography and meteorology, and his system of recording oceanographic data was adopted globally. He wrote *The Physical Geography of the Sea*, the first oceanographic textbook, in 1855.

Gerard Mercator

(Flanders, 1512–1594) Gerard Mercator is one of the most famous of all cartographers thanks to two innovations. He was the first man to use the word 'atlas' to describe a book of maps (in 1585), and in 1569 he invented the projection named after him. Mercator's world map was a remarkable mathematical feat, being proportioned in such a way that a course of constant bearing at sea could be plotted on the map as a straight line. After the projection had been further explained by the Englishman

Thomas Wright in 1599, it became the standard projection for world maps for ocean navigation and later for world maps in general.

Charles Joseph Minard

(France, 1781–1870) Charles Joseph Minard trained as a civil engineer before following a career dedicated to building waterways, bridges and dams throughout French-governed Europe. In the 1840s he began experimenting with graphics to show information, and after his retirement in 1851 his interest grew and he experimented with a wide range of pioneering visualizations in fifty-one thematic maps, including the first to use pie charts to convey data. Of his most famous work, the map of Napoleon's Russian campaign of 1812–13 (1869), the designer Edward Tufte said, 'It may well be the best statistical graph ever drawn.'

Herman Moll

(Germany/Netherlands, 1654–1732) Either Dutch or German by birth, Herman Moll spent part of his career in London and later worked for the Dutch. His earliest maps were produced and printed in London, and he worked as an engraver for others before publishing his first map, *A System of Geography*, in 1701. His most famous work, the so-called '*Beaver Map*', was published in 1715 during disputes between Britain and France over the borders between their North American colonies.

John Ogilby

(England, 1600–76) The cartographer John Ogilby was a dancing instructor who founded Ireland's first theatre and fought in the Irish Rebellion of 1641 before setting up a printing press in London, where he published atlases by Wenceslaus Hollar and others. Appointed by Charles II 'His Majesty's Cosmographer and Geographic Printer', Ogilby produced the first road atlas of Britain in 1675.

Abraham Ortelius

(France, 1527–98) Born in Antwerp, Abraham Ortelius became geographer to King Philip II of Spain in 1575, despite doubts about his orthodoxy. He travelled widely and trained as a map engraver before publishing his first map in 1564, under the influence of his friend Gerard Mercator. In 1570 he published the *Theatrum Orbis Terrarum*, with fifty-three maps (most of which were copies). The book, which is recognized today as the first modern atlas, was a huge success: before Ortelius's death it ran to twenty-five editions, during which he corrected and expanded the contents. Ortelius was one of the first geographers to suggest that the continents had once all been joined, but had subsequently broken apart. His fame was such that his death was marked by public mourning in his home town.

Matthew Paris

(England, c.1200–59) Matthew Paris was a Benedictine monk at St Albans Abbey in England, where he wrote and illustrated historical works including *Chronica Majora*. His illustrations include four maps of Britain and an itinerary of the pilgrim route from England to the Holy Land.

Piri Reis

(Turkey, c.1465–1553) Piri Reis (Captain Piri) was a Turkish privateer who became an admiral in the Ottoman Navy, campaigning in the Indian Ocean and the Persian Gulf. His *Book of Navigation* was published in 1521, and became one of the leading cartographical works of the time. Piri Reis drew two world maps, in 1513 and 1528; the first is one of the earliest depictions of America. He was beheaded at about the age of ninety for refusing further service to the emperor.

Petrus Plancius

(Flanders, 1552–1622) The Flemish Protestant minister Petrus Plancius moved from his native Brussels to Amsterdam, where he developed an interest in trade that led him to become both a cartographer and a founder of the Dutch East India Company. A particular expert on sea routes to Asia, he drew on Portuguese maps and was the first cartographer to use the Mercator projection on nautical charts. One of his particular interests was mapping the southern constellations, which he incorporated into maps and globes.

Claudius Ptolemy

(Egypt, c.90–c.168) A Greek-Egyptian scholar from Egypt, Ptolemy worked at the Royal Library in Alexandria, where he applied geometry and the principles of mathematics to the problem of projecting the globe on a flat piece of paper. His textbook *Geography* (c. AD 150) mapped the inhabited world, using a grid of lines of latitude and longitude, and shaped the production of maps until at least the thirteenth century, when the first known Ptolemaic map was produced.

Diogo Ribeiro

(Portugal, active 1518–32) The Portuguese seafarer Diogo Ribeiro began working as a cartographer for Charles V in Spain in 1518; he later became the royal cosmographer. His maps recorded and aided the voyages of discovery that were then being made. In 1527 Ribeiro completed a scientific world map, the *Padrón Real*, that served as a template for the maps used on all Spanish ships.

Matteo Ricci

(Italy, 1552–1610) The Jesuit priest Matteo Ricci began his mission to China after serving in Goa,

India. Arriving in Macau in 1582, he began learning Chinese language and customs; he eventually compiled two Chinese–Portuguese dictionaries and became one of the first Westerners to study the Chinese language. He introduced many aspects of European science and mathematics to China, including drawing the first world map to introduce Western discoveries to East Asia. He was made a scientific advisor to the Wanli Emperor, and was the first Westerner to visit the Forbidden City and the first to be buried in Beijing.

Christopher Saxton

(England, c.1543–c.1610) The English surveyor Christopher Saxton made the first systematic maps of English and Welsh counties in the 1570s, possibly after being inspired by a local clergyman, John Rudd, on whose originals he may have based his work. Sponsored by Queen Elizabeth I and a court official named Thomas Seckford – their coats of arms appear on the maps – Saxton sold his maps individually before combining all thirty-five in the highly influential *Atlas of the Counties of England wand Wales* (1579).

William Smith

(Britain, 1769–1839) From humble roots – his father was a blacksmith – William Smith became a surveyor whose work on coal mines near Bath in Somerset led him to realize that rock strata followed predictable patterns, which would allow him to map where they would occur. In 1799 he published a geological map of the area around Bath, before a chance encounter with a vegetation map gave him the idea of using colour to indicate where outcrops of rock would occur. In 1801 Smith began travelling around Britain, gathering information to compile the first geological map of Britain, and the largest geological map then published (1815). Smith's business dealings were disastrous – his map was widely copied, while he ended up in debtor's prison – but in 1831 the Geological Society of London honoured him and labelled him 'the father of English geology'.

John Snow

(Britain, 1813–58) Celebrated as one of the outstanding physicians of history, John Snow moved from his native Yorkshire to study in London, where in 1750 he helped to found the Epidemiological Society of London to research the spread of disease. He was a pioneer of anaesthesia, and personally attended Queen Victoria during the births of two of her children. Snow's celebrated map of the locations of deaths during an outbreak of cholera in Soho, London (1854), led him to identify the source of the outbreak as an infected water pump, thus disproving the prevailing theory that disease spread via 'miasma' or 'bad air'.

John Speed

(England, 1542–1629) John Speed trained as a historian under noble patronage, but it became apparent that his real talent was for cartography. Leaning heavily on previous work, he drew the first set of individual county maps of England and Wales (1610/11), many of which incorporate town plans. In 1627 he published the first English atlas, *Prospect of the Most Famous Parts of the World*.

Saul Steinberg

(United States, 1914–99) The Jewish Romanian-born cartoonist Saul Steinberg worked for more than a century for the *New Yorker*, which first published his work in 1941. The newspaper sponsored his immigration to the United States the following year, when he was a refugee from anti-Semitism in Europe.

Alexander Georg Supan

(Austria, 1847–1920) Alexander Georg Supan was an Austrian academic geographer who spent most of his career as a professor of geography; he was also editor of the geographical journal *Petermanns Geographische Mitteilungen* (Petermann's Geographical Announcements) and wrote *Principles of Physical Geography* (1884). Supan's map of the world's ocean floors (1899) proposed a system of terminology for naming undersea features after related geographical features which was adopted in 1904 by an international gathering of geographers, leading to the creation of the first standard bathymetric chart of the oceans.

Marie Tharp

(United States, 1920–2006) Marie Tharp obtained degrees in geology and mathematics before working at the Lamont Geological Laboratory in New York, at first locating aeroplanes lost at sea during World War II. She and her colleague, Bruce Heezen, began the systematic mapping of ocean-floor topography, Heezen collecting data from research ships and Tharp mapping the results. In 1977 they published their landmark map of the whole ocean floor, painted by the Austrian cartographer Heinrich C. Berann.

Tupaia

(Society Islands, c.1725–70) Tupaia was a Polynesian navigator who joined Captain James Cook as translator on the *Endeavour*'s voyage of 1769 to New Zealand and Australia. Relying on personal experience and family knowledge, Tupaia impressed Cook's colleague Sir Joseph Banks with his geographical knowledge, although Cook himself preferred to rely on his own explorations.

Sébastien le Prestre de Vauban

(France, 1633–1707) While serving in the French army in the 1650s, Sébastien de Vauban was apprenticed to the military engineer Chevalier de Clerville and became in turn the leading designer of fortifications of the late seventeenth century, employing a system of pointed walls and parallels. He was also an effective military commander, taking charge of French sieges of enemy cities and developing new tactics for overcoming defences.

Pietro Vesconte

(Italy, active 1310–30) Although he was from Genoa, Pietro Vesconte spent most of his career in Venice, where he pioneered the production of portolan charts of the Mediterranean and the Black Sea.

Juan Bautista Villalpando

(Spain, 1552–1608) Juan Bautista Villalpando worked as an architect for the Jesuits, whom he joined in 1575 before becoming a priest and publishing scholarly commentaries on the Old Testament, particularly on the Book of Ezekiel. Villalpando illustrated his work with drawings and maps, including a reconstruction of the Temple of Solomon and a map of Jerusalem that showed a city based on the rules of classical architecture. In 1604, accused and cleared of heresy by the Spanish Inquisition, Villalpando moved to Rome, where he spent the rest of his life.

Johannes Vinckboons

(Netherlands, c.1616–70) The son of the painter David Vinckboons, Johannes was a proficient artist – he worked as a watercolourist for the cartographer Johannes Blaeu – who produced a range of maps and scenic paintings of the discoveries of Dutch mariners in the seventeenth century. Working in Amsterdam with his five brothers, Vinckboons based his maps on the latest reports from the Dutch East India and West India companies. His work was highly popular: a three-volume atlas containing 130 watercolours was bought in 1654 by Queen Christina of Sweden.

Alfred Wainwright

(Britain, 1907–91) A lifelong walker, Alfred Wainwright spent much of his life documenting the fells of the Lake District in north-west England in books that were published as facsimiles of his manuscript, with handwritten text and hand-drawn maps that he produced at the rate of one page a day. The seven-volume *A Pictorial Guide to the Lakeland Fells* was published between 1955 and 1966, and remains the standard guide for walkers.

Martin Waldseemüller

(Germany, c.1470–c.1521/22) In 1507 the German cartographer Martin Waldseemüller drew a globe and a twelve-panel world map that included the first use of the name 'America', after the explorer Amerigo Vespucci. The maps, which were based on the voyages of Columbus and Vespucci, were accompanied by a book, *Cosmographiae Introductio* (Introduction to Cosmography). By the time of his death, Waldseemüller was a canon at a church in the Vosges Mountains near the Rhine in eastern France.

GLOSSARY

Astrolabe
An early astronomical instrument used to measure the altitude of stars and planets, usually for navigation.

Atlas
A collection of maps or charts, usually in the form of a printed book.

Bathymetry
Originally the study of the ocean's depth relative to its surface, bathymetry – named from the Greek for 'deep measure' – has come to mean the study and measurement of the floors or beds of oceans, seas, lakes, rivers and streams.

Cadastral survey
A land survey carried out for the purpose of defining property boundaries to establish land ownership.

Cartogram
A map in which the geometry or shape of regions or countries are distorted in order to show statistical information in a graphic way.

Cartouche
A framed graphic element on a map – often in the shape of an oblong scroll or an oval shield – that contains an inscription, typically the map's title and date, a dedication or a scale; many cartouches have elaborate frames.

Chart
A navigational map of an area of water that shows coastlines, water depths and other practical information for sailors.

Chloropleth
A thematic map in which areas are shaded or coloured in proportion to a statistical variable, such as a percentage of the population.

Chronometer
A highly accurate timepiece used for marine navigation and designed to remain constant even in the conditions on board an early ship.

Compass
An instrument used for navigation and orientation with a magnetized pointer that indicates the direction of magnetic north, from which other bearings can be derived.

Compass rose
A graduated circle printed on a map or chart from which bearings can be taken; they can be highly elaborate and are often annotated with letters to indicate the four cardinal points: north, east, south and west.

Constellation
A group of stars in an identifiable shape, after which the constellation is usually named; different cultures typically have their own constellations.

Contour line
A line on a map that joins points of equal height above or below sea level.

Coordinate
One of a pair of numbers used to indicate the position of a location on a map or on the Earth; coordinates are usually expressed in terms of north-south and east-west.

Cordiform
Describes a map projection that is heart-shaped.

Cosmography
The representation of the features of the cosmos or universe; cosmography is also the branch of science that studies and maps the general shape of the universe.

Dead reckoning
A process of calculating one's position at sea by estimating one's speed and the distance and direction of travel.

Digital mapping
A contemporary branch of cartography that compiles data into a virtual image that may be printed but is not initially created in a concrete form.

Elevation
The height of a geographical point or feature above sea level.

Equal area map
A map projection in which the area of quadrilaterals formed by meridians and parallels is proportional to their area on the globe, so the quadrilaterals are larger close to the Equator.

Escape map
A map issued to military personnel for use in case of capture by the enemy.

Geodesy
A branch of applied mathematics concerned with the study of the shape and area of the Earth or its regions.

GIS
Abbreviation of Geographic Information System, a computerized system for gathering, storing, retrieving and analysing spatial and geographic data. GIS information is often displayed in the form of a map.

GPS
Abbreviation of Global Positioning System, a space-based navigation system that uses satellites – a minimum of four – to provide location and time anywhere on Earth.

Graticule
A grid of lines representing meridians and parallels on which a map can be drawn.

Gyoki map
Named after the eighth-century Japanese Buddhist priest Gyoki, these maps depict Japan's provinces as a series of round or oval shapes rather than mapping their real shapes.

Hachure
A method of representing relief on a map by using short lines to shade and indicate the direction of steepness of a slope.

Hydrography
The science of surveying and charting oceans and other bodies of water; a hydrographic survey maps features that affect navigation or other human activity on the world's oceans.

Hypsometry
The science of measuring height, particularly in terms of distance above sea level.

Isopleth
A line drawn on a map to connect features that all share a particular measureable quality, such as average rainfall.

Itinerary
A detailed plan of a journey, which often details distances and places to be visited.

Land use classification system
A system of nationally accepted names for defining types of land use and land cover features, such as heathlands or forests.

Latitude
The position of a point on the Earth's surface expressed as an angle in terms of its position north or south of the equator.

Legend
The part of a map that explains the meanings of the symbols used on it; sometimes also known as a key.

Line copy
A map or other image that has only two ungraduated full tones – black and white.

Lithography
A method of printing in which an image is created on a flat stone in oils or greases and then used to make ink impressions on paper.

Longitude
The position of a point on the Earth's surface expressed as an angle in terms of its position east or west of the prime meridian.

Mappa mundi
Latin for 'map of the world', the term refers to any medieval world map.

Meander line
An irregular line drawn by a surveyor following the outline of a stream, pond or swamp, usually in order to survey bordering properties.

Meridian
A circle that joins places of constant latitude, passing through both poles and a given place at the equator.

National survey
An official survey carried out on behalf of a government and used for official purposes.

Neatline
A line that indicates or frames the edge of the geographic part of a map.

Ordnance Survey
An official country survey in the United Kingdom responsible for preparing large-scale maps of the whole country; it was originally the responsibility of the Master of the Ordnance.

Orientation
The arrangement of a map on a page, in particular the direction shown at the top of the map and the point placed in its centre.

FURTHER READING

Orthophotograph
An aerial photograph that has been geometrically corrected to remove depth from the features and present the same flat, accurate perspective as a map.

Parallel
An imaginary circle drawn around the Earth that connects places of the same latitude.

Photomap
An aerial photograph of the ground, to which gridlines, labels and other data have been added.

Planimetric map
A map that does not show any kind of relief, but rather shows features as being flat, as if seen from directly overhead.

Planisphere
A map formed by projecting a sphere or part of a sphere on to a flat surface; particularly used to describe a circular map of the stars.

Portolan
A hand-drawn early navigational map for seafarers that indicates coastlines and ports, with compass lines for plotting bearings.

Prime meridian
The meridian line designated as 0 degrees latitude, from which other latitudes are measured; Earth's prime meridian runs through Greenwich, south-east London.

Projection
A system of intersecting lines – such as a grid – that allows the surface of a sphere to be depicted on a flat surface such as a map.

Public Land Survey System (PLSS) The main surveying method used throughout the United States to divide land into parcels before designation of ownership; also known as the rectangular survey system, because it uses primarily regular lines.

Relief
A system that uses shading rather than contour lines alone to indicate hills and valleys on a map.

Rhumb line
An arc drawn on a map or globe that crosses all the meridians of longitude at the same angle, providing a constant bearing with regard to magnetic north.

Scale
The proportion between the size of a representation on a map and what it represents, usually expressed as a ratio.

Spot elevation
A point on a map marked by a dot and a number representing its elevation, usually above sea level; spot elevations normally mark high points.

Stick map
An indigenous sea chart from the South Pacific islands that uses sticks to indicate the direction and strength of ocean currents, and pebbles to represent islands and atolls.

Survey
The measurement of the shape, size and location of an area by measuring lengths and angles and applying mathematical techniques such as geometry.

Theodolite
A surveying instrument with a rotating telescope for measuring horizontal and vertical angles.

T-O Map
A medieval world map that divides the world into three continents separated by a 'T' of water inside a circular 'O'.

Topographic
Describes a detailed and precise map of the features and relief of the Earth's surface.

Toponym
A place name, often derived from a topographic feature.

Triangulation
A method of surveying by tracing a series of triangles over an area, usually by measuring one side of the triangle and using this base line to calculate the angles and length of the other two sides.

Zodiac
A belt of the sky around the elliptic that contains all the apparent positions of the sun, moon and planets. It is divided into twelve equal divisions, each known by a name such as Cancer or Sagittarius.

Ackerman, James
Maps: Finding Our Place in the World. Chicago: University of Chicago Press, 2007

Barber, Peter
The Map Book. London: Weidenfeld & Nicolson, 2005

Barber, Peter, and Tom Harper
Magnificent Maps: Power, Propaganda and Art. London: The British Library, 2010

Black, Jeremy
Visions of the World: A History of Maps. London: Mitchell Beazley, 2003

Brotton, Jerry
A History of the World in Twelve Maps. London: Viking, 2012

Brotton, Jerry
Great Maps: The World's Masterpieces Explored and Explained. London: Dorling Kindersley, 2014

Bryars, Tim, and Tom Harper
A History of the 20th Century in 100 Maps. London: The British Library, 2014

Dym, Jordana, and Karl Offen (eds.)
Mapping Latin America: A Cartographic Reader. Chicago: The University of Chicago Press, 2011

Foxell, Simon
Mapping London: Making Sense of the City. London: Blackdog Publishing, 2007

Jacobs, Frank
Strange Maps: An Atlas of Cartographic Curiosities. London: Viking Studio, 2009

Harmon, Katharine
You Are Here: Personal Geographies and Other Maps of the Imagination. New York: Princeton Architectural Press, 2004

Harmon, Katherine
The Map as Art: Contemporary Artists Explore Cartography. New York: Princeton Architectural Press, 2009

Hessler, John
A Renaissance Globemaker's Toolbox: Johannes Schöner and the revolution of modern science, 1475–1550. Washington, DC: Library of Congress, 2012

Huffman, Daniel P., and Samuel V. Matthews
Atlas of Design, volume 2. Milwaukee, WI: North American Cartographic Information Society, 2014

Mitchell, Rose, and Andrew Janes
Maps: Their Untold Stories: Map treasures from the National Archives. London: The National Archives/Bloomsbury, 2014

Moreland, Carl, and David Bannister
Antique Maps (3rd edition) London: Phaidon Press, 1994

Nebenzahl, Kenneth
Mapping the Silk Road and Beyond (2nd edition). London: Phaidon Press, 2011

Obrist, Hans Ulrich (ed) *Mapping it Out: An Alternative Atlas of Contemporary Cartographies.* London: Thames and Hudson, 2014

Pflederer, Richard
Finding their Way at Sea: The Story of Portolan Charts, the Cartographers Who Drew Them and the Mariners Who Sailed by Them. Houten, Netherlands: Hes and de Graaf Publishers, 2012

Reinhartz, Dennis
The Art of the Map: An Illustrated History of Map Elements and Embellishments. New York: Sterling, 2012

Schulten, Susan
Mapping the nation: History and Cartography in Nineteenth-century America. Chicago: The University of Chicago Press, 2012

Seed, Patricia
The Oxford Map Companion. One Hundred Sources in World History. Oxford: Oxford University Press, 2013

Times Atlases
The Times History of the World in Maps: The rise and fall of Empires, Countries and Cities. London: Harper Collins, 2014

Virga, Vincent
Cartographia: Mapping Civilisations. London: Little Brown, 2007

INDEX

PICTURE CREDITS AND ACKNOWLEDGEMENTS

Every reasonable attempt has been made to identify owners of copyright. Errors and omissions notified to the Publisher will be corrected in subsequent editions.

A2GA2: 21; Lella Secor Florence and P. Sargent Florence, © Adprint Ltd. Photo: Ian Bavington-Jones: 170; Ai Weiwei: 133; akg-images/British Library: 226; © Photo 12/Alamy: 24; © Images & Stories/Alamy: 154, 326(cl); Bibliografía: Berwick y Alba, 1892, Documentos Colombinos: 126; Cinta Arribas: 271; SCMP/Adolfo Arranz: 31; The Bancroft Library, University of California, Berkeley, G4370 1852.K6: 118; Map image courtesy of Barry Lawrence Ruderman Antique Maps: 145, 235, 252, 253, 330(r), 331(ct); Photo: Ian Bavington-Jones: 22; Guy Debord. Beinecke Rare Book & Manuscript Library, Yale University: 192; Justin Benttinen/PBA Galleries: 32; Stephen T. Benzek, Independent Researcher and Adjunct Professor, University of Redlands, Redlands, California: 85; Florence, The Biblioteca Medicea Laurenziana, ms. Plut. 9.28, c. 93r. Reproduced with permission of MiBACT: 138; Bibliothèque nationale de France: 42, 64–65, 90, 91, 152, 158, 232, 255, 323(r), 324(cb), 326(r), 328(c); Photo et Coll. Bibliotheque Nationale Universitaire de Strasbourg: 38; Koninklijke Bibliotheek van België: 137, 325(l); BPK-Bildagentur für Kunst, Kultur und Geschichte: 69; The Bodleian Libraries, University of Oxford: MS. Arab. c. 90 fols. 30b–31a: 220; MS D'Orville 77, fol. 100r.: 166, MS. Selden Supra 105: 288; © Bollmann-Bildkarten-Verlag GmbH & Co. KG: 33, 337(c); Courtesy of the trustees of the Boston Public Library: 205; © Mark Bradford. Courtesy the studio: 297; Bibliotheque nationale de France, Paris/Bridgeman Images: 14–15, 325(r); © British Library Board. All Rights Reserved/Bridgeman Images: 208; Brooklyn Museum Collection/Bridgeman Images: 147; Photo © Christie's Images/Bridgeman Images: 43, 99; De Agostini Picture Library/Bridgeman: 130; © Humboldt-Universitaet zu Berlin/Bridgeman Images: 50; © Look and Learn/Elgar Collection/Bridgeman Images: 215; Map House, London, UK/Bridgeman Images: 60; Museo Naval, Madrid, Spain/Bridgeman Images: 153; © Courtesy of the Warden and Scholars of New College, Oxford/Bridgeman Images: 264; Newberry Library, Chicago, Illinois, USA/Bridgeman Images: 77; Pictures From History/Bridgeman Images: 97, 290; The Stapleton Collection/Bridgeman Images: 175; © The British Library Board: 92, 236; © The Trustees of the British Museum: 74, 75, 322(l); Gift of Marcia and John Friede, Brooklyn Museum: 113; Courtesy of Bill Bunge and Gwendolyn Warren: 210; Courtesy of Paul Butler/Facebook: 110; Cambridge University Library: 140; Courtesy of the Canadian-American Center, University of Maine: 115; City of Portland Archive: 35; Daniel E. Coe, courtesy of Oregon Department of Geology and Mineral Industries: 101; Courtesy of the Laboratory of Neuro Imaging and Martinos Center for Biomedical Imaging, Consortium of the Human Connectome Project: 111; Becky Cooper, *Mapping Manhattan: A Love and Sometimes Hate Story in 75 Maps*, Abrams Image 2013. Matt Green(l), (r, from top): Neil deGrasse Tyson, Anon., Markley Boyer, Patricia Marx): 108; Extract from Chart C1 The Thames Estuary by permission of Imray Laurie Norie and Wilson Ltd, additions by permission of crossingthethamesestuary.com: 66; Daniel Crouch Rare Books: 44, 52, 79, 96, 139, 209, 212, 262, 292–293, 322(r), 324(l), 328(l), 331(l), 335(l); David Rumsey Map Collection: 10, 19, 30, 51, 70, 81, 82, 104, 129, 131, 151(l), 162, 187, 191, 197, 241, 242, 272, 275, 279, 294, 333(cb), 334(c), 335(r), 337; Courtesy DC Moore Gallery, New York/Photo: Kevin Noble/© the artist: 305, 338(r); © 1976 Agnes Denes, *From Isometric Systems in Isotropic Space–Map Projections*, Visual Studies Workshop, 1979: 159, 337; © Disney: 307; © DONG Zheng/China Railway Publishing House: 58–59; École nationale des ponts et chaussées: 89, 333(ct); Courtesy of Egmont and Reproduced with permission of Curtis Brown Group Ltd, London on behalf of The Shepard Trust, © The Shepard Trust: 260; Esri, USGS, ESA, GEO, WorldClim/Esri, Delorme: 225; ETH-Bibliothek, Hochschularchiv, Reproduced by permission of swisstopo (BA15021). Courtesy of Béatrice Imhof: 196; FAMA Collection: 86; Eric Fischer, using data from the Flickr and Picasa search APIs. Base map data © OpenStreetMap contributors, CC-BY-SA: 269; © FLC/ADAGP, Paris and DACS, London 2015: 313; Flowminder Foundation and WorldPop project: 213; Arquivo F. Freudenheim: 57; The Fuller Projection Map design is a trademark of the Buckminster Fuller Institute. © 1938, 1967 & 1992 All rights reserved: 231, 336(cl); Courtesy Galeria Fortes Vilaça, São Paulo; Hauser & Wirth; Sperone Westwater, New York Photo: Jorge Miño: 296; © 2015 Geographers' A–Z Map Company Limited. Photo: Ian Bavington-Jones: 189; Geographicus Fine Antique Maps: 116; Courtesy of Germanisches Nationalmuseum: 172; Historic Map Works LLC/Getty Images: 78; DEA Picture Library/De Agostini/Getty Images: 136; DeAgostini/Getty Images: 188, 322(c); Image © 2015 DigitalGlobe, © 2015 Google earth, Data SIO, NOAA, U.S. Navy, NGA, GEBCO: 309(tl); Image © 2015 DigitalGlobe, © 2015 Google earth, Data SIO, NOAA, U.S. Navy, NGA, GEBCO: 309(tr); Image © 2015 Google: 309(cl); © 2015 Google: 309(mr); © 2015 Google: 309(cl); © 2015 Google: 309(br), 339(l); Map Data ©2015 Google: 310(t): Imagery © 2015 Aerodata International Surveys, Cnes/Spot Image, DigitalGlobe, Lantmäteriet/Metria, Scankort, Map data © 2015 Google: 310(b); Paul Scruton/Syndication Guardian News & Media Limited: 71; courtesy-richard hamilton estate, © R. Hamilton. All Rights Reserved, DACS 2015: 141; © Mona Hatoum, Courtesy White Cube and Anadiel Gallery, Jerusalem: 143; Henry E. Huntington Library and Art Gallery, San Marino, California: 258; Hema Maps: 157; © Hereford Mappa Mundi Trust and Dean and Chapter of Hereford Cathedral: 13; © Estelle Hogan, courtesy of Spinifex Arts Project/National Gallery of Victoria, Melbourne: 259; Courtesy Jason Hubbard: 180; IBRU, Durham University, UK: 281; Imperial War Museum: 236; Indiana University: 165; Courtesy of Alfredo Jaar, New York, Photography: Agostino Osio: 37; © Tom Jarrett (IPAC): 285; © JAXA/ESA: 227; © The Jewish National and University Library & The Hebrew University of Jerusalem: 27; Courtesy of Aaron Koblin: 20; Koninklijke Bibliotheek, National Library of the Netherlands: 125; Collection of Guillermo Kuitca | Courtesy Galeria Fortes Vilaça, São Paulo; Hauser & Wirth; Sperone Westwater, New York, Photo: Jorge Miño: 296; Library and Archives Canada/Bibliothèque et Archives Canada: 267; Library of Congress Geography and Map Division Washington, DC: 39, 40, 80, 102–103, 114, 119, 120–121, 142, 146, 183, 186, 218, 219, 200–201, 203, 214, 233, 228, 229, 238, 239, 240, 266, 274, 289, 306, 312, 327(l), 329(l), 332(r), 333(l), 335(c), 336(l), 336(r); Library of Congress Prints and Photographs Division Washington: 244; London Metropolitan Archives: 84; © TfL from the London Transport Museum collection: 298; © Tate, London 2015, © Richard Long. All Rights Reserved, DACS 2015: 195; Copyright © 2014 MapMyFitness, Inc/Map data © 2015 Google: 268; © Maya Lin Studio/Photo: Gordon R. Christmas/courtesy Pace Gallery: 49; © 2012 Kate McLean: 109; Larry McNish, Calgary Centre of the Royal Astronomical Society of Canada: 320–321; Mcor: 311; *Miroir-Sprint*. Photo: Ian Bavington-Jones: 23; Mitchell Library – State Library of New South Wales, call Number Safe/M2 470/1617/1: 62; Aleksandra and Daniel Mizielinska: 261; Copyright Musée d'ethnographie de Genève (MEG)/Photo: M. Johnathan Watts: 182; Dr. Chris Mullen, The Visual Telling of Stories website: 277; Museo Amparo: 112; Museum Rotterdam/Atlas Van Stolk: 263; NASA: 287; 295 Nasser D. Khalili Collection of Islamic Art. MSS 745.1 © Nour Foundation. Courtesy of the Khalili Family Trust: 206; The National Archives, Kew: 216, 217; National Archives, Maryland: 198; Courtesy the National Diet Library, Japan: 181; National Gallery of Victoria, Melbourne Felton Bequest, 1980: 207; National Geographic Creative: 53; National Library of Australia: 63, 256, 328(r), 333(r); Courtesy of the National Library of Scotland: 202; Ne boltai! Collection: 265; Berg Collection, The New York Public Library/John Sampas, Literary Rep: 273; The Newberry Library: 173, 190; NOAA Central Library Historical Collection/National Oceanic and Atmospheric Administration/Department of Commerce: 160, 169, 164; Courtesy of the Norman B Leventhal Map Center at the Boston Public Library: 18, 150, 251, 327(r), 334(l); Courtesy of Oliver O'Brien, Dept of Geography, University College London: 83; Ordnance Survey: 308, 339(c); Paulus Swaen Old Maps: 284, 329(c); Courtesy the artist, Paragon Press and Victoria Miro, London © Grayson Perry. Photography: Stephen White: 107; © 2015 Mrs Arno Peters. Represented by Huber Cartography, Germany. Cartography by Oxford Cartographers, UK. North American distribution & licencing by ODTmaps, Amherst, MA, USA: 156; Pitt Rivers Museum, University of Oxford: 41; Poitiers, Bibliothèque universitaire, Fonds anciens: 278; Historic Maps Collection, Department of Rare Books and Special Collections, Princeton University Library: 179, 204, 283; Courtesy Bill Rankin: 34, 199, 336(cl); Rare Maps Collection, M0433, Alaska and Polar Regions Collections, Rasmuson Library, University of Alaska Fairbanks: 280; Photo © BnF, Dist. RMN-Grand Palais/image BnF: 128; Reproduced by permission of the Royal Engineers Museum, Library & Archive: 88; Royal Geographical Society (with IBG): 61, 29, 48, 117, 319, 331(r); Royal Library of Belgium, Rare Books Department, VB 11.283 E 2 I: 132; Rubin Museum of Art: 270; Courtesy of Russian State Library from Nikolay Petrovich Rumyantsev collection (holding 256, No.346): 94, 330(l); Tom Van Sant: 123; © 2015. Photo Scala, Florence: 36, 144, 149, 323(l), 326(r); © 2015. The British Library Board/Scala, Florence: 25, 174, 176, 316, 324(ct); AGF/Scala, Florence/Foto: Mimmo Frassineti. © DACS 2015: 122; © 2015. Photo Scala, Florence/bpk, Bildagentur fuer Kunst, Kultur und Geschichte, Berlin: 148, 177, 324(r); Christie's Images, London/Scala, Florence: 55; © 2015. DeAgostini Picture Library/Scala, Florence: 28, 76, 223, 314, 326(cr), 327(c); Photo Fine Art Images/Heritage Images/Scala, Florence: 26; © 2015. Digital image, The Museum of Modern Art, New York/Scala, Florence, Publisher: New York City Transit Authority, New York, NY. Gift of the designer. © 2015 Massimo Vignelli: 299; © 2015. Image copyright The Metropolitan Museum of Art/Art Resource/Scala, Florence: 315; Digital image, The Museum of Modern Art, New York/Scala, Florence, © Jasper Johns/VAGA, New York/DACS, London 2015: 243; © 2015. British Library board/Robana/Scala, Florence: 12, 98, 134, 221, 257, 291, 302, 318, 323(c), 329(r), 331(cb); White Images/Scala, Florence: 155; British Library/Science Photo Library: 72, 127, 286, 332(l); Library of Congress, Geography and Map Division/Science Photo Library: 73, 247; Library of Congress, Rare Book and Special Collections Division/Science Photo Library: 254; NASA/Science Photo Library: 47; Stephen A. Schwarzman Building/The Lionel Pincus and Princess Firyal Map Division/New York Public Library/Science Photo Library: 167; Royal Astronomical Society/Science Photo Library: 282, 330(c); Science Source/NASA/Science Photo Library: 105; Madiha Sikander/Bachon se Tabdili (Change Through Children) with Fifth Grade Students of B. F. Cabral Government Boys Primary School: Zahid Jamshed, Abdul Qadir, Muneer Abdul Latif, Haleema Babu Khan, Roshana Mohammad Nadeem, Maida Adil, Armeena Khaimji, Aisha Mohammad Arif, Umme Khadeeja, Abdul Kareem, Parmeen Gul Khan, Ali Mohammad, Usman Mohammad Aslam, Shafiullah Rahim Gul, Tayyab Siddiqui, Amjad Khan, Sana Abdul Wahid, Ghulam Haider, Deshant Krishan, Safiullah Siraj, Bilal Mohammad, Shoaib Mohammad Sadiq, Asim Sabir, Abdul Karim Aslam, Hamza Imran, Uns Ahmed Ali, Sharif Jan, Imtiaz Daad, Zaid Shakoor, Umer Farooq, Ansar Ahmed, Ghulam Mohammad, Aftab Mohammad Abid, Urmeela Khimji, Sameer Tanveer, Abdul Ghafoor: 56; Image courtesy Stanford University Libraries: 250; © The Saul Steinberg Foundation/Artists Rights Society (ARS), NY/DACS, London 2014: 11; Courtesy of the artist, neugerriemschneider, Berlin and Tanya Bonakdar Gallery, New York.

Photo: Tanya Bonakdar Gallery: 17; Marie Tharp Maps, LLC: 161, 338(l); Design and coloring – Snorri Þór Tryggvason, Drawing – Pétur Stefánsson: 135; Tweetping.net: 16; Universitäts- und Forschungsbibliothek Erfurt/Gotha: 68; Benson Latin American Collection, University of Texas at Austin: 246; University of Otago, New Zealand: 168; Uppsala University Library, Sweden: 184; USGS: 45, 339(r); Vatican Museums and Galleries, Vatican City, Italy: 67; © Victoria and Albert Museum, London: 304; Fernanda Viégas and Martin Wattenberg: 163; *A Pictorial Guide to the Lakeland Fells Book One: The Eastern Fells* by Alfred Wainwright, published by Frances Lincoln, copyright © The Wainwright Estate 1955. Photo: Ian Bavington-Jones. Reproduced by permission of Frances Lincoln Ltd.: 194; © D.A. Walker: 171, 338(c); The Walters Art Museum: 100; Courtesy of Warrug.com: 87; Warwickshirewickshire Museum Service: 303; David Wilson, courtesy of Bill Rankin and Census 2001, Statistics South Africa: 249; Denis Wood, published by Siglio, 2013: 193; © Worldmapper.org: 93.

Cover images
Front: (from left to right, top to bottom) *Figuritive Map of Losses of the French Army*, École nationale des ponts et chaussées: 89; *Vélib Docking Stations*, Oliver O'Brien, Dept of Geography, University College London: 83; *Map of Venice*, © 2015. Photo Scala, Florence: 36; *New York Subway Map*, © 2015. Digital image, The Museum of Modern Art, New York/Scala, Florence, Publisher: New York City Transit Authority, New York, NY. Gift of the designer. © 2015 Massimo Vignelli: 299; *Earth Seen Through the Sphere of the Stars*, Paulus Swaen Old Maps: 284; *Come All the Way! (Caminos Santiago)*, Cinta Arribas: 271; *Mundus Subterraneus*, Poitiers, Bibliothèque universitaire, Fonds anciens: 278; *Hurricane Katrina Flooding*, NOAA Central Library Historical Collection/National Oceanic and Atmospheric Administration/Department of Commerce: 169; *World Map*, Pictures From History/Bridgeman Images: 290; *Map of All Under Heaven*, British Library/Science Photo Library: 72; *A Taxonomy of Transitions*, Courtesy Bill Rankin: 211; *Survival Map 1992–1994 (The Siege of Sarajevo)*, FAMA Collection: 86; *Tabula Selenographica*, courtesy of Barry Lawrence Ruderman Antique Maps: 235; *Pictorial Map of the City of Mexico*, David Rumsey Map Collection: 129; *World Ocean Floor*, Marie Tharp Maps, LLC: 161; *The Whole World in a Clover Leaf*, Map Reproduction Courtesy of the Norman B Leventhal Map Center at the Boston Public Library: 18; *Trade Wind Chart of the Atlantic Ocean*, David Rumsey Map Collection: 162; *Death to Fascism*, Ne boltai! Collection: 265; *Icelandia*, © 2015. British Library board/Robana/Scala, Florence: 134; *Deaths from Cholera in Soho*, © 2015. British Library board/Robana/Scala, Florence: 212; *Delineation of the Strata of England, Wales and part of Scotland*: 46; *Map of the River Nile from its Estuary South to Cairo*, The Walters Art Museum: 100;

A Map of Vesuvius, University of Otago, New Zealand: 168; *Jerusalem as the Center of the world*, Photo Fine Art Images/Heritage Images/Scala, Florence: 26; *Map of Tenochtitlan and the Gulf Coast*, Newberry Library, Chicago, Illinois, USA/Bridgeman Images: 77; *Flight Patterns*, Aaron Koblin: 20; *Dukes Plan New York*, © 2015. British Library board/Robana/Scala, Florence: 98; *World Map*, Daniel Crouch Rare Books: 139; *Maritime Jurisdiction in the Arctic Region*, IBRU, Durham University, UK: 281; *Burlington Route*, Library of Congress Geography and Map Division Washington, DC: 274; *Geological Investigation of the Alluvial Valley of the Lower Mississippi River*, courtesy Bill Rankin: 199; *Ethnographic Map of the Austrian Monarchy*: 95 (background).

Front Flap: (from left to right, top to bottom) *Imperial Federation*, Map Reproduction Courtesy of the Norman B Leventhal Map Center at the Boston Public Library: 150; *Osaka to Nagasaki Sea Route*: 54; *Outline of Plant Geography*, David Rumsey Map Collection: 51.

Spine: (from left to right, top to bottom) *City of Anarchy*, SCMP/Adolfo Arranz: 31; Illustrated map of London © 2015. DeAgostini Picture Library/Scala, Florence: 28.

Back: (from left to right, top to bottom) *Plan of Hesdin*: 106; *Bird Migration in the Americas*, National Geographic Creative: 53; *Jagannath Temple and City of Puri*, DeAgostini Picture Library/Scala, Florence: 314; *A Chart of Frobisher Bay*, Geographicus Fine Antique Maps: 116; *The Heart of Canyonlands National Park, Utah*, Tom Patterson, US National Park Service: 224; *2MASS Redshift Survey*, © Tom Jarrett (IPAC): 285; *Sir Francis Drake's Raid on St Augustine*, Library of Congress, Rare Book and Special Collections Division/Science Photo Library: 254; *Map of Edo, Japan*, Pictures From History/Bridgeman Images: 97; *Mumbai*, © JAXA/ESA: 227; *Birdseye view of the National Capital*, Historic Map Works LLC/Getty Images: 78; *Wallis's New Game of Wanderers in the Wilderness*, Daniel Crouch Rare Books: 52; *Los Angeles*, Library of Congress Geography and Map Division Washington, DC: 80; *Cantino Planisphere*, DeAgostini Picture Library/Scala, Florence: 223; *Johannesburg: Population Density by Race*, David Wilson, courtesy of Bill Rankin and Census 2001, Statistics South Africa: 249; *German Bombing Map of Liverpool*, © The British Library Board: 236; *Mappa Mundi*, Photo By DEA Picture Library/De Agostini/Getty Images: 136; Keicho map of Japan, Courtesy the National Diet Library, Japan: 181; *Greater Yellowstone*, David Rumsey Map Collection: 197; *Isometric Systems in Isotropic Space - Map Projections: The Doughnut*, © 1976 Agnes Denes, From the book *Isometric Systems in Isotropic Space—Map Projections*, Visual Studies Workshop, 1979: 159, 337(l); *The Administritive and Political Divisions of Korea*, Library of Congress, Geography and Map

Division/Science Photo Library: 73; *The Course of the River Nile*, Photo et Coll. BNU Strasbourg: 38; *Europe Divided into its Kingdoms*, © 2015. British Library board/Robana/Scala, Florence: 318; *Great Britain: Her Natural & Industrial Resources*, Courtesy of the trustees of the Boston Public Library: 205; *Panorama of the Washoe Region from the Summit of Mount Davidson*, David Rumsey Map Collection: 279; *Fijian World Map*, © The Trustees of the British Museum: 75; *Franklin-Folger Chart of the Gulf Stream*, Royal Astronomical Society/Science Photo Library: 283; *Map of Amsterdam*: 185; *Diagram of the south part of Shaker Village*, Library of Congress, Geography and Map Division/Science Photo Library: 247; *Satellite Map of Earth*, Tom Van Sant: 123; *Tweeting*, Tweetping.net: 17; Mars, USGS: 45 (background).

Back Flap: (from left to right, top to bottom) *Route of Zheng He*, Library of Congress Geography and Map Division Washington, DC: 289; *Chicago, USA*, David Rumsey Map Collection: 191; *Terror in Afghanistan*, Stephen T. Benzek: 85; *Beijing-Shanghai High-Speed Railway*, © DONG Zheng/China Railway Publishing House: 58–59.

PUBLISHER'S ACKNOWLEDGEMENTS

A project of this size requires the commitment, advice and expertise of many people. We are particularly indebted to our consultant editor John Hessler for his vital contributions to the book, and to the members of our international advisory panel for their knowledge, passion and sound judgement: Lauren Beck, Daniel Crouch, Catherine Dunlop, Daniel Huffman, Kimberly Kowal, P.J. Mode, Peter Nekola, Richard Pflederer, Dennis P. Reinhartz, David Rumsey, Susan Schulten, Patricia Seed and Ruth Watson. Thanks are also owed to Marcia Kupfer, Massimo De Martini and Chet Van Duzer for their advice.

We are grateful to the following contributors for their texts: Mirela Altic: 130, 202, 263; Lauren Beck: 12, 26, 77, 112, 125, 128, 136,219, 240, 246; John Blake: 54, 61, 106, 116, 117, 176, 218, 255, 256, 257, 288, 289; David Bower: 303; David Buissert: 88, 172, 173, 174, 233; Kris Butler: 19, 22, 23, 32, 35, 43, 81, 82, 86, 108, 113, 114, 129, 147, 187, 191, 232, 237, 241, 242, 245, 247, 250, 261, 268, 269, 275, 286, 304, 314, 315, 317, 319; Mario Cams: 132; John Cloud: 115, 118, 160, 204, 221, 238, 283; Peter Collier: 29, 47, 48, 62, 84, 92, 104, 188, 217, 227, 236, 267, 282, 291, 301; Tim Cooke: 25, 38, 45, 56, 57, 87, 99, 142, 151, 177, 201, 206, 207, 235, 266, 287, 311, 316, 321; Daniel Crouch: 28, 36, 96, 139, 184, 185, 209, 262, 293, 302; Kenneth Field: 31, 33, 60, 79, 83, 90, 103, 109, 134, 135, 140, 189, 194, 197, 212, 224, 243, 260, 264, 298, 299, 310, 318; John Hessler: 17, 20, 34, 39, 69, 71, 93, 110, 111, 163, 169, 171, 182, 192, 213, 225, 231, 259, 270, 272, 273, 309; Jason Hubbard: 179, 180; Daniel Huffman: 59, 101, 170, 193, 196, 210, 211, 294; Laura Beltz Imaoka: 97, 181; Carla Lois: 52, 168, 284; Gregory McIntosh: 15, 41, 68, 72, 76, 80, 98, 100, 121, 126, 127, 150, 153, 154, 178, 186, 208, 226, 229, 230, 234, 239, 258, 276, 290, 306; David B Miller: 53, 78, 85, 161, 214, 215, 253, 254, 281, 307; Rebecca Morrill: 16, 37, 49, 107, 122, 133, 143, 159, 195, 296, 297; Toby Musgrave: 175; Peter Nekola: 40, 46, 50, 51, 95, 162, 164, 165, 167, 190, 198, 199, 274; Thomas O'Loughlin: 11, 13, 24, 27, 74, 137, 138, 144, 145, 148, 166, 271, 277, 278; Richard Pflederer: 65, 66, 149, 152, 222, 223; Alex Rayner: 21, 55, 141, 203, 305, 308, 313; Dennis P. Reinhartz: 63, 89, 252, 312; Patricia Seed: 42, 44, 67, 73, 75, 94, 105, 119, 124, 146, 183, 220, 248, 249, 295; Susan Schulten: 10, 30, 70, 91, 131, 205, 244, 251, 265, 279 and Ruth Watson: 18, 23, 155, 15, 157, 158, 228, 280, 285.

Special thanks are also due to Sarah Bell and Emmanuelle Peri for their careful picture research and to Capucine Coninx for her tenacious research and editorial assistance.

Finally, we would like to thank all the cartographers, map-makers, artists, collectors, libraries and museums who have given us permission to include their maps.